Fighting With JEB Stuart

Major James Breathed and the Confederate Horse Artillery

Fighting With JEB Stuart

Major James Breathed and the Confederate Horse Artillery

David P. Bridges

Cataloging-in-Publication Data is available from the Library of Congress.

ISBN 0-9774508-0-5

Breathed Bridges Best, Inc.
2600 South Veitch Street, #411
Arlington, VA 22206
Phone: 703-486-4275
Fax: 703-521-1867

For more details contact Breathed Bridges Best, Inc, or you may e-mail the author at DPBridges@aol.com, or visit my website at www.davidpbridges.com for additional information.

Printed in China.

This book is dedicated to the
following cousins of Major James Breathed:

Emily Jane Williams Perry, Rodger Loren Perry, and
Herbert Ramsay Tobias, Jr.;

Civil War historian William Harold Perry;

and to the men of the 2nd Virginia Cavalry and
the Stuart Horse Artillery, then and now.

A charcoal rendering of Major James Breathed, C.S.A.

Contents

Contents (continued)

Maps, Photographs, and Tables

Maps, photographs, and illustrations are located throughout this work for the convenience of the reader.

Foreword

I have spent much of my adult life studying cavalry operations in the American Civil War. Until recently, the horse artillery has received scant attention when compared to the exploits of the horse soldiers of both sides. With the exception of Major John Pelham, the handsome young West Pointer who was mortally wounded at Kelly's Ford on March 17, 1863, the horse artillery has been largely ignored. In recent years, historian Robert J. Trout has brought the accomplishments of the Stuart Horse Artillery of the Army of Northern Virginia to light with his outstanding history *Galloping Thunder*. At last, Trout has focused attention on the important role these dedicated artillerists played in the cavalry battles of the war's Eastern Theater. Trout's efforts brought to light the exploits of Pelham's successors—Robert F. Beckham, Roger Preston Chew, and James Breathed, the subject of this study.

James Breathed was trained as a physician, but instead of finding fame as a healer he gained immortality as an artillerist. Were it not for his service with Lee's Army of Northern Virginia, no one would find his life worthy of a biography. Personally recruited by J. E. B. Stuart, Breathed joined a Virginia cavalry regiment before transferring to the newly-formed Stuart Horse Artillery. Breathed quickly discovered that he had a true gift for dealing out death and destruction, perhaps more than any gift he might have had for healing. By the end of the Civil War Breathed was in command of one of the two battalions of the Stuart Horse Artillery. He was a man who lived by a clear code of honor, and had gained the respect of friend and foe alike.

Personally fearless, Breathed suffered numerous combat injuries, including a gunshot wound that would have killed almost any other man. He not only survived this wound but returned to duty and honorably served for the balance of the war. Leading by example, Breathed proved to be a brave and inspirational leader whose men would follow anywhere he asked them to ride. Breathed refused to surrender at the end of the Civil War, deciding instead to simply ride away from the tragedy at Appomattox Court House and hang up his uniform on his own terms.

David P. Bridges, a relative of the subject of this book, has penned as comprehensive account as currently possible on the life and accomplishments of Major Breathed. In doing so, he has brought an important but too often overlooked figure of the Civil War the level of attention he has long deserved. Bridges draws upon previously unpublished family papers to highlight the remarkable and but little-known story of the man who set aside his scalpel for a saber and used it on behalf of the Confederacy for four long years. It is a story that has remained untold for too long.

Eric J. Wittenberg
Columbus, Ohio

Preface

A confluence of events inspired the writing of this book. For me at least, they were rather remarkable. As an eleven-year-old boy I visited the home of my cousin, Virginia Carmichael, in Hagerstown, Maryland. She lived in an old Victorian house, the kind filled with all sorts of memories. I immediately fell under the spell of the relics, sabers, guns, and antiques Virginia had amassed. In a remote room upstairs I remember a pair of scissors sitting on a dresser. When I picked them up, the outline of where they had rested for years showed in the thick dust. It was as if the scissors in my hand had never left the dresser. The present and the past often seem to merge in much the same way.

I also remember seeing a photograph of General Robert E. Lee hanging over the downstairs fireplace. It was the familiar image of the general taken on his back porch in Richmond the last time he wore his Confederate uniform. A photo of Lee hanging in a Southern home was not exactly a rare occurrence. This one, however, was inscribed to a Major James Breathed. The photograph had been presented to Breathed's father, Judge John W. Breathed, sometime between 1865 and 1870. As I would later learn, General Lee had once proudly proclaimed that the judge's son was "the hardest artillery fighter the war produced."[1]

When I was a young boy James Breathed was not a household name; nor is it today. Someday, I told myself, I would learn more about the doctor-turned-warrior.

The years passed until I was an adult far removed from my cousin Virginia's Victorian home before I gave serious consideration to studying Major Breathed more closely. When I finally got around to opening books about the Army of Northern Virginia, however, I was surprised on how little there was about him. The scattered references included a few words here, a sentence or two there, but little more. It quickly became obvious that there was no single place to read a detailed account of the artillerist whom General Lee had so highly praised. No one, it seemed, had considered Breathed worthy of a biography. Still, the tantalizing tidbits I read about him sketched a soldier brave to a fault, a fearless leader of men respected by those he commanded and by his own superiors—a warrior of some renown. But who was James Breathed?

Research into the *Official Records* of the war and uncovered enough references to Breathed for me to realize he was indeed someone who mattered. Colonel Thomas T. Munford, an officer with the 2nd Virginia Cavalry who served with Breathed, wrote: "A more dashing gallant, generous hearted Confederate soldier never drew a saber or fired a cannon. He was 'recklessly brave' himself, and ever ready to lead his batteries where few artillery officers would be willing to risk their guns, and then he would turn over his guns to the next officer under him and dash and lead the cavalry in a charge." Breathed, remembered Munford, "loved to hear the roar of artillery and witness the flashing of the guns . . . but while he 'slashed and dashed' in and out of a battle he was generous as he was brave, and having been a doctor before the war he often ministered to the men who a short time before had stood up before his guns and fallen in the fight he had led against them." Once I read those words I admit to becoming intrigued with the true history of my long-dead Great-Great Uncle.[2]

I decided that I would undertake the task of chronicling his life and military career. My immediate concern, of course, was whether there were enough archival sources upon which to base a respectable work of history. My research turned up some interesting and helpful sources, but the treasure trove of Breathed letters or a wartime diary, if one ever existed, eluded my efforts. Still, there seemed to be enough material to produce at least a slim biography, which I was convinced this Confederate officer deserved. So I continued my efforts, traveling to every battlefield where Breathed fought, visiting archives in several states, and talking with a wide variety of students of the war in general, and cavalry and artillery historians in particular. I also visited Bai-Yuka, Breathed's boyhood plantation home just ten miles from the Sharpsburg battlefield. Breathed and his eight siblings grew up at Bai-Yuka; four of them served the Confederacy.

Major Breathed reflected the cultural values of the antebellum South, which held that individuals—rather than society as a whole—determined their level of success or failure in life. "[What] really counted were not social institutions, but one's own virtue, will, convictions of duty and honor, religious faith in a word, one's character," wrote one historian who has studied such things in great detail. "God controlled human destiny, but God helped those who helped themselves." This was a popular and powerful notion among Protestants. Americans before and after the Civil War believed as Horatio Alger did, that the poor were that way because they did not help themselves. The key to success depended on hard work.[3]

The chivalric ideal for aristocratic men helps explain how the South and, for our purposes at least, the Army of Northern Virginia, fought in the Civil War. While the politicians and captains of industry in the North spurned such notions as archaic, these ideals stayed very much alive in the South. In Virginia, being a "gentleman" meant a man was always courteous to women; dealt fairly with other gentlemen; was magnanimous toward those of lower birth; avoided displays of excessive emotion (unless honor was at stake, particularly the honor of a lady); and behaved calmly in the face of death. However outmoded those concepts sound today, to a large degree they defined many officers who served in Lee's Army of Northern Virginia, and one of those was James Breathed.

My research helped me grasp several important (to me, at least) conclusions about the war. To study Breathed and his comrades is to understand how the mix of chivalry and independence was stamped into Confederates of different ranks. It still amazes me that the two meshed as well as they did for as long as they did. If Breathed and other officers in the Army of Northern Virginia fought out of a sense of honor, the men in the ranks had their own reasons for going to war. To know the Confederate States of America is to appreciate the powerful interplay of abstract and emotional motivations that caused men to make the ultimate sacrifice of their own lives.

According to James M. McPherson, "*Subjugation* was the favorite word of Confederate recruits. . . . [I]f the South remained in the Union or was forced back into it . . . 'our property would be confiscated . . . & our people reduced to the most abject bondage & utter degradation.'" The cause, however defined, induced Southern soldiers to undertake extraordinary acts of bravery. Of course many men shirked their duty or deserted, but there was a preoccupation in the ranks with honor. Peer pressure was a powerful motivational factor. Fighting next to one's brother, cousin, or neighbor meant that any cowardice would be reported to those waiting for news back home. At least publicly, no one tolerated cowardice or slacking. "Skulkers, sneaks, beats, stragglers, or coffee-coolers," McPherson concluded, were despised nearly as much as deserters. If the South seemed to fight harder, it was in part the product of a sense of honor—and the corresponding fear of being considered a coward.[4]

It is ironic that the birthplace of individualism in the Western world was also home to slavery. While I have not found much evidence that Breathed fought specifically for the preservation of slavery, his family was wrapped up in that cruel and objectionable issue. Along with his fellow Southerners, Breathed fought for Southern independence and against what he and others perceived to be Union tyranny. This marks Breathed as a product of his time, as does his family's acceptance of slavery. Had Breathed lived longer, perhaps his views on race would have changed, just as they had for Generals James Longstreet and Wade Hampton. But as a young soldier in his twenties Breathed did not question the practice of denying freedom to some—and I am duty-bound to note that silence.

According to one National Park Service historian, the primary reason why no biography of James Breathed had been written was the lack of primary source documents. Serendipitously, in 2000 another cousin came forward with four scrapbooks stuffed with articles relating to the war in general, and Breathed in particular. Some were eyewitness accounts or recollections, and all of them helped me flesh out many aspects of Breathed the man and Breathed the soldier. Without them, I do not think this book could have been written. Perhaps somewhere in an attic is Breathed's personal correspondence from the war or the collection of papers from Breathed's Battery salvaged after the war but long since lost. Unfortunately, I have been unable to locate them.

When I began this project I knew very little about cavalry or artillery. In order to get a fuller feeling about what my subject experienced, I decided to join the 2nd Virginia Cavalry/Stuart Horse Artillery, a reenactment group based in Roanoke, Virginia. This helped me learn about handling horses, field artillery, caissons, limbers, and the cavalry charge! I learned about horse artillery and how to fire cannon, and what horse holders were expected to do. I learned lessons about the role dismounted cavalry played during the war and what it was like to charge on horseback. I even discovered how to execute a "prolonge maneuver," i.e., pulling an artillery piece by rope to a new position, thereby avoiding having to tow the gun by limbered horses to a new spot in the heat of battle. I was now able to put word and action together thanks to this dedicated and sincere group of reenactors from "Old Virginia." I am indebted to each of them, some of whom also have Confederate ancestors.

Although I do not share the negative image Tony Horwitz paints of Civil War reenactors in *Confederates in the Attic*, Horwitz is right about one thing: even the most intense reenacting comes to an end after a few days or a week, and everyone returns to the present. Our self-inflicted hardships, without real combat, real wounds, and death, are fleeting. The men who fought in the Civil War experienced these hardships (and so many others that we cannot even imagine) for months or years on end.

As I was finishing Breathed's story his charcoal "ghost-type" portrait, which had been lost for more than a century, resurfaced in a private collection. There is no rational explanation for why it came up at this time, just as there is no easy way to explain why the visit to my cousin Virginia meant so much to me when I was young and lingered inside me for many years. As I have discovered, life is an interesting series of confluences that we are unequivocally left to accept. The confluences of my life dictated that I work to the best of my ability and set forth the story of James Breathed. I did the best I could with what I had to work with, and my hope is that this book adds something worthwhile to the literature of the Civil War.

Acknowledgements

I am grateful to all the people who assisted me in bringing this book to fruition. I hope I will be forgiven if I neglect to include anyone. Robert J. Trout read several versions of this manuscript and offered valuable suggestions and advice. His book *Galloping Thunder: The Story of the Stuart Horse Artillery Battalion* is the complete history of that redoubtable organization; Robert K. Krick reviewed the manuscript and offered much of value; Dr. Richard R. Duncan for his review of the manuscript and suggestions; Judge Richard Abell encouraged me to write this history and reviewed portions of it; Ellen Roberts offered continuing encouragement and vital support throughout the project; Dr. Douglas Bukowski of the University of Illinois at Chicago offered important editorial suggestions; Daphne Butas helped verify sources; Eric J. Wittenberg, who is recognized as one of the country's finest cavalry historians of the war, offered extensive suggestions and editorial advice. I highly recommend that everyone interested in cavalry operations read Eric's books, particularly *The Union Cavalry Comes of Age* and *Glory Enough for All.* They are masterfully written and include groundbreaking research. I must also thank him for agreeing to write the Foreword; my friend, William H. Perry spent countless hours reviewing and commenting on the final version of the manuscript, and demonstrated a sincere love for Major Breathed and the Civil War. Bill is a friend who took the time to tour many battlefields with me over the years. I could not have done this without him.

So many others also assisted: Dr. Rod Clare for his valuable research assistance at Duke University and at the University of North Carolina libraries; James B. Couch for his research assistance with the Southern Historical Society Papers; James Burgess of Manassas National Battlefield Park, who reviewed relevant portions of my manuscript; Dr. Carole Sargent for her editing assistance; Dr. Edward G. Longacre for his invaluable assistance along the way, for his outstanding books on both Union and Confederate cavalry, and for agreeing to pen the Introduction for this book; Irvine Rutledge, God rest his soul, accompanied me on my initial tour of the Antietam Battlefield; Col. Walbrook Swank, a prolific writer on Civil War matters, took me on a tour of Trevilian Station; Michael Lucas did the same at the High Bridge battlefield; Virginia Morton helped me understand Culpeper, Virginia, and the surrounding area; Dave Goetz guided me over the Aldie, Middleburg, and Upperville battlefields.

I would also like to thank members of the 1st Maryland Artillery reenactment group for taking a season to teach me how to fire a 12-pounder howitzer; the 2nd Virginia Cavalry/Stuart Horse Artillery reenacting group for allowing me to participate in their Confederate family and for teaching me authentic horse artillery maneuvers.

I must also thank Maxine Newbraugh, Reverend David Miller and the Reverend George Pera for their continued support of my writing in general; Herbert R. Tobias, Jr., for his wisdom and genealogical research of the Breathed family. The outstanding staff at the Library of Congress, National Archives, Virginia Historical Society, The Museum of the Confederacy, Valentine Richmond History Center, Virginia State Library, Maryland Historical Society, Enoch Pratt Library, Baltimore, Maryland and all the other local historical societies that have aided my research, especially the Hancock Historical Society, Lexington Park Public Library, Lexington Park, Maryland, and the Wilderness Road Regional Museum, Pulaski, Virginia. The members of the Sons of Confederate Veterans, General Robert E. Lee Camp #726, as well as the members of the Military Order of the Stars & Bars, General Samuel Cooper Chapter, for their efforts at continuing education. Finally, the Brandy Station Foundation for locating and enabling me to bring before the public both the ghost-type photograph of Maj. James Breathed and the Breathed Scroll from the Graffiti House in Brandy Station, Virginia.

Introduction

Among the countless unsung heroes of the Confederacy, James Breathed of Maryland remains one of the most deserving of historical attention and military recognition. From 1861 to 1865, Breathed was a leading light of the Stuart Horse Artillery, a critical component of the cavalry branch of the Army of Northern Virginia. In scores of battles and skirmishes his polished leadership, bulldog tenacity, coolness under fire, and professional skill earned him the praise of friend and foe alike. Although largely forgotten today, he ranked behind only John Pelham, the founder of J.E.B. Stuart's artillery arm, as the most notable Confederate horse artillerist in the Eastern Theater of operations. And it was Breathed who, following Pelham's tragic death in battle midway through the conflict, almost single-handedly maintained the power, poise, and professionalism of the fallen hero's unit. His tactical and strategic expertise enabled the Stuart Horse Artillery to make critical contributions to the fortunes of Robert E. Lee's army up to and including its final battle at Appomattox Court House.

Breathed was neither a born soldier nor a trained one. Prior to the outbreak of the war, he was a physician with a flourishing practice in Rushville, Missouri. Soon after the war's start, however, the doctor—a Southern patriot of the first rank—happened to occupy a seat beside then-Col. James Ewell Brown (Jeb) Stuart on an eastbound train carrying men from points west. Their casual acquaintance developed into a mutually advantageous military association. Under Stuart, who would become the war's most famous cavalry leader, Breathed not only learned the tactics of his acquired branch with remarkable speed, but just as quickly developed a unique style of leadership that immediately identified his Virginia battery on every field of combat. One of Breathed's most accomplished opponents, Captain Alexander C. M. Pennington, a skilled West Pointer and the commander of Battery M, 2nd United States Artillery, could tell within seconds of coming under Breathed's shelling that he was opposing one of the most deadly accurate units of horse artillery in Confederate service. From his earliest encounters with Breathed's Marylanders, Pennington acknowledged that he dreaded facing them in battle. Many of his comrades in the Army of the Potomac shared his view, although most lacked Pennington's candor in admitting it.

Breathed's own artillerymen echoed the praise the enemy bestowed upon him. After the war, one of the major's gunners, H. H. Matthews, declared, "History has no parallel in modern warfare that equals the valor the achievements of this battery. Breathed was in it from early dawn to dewy eye. He was in his best element [in combat]. Nothing gave him more pleasure than to be among bursting shells and the zip of the minie [ball]. Artillery duels had no terror for him. He was in his second heaven, especially if the opposing battery was battery M, 2nd U. S. . . . ."

If Breathed was well-known to both friend and foe in his time, his fame has not survived him. While Pelham's name continues to evoke recognition among historians and students of the war, Breathed's has been unfortunately lost in the passage of time. Not surprisingly, this is the first and only book-length biography of the man. The author, David P. Bridges, is a relative of Breathed. He has done an admirable job of restoring the fame once accorded to his kinsman and later denied to him. Bridges offers a detailed, balanced, well researched, and straight-forward account of James Breathed's life. The result is a tribute long overdue and a story well worth reading.

Edward G. Longacre

Chapter 1

The Early Years:
To the Threshold of War

The Breatheds were a prosperous plantation family with deep Southern roots. Judge John W. Breathed, James's father, counted among his relations Andrew Jackson's private secretary and the eleventh governor of Kentucky. Judge Breathed married Ann Macgill Williams, a descendant of Sir James Macgill, a Reformation-era provost of Edinburgh, Scotland. In 1728, the Anglican Bishop of London sent Ann's ancestor, the Reverend James Macgill, to start Somerset Parish in Somerset County, Maryland. Two years later, Reverend Macgill was transferred to Queen Caroline Parish, Anne Arundel County, in what is now Howard County. He served there for 46 years and retired during the American Revolution, when established churches lost their operating subsidies from the English government. Reverend Macgill married a descendant of Humphrey Williams, who came to America in 1635. Among Ann's relations was Governor Claiborne F. Jackson who was governor of Missouri at the opening of the Civil War. Also, soon to be Brigadier General John S. Marmaduke who served as the commander of the Confederate Cavalry Corps of the Army of the Trans-Mississippi.[1]

Kentucky governor (and relative) John Breathitt arranged a West Point commission for his cousin John, who turned down the appointment in favor of seeking adventure out West. Once the urge passed and the

Dr. Robert Strauch

Bai-Yuka, the Breathed plantation home in Maryland.

travel was behind him, the young man returned home and entered the mercantile business in Berkeley Springs, Virginia. In 1837, John and Ann married. From 1837 to 1848, they lived at Fruit Hill Manor in Morgan County a few miles above Berkeley Springs. During this time, John represented his county in the state legislature.[2]

John and Ann's first child, James, was born December 15, 1838. He was followed by eight siblings: John Jr., 1840; Priscilla, 1842; twins Jane and John, who were born in 1844; Isaac, 1847; Francis, 1848; Elizabeth, 1852; and Edward McGill, 1859. In 1838, Martin Van Buren was the nation's eighth president and Jefferson Davis was a Mississippi planter. In Boston, William Lloyd Garrison began publishing his abolitionist paper The Liberator. The forces Garrison helped stir would eventually compel James to define himself as a "Davis man" more than two decades later.[3]

By 1848, the Breatheds had moved from Morgan County to Maryland, and their new plantation home, Bai-Yuka, an Indian name meaning "fountain rock." The home was on property that was once part of the estate of General Samuel Ringgold, a gentleman of great wealth during the late colonial period, who was a commander in the

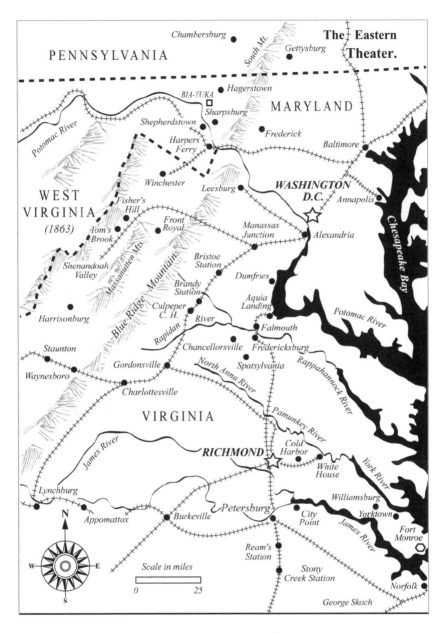

Revolutionary War. Bai-Yuka was built in 1825 for Maj. Samuel Ringgold, the son of General Ringgold. The major was a commander of horse artillery in the Mexican War. In 1848, John exchanged land holdings with his brother to acquire the estate, which had a pillared front

Reverend Doctor
John B. Kerfoot

St. James School

porch in the Greek Revival style, a grand interior, and picturesque lands which offered a stunning sight to everyone who visited the home.[4]

While living in Maryland, the Breatheds were swept up in the Second Great Awakening, a religious movement that flourished in America during the early 19th century. Like its colonial predecessor, the Second Great Awakening fostered an intense personal relationship between the individual and God. Both black and white Americans took part.

"It is high times for our sakes & for the sake of the people that the College should evangelize this neighborhood," wrote Reverend John Barrett Kerfoot, Provost to the Reverend Bishop William R. Whittingham, D.D., on February 21, 1848. "Regular services may induce some nominal attendants in town to attend nearer them. . . . Until now I had not health—now I can preach & there are enough besides or will be to preach & our older and serious boys ought & need to learn to do good to others by teaching Sunday School. . . . We grow selfish in our religion—& the boys grow up to think that the Church is meant only for gentlemen." Reverend Kerfoot may have sparked the impetus for the building of St. Mark's Episcopal Church at Lappan's Crossroads. However, it was the Maryland Bishop Whittingham who desired the creation of a seminary to educate boys and turn them into scholars and priests to supply the needs of the Episcopal Church in Maryland.[5]

Because Judge Breathed wanted to cultivate both the minds and souls of his children, he volunteered to be a part of the building committee for Saint Mark's. His motives also included a practical reason: the nearest church was eight miles away, an uncomfortable distance for anyone concerned with issues of salvation. In April 1849, Bishop Whittingham laid the cornerstone of the new church and consecrated the building three months later. The intent, as the church's historian wrote, was "to build the most beautiful church possible in which they could meet and worship." John contributed $275, one of the largest donations for a project totaling $1,385. On May 6, 1849, Reverend Joseph Clarkson Passmore became the first rector with an annual salary of $80. Now, in addition to a place to educate his children, the judge now had a new Episcopal church nearby, which included a slave gallery for separate, if equal, worship.[6]

The College of St. James opened in Washington County in October 1842, through the efforts of Rev. A. B. Lyman and the Right Rev. William Robinson Whittingham, Bishop of Maryland. Lyman and Whittingham were among the early leaders in the movement to establish Episcopal Church schools in the United States. They started the facility by purchasing a mansion (a house of General Samuel Ringgold, later to become Bai-Yuka of the Breathed family) and some property from an insolvent estate for the sum of $5,000. Construction funds came primarily from Washington County Episcopalians.[7]

At the time of the church's founding, Reverend Kerfoot was part of the faculty of St. Paul's School in Flushing, New York. Transferred and given charge of the College of St. James, Kerfoot made little effort to hide his Unionist beliefs. The families of children enrolled in the school appreciated his transparent honesty and firmness. He had a generous consideration for the views of others and was therefore able to continue as the head of the college. The trustees began an effort to raise an endowment of $250,000 for professorships and scholarships. While the College of St. James retained its character as the local diocesan school for boys and seminary, it was in reality a private school for children of privileged families. John Breathed served on the board and helped the college by filling several positions over the years.[8]

The college was located across the road from Bai-Yuka. In the trifecta ruling the world of real estate, John had picked a perfect home for his children. Young James was ten years old when the Breatheds moved into Bai-Yuka. His brothers Francis, John, and Isaac later matriculated at the college.[9]

James attended the school from 1848 to 1855. Area residents who sent their children to the school were mostly Southern in their sympathies. Fully three-quarters of the students hailed from Southern states. The faculty, however, was predominantly Unionist in sentiment. Doctor Kerfoot's Northern loyalist persuasions apparently did not bother young James or his father, who acted as the bursar at the college. His official titles were Secretary of the College and Curator of the Students.[10]

The school year opened each year in October and ended in early July. During the time James attended, the school enrolled 104 boys, two-thirds of whom attended the collegiate division, which was intended for students interested in the Episcopal priesthood. However, James' interests lay in areas other than divinity studies.[11]

A few years after James attended St. James, a student named W. Wilkins Davis enrolled there. For all practical purposes, Davis (or Wilkins, as he was often called) and Breathed enjoyed parallel experiences, if not lives. Wilkins arrived at St. James after attending a small school in Medfield, near the mill town of Hampden-Woodberry on the edge of Baltimore County, Maryland. Five letters survive from his time there. It must not have been a particularly happy experience, given how Wilkins's mother forbid him to take dancing lessons because of their "evil associations and intense love of the world."[12]

Doctor Kerfoot employed recent graduates of the college to teach and live among the boys. Acting as elder brothers within the school family, many of them later went into the ministry. Wilkins's mother may have wanted to employ one of these men to help her son memorize Scripture so that he, too, could enter the ministry. But, like James Breathed, Wilkins chose a different path.[13]

During Holy Week each year, the usual pattern of school changed considerably. Some studies were set aside—Caesar, Virgil, Xenophon— and others taken up in their place. Students were required to memorize (in

St. James School

Chapel of the current St. James School.

Latin) the Creeds, Te Deum, Pater Noster, and other historical hymns. They read parts of the New Testament in Greek and, instead of the usual work in algebra or geometry, were instructed in the history and use of the church calendar. There were extra chapel services during the week and special lectures on such subjects as "the destruction of Jerusalem, the prophecies of Daniel, and the history of sacrifice." Happy memories of these difficult schoolboy routines would return to many of these young men years later on the battlefield.[14]

On April 2, 1858, Wilkins described the activities of Holy Week in a letter to his father. "We have had some change in our studies. Instead of our usual lesson in Greek we have been reading the betrayal and crucifixion of our Lord from a Greek Testament. We have had chapel three times a day this week, two times voluntary and one a lecture from Dr. K[erfoot] on the history of the prayer book. We have had a sermon every day and some of them as good as I would wish to hear especially Dr. Kerfoot's sermons." A little more than two months later, Wilkins admitted in a letter to his mother, "I cannot say that I am prepared for confirmation, but hope by the Grace of God to be prepared by commencement. Dr. Kerfoot has promised me that I shall have the benefit of his prayers and advice. I expect that Dr. Kerfoot will very soon form a class of all those who wish to be confirmed."[15]

Students enjoyed one or two hours of recreation each afternoon, most of it spent eating meals or in chapel. Wilkins wrote to his sister Rebecca, "attendance at Morning Prayer and Evening Prayer was mandatory, the service at noon voluntary." The Alumni Award was for exactly those outstanding undertakings described by Wilkins in his letter. The contest was held every year, alternating annually between Latin and Greek.[16]

On October 10, 1858, Wilkins wrote home to his father about his exacting scholastic requirements:

> My studies this year are Virgil which we have nearly finished, Homer, English Composition, Geometry, Algebra, History, and French, which studies combined, give abundance of exercise to my intellectual powers.
> The Alumni have offered a premium of 50 dollars to the boy who will be able to read any part of the first four books of the Annals of Tacitus fluently, and answer the most difficult questions upon them which a committee of seven shall be 'De Caesaris Morte.' As Tacitus is studied by the Senior Class, the contest lies only between

the select of the Junior and Senior Classes. . . . The College appears to be hard up for money this year in consequence of which we have not quite so good a table as last year.

In July, Bishop Whittingham awarded "Alumni Prizes," the school's principal and most prestigious awards for outstanding performance in Greek and/or Latin. St. James based its educational philosophy on the classics, and rewarded accordingly.[17]

The boys were required to translate the Gospel of John from a Greek testament at the rate of 10 verses a day or translate long Latin hymns and learn "Mediaeval Drama" in English literature. These were short morality plays aimed at reinforcing Episcopal teachings for essentially illiterate audiences. Wilkins again wrote Rebecca in May 1860, this time about his confirmation: "I should advise you, by all means, so to do, unless you feel yourself totally unfit to receive that solemn rite, and unworthy to partake of the blessed body and blood of our Savior Jesus Christ. It is indeed a dreadful thing to receive the Holy Communion unworthily, and I fear we poor mortals are too prone to underrate the great privilege granted to us . . . ."[18]

Wilkins read the first two volumes of the Bridgewater Treatises on the power, wisdom, and goodness of God, as shown toward the Creation. These volumes gave a general view of the history, habits, and instincts of animals. This, as much as anything, was part of his pre-med training. Education in 1860 tended to be more intensive than extensive.[19]

Intensive studying notwithstanding, the students paid attention to the growing sectional strife engulfing the country. "Congress has at last met and the great problem will soon, I have no doubt, be solved, whether this grand experiment of Republican government shall, or shall not succeed," Wilkins wrote Rebecca on December 5, 1860. By this time, the nation's political turmoil was the major issue on campus. With the impending war crisis, school administrators tried to keep their students focused on studies, not sectional strife. Reverend Kerfoot asked the boys to refrain from giving speeches or writing essays on political topics. Although he privately believed three-quarters of the student body was pro-Union, his judgment would soon prove erroneous.[20]

On May 22, 1861, Wilkins announced himself as a "Southern Rights" man. While much of the school faculty and Reverend Kerfoot tilted North, more than a few of their charges were heading in the opposite direction. An advance guard of 1,500 Virginians was now encamped only four miles away at Williamsport; the group may have included James Breathed. Wilkins also expected 10,000 Union troops at Hagerstown, only six miles to the north. With so many students visiting the Virginia camp, Kerfoot delivered a speech on the subject. He claimed to have spies out in the direction of Williamsport and that anyone caught heading off in this direction would face immediate dismissal from the College of St. James.[21]

By the end of the 1861 school year that crucial summer, Wilkins wrote, "I have some idea of going into the apothecary business next year, in order to study Chemistry and Materia Medica practically, preparatory to my commencing the study of Medicine regularly." In the fall, he enrolled at the School of Medicine at the University of Maryland. Much to his liking and perhaps surprise, he found many of the faculty there expressing anti-Lincoln sentiments.[22]

Wilkins again followed Breathed's lead. Just like James, Wilkins found himself under the careful guidance of Doctor Nathan Ryno Smith. "Once a week, students watched Smith perform impressive feats in the operating theater. At other times, they followed him on his rounds to see the results of his work," he wrote. Wilkins found him to be "a redoubtable and inspiring figure." But the similarities between the two Southern

students did not extend to matters of health. Physical problems forced Wilkins to leave medical school and move to Minnesota. On February 29, 1866, he died of consumption

Dr. Nathan Ryno Smith, professor of surgery at the School of Medicine, University of Maryland.

Medical Alumni Association, University of MD

(tuberculosis). Breathed, who finished his medical studies, was destined to an entirely different existence thereafter.[23]

*   *   *

Located across the road from the college, Bai-Yuka was well suited for the cattle, horses, and crops the Breatheds raised on their land. The judge made his living from agriculture, in addition to the positions he held at the college. James was comfortable in the saddle at an early age. As the eldest boy, he was expected to help manage the cattle and other livestock on the plantation, and this he did with expertise. All the Breathed children lent a hand in the daily operation of the plantation. So, too, did the family slaves.[24]

According to the July 16, 1860 slave census of Washington County for the Williamsport District of Maryland, Judge Breathed owned eight slaves, apparently all from the same family. These included an 8-month-old male, a 7-year-old female, a 14-year-old female, a 16-year-old male, a 19-year-old male, a 20-year-old female, a 40-year-old female, and a 50-year-old male. No names were recorded. Their tasks included working in the fields around Bai-Yuka and tending to the cattle. It is not known whether any of the Breathed slaves helped raise the children born at Bai-Yuka, who included James' siblings Elizabeth, 1850; Kitty, 1851; Kate, 1854; William, 1856; and Edward, 1859.[25]

Along with his other occupations, Judge Breathed also worked as the first agent of the Baltimore & Ohio Railroad at Breathed's Station, and as the "president of a turnpike company." John also served as a "Judge of the Orphans' Court" for four years, where he reviewed wills that had to be probated. This was an important position in the county because it determined who ultimately owned tracts of land and other forms of wealth. As a churchgoer, school administrator, and public official, John made himself an essential part of his community. No doubt his children were raised with the same expectation of service to others, which in some ways helps explain James' choice of a medical career.[26]

James interned and studied medicine with his relative, Doctor Charles Macgill of Hagerstown. A graduate of the School of Medicine in the University of Maryland's class of 1828, Macgill began his career in Martinsburg, Virginia (now West Virginia), and practiced there for some

Dr. Charles and Mary Ragan Macgill after 50 years of marriage. James Breathed interned with Dr. Macgill for two years.

David Bridges Private Collection

five years. In 1833, his brother Doctor William Macgill died, leaving his Hagerstown practice to his brother Charles.[27]

Charles also became active in Maryland politics in the 1836 presidential election of Martin Van Buren. He remained close friends with Nathan Ryno Smith and Francis Thomas (one of Maryland's future governors). He also had deep connections to Southern politicians as well as a growing sympathy for the Southern cause. Doctor Macgill married Mary Ragan, daughter of a successful Hagerstown merchant. The couple had 11 children, including Mary Mollie Ragan Macgill, born on February 28, 1839.[28]

From 1855 through September 1858, James interned with Doctor Macgill. At some point, the robust and handsome James fell in love with Miss Mollie, "the [doctor's] young and attractive daughter," as his sister Priscilla Breathed Bridges recounted many years later. Mollie was just a few months younger than James. The two teenagers visited back and forth between Bai-Yuka and Hagerstown. Most likely, James roomed with Macgill so the two could make house calls together in Hagerstown and in the Maryland countryside.[29]

Whenever James managed to free himself from his studies, he busily courted Mollie. Although reserved in the company of strangers, she was warm-hearted with a radiant beauty, and so attracted the eye of many

David Bridges Private Collection

Mollie Ragan Macgill, at age 35, March 18, 1874.

suitors. But Mollie remained steadfastly interested in James. The young couple soon found themselves the talk of town and countryside.

In September 1858, after three years of studying medicine under Doctor Macgill, James moved to Baltimore, where he enrolled at the School of Medicine, University of Maryland. The fifth oldest medical school in the United States, its program dated to 1807. The inspiration for the school can be traced back to 1789, when a group of physicians organized the Medical Society of Baltimore. The society founders, wrote one historian, "tutored young students in the physicians' homes with lectures on anatomy, surgery, and chemistry." The society's practice of medicine was so elementary that they resorted to the use of everyday knives to perform surgery.[30]

The surgeons met with strong community complaints over the use of human cadaver dissections. Consequently, the physician-teachers deliberated with the Maryland legislature to construct a more legally secure and protected medical college. In 1807, the "Act for Founding a Medical College in the City or Precincts of Baltimore for the Instruction of Students in the Different Branches of Medicine" was passed. The charter incorporated the College of Medicine of Maryland, and in 1812 was re-chartered as the School of Medicine of the University of Maryland. It held the unique distinction of being the only medical school in the United States to have a university system built around it.

American medicine was a very inexact science when James enrolled to study medicine. The trial testing of medicines was an unheard of practice, and the dangers of infection were but little understood. Treatments were often as severe as the illnesses they were intended to cure. It was no wonder that patients dreaded the idea of seeing a doctor. Remembering how his typhoid was treated, a Civil War veteran recalled in 1905, "Darkness and fog surrounded the medical profession. The doctors were then feeling their way thru their duties, as a blind man gropes his way along a strange street." He concluded that "Dr. seems to have been the executioner indirectly."[31]

James may have received his best instruction from Doctor Nathan Smith, who had been chair of surgery at the university since 1827. Smith's removal of a goiter from a patient was the first procedure of its kind in Maryland, and only the second thyroidectomy in the country. Smith became the first surgeon to resect the parotid gland for a neoplasm. Yet another innovation would have a direct connection with the coming war. Smith was known as the "inventor of the anterior splint for fractures of the lower extremities." His valuable invention for the treatment of compound fractures was perfected just a year before the outbreak of the Civil War (where it saw extensive use), when it was made available for widespread use. Smith considered the splint to be his greatest contribution to the field of medicine.[32]

Of the 150 medical students in James' class, only about one-third of the class were actually college graduates. The University of Maryland— 53rd Annual Circular of the School of Medicine, Session, 1860-61 offers a sense of a medical student's life on the eve of the Civil War. Each utilized textbooks for anatomy and physiology, surgery, chemistry and pharmacy, obstetrics, diseases affecting women and children, principles and practice of medicine, materia medica, and therapeutics. Class fees ranged from $10 to $15.[33]

The Dean of the School of Medicine stated in the Annual Circular that the school:

> [D]esired to . . . furnish such a course of instruction as they consider best adapted to be useful to those who are preparing to enter upon the duties of the Medical Profession. . . . [and] will best qualify the young physician to commence with safety the treatment of diseases, and will also best prepare him to derive from his own observation and experience the clinical skill and sagacity which in their highest degree can never be learned from teachers. The important truth is recognized and ever kept in view, that the most valuable portion of all preliminary education is that which prepares the pupil to become his own instructor.

If nothing else, Breathed's medical training laid the foundation for his military career. His fine education trained his mind and made him a quick study with the cannon.[34]

After completing his required three years of study, James devoted his thesis to the subject of pneumonia. "The word 'pneumonia' is applied to inflammation of the substance of the Lungs," he wrote. "It is therefore a disease, in which the eye fails, and the touch cannot guide us to its true condition, then what have we left, but the ear to give us some information reflecting the nature of this great disease. It is a curious, but well known fact," he noted, "that the right lung is greatly more subject to attacks of this disease than the left. (Why this is, we know not.)"[35]

James believed in treating the disease with "great tenacity and vicissitudes," and recommended bleeding the patient as the first course of action. If that failed to produce the desired results, pharmaceutical remedies might help: "tartar-emetic & mercury and or calomel & opium and or carbonate of ammonia, Sulphate Quinea, Brandy and oil of turpentine and the diet should be nutritious." Though bleeding was hardly helpful and usually harmful, James was a product of his times and education. He was a gifted student who ranked near the top of his class in medicine, as well as politics.[36]

In March 1860, at the age of twenty-one, Breathed received a degree and graduated "meritoriously." His commencement outlay was $20, while his overall education cost his family $140. After graduation, he made his way to Rushville, Missouri, located outside St. Joseph, to start his practice. One of the draws west was the presence of two prominent relatives, Governor Claiborne F. Jackson and the West Point man John S. Marmaduke. James' desire was that Mollie would soon join him.[37]

It would be interesting to know what James Breathed was doing politically in the year before Virginia seceded from the Union. One thing is certain, St. Joseph was no quiet backwater away from the tensions that were about to rend the United States. Missouri was a slave state and ten percent of Buchanan County (where St. Joseph and Rushville were located) were in bondage. Across the Missouri River was the "free land" of Kansas. Tensions were high. This was the land of John Brown, whose Harpers Ferry attempt at insurrection and subsequent hanging in Charlestown, Virginia would have been local events for the Breathed family the year before James left to go West. [38]

St. Joseph was also the gateway to the West. The California Gold Rush of 1849 had turned St. Joseph from a one-horse trading post into the second largest city in Missouri by 1860. People from all over the United States flocked to St. Joseph to either homestead or set up shop for those that did. Thus, with a diverse population, there were Northerners as well as Southerners rubbing elbows in St. Joseph, although the Southerners were the most numerous. By the time James Breathed was getting ready to go back East, the nations newspapers had carried leading articles about the sectional clashes of the citizens of St. Joseph and environs. However, this turmoil would still not stop the Pony Express from inaugurating its mail service from St. Joseph in the Spring of 1861.[39]

Whatever James Breathed's plans might have been, they did not hold together long. James was only able to practice medicine for about a year before Southern guns opened on Fort Sumter and Virginia seceded from the Union. When it came time to choose sides in the war, James' alma mater divided its loyalty this way: 30 percent of the recent graduates threw their lot in with the Confederacy, 10 percent with the Union, and the remaining 60 percent scurried out of harm's way entirely.[40]

James' sentiment would probably have been very similar to that of his relative, Governor Claiborne Jackson, who responded to Lincoln's call for troops by saying that the President's request was, "illegal, unconstitutional, and revolutionary in its object, inhuman and diabolical, and cannot be complied with. Not one man will the State of Missouri furnish to carry on any such unholy crusade." With Virginia's secession, James was headed East, confident that Maryland would soon follow suit.[41]

Just as James Breathed had done, so too did multitudes of other young men above and below the Mason-Dixon Line have to chose sides and their destiny. Ideology triumphed over all else. Little else mattered—certainly a career did not. Even family issues or love often took second place to cause and country. For Northern patriots, the Union had to be saved. Secessionists believed, with equal passion, that the South had to win its independence on the battlefield or otherwise submit to what had become despotic rule. And so the men went off to war.

James Breathed, at least, packed his bags with the benefit of a quality education. One school had taught him how to pray, and the other how to heal. Enlistment entailed far more deadly lessons, which he would learn well over the course of four years with the Confederate Army in Virginia.

Chapter 2

Lancet or Sabre?
Surgeon or Cavalry?

D uring Breathed's formative years, Northerners, and especially abolitionists, manufactured a myth about the South. In their fiction, the South was the "land of the lash," where every owner beat his slaves and begat children by them. Northerners who subscribed to this view considered Southerners hypocrites—attending church while keeping blacks in bondage. To them, the South was a backward land: crude, uncivilized, with no respect for education, industry, or progress. Its people, so the tale went, were ignorant and immoral.[1]

The South had its view of the North. As one writer commented, the North was characterized as "a land of money-grubbing, materialistic, rude people, with no sense of courtesy or hospitality." They lived for Mammon, not God, and, instead of making money through genteel farming, many Northerners chose market speculation. They operated factories where men, women, and even children toiled for low pay in dirty, uncivilized conditions for long hours. Yet the Northerners, according to this view, were hypocritical enough to condemn Southerners as "Slave drivers." Southerners lived among blacks and provided their food, clothing, and shelter, while Northerners despised blacks and excluded them from their social world altogether.[2]

With the outbreak of war, both James and Mollie "yielded to the advice of their parents to come home." The pair lived separately because they were not yet married, Breathed practicing in Missouri and Mollie visiting friends in Galveston, Texas. While waiting at Chambersburg, Pennsylvania, during the long train ride east from Missouri, Breathed fell under the surveillance of wary Federal authorities. After a short detention, during which his trunks and baggage were thoroughly searched, he was permitted to proceed to his destination: Bai-Yuka. Breathed waited until his native state of Virginia passed an ordinance of secession and then "quitted his new home and his profession and hurried back [to Bai-Yuka] . . . and for several weeks remained at home, awaiting the action of Maryland, whose Legislature was about being convened in extra session." The Maryland legislature condemned the Federal government's actions against the Confederate states but, unlike Virginia, Maryland did not call a convention to consider the issue of secession.[3]

Breathed burned with the excitement of war and its perils, anxious to do his part; remaining inactive was simply not in his makeup. On the train ride home from Memphis to Pennsylvania, he had ridden next to one James Ewell Brown Stuart. The future Southern cavalryman was an 1854 graduate of West Point. Stuart, a fellow Virginian, was returning from the Western frontier to offer his services to John Letcher, the governor of his native state. Like Breathed, Stuart had found Lincoln's call for 75,000 troops to quell the rebellion in the Southern states unsettling enough to resign his commission in the U. S. Army and offer his sword in defense of his native state. Breathed and Stuart hit it off from the start and quickly became good friends. As one writer put it, both men were "journeying toward Virginia and for the same purpose, but each retaining his secret from the other." They would have courted arrest had they openly voiced their true allegiance. According to historian James McPherson, "Many soldiers enlisted for patriotism and ideology, some for adventure." For Breathed and Stuart, all three reasons applied.[4]

After Breathed's return to Bai-Yuka, he rode his horse south across the Potomac River at Williamsport, Maryland, and continued on to Martinsburg, Virginia. There, on April 19, 1861, he enlisted for one year as a private in the Berkeley Troopers of Cavalry, which eventually became Company B of the 1st Virginia Cavalry Regiment. Like his compatriots, Breathed was determined to fight for the Confederate cause and the Southern way of life. As one historian notes, "combat

LC

James Ewell Brown (JEB) Stuart encouraged James Breathed
to enlist with the South and fight for the Confederacy.

motivations were not unrelated to the complex mixture of patriotism,
ideology, concepts of duty, honor, manhood, and community or peer
pressure that prompted [Civil War soldiers] to enlist in the first place." In
addition to these reasons, many Confederate soldiers fought to defend

their homeland, an impulse many historians have labeled as one of the "strongest of combat motivations." Breathed's allegiances may have been divided between his native state of Virginia and his home state of Maryland, but regardless with which state he aligned himself, he was ready for a fight.[5]

Having grown up with horses at Bai-Yuka, Breathed was a proficient rider. At this stage of the war, Southern cavalrymen tended to be more experienced and skilled in the saddle than their Northern counterparts. Exactly why Breathed chose to enlist as a cavalryman instead of utilizing his medical training to become a surgeon for the Confederate army is unclear. It would have been logical for a fully educated and trained physician to enter Confederate service as a doctor. Breathed decided otherwise.

Stuart—now a lieutenant colonel in the Provisional Army of Virginia, which would later be folded into the Confederate army—rode with eight companies of cavalry to Harpers Ferry on May 11, 1861. The Berkeley Troopers were assigned to picket nearly fifty miles of the Potomac River. As one of Breathed's comrades later wrote, "Stuart frequently detailed Breathed for scouting duty and other detached service, then considered responsible and perilous, and so well were these duties discharged, that he rose at once in favor." Breathed's expert knowledge of the terrain, together with his quick wit and intelligence, paved the way for future success and promotions. On May 14, Stuart wrote his wife, "I have changed my headquarters to Bolivar, a suburb of Harper's Ferry today where I have the Cavalry concentrated (3 companies). The remaining five of my command are detached—two at Point of Rocks 12 miles below—one at Berlin Bridge on the Virginia side six miles below—one at Shepherdstown, and one at Martinsburg."[6]

Brig. Gen. Joseph E. Johnston traveled to Harpers Ferry to incorporate the neophyte cavalrymen, along with Col. Thomas J. Jackson's Virginia infantry brigade, into the main Confederate army. Breathed was about to receive his baptism into army life. An 18,000-man Union force led by Maj. Gen. Robert Patterson, meanwhile, was poised to cross the Potomac River at the spot where Stuart had bivouacked one-third of his men. The "real" war was about to begin.

*   *   *

On July 1, 1861, at 7:30 A.M., Patterson's troops crossed the Potomac at Falling Waters and headed toward Hainesville, Virginia. Ironically, Falling Waters was just a short six miles from Breathed's boyhood home. This would not be the last time he would be called upon to fight within close proximity of his home.[7]

Stuart quickly apprised Jackson of the Union advance, and Jackson's infantry moved to support Stuart's cavalry with 380 men and one piece of artillery from Col. Kenton Harper's 5th Virginia Infantry and Capt. William N. Pendleton's 1st Rockbridge Artillery. The reinforcements marched rapidly to Hainesville to meet Patterson's thrust, while Stuart unsuccessfully attempted to turn the Federal flank.[8]

Stuart's troopers encountered Union infantry shielding Patterson's main body. When Stuart emerged from a stand of timber, he discovered a company of enemy infantry belonging to the 15th Pennsylvania Infantry. The inexperienced soldiers were crouching behind a rail fence. The Southern commander, as were many Confederates early in the war, was still dressed in his blue United States Army uniform. He trotted forward on his horse and ordered the Unionists to drop their arms and come out into the pasture. The soldiers thought Stuart was an Union officer and obeyed immediately. Within seconds Stuart's troopers, including Breathed, rode forward and ordered them to surrender. The unarmed Pennsylvanians had no choice but to comply or be killed on the spot.[9]

Breathed's company experienced its first skirmish at Falling Waters, but the action was almost over before it began. It marked the first time the doctor-turned-soldier saw blood spilled, other than that which he had drawn with his scalpel on the surgical table at the School of Medicine, University of Maryland. Stuart's tactical audacity on the battlefield was demonstrated early, and Breathed absorbed the experience of how the soon-to-be-famous Confederate cavalryman conducted field operations. With only a small command and with very little bloodshed, Stuart delayed Patterson's advance by forcing the Union general to deploy an entire division.

The number of men in General Johnston's command grew to nearly 12,000 during the month of July. By the 16th of the month, the 1st Virginia Cavalry was composed of 13 companies and had appointed its field officers. Breathed, equipped with horse and saber, was now part of a large regiment. Although they did not yet know it, he and his fellow cavalrymen were about to become engaged in their first full-scale battle.[10]

For a short time, the Confederate forces were deployed at Darkesville, where they hoped to draw Patterson out for a fight. They would soon get all the fighting they wanted. Union Brig. Gen. Irvin McDowell was moving some 35,000 men out from the defenses of Washington, D.C., toward Centreville and Manassas, where Confederate Brig. Gen. P. G. T. Beauregard's 20,000 men awaited their advance. McDowell hoped to smash Beauregard's army, capture the Confederate capital at Richmond, and bring the war to a swift end. Unfortunately for the Union, it was not to be.

*   *   *

On July 18, Johnston's Confederate army began tramping down the road through Ashby's Gap en route to Manassas. Stuart masked the move from Patterson by picking and prodding at the enemy, who was largely hemmed in around Charles Town, Virginia. When Johnston was well away and his mission complete, Stuart rode his command toward Manassas Junction with Pendleton's artillery and the 1st Virginia Cavalry, leaving behind a small detachment to continue screening the lethargic Patterson. Jackson's men, meanwhile, boarded trains at Piedmont Station and traveled to Manassas Junction, adding their weight to Beauregard's command.

The muster roll of Company B, 1st Virginia Cavalry reported Breathed as present, but noted he was "sick." Someone issued the ill cavalryman a blanket before he set out for Manassas. After 36 hours in the saddle, during which Breathed was sick throughout, the men of the 1st Virginia Cavalry finally bivouacked for the night. The next morning, while camped on Bull Run, a creek meandering near Manassas, Breathed woke to the sound of musketry and a bugle. "Boots and Saddles" blared out while he was at the creek, washing his face and hands and watering his horse. Company B fell in line behind the Rockbridge Dragoons, and a scouting party was dispatched to ascertain the enemy's position. Breathed, if not entirely recovered from his illness, was nonetheless ready to participate in the upcoming combat.[11]

McDowell's troops had crossed Bull Run at Sudley Ford and Catharpin Run at Sudley Springs Ford, their advance aimed at the

Confederate left flank. As the battle raged, Stuart spent much of the day pacing and awaiting orders, hoping for an opportunity to pitch into the enemy. When a courier finally arrived, it was with a vague message that he should attack where he found the fighting the "hottest." Stuart gleefully complied and rapidly mounted his horse soldiers. The troopers quickly made their way to the extreme left of the Confederate line.

The Union army's attack had initially met with success when McDowell's flanking maneuver caught the inexperienced Southerners by surprise. After driving Beauregard's men back, the victorious Federals surged onto a local eminence called Henry Hill. Here, the men of the 11th New York Infantry, also known as the "Fire Zouaves," were supporting two batteries of artillery. Dressed in the style of France's elite North African troops, they wore baggy red pants, blue jackets, and red caps. These men were members of the Fire Department of New York, which provided the source of their unique moniker. The perspiring New Yorkers hustled into a line of battle at the double-quick. As they advanced toward a tree line, withering Confederate volleys scythed through their ranks. Jackson, who was now a brigadier general, was not about to yield Henry Hill without a fight. The Virginian and his regiments stood tall that day, where Jackson made his stand "like a stone wall," giving rise to his new nickname. The bullets flew all around him,

LC

The 1st Virginia Cavalry.

with one shot hitting a finger. Still, it was not yet his time to die, or so Jackson, a devout Presbyterian, might have believed.

Heedless of their officers' entreaties, some Zouaves returned fire, while others dropped to the ground or stumbled back down the slope in confusion. The rearmost companies were still attempting to deploy when, out of the woods on their flank, thundered 150 Confederate horsemen flourishing sabers and firing pistols and carbines. Lt. Col. Stuart launched his troopers at the disorganized mass of New Yorkers "like an arrow from a bow." Stuart, still wearing his prewar blue United States Army uniform, eagerly plunged his horse into the melee with Breathed just a stone's throw away.[12]

The field was so littered with Confederate and Union dead and wounded that the Southern horsemen had to pick their way through the human debris field. Many bodies, still and crumpled, lay with rifles yet grasped in their hands, while grievously injured soldiers cried for assistance. Cannon shells exploded all around Stuart's charging troopers, leaving a smoky purple fog hanging on the battlefield that made it difficult for the riders to find their way.

Stuart, according to one witness, "led the charge into the Zouave formation. A ragged volley brought down several horses and their riders, but Stuart's Virginians slashed their way through the New Yorkers, causing chaos. Lt. William Blackford felled one Zouave with a point-blank blast from his carbine, and others were cut down and trampled underhoof." Stuart's timely action routed the New Yorkers. His performance rivaled or overshadowed that of any other regimental commander on the battlefield. The terrified and broken Zouaves fled, which helped precipitate the crumbling of the entire Union line. The balance of McDowell's army would fare little better. Before the day was out, much of it would be streaming back toward Washington in panic, terrified that the dreaded Confederate "Black Horse Cavalry" would suddenly appear and decimate their ranks.[13]

*   *   *

A few days later, the 1st Virginia Cavalry formed pickets on the Virginia side of the river facing the Washington defenses at Fairfax Station, Falls Church, Mason's Hill, Munson's Hill, and Upton's Hill. Stuart established his headquarters at Munson's Hill, within sight of the enemy capitol. The stunning Confederate victory at Manassas had endowed Southerners with a belief that the war was all but won, and that they could outfight Northerners under any conditions and on any field. Nearly all of the troops engaged at Manassas had "seen the elephant," as the experience of battle was colloquially called, for the first time. A bizarre feeling of brotherhood developed between enemy and friend afterward. The "elephant," after all, separated the fighters from the skulkers.[14]

For the balance of the summer, Stuart and his cavalry drilled, picketed northern Virginia, and honed their abilities in the field. As the weeks passed, it became obvious that the summer victory would not end the war any time soon. On September 11, Stuart moved to confront a Union reconnaissance-in-force moving toward Lewinsville. The enemy movement was under the command of Col. Isaac I. Stevens of the 79th New York Infantry. Stuart moved out with 305 men of the 13th Virginia Infantry, one section from Lt. Thomas L. Rosser's artillery company, and two companies of the 1st Virginia Cavalry.

Breathed, a veteran of the skirmish at Falling Waters and the heavy fighting at Manassas, was growing increasingly comfortable in his new role as a combat trooper. If he was itching for a sharp fight he was disappointed, for Lewinsville ended up as little more than a skirmish. Stuart's men rode against the Union right flank and brushed up against a Northern skirmish line that was covering an enemy already in the act of withdrawing. The Union troops pulled back from Lewinsville with only a few casualties, and the Confederates withdrew without suffering a single loss.

On September 24, Stuart was promoted to brigadier general and was assigned to lead a cavalry brigade that included his old regiment. Col. William E. Jones, better known as "Grumble Jones," was elevated to command the 1st Virginia Cavalry after Stuart's promotion. Jones, a competent West Pointer, richly deserved his nickname: he was gruff and irascible, and had little tolerance for pageantry or showmanship. He and Stuart did not like one another, a situation that would eventually lead to problems between the two headstrong officers. The change in personnel and leadership styles could not have been more dramatic. Exactly what Breathed thought of the change is unknown.[15]

By October of the war's first year, Breathed's former medical mentor, Dr. Charles Macgill, was having some problems of his own in

Hagerstown. The doctor was arrested at his home on South Potomac Street for refusing to take an oath of loyalty to the United States. When Union troops came to arrest him, his daughter Mollie was prepared for their visit and "tried to beat the soldiers away with a riding whip. The soldiers drew pistols and only interference by the cool-headed Captain precluded an ugly incident. Miss Macgill's brother and father were both arrested." Doctor Macgill was incarcerated at Williamsport, Maryland.[16]

Despite his incarceration, Macgill's loyalty remained firmly with the South. His sons, William D. (Barlow) and David (Pat) fought with the Confederacy in the 1st Maryland Cavalry. All of Doctor Macgill's daughters became romantically involved with Confederate officers and Mollie, in keeping with the family's sympathies for the Southern cause, was no exception. Her love for Breathed had only grown deeper during his absence.[17]

On November 11, Thomas "Stonewall" Jackson, now commanding all Confederate forces in the Shenandoah Valley, granted permission for Capt. Roger Preston Chew and Lt. Milton Rouss to form the Ashby Horse Artillery Battery in Flowing Spring, Jefferson County, Virginia. Theirs was the first horse artillery battery formed in the Confederacy. In Martinsburg, Virginia, meanwhile, Stuart talked with Breathed about his role in the 1st Virginia Cavalry and his future plans. The exact conversation between them will never be known with certainty. Perhaps

LC

Horse artillery being whipped into action.

The Museum of the Confederacy

Captain Roger Preston Chew, shown here
as a lieutenant colonel.

they reminisced about their meeting on the train south from
Pennsylvania. Stuart, as events would prove, had plans for the doctor in
gray who had already proved his valor as a trooper.

Jackson's Ashby Battery was formally organized on November 13,
1861, with 33 enlisted men and four officers. Its official status gave
Stuart the impetus he needed to formalize his own efforts to create horse
artillery units. On September 18, Stuart had asked Virginia Governor
John Letcher for two guns so he could form his own horse artillery
battery. The wheels of bureaucracy moved slowly and the guns were not
immediately forthcoming. By November, however, the Stuart Horse
Artillery moved from idea to reality. On the 18th of the month—five days

after the Ashby Battery organized—Breathed received a 2nd Lieutenant's commission from Stuart. According to the muster roll for Company B, two days later Breathed was transferred to "Stuart's Artillery." From that day forward, he would fight for the South as an artilleryman, and not as a cavalryman.[18]

While the Stuart Horse Artillery was being formed, Reverend Henry H. Tucker delivered a sermon to the Georgia legislature at the state capital at Milledgeville. On November 15, this professor of belles lettres at Mercer University in Macon preached "God In the War," an oration lamenting the Confederacy's losses and the horrors of the war in which Breathed and his comrades were engaged:

> Desolation! Desolation! Thousands of our young men have been murdered. Thousands of fathers and mothers among us have been bereaved of their sons. Thousands of widows are left disconsolate and heart-broken, to struggle through life alone. The wail of thousands of orphans is heard through the land, the Aegis of a father's protection being removed from over their defenseless heads. Thousands of brave men are at this moment lying on beds of languishing, some prostrated by the diseases incident to the army and camp, and some by cruel wounds . . . [19]

The war was no longer an imaginary ideal in the minds of Southern aristocrats; it was a bloody reality. First Manassas served as a reminder that more brave young men would have to die if the Confederacy was to have a future. The war would not be settled with one or two great battles. The generals of both sides had equipped their soldiers to the best of their abilities, but new tactics and strategies were required to achieve an edge on the battlefield. Stuart knew that horse artillery had been effective during the Mexican War, and he hoped its proper implementation on the battlefield would help facilitate the South's ultimate victory.

The North was also aware of the value of horse artillery. Captain Henry J. Hunt, who would eventually command all of the Army of the Potomac's artillery, had served in the horse artillery during the Mexican War and was well acquainted with the critical role that so-called "flying batteries" could play in the fluid atmosphere of a battlefield. Hunt became a driving force behind the formation of Northern horse artillery. About the same time the Stuart Horse Artillery was being formed, the Union army organized Company A, 2nd Regiment, Field Artillery,

United States Army. It was the first horse artillery unit created for the newly christened Army of the Potomac.

*   *   *

The concept of field artillery stretches back several centuries. Sweden's King Gustavus Adolphus introduced the idea in the early 1600s during the Thirty Years' War. Field artillery grew in importance as the science of military warfare evolved. Frederick the Great improved the system, enlarged the caliber of field guns, and introduced "horse artillery" into his armies from 1740 through 1786. Napoleon elaborated upon the use of "flying artillery" by generally improving its tactical use on the battlefield. Mounted artillery operated with infantry in the field. When the guns needed to rapidly change their position, the cannoneers simply climbed onto the limber chests and caissons and rolled to another location.[20]

During the American Civil War, horse artillery units were usually attached to specific brigades of cavalry. A typical horse battery was equipped with four 12-pounder guns, sometimes Napoleons and Howitzers, sometimes 3-inch rifles. The guns were each pulled by either four or six horses, depending on the availability of horses. Each set of teamed horses had a driver on the left horse. The drivers were appropriately named lead, middle, and wheel drivers. Caissons, which held gunpowder, ammunition, fuses, and equipment for firing the pieces, were assigned one per gun. The limber chest held up to 50 rounds of ammunition. When all the limber's ammunition was expended in battle, another limber was moved to the gun to replenish its supply of projectiles.

In a mounted field battery (the typical artillery unit assigned to serve with the infantry), horses pulled the guns. The men who manned those guns, however, were not mounted. They either walked from place to place or rode the limbers. Horse artillery batteries differed from the mounted field batteries in this respect. In horse units, the cannoneers rode their own horses. For each gun there were at least two extra men to hold the cannoneers' horses when the pieces were firing. During an action, horse artillery could change its position at a gallop, explained one veteran, as "frequently as practicable to save the men and horses when the enemy got their range to accurately." In an emergency, a crew could "prolonge," i.e., move the guns with a heavy rope that could be used to drag them short distances.[21]

At long range, the guns fired shell, case, or solid shot. Shells had fuses that were ignited when the cannon fired. The fuses were cut to burn a certain number of seconds, timed so the shells would explode over the enemy position. Some types of shells detonated upon impact, sending iron or lead balls packed inside and iron pieces of the outer skin flying like a giant shotgun blast in all directions.

Canister and grapeshot were designed for use when the enemy moved within close range and an anti-personnel weapon was required. These projectiles were essentially giant shotgun shells. Canister was packed with ½-inch to 1-inch solid balls, while grapeshot contained 10 to 12 larger balls of iron. Their purpose was to rip apart lines of infantry. The artillerists held the cannon muzzle level as the approaching enemy infantry or cavalry moved into range and then discharged their guns. As one Confederate veteran recollected, "The shriek of a shell is the wickedest sound in war, but nothing makes the flesh crawl like the demonic, singing, purring, whistling grapeshot and the serpent like hiss of canister. Men's legs and arms are not shot through, but torn off; heads are torn from bodies and bodies cut in two. Grape and canister mow a swath and pile the dead on one another." The carnage created by canister and grape shot was fearful, and the wake of dead and maimed men it left behind was often immense and sobering.[22]

When Breathed joined the Stuart Horse Artillery, he knew little about such matters. Given his lack of artillery experience, the 22-year-old trooper-physician must have made quite a favorable impression on Stuart to earn his prestigious new assignment. Breathed was ordered to report directly to Lt. John Pelham, commander of the newly formed Stuart Horse Artillery. It was up to Breathed to learn the intricacies of gunnery.

Pelham, a fresh-faced, handsome Alabamian whose West Point training had been cut short by the war's outbreak, probably tutored Breathed in the science of artillery. In order to accomplish his goals, Pelham needed top recruits to join his battery team. He had under his command a number of Frenchmen from New Orleans, Louisiana. The Creoles, known as the "French Detachment," often sang the Marseillaise when in camp. Another large body of artillerymen came from Floyd County, Virginia, outside the railroad town of Roanoke.[23]

James Flanagan

The "Gallant Boy Major" assumed command of the
Stuart Horse Artillery while still a captain.

A team ranging in size from four to six horses pulled each of the guns of Breathed's section of the Stuart Horse Artillery. Horseflesh was plentiful at the onset of the war, but as the months passed the beasts became critically scarce. It took approximately 10 men to operate each artillery piece. Although Breathed was new to artillery, his intelligence enabled him to grasp quickly the fundamental tactics of horse artillery. Among other vital skills, he had to become proficient at measuring the distance from the cannon to its target. Equally important, he had to learn how to judge fuse lengths. If a fuse was too short, a shell might burst over friendly troops. If it was too long, it would explode harmlessly behind the target. Even the most skilled Civil War artillerists could not always guarantee the accuracy of their firing. Artillery ammunition, especially Southern ammunition, was often defective and would either explode too soon or not at all. Breathed spent the last days of November and much of December training with his pieces. His chance to see combat would come sooner than he expected, though he was again destined for disappointment.

*   *   *

By the time the first December of the war arrived, four months of near-bloodless faux warfare had passed since the Union debacle at Manassas. October had witnessed a failed Union excursion thrown back at Ball's Bluff, but little else interrupted the war in the Eastern Theater. With winter upon them, both armies suffered from a want of forage for their animals. On December 20, both sides dispatched large foraging missions into the same area near Dranesville, rich farm country between Alexandria and Leesburg in northern Virginia. A clash, therefore, became almost inevitable. Stuart took 1,600 infantrymen, a battery of artillery, and 150 cavalry on a mission to protect the army's wagons. Breathed went along for the ride and to help collect much-needed forage for the horses.

Near Dranesville, Stuart ran headlong into Union Brig. Gen. Edward O. C. Ord's brigade of Maj. Gen. George A. McCall's division. Capt. A. L. Pitzer, commanding the advance guard of Stuart's cavalry, reported that the enemy occupied Dranesville and had driven Stuart's pickets out. Ord, meanwhile, holding the high ground, deployed his guns and men to meet an expected Confederate attack. Neither commander had a good grasp on the developing situation. Seeking to assure the safety of the wagons, Stuart engaged Ord in a confused meeting engagement. He finally withdrew after two hours of fruitless fighting, having suffered nearly 200 casualties to Ord's 68. Stuart's decision to extricate himself was timely, for McCall's two other brigades were moving onto the field. Another hour of fighting and the Confederates might well have been surrounded. Stuart bivouacked about five miles from Dranesville. Breathed's role at Dranesville was more as an observer than a combat participant. Still, he was able to witness the movement of men and guns under fire and watch Stuart handle his command.

Elijah Viers White, commander of the 35th Virginia Cavalry was one of James Breathed's cousins. He is shown here in a lieutenant colonel's uniform.

LC

Breathed was not the only member of his immediate family serving in the Confederate army. His younger brother, John W. Breathed, Jr., had enlisted as a private in "White's Rebels," a cavalry outfit that on October 28, 1862, would be formally designated as the 35th Virginia Cavalry Battalion. Breathed's cousin, Elijah Viers White, commanded this fine Virginia unit, which would come to the aid of Breathed and his compatriots in the Stuart Horse Artillery many times throughout the course of the war. Young John must have had some sense of security serving under his cousin. Elijah White began his life in Montgomery County, Maryland, outside the small town of Poolesville. He hailed from a prosperous plantation family, and was born and raised at a beautiful plantation home called Stoney Castle. Because John, James, and Elijah were all descended from the Williams family, all three could trace their common ancestry back to the colonization of Maryland.[24]

If Breathed worried for his younger brother's life his concerns were misplaced, for tragedy struck from a different quarter. On March 14, 1862, the Breathed family suffered the heart-wrenching loss of Breathed's beloved mother, Ann McGill Williams Breathed. "The sudden death of this estimable lady is a cause of deep sorrow, not only to her family, but also to a very large circle of acquaintances and friends," lamented one mourner. "As a wife and mother, Mrs. Breathed was all that could be wished. But, more than this, she was a true Christian; and her friends have the best possible assurance that she is now safe in the

Paradise of God." We don't know whether Breathed was able to attend his mother's funeral at St. Mark's Church. Given its location and the timing of her death, it is unlikely he did so.[25]

A few days after the death of Breathed's mother, the young officer was promoted to 1st lieutenant, to rank from March 23, 1862. Two more 12-pounder howitzers were added to the Stuart Horse Artillery. Pelham's batteries were beginning to take shape. Elections were held and, according to the Compiled Service Records, "Pelham was elected Captain; Jim Breathed, first Lieutenant; William M. McGregor, second Lieutenant; William C. Elston, third Lieutenant; James S. T. Shepard, from Charles Town, Virginia, fourth Lieutenant; and Charles E. Ford, from Fairfax, Virginia, sergeant." Elections were a common practice during the early days of the Civil War. In most volunteer regiments, the rank and file selected their own officers, even though most of them had no combat experience. The election of officers was often a popularity contest that had little or no bearing on military qualifications. Although Breathed had engaged in combat as an enlisted man, he was a trained doctor and not an artillery officer. Still, the men thought enough of him to elect him second in command of the Stuart Horse Artillery.[26]

Pelham, the dashing commander of Stuart's guns, thought highly of Breathed. "Capt. Pelham was struck and impressed with Private [sic] James Breathed's high personality and his sense of great moral courage that makes the true man and the ideal soldier," recalled Private H. H. Matthews, a member of the battery who had ample opportunity to watch both Pelham and Breathed in camp and on the field. It was Pelham who had personally requested Breathed be elected as 1st Lieutenant, and he would not have done so had he not been convinced of Breathed's coolness under fire. "The ultimate test of leadership was combat," wrote one recent historian. "No officer could pass this test unless he demonstrated a willingness to do everything he asked his men to do. . . . The only thing respected in young officers was personal courage." In the Civil War, bravery was not the only quality required of an officer, but it was perhaps the most important quality. Officers were well aware of this fact. Breathed had already proven himself to be a man of action who fought at the front with his men. His behavior bred loyalty and instilled in his men a willingness to follow him anywhere. Confederate officers dwelt on the importance of leading by example even more than their

Union counterparts. Cowardly actions quickly earned officers the contempt of their soldiers and undermined their authority as leaders.[27]

1862 Peninsula Campaign

The deep winter months of January and February passed relatively quietly. Pelham and Breathed spent the time drilling their men and becoming familiar with the equipment they knew they would take into combat as soon as the weather warmed and the roads dried. That March, lashed by heavy rains and hampered by mud, Captain Pelham's inexperienced battery, as part of Stuart's Brigade, trekked to the environs of Yorktown on the tip of a peninsula between the York and James rivers. Stuart's Brigade consisted of 1,148 troopers plus 141 artillerymen and eight guns of Pelham's horse artillery.

"The march was a most intensely disagreeable one," remembered Private Matthews. "The roads were in a horrible condition, caused by the spring thaw—and constant rain. The entire army had preceded [us]." The rains had turned the dirt roads, such as they were, into rivers of deep sticky mud into which the heavy wagons and artillery pieces sank. "Apparently there was no bottom to them. We had to travel very slowly, owing to the snail like pace of the infantry ahead of us," recalled the private. Often the men had to wait on the side of a swollen stream until the swift flowing water subsided enough to cross. "On one instance at Rapidan Station on the old Orange and Alex R. R. bridge, we utilized everything in the shape of plank, and succeeded in putting a floor on the bridge so that the battery crossed safely," wrote Matthews. The cavalry swam their horses over the ford below the bridge.[28]

The difficult journey to Yorktown from near Centreville in northern Virginia ended for a time at a camp established on the Brook Turnpike about two miles from Richmond. Private Matthews remembered what took place there: "After remaining in this camp until we had obtained necessary supplies, additional horses and two rifle guns, a Whitworth and a Blakely, both English, we again took up our line of march, passing through Richmond to the Williamsburg road, crossing the Chickahominy River at the Bottom Bridge, through New Kent Ct. House, reaching our position at last on the right of our army near Yorktown at Dam No. 2."[29]

Stuart's move to southeastern Virginia was intended to reinforce the troops gathered there under Brig. Gen. John Magruder to oppose the latest major threat to the Confederate capital at Richmond. This one was in the form of a large and well-organized and well-equipped Union army under Maj. Gen. George B. McClellan. The new commander, known as "Little Mac" to his soldiers, had replaced Irvin McDowell in command of the Federal forces in the East during the fall of 1861. In a new bid to capture Richmond, McClellan landed his army (the first elements marched ashore on March 17 at Fort Monroe), which he had named the Army of the Potomac, on the peninsula between the York and James rivers. The Union advance ground to a halt on April 5 after McClellan marched up the narrow neck of land and encountered Magruder's skimpy Confederate army at Yorktown. To Magruder's relief, advance elements from Joe Johnston's army began arriving at Yorktown the next day. Convinced he was facing a significant enemy force, and upset that President Lincoln decided to hold back McDowell's corps at Fredericksburg instead of allowing him to march south, McClellan halted outside Yorktown. An inconsequential standoff ensued. On the night of May 3, before McClellan could unleash a massive assault planned for the next day, Johnston slipped his army out of Yorktown and marched up the peninsula toward Richmond.

The peninsula was not a pleasant place, especially in the spring of 1862. Too many men and animals were packed into a small area cut by sluggish, malarial streams, muddy roads, and swampy terrain. Many men on both sides fell sick from drinking bad water; dysentery spread through the armies and killed far more men than bullets. Stuart's men remained at Dam No. 2 for a few days. Their spirits remained high, but the conditions under which they lived were anything but ideal. The soldiers stayed busy moving their horses from point to point to keep them out of the mud, protect their health, and to forage for supplies.

On May 2, Pelham and Breathed, together with six guns, reported to Col. Fitzhugh Lee at Bigler's Wharf. Breathed and Lee, who had fought side-by-side at Manassas, knew and liked one another. Their goal was to help screen the withdrawal from the Yorktown defenses planned for the following night. A detached section of the Stuart Horse Artillery consisting of a pair of mountain guns under Lt. James T. Shepherd also reported to brigade headquarters. The next day, Shepherd took position on a small stream near Grove Landing. When Union skirmishers were

Fitzhugh Lee, a capable
Southern cavalry leader
and friend of James
Breathed

USAMHI

spotted in the distance, Shepherd fired three rounds of case artillery shells before slowly retiring. Though utterly insignificant, the shots marked the first time the Stuart Horse Artillery saw action as a cohesive unit.[30]

On May 4, Union troops marched into the empty defenses of Yorktown. With Johnston's army on the move, the campaign entered a more mobile phase. The Confederate commander knew he had to slow down McClellan's advance, so he stopped his rearguard in some prepared defenses at Williamsburg. In a driving rain on May 5, elements of the Union army assaulted them there while the balance of Johnston's divisions continued their withdrawal toward Richmond.

Pelham's Battery was equipped with enough men to crew eight guns, but securing enough strong horses to pull them was always a challenge. Ideally, six horses were used to haul each piece, and each gunner required a mount of his own. On the morning of May 5, Pelham received orders to move immediately to Williamsburg. Apparently short of horseflesh, he left behind five guns and rode forward with two 12-pounder howitzers and a single 12-pounder rifled Blakely (an English-manufactured artillery piece produced in 1860-1861). Pelham reached his destination at 2:00 P.M. and reported directly to Stuart.

The Confederate gunners took up a position to the right front of Fort Magruder, the primary Southern fortification on the battlefield. Pelham opened fire on advancing Federals moving through woods along the road to Lebanon Church. Pelham's own words describe what he and his men experienced:

> Here I detached Lt. Elston, with two men, to bring off some captured artillery. In a few minutes they returned on foot, their horses having been shot down as soon as they made their appearance at the guns. I held this position under a heavy fire until Gen. [Ambrose P.] Hill's brigade moved up and deployed in front of my battery, when I moved to the left and took position on the Yorktown road, to enfilade the enemy's lines. Here the metal bed of the elevating screw of my Blakely gun gave way; but it was retained on the field and did good service. I remained in this position until 5 PM, when I withdrew for want of ammunition. I fired 286 rounds of spherical case and 4 of canister from the 12-pounder howitzers and 40 percussion shell and 30 solid shot from the Blakely gun. Total of 360.[31]

Breathed, McGregor, and Elston led by gallant example at Williamsburg, firing their pieces and urging their men to stand their ground. Each continually exposed himself to enemy fire in an effort to hold back the Federals as long as possible. "Self-preservation is the first law of nature," observed one veteran. "The man who does not dread to die or to be mutilated is a lunatic. The man who, dreading these things, still faces them for the sake of duty and honor is a hero." Duty and honor were indeed powerful motivating forces, and created many heroes in confused fighting at Williamsburg. When darkness fell, some 2,200 Federals and 1,700 Confederates were casualties.[32]

The Confederates continued their withdrawal that night and early the next morning. Pelham's artillerymen left Williamsburg and encamped at a brick schoolhouse half a mile from Burnt Ordinary. "About 10 A.M., May 7, I received orders from the brigade commander to return to the rear, with a rifled gun and howitzer," reported Pelham. "The howitzer was left at the Methodist Church, about 1½ miles beyond Burnt Ordinary, under Lieutenant Breathed; the rifled gun was placed in position about a mile farther on. The enemy's cavalry made their appearance in the edge of the woods in front of us, and I fired five shots at them. The shot fell, well scattering them, but I could observe no other effect. I then retired in the rear of the main body of our forces."[33]

Stuart ordered his cavalry to pursue the fleeing Unionists. When fresh Northern troops opened fire on the Southern horse soldiers, Stuart ordered Pelham into action. The gunner was already on scene and had opened a blistering fire before he received Stuart's directive, for the enemy was only some 200 yards distant. Breathed and his gunners joined in and maintained a continuous fire as the Federals fell back. Although Pelham was typically modest in his battle reports, Stuart's praise was glowing. Pelham's intensive training of his men had paid off, and the captain was justifiably proud of the tenacity with which his men fought. The Stuart Horse Artillery withdrew to Kent Court House, stopping several times to unlimber and fire a few shots in the direction of the enemy in a series of small-scale rearguard encounters.

By May 14, Breathed and his men were at Bottom's Bridge on the Chickahominy River, just a handful of miles outside Richmond. Their orders were to set the bridge ablaze. The steady rains, however, had soaked the bridge and made it impossible to fire. Unable to complete their mission, they instead threw up earthworks on the river and prepared to hold their position.

The new horse artillerists had offered a solid account of themselves in their first actions against the enemy. Only in the fighting at Williamsburg had they suffered any losses. There, two men were wounded, four horses killed, three wounded, and 13 had "escaped from horse holders." Unfortunately, the light losses were about to become a thing of the past.[34]

* * *

Although Johnston had conducted a well-crafted retreat, McClellan's army was now at the very doorstep of the Southern capital. Pressured by President Davis to strike out, Johnston finally turned on the enemy and struck McClellan at the Battle of Fair Oaks (also known as Seven Pines) on May 31. The opportunity facing Johnston was a good one, for McClellan's army was divided by a swollen Chickahominy, two corps below it and three above. Johnston's plan was to converge on the pair of isolated Union corps and destroy them. Unfortunately for the Confederates, his battle plan was too complex for his officers to carry

General Robert E. Lee

out. Orally delivered orders, a confusing road network, and inexperience in handling large bodies of men doomed the offensive. Pelham's Battery was ordered onto the field, but its involvement was negligible. To

Breathed's frustration, the men were not able to bring their guns to bear on the enemy. Swampy terrain also prevented the Stuart Horse Artillery from moving into position and joining the fight.

Although the battle was tactically a draw, it had important consequences for the course of the war. Near the end of the first day of fighting, Johnston was severely wounded by a shell burst. His second in command, Gustavus Smith, assumed the reins of the army, but it became quickly clear during the fighting on June 1 that Smith was not the man to command in the field. Later that day, President Davis appointed Robert E. Lee to command of the army, which would soon be known as the Army of Northern Virginia. No one, not even the Confederate president, could have guessed the success Lee and his army would soon enjoy.

The choice of Lee was not a popular one. Many people held the general in low esteem after his mediocre early-war performance in western Virginia. His credentials, however, were impeccable. Lee graduated second in the West Point class of 1829 with no demerits and spent most of his antebellum career as a military engineer. His distinguished service as a staff officer in the Mexican War, which contributed greatly to the capture of Mexico City through the method of mobile flanking movements, presaged the martial talent he would display in the Civil War. When secession came Lee sided with his native state, Virginia— even when envoy Francis P. Blair Sr., a publisher and close associate of President Lincoln, offered Lee command of the Union army then gathering around Washington to suppress the rebellion.

The elevation of Lee was indeed a turning point of the war in the Eastern Theater.[35]

Chapter 3

Reconnaissance

General Lee was determined to keep Richmond out of McClellan's grasp, and was not afraid to risk his new command to save the Confederate capital. Rather than await his opponent's next move, Lee resolved to strike first. The only question was where to attack, and when.

The Union right flank stretched well north of the Chickahominy River, and seemed vulnerable to a turning movement. Before he could launch his counteroffensive, however, Lee needed to ascertain McClellan's numbers and dispositions. He turned to Stuart to gather this vital information. Stuart's subsequent reconnaissance, known to history as the "Ride Around McClellan," took place between June 12 and 15. The expedition was quickly recognized as a great cavalry exploit. It also demonstrated the potential value of horse artillery, for regular artillery would not have been able to keep pace with Stuart's hard-riding troopers. "Perhaps nothing that occurred during the early days of the war so awakened the Army to the possibilities of the more mobile guns as did this raid around McClellan," observed one historian.[1]

In his instructions to Stuart, Lee stressed the vital importance of gaining information about McClellan's dispositions: "You will return as soon as the object of your expedition is accomplished, and you must bear constantly in mind, while endeavoring to execute the general purpose of your mission, not to hazard unnecessarily your command. ...Remember that one of the chief objects of your expedition is to gain intelligence for the guidance of future operations."[2]

Wisely, Stuart took very seriously another part of Lee's order, "I recommend that you only take such men and horses as can stand the expedition..." Stuart's reconnaissance force included detachments from the 1st Virginia Cavalry, led by Col. Fitzhugh Lee (the army commander's nephew); the 9th Virginia Cavalry, commanded by Col. W. H. F. "Rooney" Lee (one of General Lee's sons); and the 4th Virginia Cavalry, whose current lack of field officers compelled Stuart to attach portions of the unit to the expedition's other two Virginia regiments. The expedition also included two Mississippi cavalry squadrons from the Jeff Davis Legion under the command of Lt. Col. William T. Martin. Stuart took with him a pair of guns from the Stuart Horse Artillery to bolster the firepower of his reconnaissance team. Pelham, probably because of an illness, did not take part in the mission; Breathed was left in overall charge of the guns. In all, Stuart had assembled about 1,200 sabers for his reconnaissance, all well mounted and fit, just as Lee had recommended.[3]

Stuart woke his troopers at 2:00 A.M. on June 12 and ordered them to mount up. The men had not been given prior warning that they would be part of an important expedition. Scouts took position on the right of the column, searching for any sign of the enemy. To prevent surprises, guards on the flanks and rear screened Stuart's force.[4]

The expedition moved out early, only Stuart knowing its true purpose. To deceive any Union spies in the area, he directed his first day's march toward Louisa, which would give anyone watching the impression he was moving to reinforce Stonewall Jackson in the Shenandoah Valley. Unlike Jackson, who routinely kept such information from his subordinates, Stuart realized his chances for success would be higher if his officers knew the objective of the raid. As a result, he quietly informed his regimental commanders of their mission. That night, the cavalrymen encamped opposite Hanover Court House near South Anna Bridge on the Richmond, Fredericksburg, and Potomac Railroad. As the men settled into camp, scouts who had left earlier on reconnaissance patrols returned with news that no serious enemy forces were to be found along the route Stuart had selected for the next day's ride.[5]

The men were awakened the next morning without bugle calls or other loud noises to avoid alerting any Union troops within earshot of

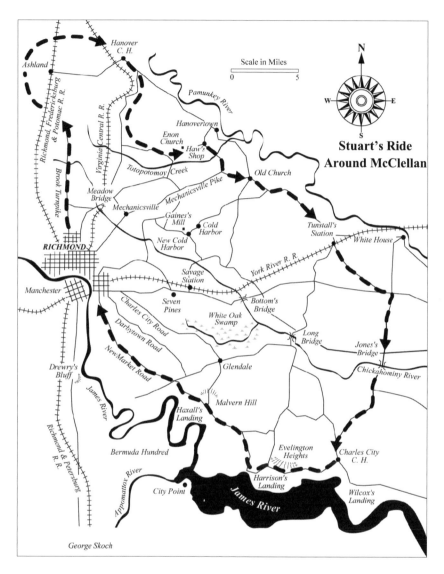

Stuart's Ride Around McClellan

George Skoch

their presence. The expedition's destination still remained, in Stuart's words, "a profound secret," known only to a small circle of chosen officers. Stuart's column rode generally southeast via Hanover Court House on the route to Old Church. The Southern cavalrymen soon discovered that Union forces occupied Hanover Court House. Uncertain of their strength, Stuart proceeded with caution. Fitz Lee's 1st Virginia Cavalry was ordered to swing around on the right and "reach the enemy's route behind him, to ascertain his force here and crush it, if possible," reported Stuart, "but the enemy, proving afterward to be 150 cavalry, did not tarry long, but left, my column following slowly down, expecting every moment to [drive the enemy] upon [Fitz] Lee; but owing to a bad marsh Colonel Lee did not reach the intersection of roads in time." Because of Fitz Lee's delay, the 150 Federals from the 6th U.S. Cavalry managed to slip away and head in the direction of Mechanicsville. Although they had escaped, their route carried them away from the direction of Stuart's march. Determined not to lose sight of his objective, Stuart let the 150 men ride away.[6]

Accompanied by their horse artillery, the Southern cavalry rode on to Taliaferro's Mill, then to Enon Church, and finally Haw's Shop, where they surprised and captured some Union pickets. Rooney Lee's 9th Virginia Cavalry led the day's march, with the regimental adjutant, Lt. W. T. Robins, in charge of the advance guard. This arrangement enabled Stuart to divide his column and thus confuse and surprise any Union force they encountered.[7]

Between Haw's Shop and Old Church, north of Totopotomoy Creek, the advance elements discovered and clashed with Lt. Edward H. Lieb's Company F, 5th U.S. Cavalry. Realizing he was outnumbered by Lieutenant Robins' Virginians, Lieb fell back, riding as fast as possible for the far side of the creek. Stuart believed the enemy would make a stand at the waterway, and the fact that they did not destroy the bridge increased his apprehension. Any significant delay would force him to cancel his mission.[8]

Skirmishers from the 9th Virginia carefully splashed across Totopotomoy Creek, "a strong position of defense, which the enemy failed to hold, confessing a weakness," Stuart later reported. He prudently deployed a small force on foot as skirmishers to cover the crossing until "the point of danger was passed."

With a small bridgehead formed, Stuart pressed Robins forward and his men waded across on foot. Up ahead, about 100 troopers from Capt. William B. Royall's 5th U.S. Cavalry were drawn up and prepared to charge, having been advised by Lieb that the Rebels were coming in force. Dismounted, Robins ordered a retreat, but when Stuart arrived upon the scene at the head of the 9th Virginia, he ordered its leading squadron under Capt. William Latane to meet and defeat the enemy cavalry. Arranged in columns of four, they trotted forward until the order to "charge!" was given. Robins and his men soon mounted and joined in the attack. Stuart was more than pleased, perhaps keeping in mind that the side that feeds in the last reserves often wins the day. A hand-to-hand combat quickly ensued with pistols and swords at close range. After the war, Matthews recalled the running action this way:

> When we reached the bridge spanning Totopotomy creek we met Lt. Lieb of the 5th U. S. Cavalry with a squadron. The ground being in the favor of the Federal cavalry, they accordingly concluded to receive our advance. Lt. Lieb halted his command near the north approach to the bridge. Adjt. Robbins of the 9th Va., threw out flanking parties, causing the enemy to retire in great confusion to the junction of the Old Church and Bethesda church roads leading to Mechanicsville. Here the command under Gen. Lieb, 6th U. S. Cavalry, was reinforced by Capt. Royal[l]'s [sic.] squadron of the 5th U. S. Cavalry, who drew up his squadron to receive the attack.

After a short fight that included several charges and countercharges, Royall was convinced he was facing an "overwhelming force" and fled the field. He left four killed and about a dozen wounded in his wake. Although Royall himself was reported mortally wounded, he was only gravely injured. On the Confederate side, Latane was killed in the brief encounter, and a few others wounded.[9]

With Pelham absent, Breathed had set up his guns in the belief that "our dogs of war [would be] a barking." However, the opportunity to engage the Union troopers never presented itself. Although a short pursuit was ordered, the Southerners were unable to catch up and engage them.[10]

The woods and fields were strewn with disoriented Union soldiers struggling to rejoin their compatriots. Knowing that speed was vital to his mission's success, however, Stuart refrained from capturing them. Taking prisoners would have wasted valuable time. As it was, Stuart reported the capture of "several officers and a number of privates," along with horses, weapons, and various other stores. He also took five enemy guidons (cavalry flags), a feat that instilled a sense of pride in the ranks. For both sides in the Civil War, the most powerful emblem of a unit's pride was its colors. The capture of an enemy's flag was one of the most honorable feats anyone could hope to accomplish.[11]

Fitz Lee, leading his 1st Virginia Cavalry, longed to share in the fruits of the victory. Like his more famous uncle, Fitz Lee had served in the 2nd United States Cavalry before the Civil War. During the action on the Old Church Road he had pleaded with Stuart to let him join in the embarrassment of his former pre-war peers. When Stuart finally granted him permission, Lee's leading squadron forged ahead to Old Church. However, Royall's disoriented command was in no shape to offer Lee the fight he desired. Fitz Lee's battalion, five companies strong, charged unopposed into the Union camp, seizing horses, weapons, and supplies. Several more Union officers and enlisted men fell into his hands. The Confederates set ablaze any supplies they could not utilize, and the expeditionary force continued its march.[12]

Stuart now made an important decision, which he termed "the turning point of the expedition." He had accomplished what General Lee wanted, and had determined that there was not any major Union force deployed in the Chickahominy and Pamunkey watershed. Now Stuart had to report back to Lee as quickly as possible. However, the question remained: what was the quickest way back? There were two routes Stuart could follow:

> the one to return by Hanover Court-House, the other to pass around through New Kent, taking the chances of having to swim the Chickahominy and make a bold effort to cut the enemy's lines of communication. The Chickahominy was believed by my guide to be fordable near Forge Bridge. I was 14 miles from Hanover Court House, which I would have to pass. If I returned, the enemy had a much shorter distance to pass to intercept me there; besides, the South Anna was impassable, which still further narrowed the chances of escape in that direction; the enemy, too, would naturally expect me to take that route.

Tunstall's Station was a mere nine miles southeast on the Richmond & York River Railroad, a major artery linking McClellan's army to the supply depot at White House Landing on the Pamunkey. Severing it and wrecking the line, thought Stuart, would be a major success. Thereafter, he could head south and cross the Chickahominy River at Forge Bridge. Once below the river on the Charles City County side, Lee's army could easily offer a diversion that would help prevent the Federals from moving to intercept the column. The enemy, he further reasoned, would not expect him to take this route. Stuart had just decided to ride completely around McClellan's army.[13]

To deceive the pursuing Federal horsemen, Stuart interrogated local civilians about the distances and routes to Hanover Court House, offering the Northerners the impression he was going to backtrack toward Richmond instead of returning via Tunstall's Station.[14]

Knowing the enemy was likely hot in pursuit, the rear of Stuart's column had now become as important as the front (and probably more vulnerable). Lt. Col. William T. Martin's Jeff Davis Legion was bringing up the rear and escorting Breathed's artillery at the same time. The Legion and guns had trouble keeping pace with the quick-moving main body, but to fall too far behind would all but guarantee their eventual capture or destruction. To Martin's surprise, a party of 25 Union soldiers emerged along the way brandishing a white flag. They mistakenly believed they were surrounded and wanted nothing more than to surrender and end the matter.[15]

Approaching Tunstall's Station east of Richmond, Stuart deployed an advance force of carefully selected men in order to capture and destroy its telegraph communications. The Confederate raiders expeditiously seized the depot and captured its garrison without firing a single shot. Within a short time the railroad tracks were blocked with timbers and other materials in an effort to intercept and wreak havoc on the next train arriving at Tunstall's Station.[16]

Unfortunately for the Confederates, stopping a train was not an easy endeavor. A troop train approached the station at full throttle just as the main body of Stuart's column reached the depot. The engine smashed into the barrier and sent debris flying in every direction from the tracks. The cavalrymen opened fire on the engine and a stray bullet killed the engineer, but stopping or otherwise derailing the train at this point was now all but impossible. Stuart later made the arrogant claim that the bullets fired by his men either killed all the passengers and crew or caused them to lay low and act as if they were dead. He hoped the engineer's death would result in a speeding train smashing into White House Landing. A fireman, however, seized the locomotive's controls and safely brought the train under control which arrived at its final destination without damage to the end of the line.[17]

The train's derailment might have been accomplished if one of Breathed's guns had arrived at the depot in a timely fashion. However, the battery's horses were exhausted and the roads too congested for the artillery to arrive and deploy in time. "We were now within four miles of

McClelland's mighty army of the Potomac's headquarters [White House Landing]," Matthews later wrote. "Danger was on all sides, but that band of heroes rode on unconscious of the danger they were in. What cared they when the intrepid Stuart rode at their head?"[18]

Although they failed to derail the troop train, the cavalrymen set ablaze a substantial wagon train before heading south toward Talleysville on the way to Sycamore Springs. Once they arrived at Talleysville, the men stopped for a short time to feed and water their jaded horses. Stuart "had great consideration for his pet—the horse artillery. They were destined to bring him out of many a close place by their determined and bull dog fighting," but the horses were tiring quickly and the last thing the cavalry leader wanted to see was the loss of his precious guns.

Freshly watered and with reasonably full stomachs, the horses carried the cavalrymen south along the Pamunkey River, where they questioned civilians and tried to glean whatever information they could about the disposition of the enemy.[19]

On June 13, one of Breathed's two guns became stuck in a mud hole. The cannoneers shouted and lashed at their horses, but the deep sticky mud refused to allow the heavy piece to roll free. A sergeant offered Breathed an idea in the midst of this frustrating situation. Heeding his advice, Breathed placed a barrel of whiskey on the gun's carriage as an incentive. The whiskey had the desired effect. According to his family's oral tradition, Pvt. James Gray, one of Breathed's gunners, was the first man to splash into the quagmire. He was closely followed by the other artillerists who had suddenly found a fresh source of strength and vigor. Within a few minutes the gun was freed and the men were enjoying their liquid reward. Breathed had just demonstrated his ability to motivate his men, however unorthodox the methodology.[20]

Martin was impressed by Breathed's unflagging efforts to keep his guns moving, and officially complimented the officer's dogged efforts. "I would take occasion to mention the energy displayed by Lieutenant Breathed in overcoming the difficulties encountered in moving his piece of artillery," Martin later reported, "and the promptness shown in preparing for action on several occasions when there was reason to believe that the enemy were about to attack."[21]

At midnight, Stuart's command rode the eight miles from Talleysville to Forge Bridge on the Chickahominy River. The men were so exhausted that many fell asleep in the saddle. Even Stuart succumbed.

Gary Gray

James Gray and wife, long after the Civil War.

When a soldier told Stuart that a ford over the river at Sycamore Springs plantation was closer than Forge Bridge, the general ordered his men to make for it. Time, after all, was of the essence, and the pursuing Federals were more likely to head for the bridge than an obscure crossing point.

When they reached the crossing point, however, the Southerners quickly discovered a swollen river with muddy banks. Fitz Lee tried the crossing and declared it too deep and swift for wagons and guns, and probably for horses as well. Stuart's men jumped into action with axes and began gathering the materials they needed to construct a makeshift bridge. Simultaneously, others tried unsuccessfully to build a ferry. By the time the sun was rising above the horizon, only a small group of riders had managed to cross. Bridge building was not a cavalryman's forte, and it quickly became obvious that if they tarried longer at the swollen crossing they would be trapped against the river by the pursuing enemy. Stuart decided to head to Forge Bridge. The river there was divided by an island, and the bridge across the northern channel was reportedly partially destroyed. Still, according to one local, enough of the structure remained to arrange for an expeditious crossing.[22]

Within a short time the Southern workers had erected a rather ramshackle pontoon-style structure across which the men began walking with their equipment. The process was painfully slow, and Stuart turned to demolishing a barn to use the wood to span the stone supports from the original bridge. So strengthened, the bridge was now ready to bear the weight of Breathed's guns and the expedition's wagons. By 1:00 P.M., the column was over the first channel and safely on the island. Fitz Lee was the last man to step off the northern bank. The south channel was also treacherous, but fordable. Stuart assigned a party to burn the northern bridge as the rest of the command walked and swam its way to safety. Although a limber was left in the swampy terrain, the entire command finally made it across the flooded Chickahominy by early afternoon.[23]

As Stuart and every man in his command realized, the successful crossing moved them beyond the reach of the pursuing enemy, or as Stuart later put it, the men had "passed the point of danger." Freed from the stress of possible annihilation, Stuart rode off to present his findings to General Lee.[24]

The cavalier's feat of riding around the enemy's entire army was amazing, and one that quickly made the name Stuart a household name. Stuart's father-in-law, Brig. Gen. Philip St. George Cooke, was the commander of the Union cavalry pursuing Stuart and his raiders. Cooke, who was in his fifties, was neither young enough nor vigorous enough to meet the task at hand, and his failure was fairly obvious to everyone. The career officer served through the remainder of the campaign, but for the rest of the war he performed solely administrative functions.[25]

On June 17, Stuart concluded in his official report to Lee regarding the reconnaissance:

> Returning to my command soon after, the prisoners, 165 in number, were transferred to the proper authority; 260 horses and mules captured, with more or less harness, were transferred to the quartermaster's departments of the different regiments, and the commands were sent to their respective camps. The number of captured arms has not been as yet accurately ascertained. A pole was broken, which obliged us to abandon a limber this side of the Chickahominy. The success attending this expedition will no doubt cause 10,000 or 15,000 men to be detached from the enemy's main

body to guard his communication, besides accomplishing the destruction of millions' worth of property and the interruption for a time of his railroad communication.

Lee himself issued a congratulatory order and praised the expedition as a "brilliant exploit." The ride, he noted, was "a signal success" and helped the Army of Northern Virginia better appreciate how McClellan had deployed his army.[26]

If his later raids are any indication, Stuart learned an important lesson about positioning horse artillery in a raiding column. Breathed's guns had not fired a shot during the "Ride Around McClellan." There were two obvious reasons for this. First, Breathed's guns were virtually always at or near the end of Stuart's column. Second, 1,200 horses had made a muddy mess of wet roads, almost resulting in the loss of one of Breathed's guns in the mud churned up by the front of the column. Trying to pull cannon through the wake of a large cavalry force was too much even for a six-horse team. In the future, horse artillery accompanying a raiding column of Stuart's would be moved closer to the van, where it could fight more effectively and move with less fatigue to the horses (and men). Learning this valuable lesson at the mere cost of one limber was a bargain.

By the time the raid concluded, Breathed was a long way from his peacetime profession of medicine. Although his guns had not yet been trained on Union targets, as they would shortly be, he was now physically and mentally a soldier in every respect. Ironically, Breathed's surgical experience may have made it comparatively easy for him to adjust to the horrors of combat. He was accustomed to seeing and handling dead bodies from his long hours in the School of Medicine's Anatomical Hall dissecting human cadavers. For the same reason, he would have gotten over any nausea at the sight of blood, if he ever had any. In all likelihood the doctor-turned-gunner carried an apothecary kit and surgical implements in his supply wagon, to practice his old trade if the fortunes of war so required.

*   *   *

The reconnaissance gave Lee the information he needed to conclude that an attack against McClellan's right flank, north of the Chickahominy

River, was the best course of action. McClellan's flank did not stretch far enough to protect the Army of the Potomac's communications. Lee's plan was bold and complex; moreover, it depended upon the precise timing of the several separate columns advancing over ground where communication was difficult. Lee decided to leave only some 25,000 men south of the Chickahominy to hold back nearly three times that number of the enemy. With his remaining 50,000, he would fall upon Fitz-John Porter's exposed corps north of the river, turn it out of its position, and destroy it. Stonewall Jackson and his 18,000 men were recalled from the Shenandoah Valley as part of the hammer and ordered to move quickly north of the river but south of the Totopotomoy Creek, outflanking McClellan and turning him away from his base of supply at White House Landing. As the movement developed, other divisions would take up the advance and strike the enemy as he was falling back in what was essentially a giant echelon attack. Unfortunately, the terrain was confusing and the plan too complex for commanders who were inexperienced in handling large bodies of men. Jackson was to have been in position by June 26, but the march took longer than expected, Jackson himself was exhausted, and the route muddy and confusing.

Early on the morning of June 25 in Stuart's Camp, the bugle sounded "Boots and Saddles" and the majority of the Southern cavalry, along with Pelham's command, moved along the Richmond, Fredericksburg & Potomac Railroad in the direction of Ashland. Their objective was to join forces with Jackson to help screen and protect his march. That evening, however, Jackson messaged Lee that he was behind schedule and had only reached Ashland, fifteen miles north of the capital. Early the next morning the two commands set out in the pre-dawn darkness moving toward McClellan's right flank by way of the Ashcake Road. Stuart's troopers rode parallel to Jackson's left flank, screening the infantry's march from any prying Federal eyes.

Stuart's advance, led by the 1st Virginia Cavalry, ran into the enemy at Taliaferro's Mill. Breathed and his compatriots of the Stuart Horse Artillery unlimbered their guns and threw a few shots at the Union cavalry, which promptly retreated. The Confederate cavalry continued to the home of a doctor named Shelton, skirmishing lightly along the way. When he discovered he had put too much distance between himself and Jackson's infantry, Stuart stopped at Dr. Shelton's and waited for Jackson to catch up. When he did so, the two generals continued on until nightfall and finally camped near Beaver Dam Creek. Jackson was close to his objective, but failed to coordinate his actions with other commanders who were themselves waiting for Jackson to open the engagement.[27]

Waiting for Jackson to attack and turn the enemy flank was Maj. Gen. A. P. Hill. Exasperated by the delay, Hill launched his own men against powerful Federal positions at Beaver Dam Creek east of Mechanicsville. The attack would have been unnecessary had Jackson arrived on time and flanked the position, but his failure to do so left the Federals in place and the impetuous Hill took action. The attacks by Hill's "Light Division" across the swampy terrain were thrown back with heavy losses.

On the morning of June 27, the Stuart Horse Artillery continued screening Jackson's left as it pressed on across Beaver Dam Creek. The Federals had left at dawn, falling back a few miles east to Gaines' Mill, where the main body of General Lee's army north of the Chickahominy (including Jackson's divisions) was gathering to attack Porter's exposed corps. The piecemeal attacks at the Battle of Gaines' Mill were thrown back with heavy losses for hours until nearly nightfall, when a concerted effort pierced the lines and forced Porter to evacuate his position. Stuart, meanwhile, intending to rendezvous with Jackson at Cold Harbor, had advanced by way of Beulah Church across a tortuous route that temporarily separated him from the infantry. The horse soldiers reunited with the army later in the day.[28]

Jackson's difficulties in reaching the field were made harder by a pair of enemy artillery batteries that had set up near the Grapevine Bridge on the Chickahominy and were shelling his men. Since Jackson's own artillery was not available, Stuart offered his horse artillery in its place. One of the gunners remembered as Pelham rode into camp. "We knew that there was work ahead, for it was invariably the case when Stuart and Pelham rode off," recalled Henry Matthews. "It meant for us trouble ahead, and plenty of it, as it proved this instance." Pelham, who cut a dashing figure on a horse, galloped up, drew his mount to a stop, and ordered his men to move out at a trot. "We immediately thundered along the road, not in a trot, but from a full run," remembered Matthews. Some of Stuart's horsemen, riding to protect the guns, fanned out to the right and left of the short artillery column. "In pressing them we would salute them in this way: 'Stay back, boys; we will settle them, and then you can come up in perfect safety.' We knew them so well that we could take this liberty without giving offense."[29]

With Pelham leading the way, Breathed guided a newly captured Napoleon and a 12-pounder Blakely into position in a clearing, where the guns were unlimbered and opened fire. Union counter-battery fire, however, was remarkably accurate and the first shots knocked the Blakely out of action, leaving "the Napoleon, with Fayette Gibson as gunner, alone to encounter the two Federal batteries to which it was opposed," wrote Matthews. Pelham ordered the crew to drag the piece out of range and he and Breathed shifted the position of the lone operational piece. Once situated, Pelham offered a short, enthusiastic speech to his gunners and the firing commenced anew. "Pelham maintained the unequal contest with the same courage which he always displayed in subsequent actions," Matthews remembered with pride. In recalling the services of First Lieutenant Gustavus Warfield (Gus) Dorsey, 1st Virginia Cavalry, Matthews also complimented Breathed: "On every battlefield in the old Virginia his [Dorsey's] sabre . . . flashed like an engine of destruction. Like his friend, Jim Breathed, he was always in the front." Jackson's own guns eventually replaced the single piece. When Stuart told Jackson about the unequal duel, Pelham was taken before Stonewall Jackson, who complimented him for his brave efforts.[30]

The course of the Seven Days' Battles changed after Gaines' Mill. Once he abandoned his position north of the Chickahominy, McClellan began an open retreat toward the James River. On the morning of June 28, Lee summoned Stuart and gave him a new mission—severing the York River Railroad, McClellan's main supply line connecting his army to the main supply depot at White House Landing on the Pamunkey River. On the back of a horse yet again, Breathed rode along with his guns as the cavalry column moved out. The troopers cut telegraph wires and ripped up some track on the line. When they reached the vicinity of Tunstall's Station, enemy cavalry supported by artillery was found deployed on the far side of a small but muddy creek. Stuart called up his guns to "disperse" the Federals. Breathed quickly opened on the enemy and assisted in placing a pair of howitzers with his characteristic perfection. Canister was used along the banks of the creek to flush out infantry hiding in ambush. "The battery did good execution, driving them [the Union] out of their works with shells, killing a goodly number,"

LC

The "White House," Rooney Lee's home, was ruined by the Federals.

remembered Matthews. The fleeing enemy left a pair of rifled guns in their wake, which Stuart promptly turned over to Pelham's Battery.[31]

When Stuart reached White House Landing, he discovered that McClellan had abandoned his base the previous day. There was now no doubt about it: the Army of the Potomac was retreating toward the James River. White House Landing was the antebellum home of Rooney Lee, and the spiteful Federals burned it to the ground before leaving. Like Stuart, Breathed watched the fire from a distance. "The conflagration raged fearfully at the White House during the entire night [of June 28-29], while explosions of shells rent the air," Stuart wrote.[32]

Stuart had approached White House Landing cautiously because he believed some 5,000 Union troops were nearby. Instead Stuart found an intriguing target, the Union gunboat *Marblehead*. "Imagination had clothed the gunboat with marvelous terrors, and at this stage of the war there was nothing that inspired more fears in the breast of a Johnny Reb than the screech of their enormous shells," Matthews explained. Stuart was determined to brush aside the fear of what he called "this Yankee bugaboo." With a howitzer from Breathed's section, the Rebel cavalry chief sent 75 dismounted troopers against the gunboat in the hope that its commander would think no one would attack it unless they had an overwhelming superiority. When the troopers opened fire, a detachment of New York troops from the gunship came ashore to engage them. It was then that Pelham and Breathed opened a steady and accurate fire, changing positions often to confuse the navy vessel. The gunboat's skipper was not prepared for a fight. When he realized the accurate fire was seriously imperiling his ship, he quickly moved out of range. Breathed spurred his horse along the bank as the artillerists moved the gun and the dismounted sharpshooters kept up their fire at the fleeing vessel.[33]

The men retired to White House Landing for the night, where they discovered ample rations and forage that the Union army had failed to destroy. Together, Pelham and Breathed sat beneath a tree and enjoyed large servings of pickled oysters and fruit. "Captain, if McClellan's troops eat like this every day, its no wonder they run away rather than fight and get killed," joked Breathed. When a pair of undamaged locomotives was discovered, Stuart asked the artillerists to disable them without permanent damage. The gunners sized up the job and determined to put a hole through each boiler. Pelham ordered up a rifled gun, and two shots took care of the matter.[34]

When the 1st Virginia Cavalry left after dark on a scouting expedition to look for any trace of Union activity between Bottom's Bridge and Forge Bridge on the Chickahominy River, Breathed joined them. If he got any sleep that night, it was probably in the saddle. The next morning, Breathed joined Stuart's command as it moved to Long and Forge bridges on the Chickahominy. It was time to rejoin the main army, which had been heavily engaged with McClellan as he slipped his way toward the James. The pickets of Fitz Lee's 1st Virginia Cavalry could see Union pickets across the river at Long Bridge. The next day only promised more riding, more hardships, and probably more fighting.

When the Confederate cavalry reached Forge Bridge, they discovered a pair of enemy guns accompanied by infantry and cavalry support waiting to obstruct their passage. Stuart ordered up the artillery to engage the Union guns and Pelham complied, shouting to everyone in the road to "Make way for the Horse Artillery!" A Napoleon was unlimbered alongside Lee's men, but its trail broke off after firing its first shot, rendering the cannon useless. The battery's Blakely had already been disabled during the skirmish at Cold Harbor, which left Stuart with

Breathed's section of 12-pound howitzers. Despite the diminished firepower, Pelham ordered Breathed to move his pieces into action, where their effective fire drove off the Union guns and once again earned Stuart's praise.[35]

Once the enemy fell back, a reconnaissance force from Martin's Jeff Davis Legion splashed across the river. There, Union cavalry drew sabers and charged them. Pelham, with Breathed's two howitzers in tow, was sent to clear the Union troopers off the road. Once across, Breathed unlimbered his guns in the midst of severe counter-battery fire from two rifled pieces. Martin described the fire of the Union guns, blasting from only 400 yards away as, "very rapid and accurate." Somehow Breathed's section was able to drive off the Federal guns in just a few minutes. Martin later reported that Pelham's men killed two of the Union soldiers and a pair of horses.[36]

On July 1, Stuart received orders to rejoin Jackson south of the Chickahominy River. Despite his efforts to catch up with Jackson's infantry, Stuart was unable to do so. This proved fortuitous for Breathed and the other members of the Stuart Horse Artillery, who otherwise might have been engaged in the one-sided Battle of Malvern Hill, the last major action of The Seven Days' Battles.

From June 26 forward, Lee had sought to turn McClellan away from the Southern capital and annihilate the Army of the Potomac. In a week of the most brutal fighting the war had yet witnessed, Lee successfully drove McClellan away from Richmond all the way back to Harrison's Landing on the James River. Although several opportunities had presented themselves, Lee was unable to execute the complex movements necessary to grasp and decisively defeat the Federals.

As McClellan's troops took position on Malvern Hill, on the road to Harrison's Landing, Lee realized he was facing his final opportunity to score a clear-cut victory. His plan was relatively simple: mass as much artillery as possible, shell the enemy guns and positions, and then attack with his infantry. The Federals, however, had amassed more than 100 guns on the crest of Malvern Hill with more in reserve, and with them and the gunships stationed on the James, smashed the Southern gunnery effort. Had Breathed's howitzers been committed to the battle, they likely would have helped swell the casualty list, but not much more. Still, Stuart's troopers were missed at the battle. Lee had wanted to look into the possibility of outflanking the Union position to the east, but without

Stuart's cavalry it was difficult to conduct a competent reconnaissance of the region.[37]

Ultimately, the battle developed into a series of doomed Confederate frontal assaults that were quite literally mowed down by the concentrated fire of the Union guns. Confederate Maj. Gen. Daniel Harvey Hill famously summarized the battle at Malvern Hill: "[T]he Confederate assaults did not move together and were beaten in detail. As each brigade emerged from the woods, from 50 to 100 guns opened upon it, tearing great gaps in its ranks, but the heroes reeled on and were shot by the [infantry] reserves at the guns...It was not war, it was murder." McClellan scored a decisive victory on July 1, thanks to a superb choice of position, which had the guns set upon the crest of a sloping open field to their front. The slaughter was a result of well-served artillery, and the willingness of his opponent to attack him with wave after wave of exposed Confederate soldiers.[38]

Brig. Gen. William W. Averell, who commanded a brigade of Union cavalry, left a vivid and moving description of the appearance of the

LC

Brigadier General William W. Averell and cavalry staff.

battlefield. All that could be heard was the agonizing shrieks from many thousands of wounded and dying men. "Over five thousand dead and wounded men were on the ground in every attitude of distress," he recalled. "A third of them were dead or dying, but enough were alive and moving to give to the field a singular crawling effect." The battlefield looked as if it was a shoreline, with three lines of dead and wounded men crawling and ebbing forward and back searching for a helping hand.[39]

That night, the opposing forces fought rearguard actions as McClellan evacuated Malvern Hill for Harrison's Landing on the James, where he believed he would be essentially immune from attack. The withdrawal, however, also offered opportunity. Stuart directed Pelham to move down the river and scout the enemy's new position, disposition, and vulnerabilities. Breathed was to command in his absence. Stuart spent July 2 and 3 dispersing his forces to try to establish a clear picture of what McClellan was doing since his withdrawal from Malvern Hill. The horse artillery, its officers, and its gunners were split up among various of Stuart's cavalry units that were sent to patrol between Haxall's Landing just below Malvern Hill all the way to Charles City Courthouse well to the east. The horse artillery was undoubtedly engaged with Union forces in piecemeal encounters, but it was not until the morning of July 3 that Stuart and Pelham located the bulk of McClellan's army at Harrison's Landing. [40]

"Harrison's Landing was a peninsula about four miles long by one and half wide, formed by Herring Creek on the northeast; running for that distance nearly parallel to the James before emptying into it," recalled Confederate artillerist Edward Porter Alexander. "At its head a small inlet from the river on the southwest left but a narrow front exposed to attack." If artillery and infantry in sufficient number held the heights, the Federals would be forced to attack into strength with an impassable creek in front, or risk being trapped. Here was potentially an opportunity to trap the entire Union army with its back against a wide and deep river! [41]

On July 3, Stuart and his cavalry, together with Pelham and his guns headed toward the high ground to occupy it before McClellan determined its value and seized it. The results of the earlier reconnaissance had been passed on to Lee, and Stuart believed infantry was following in his wake. When he spotted a squadron of Federal cavalry on the previously unoccupied hill, Stuart brushed them aside and occupied Evelington Heights himself. It was about 10:00 A.M. Without waiting for infantry to control the dominant terrain feature, Stuart ordered Pelham to shell the encamped enemy. (Confederate infantry was indeed moving to support Stuart, but had taken the wrong road and would not arrive in time.)

The single gun was unlimbered on the River Road and methodically threw a handful of shells at the surprised enemy for several hours. "Judging from the great commotion and excitement below, it must have had considerable effect," Stuart later reported. It has frequently been argued that Stuart's hasty decision only prodded McClellan to act fast to gain control of Evelington Heights and that if Stuart had waited for his infantry support McClellan's army could have been completely destroyed. Whether Stuart was premature or not, what happened was that McClellan attacked Stuart in overwhelming force. Left with little choice, Stuart and his command evacuated Evelington Heights, effectively ending the week of fighting.[42]

After the excitement of July 3, Stuart's command bivouacked near the Phillip's Farm. Breathed and his fellow battery men finally had an opportunity to enjoy a few days of rest. When word of a grounded enemy steamer reached them, Stuart dispatched his gunners to Wilcox's Landing, a few miles from Harrison's Landing. There they found the Federal transport *Juniata*, trapped on a sandbar. Pelham's guns pounded the *Juniata*, killing and wounding a handful of men before the ship managed to clear the sandbar and slip out of range.[43]

Lee's aggressive strategy and tactics were exactly what the Confederacy needed to save its capital, but the price of his audacious campaign was high. Southern losses were more than 20,000: 3,500 killed, 16,000 wounded, and another 1,000 missing. McClellan's losses were nearly 16,000: 1,750 killed, 8,000 wounded, and 6,000 missing.[44]

The campaign offered an opportunity for the officers and men to display their talents (or lack thereof). Both Stonewall Jackson and Stuart have come in for criticism for their efforts during The Seven Days' battles. Perhaps that was inevitable, given that Jackson's Valley Campaign and Stuart's Ride Around McClellan were difficult to equal, let alone exceed. Stuart was criticized for premature shelling from Evelington Heights without sufficient support to inflict the maximum damage on the Federals. He was also criticized for ranging too wide afield from the main body of Lee's army. If there was a lesson to be learned from Evelington Heights it has still to be determined exactly what it was. However, Stuart's propensity to wander off into local actions independent of the battle plan would be seen again, with more serious consequences.

It cannot be denied that Stuart frequently did not know where Jackson's forces were, even though Stuart's orders were to screen Jackson's flank. However, the Peninsula, as was seen in earlier actions, was still far too soggy for massed cavalry actions. Swamps abounded; roads were few, bridges scarce. Stuart was always impetuous, and would remain so until his death. Therefore, if Stuart found himself idle and an opportunity to discomfort the enemy arose, he would usually take the opportunity afforded. It was his strength; it was his weakness.

The horse artillery, on the other hand, had performed well. The batteries were learning to work independently with small units and had contributed decisive force on some occasions. Pelham and Stuart were learning to work together in battle. Things looked promising. The men of Pelham's Horse Artillery Battery, including its commander John Pelham, had fought valiantly during the recent combat. They were no longer green recruits, but veterans who had experienced the hardships of combat without failing in the hour of need. Although no promotion came his way because of The Seven Days' battles, James Breathed had clearly earned the $100 paycheck he received from the Confederacy.

Breathed had also learned some hard lessons of war. He learned firsthand the relentless effort required to move, position, and fire his guns. He had led his weapons with authority and exercised sound discretion. Now it was time to rest, refit, and recall the battles around campfires as the generals and politicians decided what to do next.

However, the war was changing, and Stuart's Cavalry was about to be reorganized to meet the new challenges.

As it became evident that McClellan's army ceased to be a threat to Richmond, there was a brief pause in action during which Lee reorganized his forces. Stuart was promoted to major general and assumed command of all of the Army of Northern Virginia's cavalry on July 25. Maj. Gen. Stuart could only justify his rank if he commanded a division; so a Division of Cavalry was created. This division required brigades, so two were created and one acquired. Who would command the brigades would be a troublesome question, but it was finally settled that Brig. Gen. Wade Hampton of South Carolina assumed command of the 1st Brigade while the newly promoted Brig. Gen. Fitzhugh Lee took command of the 2nd Brigade. The "Third Brigade" was Turner Ashby's famed command. It had been operating under the command of Stonewall Jackson. But Ashby was dead. He was replaced by Brig. Gen. Beverly Robertson. But Jackson thought Robertson incompetent. (Visiting Jackson after August 8, Stuart was of the same opinion as Jackson.) However, before a replacement for Robertson could be found events compelled Stuart and his cavalry back to the field.[43]

For better or for worse, about the beginning of August 1862 the official organization of the Cavalry of the Army of Northern Virginia was as follows:

Cavalry Division: Major General JEB Stuart

1st Brigade: Brig. Gen. Wade Hampton
1st NC Cavalry, Col. Laurence S. Baker
Hampton Legion, Col. Matthew C. Butler
Cobb's Legion, Lt. Col. Pierce M. B. Young (wounded)
Maj. William G. Delony (acting)
10th VA Cavalry, Lt. Col. Zachariah S. McGruder
Jeff Davis Legion, Lt. Col. William T. Martin

2nd Brigade: Brig. Gen. Fitzhugh Lee
1st VA Cavalry, Lt. Col. L. Tiernan Brien
3rd VA Cavalry, Col. Thomas F. Goode
4th VA Cavalry, Col. Williams C. Wickham
5th VA Cavalry, Col. Thomas L. Rosser
9th VA Cavalry, Col. William H. F. "Rooney" Lee

Around this time Stuart's command was officially supplemented (on paper) by a third brigade, the Ashby Brigade:

3rd Brigade: Brig. Gen. Beverly H. Robertson
2nd VA Cavalry, Col. Thomas T. Munford
6th VA Cavalry, Col. P. S. Flourney
7th VA Cavalry, Col. William E. "Grumble" Jones
12th VA Cavalry, Col. A. W. Harman
17th VA Cavalry Bn., Maj. Oliver R. Funsten, Sr.[44]

LC

South Carolinian Wade Hampton, one of
the finest Southern cavalry commanders of the war.

The horse artillery was in theory attached to the division, but in practice was generally assigned to a brigade on the march, with batteries frequently assigned to smaller detachments as the vicissitudes of battle required.

Cavalry Artillery Battalion: Maj. John Pelham
1st Stuart Horse Artillery, Capt. James Breathed
Washington (SC) Artillery, Capt. James Franklin Hart
Ashby Battery, Capt. Roger Preston Chew[45]

What is not obvious from the above reorganization was how many of these battalion and battery commanders would make the Stuart Horse Artillery the legend it would soon become. The leadership that the Stuart Horse Artillery would draw upon throughout the remainder of the war was, with few exceptions, fully assembled.[46]

In addition to Pelham and Breathed, there was Roger Preston Chew of Ashby's Battery, who had been the commander of the first Confederate horse artillery unit to take the field. One topic that always started a lively discussion any time "Lee's Miserables" gathered after the war to reminisce was "Who was the best horse artillery commander?" Invariably, Chew's name would be mentioned together with the deeds to back it up. It was not long before Ashby's Battery was referred to as Chew's Battery.

James Franklin Hart was the commander of the Washington Battery of South Carolina, which had just been converted to horse artillery. Because these men and guns hailed from the Palmetto State, Hart's Battery would frequently support Wade Hampton's cavalry units. Hart would prove his mettle through most of the war until he was severely wounded in 1864.

Mathis Winston Henry, who had been with the Stuart Horse Artillery from the beginning, had often supervised training. When it was decided to create a 2nd Stuart Horse Artillery, Henry got the command. Within months his gallantry earned him a major's rank and a command in the regular artillery with Longstreet's Corps.

William Morrel McGregor would rise to command a battalion before the end of the war. McGregor learned to fight beside the very best: Pelham, Breathed, and Henry. McGregor fought as hard as anyone and even after several wounds never lacked in bravery and leadership. It was often said of McGregor that he would take guns where even Breathed and Pelham would not.

Philip Preston Johnston, who had recently re-enlisted in Pelham's Horse Artillery, would fight on many fields and advance to the rank of major. His promotions were always accompanied by reports of his conspicuous gallantry under fire.

James Walton Thomson had been a student at VMI in 1860. If there was anyone in the Stuart Horse Artillery who rivaled Breathed in fearlessness and recklessness, it was Thomson. If he could not bring his guns to bear on the enemy, Thomson would do his best to find the nearest cavalry charge and join in. He fought that way throughout the war and would die that way just three days before Lee's surrender.

Before he joined the Stuart Horse Artillery, Marylander Daniel Shanks had already been cited by his commanding general for conspicuous gallantry with the 1st Maryland Infantry. Shanks' name was destined to appear time and again in reports citing his bravery. Near the war's end, Shanks would be named the last commander of his battery.

All of these gallant officers and soldiers were now being brought together by this reorganization of the horse artillery. The time for great deeds was now fast approaching.[47]

* * *

While the reorganization proceeded, field operations for Stuart's Cavalry did not cease, although the units were spread out all over central Virginia. Chew's Battery was still supporting Robertson's Brigade with Jackson's new Corps. Chew would not reunite with Stuart until after the Battle of Cedar Mountain. Hart's Battery was still with Hampton's Brigade, presumably learning how to be horse artillery (Hart turned out to be a fast learner). Pelham and Breathed were with Fitz Lee's Brigade.[47]

If McClellan had been quiescent at Harrison's Landing since early July, other Federal units had not. Federal raiding units operating out of the Fredericksburg area were trying to disrupt the Virginia Central Railroad. The depredations had to be stopped since the Virginia Central was a vital link to Jackson's troops. By August 4 the roads had dried out enough for Stuart to lead a counter-raid.[48]

Stuart put together a force from Fitz Lee's Brigade, supplemented by two guns from Pelham's Battery, commanded by Pelham and probably Breathed. Stuart moved his force by way of Bowling Green to Port Royal on the Rappahannock just east of Fredericksburg. As they moved west the next day towards Fredericksburg, Capt. Peyton R. Berkeley of the 3rd Virginia Cavalry captured several wagons and a number of prisoners, from whom it was learned that two Union infantry brigades with cavalry had already gone south to tear up the Virginia Central. The main body of Federal raiders had already passed, but their wagon train still lagged behind. Stuart decided to attack the larger Federal force by striking their flank near Massaponax Church. When Stuart's column reached the Fredericksburg Road, his men drew sabers and charged with his main body. He held some of his troopers back as a reserve, but committed the rest of his command to the fighting. Pelham and his guns dashed through fields along either side of the road while a regiment was sent in the opposite direction to ransack the Union wagons.[49]

The 3rd and 4th Virginia Cavalry, with the horse artillery in support, smashed into the back of the Union wagon train, capturing much of it. It took only a few shots from the Blakely before its elevating screw was disabled again. Stuart had caused such damage that the Union column was forced to turn from its raiding and deal with the problem in their rear. Stuart's forces were insufficient to deal with the concerted attentions of two Union infantry brigades, so a withdrawal was in order. Stuart turned down the Bowling Green Road a few miles from Massaponax Church. A brisk engagement occurred. Pelham's one remaining operable cannon was staged back from hill to hill to slow the Union advance. In the event, the Union forces could not effectively pursue Stuart or liberate his Union prisoners, and the engagement ended.[50]

Stuart returned with 85 prisoners, 11 wagons captured and a mission accomplished (although another Union column operating out of Spotsylvania had successfully torn up two miles of the Virginia Central that same day.) Pelham's horse artillery had some practice covering a disputed withdrawal, as well as some more experience with the temperamental nature of cannons of the Blakely design.[51]

*   *   *

Stuart returned to his headquarters at Hanover Court House to find a rapidly changing military situation. McClellan was showing signs of evacuating the Army of the Potomac from Harrison's Landing. A new Union army under the command of Maj. Gen. John Pope, largely composed of the remnants of the Federal troops Jackson had defeated in his Valley Campaign, were setting up for battle east of the Blue Ridge Mountains. Pope was considered a braggart from the West by both sides.

What was worse in Lee's eyes, Pope treated the citizens of northern Virginia harshly, encouraging depredations against the populace. If Lee could strike Pope's 50,000 man army before McClellan could move north to reinforce Pope, there was an opportunity to defeat the Union forces decisively in detail.

The first problem Lee had before he could strike Pope was to reunite the Army of Northern Virginia. Jackson's main force was around Gordonsville, but some of his forces, including Robertson's Brigade and Chew's Battery were still coming out of the Shenandoah Valley. Longstreet's Corps was still around Richmond, screened on the east by Hampton's Brigade and on the north by Fitz Lee's Brigade. However, the activity of Pope would force Lee to attack piecemeal, Jackson first.

Even as Jackson's troops were engaging Nathaniel Banks at Cedar Mountain, Stuart was making his way to Jackson on a tour of inspection. The sharply fought meeting engagement was edging toward catastrophe for Jackson when A. P. Hill's Light Division arrived on the field after a hard march and drove the Unionists back and eventually off the field. Robertson's Brigade did little at Cedar Mountain, however, and horse artillery was not seriously involved.

As Lee moved to try to trap Pope's Army between the Rapidan and Rappahannock Rivers, Stuart's cavalry was ordered to screen the Confederate consolidation along the front with Pope. On August 17, in response to his orders to shield and scout, Stuart ordered Fitz Lee's men to advance to Raccoon Ford on the Rapidan River. When Fitz Lee did not arrive at Verdiersville, Stuart dispatched Maj. Norman FitzHugh, who was carrying orders from R. E. Lee, to search for Fitz Lee's wayward brigade. A detachment of Union cavalry captured Major FitzHugh, and the orders fell into the hands of Maj. Gen. John Pope. With the Union high command in knowledge of Lee's entire plan and dispositions Pope was able to escape from Lee's trap. Stuart barely escaped capture, although his famed plumed hat was not so fortunate.

On August 20, Fitz Lee finally arrived at Raccoon Ford. Lee's and Brig. Gen. Beverly H. Robertson's brigades crossed the Rapidan River in search of Pope's withdrawing columns, with Chew's Battery and Munford's Brigade covering Jackson's left flank. Breathed's Battery was assigned to Fitz Lee's Brigade. Fitz Lee ran into the Union army shortly after crossing the Rapidan ahead of Longstreet's Corps.[52]

Colonel
Judson Kilpatrick,
commander of the
2nd NY Cavalry

LC

Pelham's Battery quickly went into action. "We did effective work, and drove the opposing column before us," recalled gunner George W. Shreve. "This was a cavalry and artillery fight." Most of the fighting took place near Kelly's Ford, where the 7th Virginia Cavalry shoved Union Colonel Judson Kilpatrick's 2nd New York back. The Union army expeditiously withdrew across the Rappahannock River as a consequence of the aggressive action by Fitz Lee and Breathed.[53]

There was fighting at virtually every ford along Rapidan and Rappahannock that day. Stuart was with Robertson's Brigade between Stevensville and Brandy Station. There, the cavalier had Brig. Gen. George Bayard's Union cavalry brigade on the run. Bayard withdrew to Brandy Station and the protection of Union artillery. Stuart wanted the horse artillery to duel with the enemy, but none of his guns were at hand The opportunity to drive Bayard had vanished by the time Pelham came up with his battery. Given the way he handled later engagements, Stuart may have taken note that he needed more horse artillery support near the fluid front lines. After things quieted down he would see about getting it. Matters that August, however, were far from quiet.

By August 22, Lee's strategy of trapping Pope before McClellan or Burnside could reinforce him was fading. McClellan had withdrawn the last of his troops from Harrison's Landing and was sailing north. Lee still hoped to turn Pope's flank, so Stuart was sent upstream to Freeman's Ford on the Hazel River. At the ford Stuart ran headlong into Brig. Gen. Robert H. Milroy's brigade and Capt. Aaron C. Johnson's 12th Ohio

Battery. An attack looked unpromising, but Pelham deployed in an excellent position and Stuart ordered him to open fire to test Milroy's intentions. The iron prodding soon erupted into a full-scale artillery duel. One of the artillerists left an interesting account of Breathed's conduct during this engagement:

> On one occasion eighteen of our boys were guarding the bridge across Hazel Run with only two pieces of artillery, when twenty thousand Yankee Cavalrymen came within three hundred yards. Major [sic. Lieutenant] Breathed placed fourteen men with sticks across their shoulders, imitating guns, over the hill behind the guns (just so the tops of their heads could be seen), like infantry. We fired two guns, which checked their advance, and they turned down the river. We moved down the river and came in contact with the same men. They brought up horse artillery and struck us some hard blows, killing four of our men. Maj. Breathed ordered us to lie down, and in this position a ball cut a line ten feet long between a comrade (George Vaughan, of Alabama) and myself, who were lying about a foot apart. . . . Major Breathed never tired.[54]

The fight was a wild one that killed or wounded four Confederate artillerymen; at times Pelham himself manned the guns. Breathed's act of deception fooled the Union brigade. As always, Breathed's fighting spirit was bold and his actions smartly executed, two traits Union men would write about for years after his death. Lee, however, judged that forcing a crossing at Freeman's Ford would be too costly and called off the attack.

Breathed moved his guns down Hazel Run and kept the Federals occupied there with some fitful long-distance shelling. The next day Pelham's men linked up with Chew's Battery and relieved Chew's tired artillerymen.

Meanwhile, Stuart conducted a raid in Pope's rear at Catlett Station, where he destroyed as much as he could. The raid, which was conducted without the support of the horse artillery because of rain-soaked roads, failed in many of its objectives but was still successful in demonstrating how easy it was to get deeply into the enemy's rear areas. General Lee decided to repeat the maneuver, this time with a larger force: Jackson's entire wing of the army.

Lee had to strike now or turn to the defensive. Pope was already being reinforced by McClellan's troops. Exactly what Lee expected to happen when he ordered Jackson to position himself behind Pope is uncertain. What actually transpired was a magnificent feat of marching and fighting. Jackson marched undetected around Pope's right flank, which was drawn up along the Rappahannock River opposite Longstreet. Once in position, Jackson destroyed Pope's line of communications. The move forced Pope to deal aggressively with Jackson's divisions. Instead of awaiting attack while holding Pope's supply base, Jackson withdrew northwest and took up a strong defensive position. Jackson's maneuver forced Pope to move away from his arriving reinforcements, simultaneously shortening the route by which Jackson's reinforcements would come. Believing that a rare opportunity was presenting itself, Pope attacked Jackson. Lee, however, arrived with Longstreet's Corps and linked up with Jackson's right flank. When all was ready, Longstreet attacked the unsuspecting Union commander, crushing the enemy and driving Pope's army from the field in one of the worse routs of the war. Lee, of course, could not have foreseen on August 25 how Jackson's flank march would turn out, but he knew that Stuart's cavalry and horse artillery had an important role to play in the unfolding drama.

Stuart's initial orders were to guard Jackson's flank and screen his movements as Jackson moved his men by the same route Stuart had used to get to Catlett Station. Stuart set in motion both cavalry brigades and all his artillery. After making his dispositions, he moved ahead to attack Pope's supply point at Bristoe Station. Near sunset on August 26, Stuart, together with Munford's 2nd Virginia, overran Bristoe Station and took control of the area, cutting Pope's rail supply line and derailing Pope's locomotives. When it was learned that Pope's main supply point was only four miles northeast at Manassas Junction, where the Manassas Gap Railroad met the Orange and Alexandria line, Jackson and Stuart converged there. Brig. Gen. Isaac Trimble's infantry met Stuart's forces just outside the junction. By dawn of August 27, Manassas Junction was in Confederate hands, as was a mountain of Union supplies.[55]

The Stuart Horse Artillery, meanwhile, was stuck in the rear of Jackson's marching column. Chew's Battery, minus his Blakely (which was out of ammunition) joined Pelham's Battery and tried to keep up with the rest of the cavalry. Once again, the problem of getting horse artillery into action when the guns trailed the main force was realized. Stuart and the cavalry brigades could, and did, cut across country to get into action at Bristoe Station and Manassas Junction. The horse artillery, however, was only able to advance on roads, forcing its batteries to

The handiwork of James Breathed and his artillery:
the Stone Bridge at Bull Run.

follow the infantry for the next few days, just out of reach of the fighting.[56]

After returning on August 27 from detached service at Haymarket against the Manassas Gap Railroad, Fitz Lee rejoined Stuart's main body and Jackson's Corps near Manassas Junction. Pelham and the horse artillery finally caught up with Stuart and Jackson at the same place later that evening, but by then the day's action was over. Pelham had some captured ordnance turned over to him, but was soon moving again on Jackson's orders. After destroying everything at Manassas Junction that he could not remove, Jackson evacuated the place. The next day he concentrated his three divisions at Groveton, north of the Warrenton and Alexandria Pike. [57]

As the Confederate forces moved northeast from the junction, Pelham and the horse artillery again found themselves at the end of Jackson's column. However, action would soon find Pelham there where he served as part of the rear guard. The Confederates crossed Bull Run Creek at the Lewis Ford, where Breathed encountered the 1st through 4th New Jersey infantry regiments. His guns destroyed the railroad bridge over Bull Run. When it was discovered that Union troops were pursuing,

Pelham detached Breathed, with one piece, to deal with them, moving on with the rest of his guns. "A few well-directed shots from Breathed's gun drove the enemy off," reported Pelham. "I moved up the Warrenton Pike, and when near the Jim Robinson house I overtook the rear of General A. P. Hill's Division, which had just left the turnpike and was moving along a by-road to the right. I moved to the right of this division and passed it. I moved on and parked my battery in a field where General Jackson had ordered all his artillery to await orders." After Breathed's menacing fire ran off the Union skirmishers, Breathed and his piece caught up with the other horse artillerymen positioned at Groveton Heights.[58]

The prelude to the battle of Second Manassas opened at sunset on August 28 with the fighting at Brawner's Farm. Jackson, mounted and alone, rode back and forth in front of the woods and an unfinished railroad embankment concealing his corps, watching a large force of Federal infantry marching along the Warrenton Turnpike. When Jackson judged the enemy was where he wanted them, he returned to his men and ordered an attack. Luckily for the Union the troops being assaulting were John Gibbon's and Abner Doubleday's brigades of Maj. Gen Rufus King's division—some of the toughest in the entire army. Gibbon's men, nicknamed "the Black Hat Brigade" because of the color of their slouch hats, had never fired a gun in anger. These men would soon be known as the Iron Brigade. The two-hour fight was at close range (often 100 yards or less) in one of the rare stand-up engagements of the war. Jackson, whose infantry was only lightly supported with artillery, called for more guns. Only Pelham, with Breathed's Battery and Chew's lone gun, was in position to respond quickly. Jackson gave Pelham the discretion to locate his artillery where it could be the most effective.[59]

Pelham moved out and reported to Maj. Lindsay M. Shumaker, chief of artillery for Brig. Gen. William B. Taliaferro's Division. By this time darkness had blanketed northern Virginia, but the fighting continued to rage. Pelham moved his guns across an unfinished railroad cut about a mile from Groveton. Most of the guns moved a short distance beyond the railroad cut, while three of Pelham's pieces took up a position on the right flank of Ewell's Division. Once the Federals discovered the enemy artillery in their front, they fired a volley into the deploying pieces. The distance was extremely short, with one soldier claiming it was only about forty paces. "I immediately engaged [the 19th Indiana Infantry]," reported Pelham. "After remaining in this position about half an hour

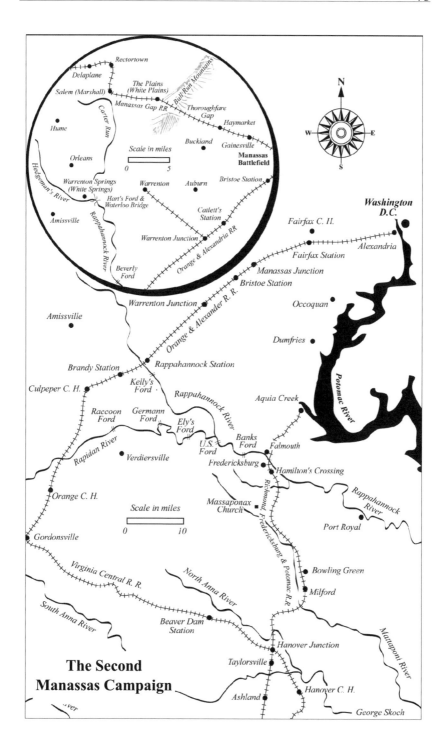

The Second Manassas Campaign

George Skoch

Major Shumaker ordered me to fall back. Owing to the pole of one of my guns being broken I could not obey the order, and continued firing until the enemy were driven back. I neglected to state that only two of my guns were engaged [3-inch rifles captured at Manassas Junction],"continued Pelham, "the other guns having lost the way because of the darkness of the night, the winding, narrow road, cross-roads." Pelham's guns helped hold back the enemy advances until darkness finally ended the fighting. Casualties were heavy on both sides, but Jackson had revealed his position to Pope, who now hurried his men forward to wipe out the pesky Confederate force. What the Union commander did not know was that Longstreet's Corps had passed through Thoroughfare Gap and was marching to join Jackson.[60]

Jackson later sang the praises of his mobile gunners: "Owing to the difficulty of getting artillery through the woods, I did not have as much of that arm of the service as I desired at the opening of the engagement," reported Jackson, "but this want was met by Pelham, with his Stuart Horse Artillery, who dashed forward on my right and opened upon the enemy at a moment when his services were very much needed." Although Jackson had called for twenty guns to be brought up, no others made it because of the impenetrable woods. Pelham, too, was justifiably proud of his gunners. "The accuracy with which my guns were fired and the rapidity with which they were served during both days [August 28 and 29] was very gratifying, and the execution they wrought was very great."[61]

Stonewall, meanwhile, withdrew to a stronger position and waited for Pope to attack him. On August 29 he did just that, advancing in long heavy lines against Jackson's front. The Stuart Horse Artillery had only four guns, and each of them went into action. When enemy troops on Pope's right were spotted moving toward Sudley Ford, Stuart placed Pelham's guns in position well beyond Jackson's right and the horse artillerymen opened fire. The guns occupied Groveton Heights west of the railroad embankment on the perimeter of a thicket. Wild grass called broomsedge covered the heights. Broomsedge grows abundantly on neglected lands in Virginia, and the hot days of midsummer made the grass dry and flammable.[62]

Supported by infantry, Pelham's barrage of shot and shell convinced the threatening Unionists that there was little they could do on this front. After remaining in position for nearly an hour, Stuart ordered two other batteries to reinforce Pelham's position, and sent Pelham to the right of the line. The men of the Breathed Battery arrived as evening approached. They unlimbered and fired with such rapidity that at times they had to interrupt their firing to allow a gun's barrel to cool. Union counter-battery and infantry fire was ineffective, but by this time the broomsedge grass was on fire and the breeze was blowing the smoke and flames toward Breathed's guns. The cries of the wounded laying in the path of the flames were heart wrenching to hear, but there was little or nothing that could be done to aid them. Richard Townsend Dodson of Stuart's Horse Artillery left a fascinating description of the action on this part of the field at Second Manassas:

> Riderless horses dashed here and there through the flames which rushed along the ground, licking up everything with their whistling of shot and shell, the venomous blasting of musket balls, the roar of great guns and the rattle of musketry presented such senses and sounds as one might expect to witness if the wide gates of hell were thrown open and the evil spirits should be seen engaged in dreadful combat. It at length became so hot that the battery was ordered to be withdrawn, fears being entertained for the safety of the ammunition chests. Just as number two gun was being limbered to the rear, poor [Wilson H. P.] Turner, of Alexandria, was struck by a shell, which seemed to explode at the same moment, for his body was completely cut in two parts.

Turner's comrades collected the unfortunate gunner's body parts, placed them on the limber chest, and started to the rear. After going a short distance, however, the jolting of the carriage wrenched loose the upper body and head portion, which fell to the ground. Unwilling to leave behind the mutilated remains of their gallant friend, the gunners stopped under a steady fire, retrieved the remains, and retired from the field.[63]

Pelham had nothing but praise for Breathed's and McGregor's fighting skills:

> It gives me great pleasure to speak in terms of the highest praise of Lieuts. James Breathed and William [M.] McGregor. The non-commissioned officers and men worthily emulated the example they set. I moved my battery to the rear to procure ammunition, but could only get a very limited supply. I held my battery in readiness on the field for action during the 30th, but it being the only battery of horse artillery, would be very much

needed in case of a retreat or pursuit. Gen. Jackson ordered me to reserve my ammunition for any emergency. [64]

An eery silence fell over Jackson's front as August 30 dawned. While Pope readied his men to attack again, Longstreet Corps waited on Jackson's right flank. It had formed there the previous day in an obtuse angle with Jackson's line. Despite warnings to the contrary, Pope seemed utterly unaware that "Old Pete" had arrived. When Pope finally renewed his attack, Longstreet opened a heavy artillery fire that ripped through Union ranks, followed by the largest infantry attack Lee's army would ever mount during the war. The assault swept Pope's army from the field in a panicked rout. Other than trying to advance in the wake of the fleeing enemy, Breathed's Battery saw little action on August 30. He was finally ordered in reserve behind Jackson's men on the Catharpin Road.

On August 31, Stuart and his men rode toward Centreville in pursuit of Pope's retreating army. Jackson's men were ordered to flank and trap the enemy before they could find shelter in the capital's defenses. A sharp rear-guard action at Ox Hill on September 1 ended the effort and brought the campaign to a close. The horse artillery was not involved. On September 2, the gunners went into camp at Fairfax Court House before riding toward Alexandria the next day. As his army rested in and around Fairfax Court House, General Lee pondered the execution of a bold new plan. The war was about to enter a new phase.

The late August fighting taught Breathed several lessons. The mobility of the horse artillery allowed it to move about the field quickly, unlimber rapidly, and engage the enemy at close range with deadly effect. The destruction wrought on August 30 by Longstreet's artillery against the left flank of the attacking Union infantry was an enduring image of the power of the long-arm. Pelham may have been thinking of this lesson when he performed a similar feat on a much smaller scale at Fredericksburg that December. The alacrity with which his batteries obeyed orders from different commanders, with little need of supervision, was not lost on his superiors. Great things would be expected of the horse artillery, and the artillerists were determined not to disappoint.

Chapter 4

The Maryland Campaign of 1862

fter the Battle of Chantilly, Virginia, Robert E. Lee had to face certain realities. The Union Army was still full of fight and about to be reinforced by 60,000 troops returned from the Peninsula. Lee could not subsist his army in Fairfax County for long because that land had been picked clean. If he retreated toward Richmond, he would still have trouble supplying his army and would be drawing the war deeper into Virginia and closer to Richmond. Another possibility would be for Lee to move west into the Piedmont around Warrenton, where he would be in a position to subsist his army and menace the Federal flank.

However, by boldly maneuvering the Army of Northern Virginia north of the Potomac, Lee hoped to accomplish better things. At the time the South was still of the opinion that Maryland could be brought into the Confederacy, which would force the evacuation of Washington. An invasion of Pennsylvania would bring the realities of war to the North, as well as provide subsistence to Lee's army. A Confederate victory in the North might well be the impetus needed to gain official recognition for the Confederacy from Britain and France. In addition, with Lee and his Army north of the Potomac, the Federal forces would have to seek him out and turn their attentions away from Virginia, thereby giving the Virginia farmers a chance to harvest their Fall crops. Lee was also aware that McClellan had been placed back in command of the Union forces.

Lee had taken McClellan's measure and believed he could count on Little Mac's lack of aggressiveness to allow the Army of Northern Virginia to recuperate even while on the move. If Lee had to withdraw, the winter would soon be upon both armies, and it was thought the campaigning season would be over until Spring.[1]

An invasion of the North presented Lee with many problems. His army had been marching and fighting for the better part of two months from the James to the Potomac. The men were tired. Horses were becoming jaded. Ammunition needed to be replenished. Not all of Lee's army was assembled. Battle casualties had been heavy, especially among the officers.[2]

Exactly when Lee decided to invade the North is not known, but on September 3 he set his army in motion to Loudoun County, Virginia, from which he could cross over into Maryland either east or west of the Blue Ridge. By September 4, Lee had determined to cross east of the Blue Ridge, and his orders spoke of moving through Maryland and invading Pennsylvania. To offset his campaign losses, Lee added three new divisions to his army and brought up Wade Hampton's Brigade. Stuart now had three brigades of cavalry under his command. On the morning of September 4 Lee started across the Potomac at White's Ford, as well as other fords upstream between White's Ford and Point of Rocks, Maryland.[3]

Immediately, Lee's army began to encounter difficulties, the most troublesome of which was straggling. Richard Townshend Dodson, Sergeant Major of the Stuart Horse Artillery, described the causes for straggling very succinctly, "The fact must ... be remembered that that army had marched from the banks of the James to this point on the upper waters of the Potomac, that it had fought in numerable severe skirmishes, had had five days of terrific battle and that it was most ill-supplied with the commonest necessities of a soldier in the way of clothing, especially of shoes. A result of all these adverse circumstances was a vast deal of straggling. Some did not want to go over the Potomac, others were anxious enough to maintain their places in the ranks, but could not stand the rapid and continuous movements of the troops, and some were cowardly and dared not go, so thousands of men who should have been with their regiments were left scattered, singly and in twos and threes upon every mile of the road from the Rapidan to the Potomac." Such was the condition of Lee's army as it splashed across the Potomac.[4]

Like most of Lee's army, the complement of the Stuart Horse Artillery had been very much reduced in men and horses by the time the Maryland Campaign began. On September 5, Stuart's men pushed across the Potomac River at White's Ford, moving toward Poolesville, Maryland, birthplace of Breathed's mother. The brigades of Hampton and Fitz Lee, along with Pelham and his battery, camped around Poolesville.[5]

On September 8, as the men celebrated their arrival in Maryland, Stuart told his Prussian mercenary aide, Major Heros Von Borcke, "Major, what a capital place for us to give a ball in honour of our arrival in Maryland! Don't you think we could manage it?" Von Borcke, with the help of the 8th Mississippi Infantry's band, staged a "Ball" in Urbana as if the war was miles away.[6]

The ball, however, was not to remain a "romantic" gala. The Army of the Potomac was also moving, with Brigadier General Alfred Pleasonton and his troopers in the lead, to intercept the Confederate forces. The music and dancing were disrupted by the news that Union troopers were attacking from the direction of Hyattstown, Maryland. Stuart's men left their partners to deal with the disturbance, grabbing their swords before the Southern belles even knew what had happened. Stuart and his men were back by 1:00 A.M., and the festivities resumed. Despite the interruption, the party picked right up where it had left off.[7]

This impromptu ball was another indication of Stuart's propensities toward flamboyance. Such antics caused the courtly Hampton to avoid participating in the enthusiastic revels of his commander. Stuart preferred jackboots, golden spurs, crimson-lined capes, and ostrich plumed hats. He liked sycophants, and had an eye for the ladies. Many thought him at best a dandy, and at worst a buffoon. However, Stuart's bias in favor of his fellow Virginians made him the most suspect in Hampton's mind. All it took to be admitted to Stuart's "inner circle" was to be a Virginian, young, high living, hard riding, and imbued with a sporting attitude toward war. Hampton, who was older and a landed gentleman from the Deep South, did not meet any of these criteria. Interestingly, Breathed was also not among Stuart's inner coterie, who, at Stuart's insistence, pitched their tents close to their commander. Most nights, Breathed pitched his tent with his men.[8]

While Lee was moving his forces into Maryland and planning how to neutralize military threats in his line of march, such as the Federal

Brigadier General Alfred Pleasonton.

garrison at Harpers Ferry, Stuart was screening the movement from Federal eyes. However, things were not going as well as had been hoped for the liberation of Maryland. Sgt. Major Dodson of the Stuart Horse Artillery describes the growing realization that the Marylanders were not rallying to the Southern Cause:

> On the 10th the column entered Hagerstown. Near this place was the home of our first lieutenant, [James] Breathed, who had confidently hoped to obtain many and good recruits for the battery in this neighborhood. But he, like many others, was greatly disappointed at finding the sentiment of the people of this section of Maryland very different from what he had expected it would be. Instead of a strong active sympathy for the Confederate cause he

encountered either ill suppressed antipathy or a careless indifference that was more unpleasant to endure. I think we obtained but one recruit and he hardly amounted to shucks. In fact the whole movement, so far as gaining accessions to the numerical strength of the army was an utter failure and we encountered far more of the Barbara Fritchie spirit than the Belle Boyd.[9]

In addition, Major Dodson continued, the horses of the horse artillery were beginning to give out:

> The long, tedious and often rapid marches of the weeks preceding the passage of the Potomac now began to tell severely upon the horses of the Stuart Horse Artillery. They became thin, spiritless and jaded, scarcely able to draw the guns and caissons. Occasionally an animal in a team gave out. It was immediately unharnessed, turned into the fields and a cannoneer dismounted, whose horse filled the vacancy. In this manner, as we approached South Mountain, nearly one-half the men in each detachment had been put afoot and the command had nearly lost its distinctive character as horse artillery thereby. . . . Captain [James S.] Oden, was directed to take a detachment of men and scour the country on either side of the line of march for the purpose of impressing mounts for the men. . . . In the course of two or three days a sufficient number of fresh horses were obtained to completely equip the command in this respect. . . . The Maryland horses—of this part of the state—were principally of a heavy, clumsy breed, commonly called the 'Conestoga' well adapted to slow movement and heavy draught, while the Virginia stock was of a smaller, more active frame, possessing a large percentage of thoroughbred blood. They combined muscular power with high mettle and great endurance. The 'Conestogas' served to carry our guns, caissons and wagons back to Virginia, but we were obliged to replace them with smaller, less cumbersome animals as soon as possible after arriving there.

The next time that Lee, Stuart and the horse artillery would invade the North, they would have the same problem, only worse.[10]

Lee gradually pulled his army back behind several mountain ranges as the Federal army advanced in mass. First Lee crossed Catoctin Mountain, west of Frederick, Maryland. Then Lee pulled the bulk of his troops behind South Mountain, one range farther to the west. Longstreet's Corps was sent up the National Road toward Hagerstown, Maryland. Jackson was sent down the Jefferson Road to neutralize

Harpers Ferry. Lee could not reunite his army to advance until Harpers Ferry had fallen.

Stuart continued to screen Lee's maneuvers. There was need. McClellan was pressing westward from behind the Washington defense to engage Lee's army. The "Maryland Ball" at Urbana may have been a typical Stuart frolic, but it had a practical aspect as well. Urbana was close to the middle of the screening and reconnaissance line Stuart had established with his three brigades of cavalry. The line ran north-south between New Market and Poolesville, with Fitz Lee's Brigade holding the north end, Hampton's Brigade the middle, and Munford's Brigade on the south. The newly promoted Col. Thomas T. Munford was now commanding what was formerly Robertson's Brigade; Robertson had been relieved of his command.[11]

By September 10, Stuart pulled his brigades back through Frederick. On September 11, Stuart screened the advance of Lee's infantry as it moved westward toward South Mountain. The Union army was at Frederick, Maryland, heading west. Early on September 13, Stuart with Hampton and Hart's Battery, retired to a gap in the Catoctin range that had been previously held by the Jeff Davis Legion. That same day, Indiana infantrymen found cigars wrapped with a piece of paper lying on the ground outside Frederick. The campaign had reached a tipping point.[12]

The paper turned out to be Lee's Special Order No. 191, which spelled out the dispositions of the Army of Northern Virginia. McClellan, who commanded the forces assigned to the defenses of Washington, was in command of the army pursuing Lee. When Special Order No. 191 was presented to him, McClellan declared, "Here is a paper with which, if I cannot whip Bobby Lee I would be willing to go home!" McClellan now knew that Lee's army was divided; Jackson was at Harpers Ferry looking to capture its garrison, and Longstreet's and D. H. Hill's commands were at Boonsboro, Maryland, on the other side of South Mountain. To get at the Confederate forces McClellan would have to force the three important gaps on South Mountain: Turner's Gap in the north on the National Road; Fox's Gap a little farther south; and Crampton's Gap to the south at Burkittsville. Stuart and his horse artillery would have to help dispute their passage.[13]

The South Mountain passes were critical to both sides. Because Fitz Lee being unable to gain the enemy's rear, Stuart was unable to determine the nature and strength of the Union movement. Accordingly, Stuart left the vicinity of Boonsboro early on the morning of September 14 and rode rapidly for Crampton's Gap. Stuart, recalled Henry Matthews, "[Left] that old ditch dog Munford at Crampton with his own two regiments of cavalry and two fragments of regiments of infantry under Mahone and instructed Munford to hold the gap at any cost." Hampton's Brigade (with Hart's Battery), fell back to Crampton's Gap to meet up with Munford (with Chew's Battery), and Confederate infantry under Maj. Gen. Lafayette McLaws. Aided partly by the steep approach from Burkittsville, this scratch force delayed the Union VI Corps until after nightfall on September 14, ensuring that the Federals at Harpers Ferry (who surrendered the next day) would not be relieved. Chew's and Hart's batteries fought at Crampton's Gap until their ammunition was exhausted or a piece was disabled (the Blakely gun, again), when they withdrew toward Harpers Ferry for refit and resupply.[14]

The Battle of Turner's Gap, which was held by D. H. Hill's Confederates, was also waged on September 14. Breathed's guns were located one mile to the south at Fox's Gap, which the Southerners had to hold if they wished to keep the enemy from pouring through Turner's Gap and dividing the army. If one gap fell, the other would quickly fall as well. Stuart dispatched Pelham's guns and Col. Thomas L. Rosser's 5th Virginia Cavalry to help bolster Fox's defenses. Pelham placed Breathed's guns at the end of Rosser's line. As the sun rose, Lt. Samuel N. Benjamin's Company E, 2nd U.S. Artillery, opened fire and the battle began.[15]

As the morning fog ascended into a clear sky, the Alabamans spotted Union troops moving in the distance. The enemy could clearly see the Southern guns waiting for them on the heights. The Jeff Davis Artillery supported Pelham's guns. However, no Southern infantry had been sent out to link up with Stuart's advanced position. Meanwhile, another Union force crept through the dense underbrush toward the right side of the Jeff Davis Artillery position. Unaware of the threat, the artillerists failed to detect the Unionists, who suddenly popped up "almost within a stone's throw" of [Capt. James W.] Bondurant's right. Bugles sounded and the Federals rapidly advanced toward the unsupported battery while "a storm of bullets from a volley flew into our [the gunners] midst." The Federals had caught the Alabamans by surprise, and the Southerners had to act quickly in order to avoid disaster.[16]

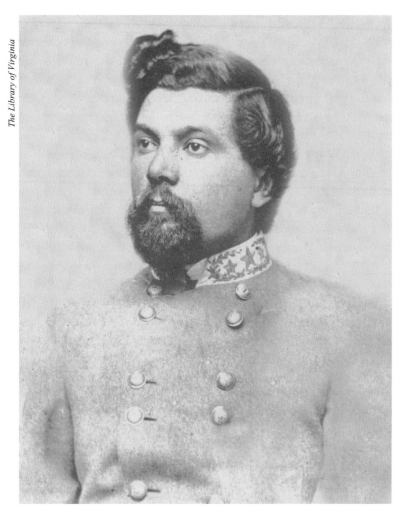

Colonel Tom Rosser, 5th Virginia Cavalry.

The Jeff Davis artillerymen bore the brunt of the attack of the 23rd Ohio Infantry while Breathed's gunners, who were to the right of the main assault, fired only a few shots. Rosser and Pelham were not engaged in the defense of the Old Sharpsburg Road until the end of the day when Pleasonton was ordered to move to Turner's Gap about noon on September 14. Most of the fighting for South Mountain took place at Turner's and Fox's gaps, where Hill's men tried in vain to stop the Union advance. By nightfall the Federals had possession of the critical latter gap. The Confederates had been unable to block the Union movement from Frederick west toward and through the South Mountain range. McClellan's success jeopardized Lee's entire army.[17]

Fitz Lee covered the withdrawal of the remainder of the infantry from Turner's Gap that evening. He took up position east of Boonsboro, where he commanded the road where it descended from the mountain. The battery secured a sound position with four pieces in support of Fitz Lee's dismounted men. He deployed skirmishers well to the front of the battery, with a squadron on each side to protect its flanks. Soon after daylight, the enemy's skirmishers advanced from the gap. Fitz Lee's skirmishers engaged them immediately, falling back very slowly until they reached the battery. As always, Pelham was not idle when there was a fight to be found. As one of his gunners recalled, his artillery hurled shell and canister into the advancing Union troops until many were made to "sleep their last sleep on the virgin soil of dear old Maryland."[18]

"At times we would hold our fire until they were up to our very guns," remembered Henry Matthews, "when the whole battery would fire into their close columns, causing them to halt for a moment. This was done repeatedly, until we were admonished that our ammunition was getting short. Lines of battle were now formed, extending beyond both of our flanks [Fitz Lee's] causing us to retire to the town [Boonsboro]. Our guns went back to a new position and our cavalry were in the act of withdrawing when the line of the enemy's ranks were suddenly opened, letting out a large body of the enemy's cavalry, which came chopping down the road."[19]

Fitz Lee, meanwhile, ordered the 3rd Virginia Cavalry to meet the Union advance. Their charge drove the Federal cavalry back onto their infantry supports. "There was such a mixture of cavalry (blue and gray) that though eager to fire we could not do so for fear of killing our own men," continued Matthews. "The pressure on Fitz Lee's rear was so great that we had to make a stand in Boonsboro with the 1st Va. cavalry in order to insure the dignified withdrawal of the balance of the brigade." Lee made one more stand on the Keedysville Road near Boonsboro before moving to Sharpsburg, where he took a position on the Confederate left covering the upper fords on Antietam Creek.[20]

Little is known for certain about the activities of Jim Breathed from the time Lee's army crossed the Potomac River until the time he deployed that army in a defensive perimeter behind Antietam Creek. In fact,

Breathed cannot be confidently placed on the field until Stuart's forces are ordered to support the left flank of Lee's position and the horse artillery are unlimbered on the Nicodemus Farm. Breathed's batteries were certainly engaged, but there is no mention of Breathed in command of them. It is only speculation, but it is very likely that Jim Breathed was temporarily away from the horse artillery at this time. The Breathed family home, Bai-Yuka, was just ten miles from Turner's Gap by road, due west. Breathed's knowledge of the road network (he had once been an apprentice to local country doctor Charles Macgill) would have been invaluable to Longstreet, who was coordinating Lee's move through Hagerstown to Pennsylvania. It would have been perfectly logical for Jim Breathed to have gone home, picked up fresh horses, and advised Longstreet on the best routes for the army to take. On the eve of the Battle of Antietam, however, Jim Breathed was definitely standing by his guns.

On the night of September 16, Lee formed his army in a one-half mile, horseshoe-shaped line protecting the intersection of the Hagerstown Pike and Smoketown Road near a small white clapboard Dunkard church. A salient at the end of the Confederate battle line was intended to economize his strength and permit a flexible response to any attacks by the enemy the next morning. However strong the line, it left a gap of nearly one mile between Jackson's left and the Potomac River. In an effort to bolster that sector, Stuart that night placed Pelham's guns on a dominating hill overlooking the Nicodemus Farm, and then advanced Fitz Lee's cavalry brigade to support Pelham's guns from the reverse slope of the hill. "Stuart with Fitzhugh Lee's Brigade of cavalry and Pelham's four guns was stationed behind the extreme left," wrote one historian of the battle. "Thus, on the line from Nicodemus Run to the Potomac, a distance of three miles, were about 20,000 infantry, 2,500 cavalry, and about 2,000 artillerymen with 108 guns." One of the most intense artillery duels of the war was about to commence.[21]

Fitz Lee's Brigade was about 650 yards northwest of Breathed, supporting the horse artillery and extending the Confederate line to the Potomac River. Breathed's section was in position at Nicodemus Heights, and his cannon opened the first Southern artillery fire of the day at about 5:30 A.M. when Major General Joseph Hooker's Federal I Corps was spotted advancing toward the Miller Cornfield. The Confederate infantry brigades of James Lawton, Jubal Early, and Isaac Trimble defended the Cornfield, while Breathed's withering enfilade fire hit

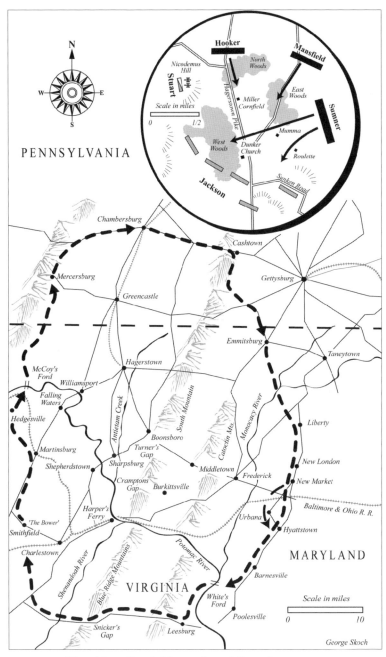

The ride to South Mountain and Stuart's guns on
Nicodemus Hill, Battle of Sharpsburg, September, 17, 1862.

Hooker's flank as it entered the tall leafy green rows. Breathed's men had to withstand the fire of six Union batteries as they stood to their pieces in an effort to slow down Hooker's infantry. "It is a fact which should become notable and historic that the great battle of Antietam was opened on the Confederate side, early on the morning of the [September] 17, and on the extreme left wing, by Breathed's guns [four guns], commanded by himself and almost within sight of the house [10 miles] where he had been reared to manhood," recalled one of his men.[22]

Henry Matthews recalled the moment:

> Pelham's battery, under the command of that terrible fighter, Jim Breathed (Pelham being on the left with the infantry batteries), followed [John] Hood in a gallop, taking position after position, firing canister into the enemy at every jump. Lieut. Breathed acted gallantly as usual . . . cheering the men by his noble example—and be it said that not a man qualified—but every man, officers and men, stood to their posts like machines, suffering and dying for their dearly loved southland. Heroes tired out [and] laid down on that battlefield . . . and the dead and dying, with the sweet consciousness that every man had done his duty to his country and to his God.[23]

Breathed remained steadily engaged until nearly 11:00 A.M., when he was relieved and the guns moved in order to avoid hitting friendly troops. One of his men met him as he withdrew, "with his guns yet warm and his face sooty with the smoke of the conflict, and although he had suffered much in loss of men and horses, he was hilarious [i.e. boisterous and gay] over the heavy gaps which his grape and canister had made in the advancing columns of the Federal troops." Breathed had withstood severe counter-battery fire from the Union I Corps Artillery. Although he came out unharmed, his battery suffered heavy losses in killed and wounded. Henry Matthews recalled that the "thunder of the artillery was terrifying—hell itself seemed to have broken loose in all its terrors."[24]

Although Breathed's men suffered heavily, they refused to leave the field until they had expended every round of ammunition. When they finally ran out just before 11:00 A.M. and were limbering up, an ammunition wagon arrived. Elated, Breathed's men quickly transferred the fresh ammunition to their limber chests and caissons and moved south about 700 yards to the Hauser Farm property, where they went into battery northwest of the Dunkard Church.[25]

The weight of superior Union numbers slowly forced Stuart's cavalrymen back from their original position. They fought against heavy odds until Brig. Gen. William E. Starke's Division of Jackson's Corps reinforced them. By late afternoon the John Bell Hood's Texas Brigade had regained some of the lost ground in the Cornfield, routing Hooker and the men of Maj. Gen. Joseph K. F. Mansfield's XII Corps, which had advanced to help reinforce Hooker. Mansfield was killed in the action.[26]

Pelham, temporarily in command of all the regular artillery on the left, had fallen back after sustaining heavy losses from the counter-battery duel on Nicodemus Heights, and Breathed found him at the Hauser Farm. It was now around noon and a new threat was looming. An attack by Maj. Gen. Edwin Sumner's II Corps was driving into the West Woods around the church and heading straight for the guns on the Hauser property. Just when it seemed the Union assault could not be stopped, several understrength Southern infantry brigades attacked and repulsed it in a close-quarters, bitterly fought engagement. A well-deserved lull settled over the northern end of the battlefield. Although Breathed and his men could not yet know it, their participation in the battle was essentially at an end. The battle raged on until nearly nightfall on other parts of the field. McClellan pierced Lee's lines in the center at the Bloody Lane, but the failure to follow it up prevented the success the attack deserved. Later in the afternoon, on the far right, another Union attack across the lower (Burnside's) bridge was beaten back at the outskirts of Sharpsburg by A. P. Hill's Light Division, which reached the field after a forced march from Harpers Ferry. Although no one then knew it, the battle was finally over. All told, some 4,700 men had been killed, another 18,400 wounded, and more than 3,000 remained missing. The red glow of the sun setting behind the Maryland hills closed out the bloodiest single day of the war.[27]

Instead of withdrawing that night, Lee decided to remain on the field the next day. With a major river behind him it was indeed a desperate gamble, though one McClellan was unwilling to match. Breathed's men, meanwhile, spent September 18 regrouping and waiting for the resumption of an attack that would never come. After defiantly staring down his opponent, Lee finally ordered his army to withdraw across the Potomac to the safety of Virginia late that afternoon. Although the enemy caught and engaged Lee's rear guard at Shepherdstown, the retreat went much better than the Confederates had a right to expect. "It is noteworthy that Breathed's guns were the last to re-cross the river at Shepherdstown, Virginia, on the occasion of General Lee's withdrawal at Antietam," recalled one of Breathed's men. "Tired with the fatigues of the previous battle and severely injured in the loss of men and horses, he had bivouacked the night of the withdrawal near the toll gate, between Sharpsburg and the river, and morning found him and his command asleep without orders." Fitz Lee covered the army's retreat to the Potomac River, keeping the enemy at bay until the entire army was across the river. The 2nd Virginia Cavalry stayed behind as the rear guard.[28]

*   *   *

There is an old saying that men fight harder when on the defensive and defending their homes. Breathed fought his guns hard at Sharpsburg knowing his plantation home, Bai-Yuka, was only a few short miles away from the battlefield. The sound of the battle was clearly audible from its porch. Some of James's siblings, as well as his father and siblings, were within walking distance of the bloody field at Sharpsburg.

The hardships of the war proved to be especially difficult for the College of St. James, Breathed's alma mater. Federal headquarters were a mere six miles from the college, and the school's enrollment had declined by nearly one quarter as a consequence of the war. Later in the conflict Confederate forces would occupy the grounds of the college, and fighting would actually take place there.[29]

On September 8, just nine days before the battle at Sharpsburg, as Confederates were moving north, students with strong Unionist sentiments were rushed away on the last train out of Hagerstown. Three days later, while en route to South Mountain, Southern troops passed by the school again. In the ranks were several former students who, according to one historian of the college, "took time to visit with the Rector." It is entirely possible that Jim Breathed was one of them.[30]

Several Confederate cavalry units operated around Hagerstown during the campaign, and at one point several horsemen passed through the grounds of the college. Their appearance prompted enthusiastic students to rush out to greet them and wave their hats. Headmaster Kerfoot and Professor Joseph Coit (who had officiated at the marriage of Robert and Priscilla Breathed Bridges the previous year) watched with dismay and disapproval, particularly of the actions of Professor Hall

Harrison, who enthusiastically joined in the demonstration. Taken with the moment, eight students, still mere boys, ran off to enlist in Lee's army.[31]

During the war years, the college had only 34 enrolled students, while only 18 graced the halls of the grammar school. "During these years the lay trustees attempted to offer assistance and issued an appeal to the Diocese for aid in helping to sustain St. James," recounted the school's historian. Judge John Breathed attempted to raise funds for the institution because some of his children still attended the grammar school. He also served as an official of the college, and remained very prominent in its affairs as late as 1864.[32]

After the Battle of Sharpsburg, St. Mark's Episcopal Church at Lappans Crossroads was used as a hospital for the injured of both sides. Many of the locals flocked to the area to help tend to the battle's thousands of casualties. Although we don't know for sure, Judge Breathed and his family almost certainly helped care for the wounded and dying men there. The Ladies Union Relief Association in Hagerstown collected supplies, donated and shredded linen tablecloths for bandages, and filled wagons with nurses bound for Sharpsburg. Breathed's love, Mollie Macgill, "provided such tender care in Sharpsburg hospitals that the men called her 'Angel of the Confederacy.'"[33]

* * *

At the same time Breathed and his men were leaving the battlefield, McClellan ordered his field cavalry commander, Brig. Gen. Alfred Pleasonton, to move his men into positions where they could determine whether Lee had actually pulled back across the Potomac. On September 19, Pleasonton's scouts confirmed Lee's retreat, prompting the Federal cavalry to pursue. The bluecoat horse soldiers moved out over the battlefield, giving them their first good look at the effects of the recent battle. The battlefield was "rife with bloated, blackened corpses, the carcasses of battery horses, and all manner of refuse," Private Daniel Pulis of the 8th New York wrote his brother. "[We saw] men with one leg, one arm, bodies without heads or with only part of a head. I saw one man . . . with the back part of his head cut entirely off. He was still alive." When they passed by a field hospital, Pulis spied "a stack of arms and legs 4 feet high." The carnage of 26,000 casualties staggered everyone.[34]

Doug Bast, Boonsborough Museum of History

Breathed's promotion, September 22, 1862.

Breathed's exemplary service in Maryland did not pass unnoticed. On September 22 he was commissioned a captain of artillery, his certificate signed by Virginia Governor John Letcher. With the promotion came added responsibility in the form of a full battery of guns that would forever after be known as "Breathed's Battery."[35]

Others similarly deserving were also promoted. Pelham's promotion to major allowed Breathed and Mathis W. Henry (who was also made a captain) to take command of the two halves of what had previously been known as the Stuart Horse Artillery. Breathed was now in charge of the 1st Stuart Horse Artillery (Breathed's Battery), while Henry commanded the 2nd Stuart Horse Artillery (Henry's Battery). Moses A. Febrey and J. Emmet Shaw were promoted to lieutenants in Breathed's Battery.[36]

On October 1, Pleasonton continued his reconnaissance mission from Martinsburg, crossing the Potomac with Lt. Alexander C. M. Pennington's Battery M, 2nd U.S. Artillery in tow. Breathed had faced Pennington before, and the men of both batteries were very familiar with each other's unique cannon "signatures of fire" on the battlefield. When

LC

Lt. C. M. Pennington's Battery M, 2nd United States Artillery.

W. H. F. Lee's cavalry reached the banks of the Opequon Creek, Pelham and Breathed were positioned on Pleasonton's left. They opened fire with a few salvos, but no large-scale engagement developed. The next day, Breathed's and Hart's batteries moved to a position near Shepherdstown. Stuart ordered Breathed to engage, prompting Breathed to hurl a few more shots at Pennington's artillery. However, the engagement did not amount to much more than a reminder that Pelham and Breathed remained ready to respond to any threat posed by Pennington and his horse artillery.[37]

The men of the four horse artillery batteries had some time on their hands after their brush with Pleasonton. Pelham renewed his acquaintance with pretty Sallie Dandridge, who lived in a beautiful nearby house called The Bower. Pelham invited Sallie and her sisters over to the artillery's camp, showing off the guns and the men under his command. "From gun to gun he would go, patting each piece as affectionately as if they were animals. He would tell them the history of each gun—how at a certain place a particular gun had wrought such

Battery M, United States Horse Artillery.

terrible execution among the Yankees, and so on to the end," recalled Henry Matthews. "No one knew the record of these guns better than our noble Captain. It was a question which he loved best, the guns or the noble band of artillery men that manned them."[38]

Breathed used the opportunity to write his sweetheart Miss Mollie back in Hagerstown. He was sympathetic to (and angered by) the plight of Mollie's father, Dr. Charles Macgill, who was still imprisoned for his defiance of the Union oath. He could not help but recall the two years he had trained with Dr. Macgill, and how the doctor had given him a start in medicine even though Breathed's medical career was short-lived because of his choice of saber over lancet. Unable to resist the call of his Hippocratic Oath, Breathed often tended any wounded Confederates he could find once the smoke of battle cleared.[39]

*   *   *

Resting and refitting in northern Virginia, General Lee had little idea what McClellan's army was doing in Maryland in the days after the battle. He needed solid information about the disposition of the Federal army, and whether his opponent was planning to move south against him any time soon. Consequently, on October 8 Lee ordered Stuart to undertake "an expedition into Maryland with a detachment of cavalry, if it can be successfully executed, [which] is at this time desirable." Always eager to go off on an adventure, Stuart promptly obeyed. He issued the following orders to his command:

> Soldiers, you are about to engage in an enterprise which, to insure success, imperatively demands at your hands coolness, decision, bravery and implicit obedience to orders without a question or cavil, and the strictest order and sobriety on the march and in the camp. The destination and extent of this expedition had better be kept to myself than known to you. Suffice it to say, that with the hearty co-operation of officers and men I have not a doubt of its success, a success which will reflect credit in the highest degree upon your arms. The orders which are here published for your government are absolutely necessary and must be rigidly enforced. The orders which will control your actions are as follows: Each commander of a brigade to detail one-third of his command to seize horses and other property of citizens of the United States subject to legal capture, while the remainder of the command must always be ready for action. Receipts must be given to all non-combatants for every article taken, in order that they might have recourse upon the Federal authorities at Washington for damage. Individual plundering is prohibited in the strongest language. The arrest of public functionaries, such as magistrates, postmasters and sheriffs, was ordered that such persons might be held as hostages for citizens of the Confederacy who had been arrested and imprisoned. The seizure of private property is prohibited in the State of Maryland.

> J. E. B. Stuart Major General.[40]

Stuart pulled together 1,200 troopers of Wade Hampton's, Rooney Lee's, and William E. "Grumble" Jones's men and set off on his way north. Major Pelham accompanied the raid, with Captains Hart and Breathed in command of the four guns rolling north with Stuart. The horse artillerists brought up the rear of Stuart's column, which crossed the Potomac close to Hedgesville, Virginia. The cavalrymen surprised and captured some Union pickets and headed farther north. Stuart passed through Washington County, Maryland, crossed the Mason-Dixon Line, and entered Pennsylvania in Montgomery Township. His men rode into Mercersburg, where Pelham deployed two of his guns in the town square in order to intimidate the local citizens. Mounted on his horse Billy, Breathed stood watch over the imposing gun tubes.[41]

Stuart captured nine prominent citizens and sent them back to Virginia as hostages while his men confiscated 600 pairs of shoes from a local tannery. Stuart filled out a receipt and suggested the owner send it to President Jefferson Davis in Richmond for payment. The cavalier also found a local map marking all of the farms in the area, which made requisitioning horses during his advance much easier. The Southern column progressed toward Chambersburg, Pennsylvania, seizing 1,200 fresh mounts along the way from some local farmers. Six hundred men swept the country on each side of the command, and every horse that could be found was taken. Gunner Henry Matthews' mule was exhausted, and he exchanged the beast for a sorrel mare, much to the chagrin of the horse's former owner. "Not having time to enter into an argument with the native on the rights of property in a hostile country I changed saddles and bid my very angry friend an everlasting adieu," recounted Matthews. Captain Breathed "fell in love with my capture, but could not persuade me that my beauty would not do me as much service as him, so I rode my mare to the end of the expedition. Nothing of any note occurred during that day except to note the astonishment depicted on the faces of the natives to see live rebels in their midst was beyond what they had even expected to see."[42]

After a long and unpleasant march through a cold rain, the column finally arrived in Chambersburg on the night October 10. Fitz Lee's Brigade established its camp in a farmyard outside of town. Colonel Williams C. Wickham of the 4th Virginia Cavalry, was a prominent planter and politician who happened to be Rooney Lee's brother-in-law. Wickham made his "couch" in a covered wagon, complaining the whole time that it was unfit for a Virginian. After watching Breathed's men helping themselves to ample supplies of corn, Wickham wrote, "Breathed's boys who were not accustomed to unlimited supplies of corn won my admiration by the frequency by which during the night they brought one sliding from the top of the pile toward the tail of the wagon by their oft repeated return for an additional feed for their horses."[43]

Before Stuart left town, he decided to burn a bridge over the Conococheague Creek, but changed his mind when the locals informed him the structure was made of iron. Instead, the grayclad horse soldiers destroyed large quantities of Union supplies and set fire to the barracks.

Wagers of hardtack were made on how long it would take to knock down the more prominent barracks buildings with Breathed's cannons.[44]

As they passed through Mercersburg, the artillerists helped themselves to ample supplies of the straw hats favored by the Pennsylvania German farmers. "The appearance of the battery was grotesque, indeed, so that Gen. Stuart on riding through the battery asked Pelham where he got all the farmers from," recalled Matthews. "The name of farmer stuck to us for quite a while. The constant rain had the tendency to make our hats quite limp, so that they resembled Shaker bonnets."[45]

After a rest, the Confederate troopers started on their return trip. By now, McClellan was aware that he had a large force of enemy cavalry operating in his rear, and all Union forces were put on alert and ordered to spare no effort in attempting to intercept Stuart's column before it could reach the Potomac and safety. The relaxed frolic thus far enjoyed by the Southerners above the river was about to end.

By this time, Stuart's force numbered about 2,000 troopers. As the column headed east in the direction of a small town named Gettysburg, they learned that a detachment of the 6th Pennsylvania Cavalry, also known as Rush's Lancers, was in the neighborhood searching for the Southern horsemen. It was time to move south—quickly. "When we got the order to move our horses, heads were turned to the west and we understood we were to retrace our steps, but before moving an order came to face front and march toward Gettysburg," recalled Colonel Wickham. Stuart quickly determined a course for his retreat. Later, Stuart told Wickham that "it was intuition not his judgment" that prompted the action. The column moved out, with Stuart relying on one of his staff officers, Capt. B. S. White, a distant cousin of Breathed's, to find a route to the river. "Thrice during the night did Stuart advise and ask White if he thought the constant rain would raise the river," recalled Matthews. "White assured him that his troopers could march as fast as the waters would flow, and that he would have ample time to cross the Potomac before the waters now falling in the mountains could swell the lower fords."[46]

After shaking off the detachment of Lancers, Stuart covered the six miles to Emmitsburg, Maryland, at sunset, having ridden more than 31 miles that day. They still had 45 miles to travel with Union cavalry nipping at the rear of the column. Soon after dark, the Confederates captured a courier carrying messages from Colonel Rush to his command. Stuart had been considering a dash into the town of Frederick, but this intelligence caused him to change his plans. "From him and his papers Stuart learned that the enemy was still unaware of his locality, although using every means to intercept him," recalled one of Stuart's staff officers, "This body of the enemy retired toward Mechanicstown. Everything now depended upon the rapidity of our march, as Pleasonton was advised of our movements, and had a shorter distance to the Ford than we had." Stuart altered his route to the east, but not before a Union scouting party spotted the Confederate column near Waynesboro, Pennsylvania.[47]

When the Confederate troopers had first crossed the Potomac on the way north, Hampton held the van, with Col. Matthew C. Butler of the 2nd

Colonel Alfred N. Duffié took part in the pursuit of
Stuart's men north of the Potomac River.

South Carolina Cavalry as his second in command, followed by the brigades of Grumble Jones and Rooney Lee. When the troopers left Chambersburg, Jones took the front and Hampton the rear, leaving Lee in the center. Lee was followed by a detail from all the commands in charge of some 1,200 captured horses. The column was long and ponderous, which made it vulnerable to being caught and torn to pieces.[48]

Matthews later described the perils of the last portion of the ride on the other side of the Potomac River. While the column was still at Hyattstown, Maryland, more than twelve miles from White's Ford, Union forces were bearing down from multiple directions. Major General George Stoneman, with a division of Union cavalry guarding the Potomac River crossings, was moving to block Stuart's march route, while Col. Alfred N. Duffié's command, along with General Pleasonton's men, blocked the mouth of the Monocacy River. Knowing the enemy was seeking him but largely oblivious to the Federal net closing around him, Stuart rode on, trusting "the great God of battles to release him from the hands of the Yankees." His adjutant, Maj. Henry B. McClellan, believed that it would be impossible for Stuart to cross the Potomac without a major fight, while many of his troopers believed that the capture of the entire force was more probable than escape.[49]

Stuart ordered Jones to form on the right of the road and send a party forward toward Pleasonton. He also ordered Wickham to push forward to take possession of White's Ford on the river, and to arrange to protect the crossing of the entire column. Wickham promptly sent a squadron to the ford, which ran off a Federal infantry picket watching the crossing. When Wickham spotted a much larger formation of Union troops—probably a brigade—forming to attack his position, he realized that the odds of crossing without a real fight had grown slim.[50]

Wickham sent his orderly galloping back to Stuart with a request for two guns. Breathed received the command and within a short time he and a pair of cannon reached Wickham. He unlimbered his pieces "and soon threw the advancing line into confusion and drove them back to the cover of the woods and repeated it whenever they appeared," recalled a pleased Wickham. "It was just before Breathed came in that Rooney Lee handed me the written demand to the Federal commander to surrender to a surrounded force and my smile was not so much one of incredulity as it was of concern that Talley would succeed in his application for the guns and of greater confidence in the efforts of Breathed's own escapades than of the General's cheeky (pardon the slang) requests."[51]

The concentrated and accurate fire of Breathed's guns helped clear the river crossing. With Breathed's guns in tow, Rooney Lee and the troopers made their way down to the riverbank. The horse soldiers and cannoneers splashed across to the southern side, the captured horses following close behind them. "Breathed put his guns in a magnificent position on the hills just opposite the ford and never during the war did I see a more beautiful artillery practice than we then had on both sides of the line of march of Stuart's column," remembered Wickham. "Infantry or dismounted cavalry were closing in and Breathed was so positioned as to enfilade each line and it was exhilarating to see he would by his well directed shots cause each line to falter and recede as they came to the line of his range thus keeping open a space through which the whole command safely marched and crossed the river." It had been a close-run affair.[52]

*   *   *

The Confederates bivouacked that night at Leesburg, Virginia, and the next day went back to their camp on the upper Opequon. Stuart had ridden nearly 120 miles through hostile territory in just three days. Once again he had humiliated and demoralized the Federal cavalry by riding all the way around the Union army without suffering any combat casualties. Along the way he secured horses and supplies, burned tons of supplies he could not carry away or use, and gathered precious information for General Lee. For the first time, the people of the North knew firsthand what it felt like to have their homes invaded.[53]

With the exception of occasional cavalry skirmishes, Breathed and his artillerists rested until McClellan finally succumbed to pressure from President Lincoln to pursue Lee's repulsed army. Grumbling that his army was not yet sufficiently recovered to move south, "Little Mac" marched the Army of the Potomac slowly back into Virginia. Stuart's cavalry deployed in McClellan's front and retarded his movements until General Lee could move the Army of Northern Virginia to a position to block the advance. "The Federals seemed to have the idea that Lee's whole army was in the valley of Va. and in order to ascertain that fact two strong columns of the enemy were sent into the valley at daylight of the

16th of October," recalled an artillerist serving with Breathed. "These two columns advanced upon us, one from Shepherdstown to Smithfield, under Brig. Gen. A. Humphreys, the other under Brig. Gen. W. S. Hancock from Harper's Ferry to Charlestown." With Stuart in personal command of Fitz Lee's Brigade and Breathed's Battery, the Confederates resisted Humphreys' advance. Matthews recalled this engagement. "At about sunset we attacked the enemy with cavalry, infantry and artillery. We had a stubborn fight, lasting until three, in which we succeeded in driving Humphreys from his stronghold." There was more skirmishing on October 17 as the Union forces withdrew toward Shepherdstown, though Breathed's Battery had not yet suffered any losses.[54]

Finally, after much prodding from Washington, McClellan began moving his army across the Potomac. Lee, convinced that McClellan would attempt to occupy the Rappahannock–Rapidan River line, reacted accordingly. In fact, McClellan was planning on moving his command to Warrenton. On October 28, Lee decided to divide his command, sending Jackson up the Shenandoah Valley and Longstreet down the Piedmont toward Culpeper, where Lee would establish his headquarters. Stuart's job was to screen these movements and conduct reconnaissance to determine the disposition and location of the Army of the Potomac. Hampton's Brigade was left behind at Martinsburg until his widely dispersed foraging units could be re-assembled, whereupon they were to join Stuart. Fitz Lee's Brigade was to accompany Stuart, moving east of the Blue Ridge to screen Longstreet. Munford's Brigade was acting as rear guard for Jackson's Corps.[55]

By October 28, Stuart, Pelham, and possibly Breathed reached Welbourne Plantation outside of Middleburg, home of Colonel Richard H. Dulany, the commander of the 7th Virginia Cavalry, where they stopped to water their horses. Dulany and his family welcomed the men into their beautiful home. Before breakfast, Pelham scratched on the parlor window, "G. C. Walker Oct 28 1862, J." Walker was Pelham's friend and aide-de-camp. The major was only able to carve his first initial "J" on the window before Mary Dulany summoned the officers to breakfast. She did not discover the inscription until later, after the men had ridden away. Although it was not very genteel of Pelham to scratch his name into the windowpane, the action certainly left a lasting memento of his visit.[56]

On October 30, Stuart and his command rode to Snicker's Gap, in Loudoun County. The next day, the horsemen attacked Union troops on the Snickersville Turnpike and drove them back to Aldie. Once again Stuart bested Pleasonton's troopers and embarrassed Battery M. However, Pennington's men were by no means demoralized.[57]

During the withdrawal from the South Mountain fighting during the Maryland raid, W. H. F. "Rooney" Lee had been unhorsed and trampled in the confusion at Turner's Gap. Temporary command of his regiment went to Colonel Wickham of the 4th Virginia Cavalry. The cavalry Wickham and his comrades led had been reduced in strength. "The brigade had been reduced to half its numbers, owing to the grease heel that had become an epidemic, consequently the gallant old brigade did not number more than one thousand men," reported Matthews. The lack of horses meant that each gun's team had to be reduced from six guns to four. "We sent our sick horses and established a horse hospital near Culpeper C. H. in charge of Lieut. Febrey," he remembered. The grease heel epidemic had reduced the strength of the horse artillery by about one-third, and the number of available troopers was beginning to dwindle rapidly. Fortunately, Wickham was a strong leader and the brigade was in good hands as it approached Snicker's Gap near Middleburg.[58]

The Confederate horsemen skirmished heavily on October 31 with Federal cavalry under command of Brig. Gen. George D. Bayard, who "suffered heavily in killed and wounded" and had one artillery piece disabled during the fluid action. During much of the first half of November, as the weather began turning chilly, a series of skirmishes erupted for the passes cutting through the Blue Ridge Mountains and in various locations in the Piedmont. These skirmishes offered Breathed and the Stuart Horse Artillery new opportunities to meet Pennington's Battery M, 2nd U.S. Cavalry on the battlefield. "Lt. Pennington was one of the best, if not the best in the Union Horse Artillery, and he and Breathed knew each other like old friends on the battlefields upon which they encountered each other," Matthews recalled many years after the war. "The Horse Artillery had met this battery on many a hotly contested fields of battle." Another testimony to the caliber of Pennington's horse artillery was penned some years after the war by Sgt. Maj. Dodson of the Stuart Horse Artillery. Dodson described events on the Aldie–Upperville Road:

we found ourselves on the left flank of Longstreet's Corps, which had passed the mountain barrier the day before. At this point we had a sharp engagement with Pleasonton's cavalry, which had come up the turnpike on a reconnoitering expedition. We had been joined by W. H. F. Lee's [Hampton's] Brigade and McGregor's Battery [Henry was still in command], so that our force numbered some three thousand cavalry and two light batteries. The fight began about the middle of the afternoon and continued almost without cessation until night put a stop to it. Eight men in our battery were wounded by the explosion of a limber chest and the gallant Captain McGregor lost a leg in the action. Here Breathed's command met for the first time a battery worthy its most gallant courage and effective work and one it was destined often to meet in future actions. This was Battery M, Second United States Artillery, a better than which did not exist in either army.[59]

The fight at Snicker's Gap began about 8:00 A.M. on October 31 when Pleasonton's Federals began deploying infantry and cavalry, together with ten artillery pieces. Angry at being embarrassed by Stuart when that general rode all the way around McClellan, Pleasonton was determined to exact revenge. Breathed posted his guns advantageously on a patch of high open ground while cavalrymen supported him by dismounting and taking up positions behind stone fences. "Pennington had taken the exact range of Breathed's guns," remembered Matthews. "Now, with the Confederate horse artillery occupying the same position Pennington's guns showered it with shot and shell. Grimly Breathed hung on." The Federal artillerists, performing better than usual, took a toll on Breathed's Battery. Unable to tolerate the blistering Union shelling for long, Breathed shifted his position at least three times that day. The Confederate gunners realized that the Federal guns and ammunition outmatched them, and so were forced to improvise as best they could to remain in effective action.[60]

While the engagement was underway, Pelham led one of Breathed's howitzers to a nearby hill, unlimbered, and opened what Stuart later called "a masked fire upon a body of the enemy's cavalry in the valley below," shocking the horsemen and "putting them to flight, capturing their flag, their arms, equipments and horses, as well as some prisoners, sustaining in this extraordinary feat no loss whatsoever."[61]

The Federal cavalry and infantry made several attempts to flank the fluid Confederate position. Years later, the events that day remained vivid to Henry Matthews:

> We were at one time firing on both flanks and in our immediate front. We were being pressed very heavily. . . . One of our caissons was exploded at this position by a shell from the enemy's artillery, killing the horses of the caisson, and burning the two men who were at the caisson at the time, Melvin Bollman and John Culbreth. The rapidity with which we were throwing iron into these Federal batteries made it necessary to have two men at the caisson—the limber of the gun being exhausted of its ammunition. A shell exploded in front of my gun (the 2nd) doing considerable damage to the piece, wounding three men.[62]

After the accurate Union fire killed two of his men, Breathed limbered up and withdrew at a gallop. The limbers and caissons rumbled through a ravine and up the other side before the gunners unlimbered yet again, forcing the Northern artillerists to descend the heights of Philomont onto the level ground recently abandoned by Breathed.[63]

In his front was the 7th Indiana, and with their usual unflappable style and combat finesse, Pelham and Breathed blasted away at the advancing infantry. One of the most amazing shots of the war was fired against these Hoosiers by Pelham himself, who sighted an artillery piece at a color bearer, "striking him down at a distance of 800 yards."[64]

It was an exhausting day of combat for everyone, but Stuart was pleased with the way his men handled themselves. "Having to watch all of my avenues leading to my rear my effective force was very much diminished, but the Stuart Horse Artillery under the incomparable Pelham and his able Lieut. Breathed," he reported, "supported by the cavalry sharpshooters, made a gallant and obstinate resistance, maintaining their ground for the greater part of the day, both suffering heavily from the enemy's shot." Superior numbers finally told, however, and the Federal infantry and cavalry flanked Stuart's position and forced his retreat. It was a stubborn withdrawal, and "every hilltop and every foot of ground was disputed so that the enemy made progress of less than a mile during the day."[65]

The cavalry and gunners bivouacked that night near Upperville, with the artillery camping at Pantherskin Creek. That night, Pennington moved his cannon to a cornfield across from Breathed's camp. Pelham, however, spotted the movement during the night and ordered Breathed to move his guns to the top of a hill. As the sun rose the next morning, Breathed and his men sent salvos ripping into the cornfield, catching the Union artillerists by complete surprise. Others from Stuart's command joined in the fighting, and the opponents moved up and down the creek, moving and firing in an effort to gain a decisive advantage that never arrived. The enemy's progress, wrote Stuart, was "obstinately and successfully resisted for nearly the entire day." Unfortunately, Wickham fell wounded when he was struck in the neck by a shell fragment. Tom Rosser of the 5th Virginia Cavalry took his place. Stuart was well aware of the role Breathed was playing in holding Pleasonton in check. "Breathed's battery," wrote the general in his after-action report, "added to its many laurels on these hard-fought fields, and was materially assisted by a battery from General D. H. Hill's command, which had been sent to reinforce me."[66]

Late that afternoon Stuart withdrew through Upperville, protecting Ashby's Gap as he did his best to slow down the advance of the probing enemy cavalry. Stuart knew McClellan was seeking to discover the disposition of the Army of Northern Virginia, and he was determined to deny him that. By November 4, the Stuart Horse Artillery occupied a position north of Markham on the crest of the hill. Sharpshooters were deployed to support the guns. The artillerists focused their attention on Union columns moving up the road. By 9:00 A.M., the Federals were advancing anew and a fitful artillery duel opened that lasted many hours. This type of intensive skirmishing filled the days between November 2 and November 10, during which time the opposing armies jockeyed for position.[67]

Tired of McClellan's cautious and grudging advance, on November 9 President Lincoln replaced him with Maj. Gen. Ambrose E. Burnside. The change in command would have far-reaching implications for the coming campaign. The new commander's performance at Antietam was sloe and inept; how he would do at the head of the Army of the Potomac remained to be seen.

*   *   *

After being incarcerated by the Union army at several unpleasant locations for refusing to take the oath of allegiance, Dr. Charles Macgill was finally released in early November. When he learned he would be freed, Macgill asked the Federal commander about the conditions of his release, declaring that if he had to raise his fingers to the brim of his hat in a gesture of gratitude, he would rather stay in jail until he died. To his pleasure, the Federal commandant answered, "I release you unconditionally."[68]

Trooper Alexander Hunter of the Black Horse Cavalry was imprisoned with Dr. Macgill at Boston's Fort Warren, and had an opportunity to observe him closely during his time there. "Nothing but skill and unremitting watchfulness of one of the political prisoners, Doctor Macgill, of Hagerstown, saved the lives of those who were so very ill that it was but a touch-and-go with them," observed Hunter. "What a noble specimen of humanity that man was! Of Herculean stature, outspoken and fearless as a lion, yet with a heart and touch for the sick as gentle as he was brave." Privates, considered expendable by many generals and usually valued only as cannon fodder, were tenderly cared for by Macgill. The doctor often sat with these prisoners through many long nights, tracking their flickering pulses and tending to them with the same fidelity and untiring devotion he would have used if these poor men were officers or generals of great importance to the war effort.[69]

*   *   *

Stuart's command was reorganized in the midst of the emerging winter campaign. Grumble Jones was given command of Robertson's old brigade and replaced Munford, who took command the 2nd Virginia Cavalry in Fitz Lee's Brigade. The cavalry arm was also getting a new brigade under Rooney Lee. The new order of battle was as follows:

Cavalry Division: Maj. Gen. JEB Stuart

Hampton's Brigade: Brig. Gen. Wade Hampton
1st NC Cavalry: Col. Laurence S. Baker
1st SC Cavalry: Col. John L. Black
2nd SC Cavalry: Col. Matthew C. Butler
Cobb's Legion: Lt. Col. Pierce M. B. Young
Phillips Legion: Lt. Col. William W. Rich

Fitzhugh Lee's Brigade: Brig. Gen. Fitzhugh Lee
1st Va. Cavalry: Col. James H. Drake
2nd Va. Cavalry: Col. Thomas T. Munford
3rd Va. Cavalry: Col. Thomas H. Owen
4th Va. Cavalry: Col. Williams C. Wickham
5th Va. Cavalry: Col. Thomas L. Rosser

Rooney Lee's Brigade: Brig. Gen. William H. F. Lee
2nd NC Cavalry: Col. Solomon Williams
9th Va. Cavalry: Col. Richard L. T. Beale
10th Va. Cavalry: Col. J. Lucius Davis
13th Va. Cavalry: Col. John R. Chambliss, Jr.
15th Va. Cavalry: Col. William B. Ball

"Grumble" Jones Brigade: Brig. Gen. William E. Jones
6th Va. Cavalry: Col. Thomas S. Flournoy
7th Va. Cavalry: Col. Samuel B. Myers
12th Va. Cavalry: Lt. Col. Richard H. Burks
17th Bn Va. Cavalry: Capt. Edward A. H. McDonald
35th Bn.Va. Cavalry: Maj. Elijah V. White

In addition to a new brigade of cavalry, Stuart added another battery to his horse artillery. The Lynchburg Battery (aka Beauregard Rifles), under Capt. Marcellus N. Moorman, was being converted to horse artillery and assigned to Stuart's command. This made five horse artillery batteries. The Stuart Horse Artillery order of battle was now as follows:

Stuart Horse Artillery: Maj. John Pelham
1st Stuart Horse Artillery: Capt. James Breathed
2nd Stuart Horse Artillery: Capt. Mathis W. Henry
Washington Artillery: Capt. James F. Hart
Chew's Battery: Capt. Roger P. Chew
Beauregard Rifles: Capt. Marcellus N. Moorman

Each brigade was generally directly supported by a specific horse artillery battery. Breathed's Battery supported Fitz Lee. Hart's Battery supported Wade Hampton. Chew's Battery supported Grumble Jones, whose Brigade would stay in the Shenandoah Valley during the coming campaign. Moorman's Battery would support Rooney Lee. That left

Henry's 2nd Stuart Horse Artillery, which was designated as the reserve, directly under the command of Pelham.[70]

Moorman was never accepted by the rest of the men in the Stuart Horse Artillery. In addition to being openly ambitious for more rank, Moorman had a tendency to exaggerate his battlefield contributions, which was exactly the opposite of the self-effacing standard of leadership that pervaded Pelham's command. Moorman was not missed when the popular John Jordan Shoemaker replaced him at the head of the battery in February of 1864.[71]

*   *   *

By November 15, Breathed's and Henry's batteries had moved east of the Blue Ridge range into the Shenandoah Valley outside Warrenton. Breathed was reattached to Fitz Lee's Brigade, which now consisted of the 1st, 2nd, 3rd, and 4th Virginia cavalry regiments. On November 18 and 19, Breathed shelled the enemy around Warrenton Springs before moving east toward Fredericksburg. Federal forces were moving east as well, signaling a new phase of the war had begun. It was now clear to Lee that Burnside was making for Fredericksburg. Lee's intelligence from Stuart was so good that Lee confidently moved his army just one day behind Burnside. Since the Rappahannock was too wide to ford at Fredericksburg, Lee knew he had sufficient time to assemble his men and dispute any attempt by Burnside to cross to the far bank. The stage was being set for the next crucial battle in the Civil War.[72]

The weeks of running fighting had worn down thousands of horses, including Breathed's. It was long past time for a new mount. "I certify that I have sold to the Confederate States one horse valued at two hundred dollars for use of the 'Stuart Horse Artillery,' by order of Gen. Stuart," Breathed certified in a handwritten affidavit while camped near Rapidan Station on November 24. He had his eye on a bay owned by Tom Rosser, and he bought her with the money the next day. "I hereby certify that I have, according to the order of Maj. Gen. J. E. B. Stuart this day purchased [of Col. Rosser] a bay horse for the use of my battery of Stuart Horse Artillery valued at $200.00." Breathed had paid for his new horse by combining this transaction with the sale of his old horse. The next day when he arrived at Fredericksburg, he was reimbursed $400.00.[73]

Chapter 5

Campaigning along the Rappahannock with Pelham

(Winter, 1862-1863)

B efore describing the actions performed by the Stuart Horse Artillery at the Battle of Fredericksburg—deeds that would make John Pelham's name a by-word in the South for his gallant behavior—it is worth explaining why the armies of both the North and South were organized the way they were.

The person most responsible for that organization was Maj. Gen. Henry Wager Halleck. Before the rise of Ulysses Grant in the East, Halleck was made head of the U.S. Army by Lincoln. Much of Halleck's fame rested in a book he wrote back in 1843 entitled *Elements of Military Art and Science*. This tome was required reading at West Point, and virtually all officers who were alumni of that institution would have had to practically commit it to memory. Halleck had the following to say about how armies in the field should be organized:

> The French Revolution introduced the system of grand divisions composed of the four arms combined; each division moved separately and independently of the other. In the wars of the Empire, Napoleon united two or more of these divisions into a *corps d'armée,* which formed a wing, the centre, or reserve of his

grand army. In addition to these divisions and *corps d'armée,* he had large reserves of cavalry and artillery, which were employed as distinct and separate arms.

If the forces be sufficiently numerous to fight by *corps d'armée,* each corps should have its own reserve, independent of the general reserve of the army. Again, if the forces be so small as to act by grand divisions only, each division should then have *its* separate reserve.[1]

Generals on both sides interpreted Halleck in different ways. In the South, Gen. Joe Johnston favored the "Grand Division" as the basic field unit. When Robert E. Lee took command, however, he found Grand Divisions too unwieldy for offensive operations. Lee utilized larger organizations and in the fall of 1862 created corps-level units. The North, on the other hand, fluctuated between variations of corps and Grand Divisions, or combinations of both. Until Grant settled the question in 1864, "army politics" resulted in either too many corps or combinations of corps and independent Grand Divisions. The structure of the Union forces in the Eastern Theater occasionally contributed to battlefield disasters. Antietam offers one of the best examples of this. The same organizational problems would contribute to defeat again, particularly at Chancellorsville.

The new commander of the Army of the Potomac, the reluctant Ambrose E. Burnside, did not believe himself competent to hold such an important position. Part of the reason he accepted the assignment was so that his rival, Maj. Gen. Joseph Hooker, would not get the command. Selected because he was a Democrat, Burnside was both popular with the men and closely associated with McClellan. Unfortunately, he was little better at devising and implementing battle plans or leading armies than his former commander. His orders from above, however, were clear: move against Lee and defeat him.

Burnside devised a plan to steal a march on Lee and place him at a disadvantage. He decided to head for Richmond via the important commercial center of Fredericksburg. The Union army would move quickly for the Rappahannock River, cross it on pontoon bridges, occupy Fredericksburg, and head south toward Richmond. The plan was a decent one, and if he had acted with dispatch it might have worked. Fortunately for the Confederates, expeditiousness was not in Burnside's nature. By the time his pontoons arrived opposite Fredericksburg, he had lost the element of surprise and Lee's army was in position on the far bank to meet the threat. Burnside's original plan had failed. However, instead of going into winter quarters or adopting another less obvious strategy, he wilted in the face of unrelenting pressure from the White House to advance on Richmond. The affable and well-liked Rhode Islander, believing he had little choice in the matter, pressed on in spite of the obvious problems waiting for him on the other side of the river.

At the beginning of what would come to be called the Fredericksburg Campaign, Burnside's Army of the Potomac numbered about 120,000 men; Lee's reinforced Army of Northern Virginia fielded a respectable 78,500. The Federals held a substantial advantage in manpower, as well as artillery. They would need all of it if Burnside's plan stood any chance of succeeding. Unfortunately for the new leader of the Union army, the Rappahannock could not be forded in front of the town; the army would have to cross on several pontoon bridges. Although he had successfully stolen a march on Lee, the pontoons were not there when the Army of the Potomac drew up in front of Fredericksburg. By the time they did arrive, Lee had fortified Marye's Heights, the dominating high ground overlooking the town.

Lee had deployed his army well. Jackson's Corps held the right side of the Southern front well below the town. Longstreet's men held the left side on the heights behind the town. Stuart and the horse artillery secured Lee's right flank at Hamilton's Crossing, a bit more than four miles south of Marye's Heights (the river ran generally north and south at Fredericksburg). In spite of the pleas of his lieutenants to attack elsewhere and not into the teeth of Lee's veterans, Burnside doggedly stuck with his battle plan even though all hope for any strategic or tactical advantage had already been lost. His plan was indeed straightforward: Maj. Gen. Edwin V. Sumner's Grand Division would cross the river into Fredericksburg, pass through the town, and assault Longstreet atop Marye's Heights; Maj. Gen. William B. Franklin's Grand Division would do the same well to the south of town and attack Stonewall Jackson's position; and Maj. Gen. Joseph Hooker's Grand Division would remain in reserve in the center. Artillery on Stafford Heights on the east side of the river would provide cover for the crossing and help prevent or break apart a Confederate attack.[2]

By the time Franklin's soldiers were across the river and aligning themselves for battle, the horse artillery batteries of Chew, Hart, Henry, and Moorman were in position at Hamilton's Crossing, guarding Lee's right flank. Breathed's Battery was deployed alone about one-half mile south and slightly west of the rest of the Confederate guns. Together, they offered a strong enfilading presence capable of punishing an attacker moving against Jackson's front. The force Franklin planned to attack with was large—some 50,000 men from the I and VI Corps, their full compliments of artillery, and the cavalry brigade of Brig. Gen. George D. Bayard, who was riding into his last battle.[3]

When it became obvious the Federals were about to attack, Jackson advised Stuart to open on Franklin's left with the horse artillery. When Stuart told his gunners to do so, Pelham asked permission to move two guns on the road from Hamilton's Crossing to a forward position near the intersection and perpendicular to the Richmond Stage Road. There, he claimed, his pieces could enfilade Franklin. Trees and hedges lined the approach roads to the spot Pelham had in mind, and would offer excellent cover as the guns bumped and rolled their way forward. Pelham's position, however, was so far beyond support that the idea of exposing guns in that manner seemed nearly suicidal. Even the audacious Stuart had reason to pause; the chances for success seemed small, while the possibility of a disaster loomed large. (Losing a gun or two was one thing, but losing Pelham and his experienced artillerists was unthinkable.) However, Pelham's entreaties finally wore Stuart down, and the cavalry chief gave him permission to do what he wanted. The Alabaman moved to the selected spot with a Blakely rifle and 12-pounder Napoleon.[4]

With his two guns in place about 500 yards from the advancing Union front line, Pelham ordered his crews to open fire with solid shot. The Union troops were moving at nearly right angles to his tubes, and were caught full in the flank by the bounding iron balls. Though they did little if any damage, they did utterly confuse the Federals. Within a few minutes enemy artillerymen responded with four batteries.[5]

The Union return fire quickly knocked out the Blakely, leaving only the solitary Napoleon to face the Union shelling. Stuart sent his aide, Major von Borcke, with instructions that Pelham could fall back any time he wished. Pelham responded, "Tell the General I can hold my ground." The Southern gunner was working his single piece so quickly that one Union commander believed Pelham had an entire battery. Two Southern gunners were hit, one killed outright and one mortally injured. All the while the enemy infantry hung back, waiting for the Federal artillery to

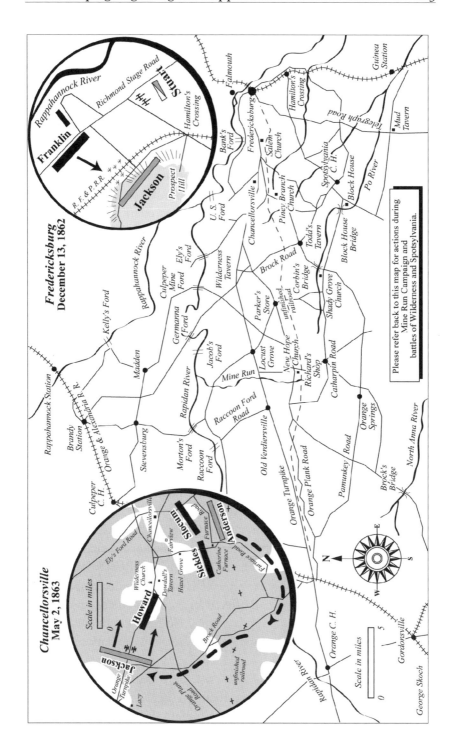

Fredericksburg
December 13, 1862

Chancellorsville
May 2, 1863

Please refer back to this map for actions during Mine Run Campaign and battles of Wilderness and Spotsylvania.

George Skoch

silence Pelham, who intended to wage the unequal fight as long as there was ammunition to do so. By the time Pelham was forced to help fire the gun himself, the bottom of the caissons were nearly visible. Stuart's third request to fall back persuaded the "Boy Major" to heed his commander's suggestion. General Lee had been watching the exchange. When he discovered the audacious gunner was Pelham he exclaimed, "It is glorious to see such courage in one so young."[6]

"The Federal line . . . had their advance checked by the Horse Artillerymen," recalled horse artillerist Sgt. George Shreve. "The Confederate generals from Lee to Jackson observed the strategic cannon fire and Lee bestowed the name 'Gallant Pelham' for his audacious maneuvers." Although Pelham gleaned the lion's share of the publicity from his exploits, Breathed and the other men of the horse artillery also did their share in halting the Union advance at Fredericksburg.[7]

Once Pelham's artillery had withdrawn, Franklin renewed his forward movement. The Federal attack was stopped up and down the Southern line by artillery and small arms fire, except for one location where a breakthrough occurred in a gap in the line. The fighting there became hand-to-hand for a time, and casualties on both sides were high before the Federals were forced back for the final time. Jackson's front, though cracked temporarily, had held. Burnside's men had even less luck against the Confederate left, where James Longstreet's men held Marye's Heights. There, thousands of Federals were mowed down line by line in a series of brave but foolhardy assaults against what was surely an impregnable defensive position. Burnside had learned little from his equally foolish narrow-front attack against the lower bridge at Antietam.

The attack and heavy enemy artillery fire forced Breathed to withdraw his battery a short distance to the opposite side of a small creek early that afternoon. By 5:00 P.M. he had moved to an 80-foot knoll close to Hamilton's Crossing overlooking the Richmond, Fredericksburg, and Potomac Railroad. This position offered an excellent vantage point from which to see the Union battle movements. He fired continuously from this point and did not stop until the fighting ended, when darkness finally obscured his gunners' vision.[8]

By the time Burnside broke off and withdrew across the Rappahannock, his army had been repulsed, his losses totaling nearly 13,000. Lee's army lost about half as many men. The fighting at Fredericksburg was a one-sided and decisive Confederate victory.[9]

After the bloodletting ended, Breathed and his men camped near Chancellorsville on the Orange Court House and Fredericksburg roads supported by some of Fitz Lee's troopers. With little to do, the men of the battery formed a choir and celebrated their victory at Fredericksburg with singing and pre-Christmas celebrations. Illness and battle losses had thinned the ranks, prompting Lt. Philip P. Johnston's trip to Richmond to find more men for Breathed's Battery.[10]

*   *   *

After its bloody rebuff at Fredericksburg, Burnside's army went into winter quarters on Stafford Heights across the Rappahannock from Lee's army. Most of the Southern army also went into winter camp, but Stuart was gearing up to raid Union supply lines at Dumfries, Virginia.

Stuart announced his intention on Christmas night. His troopers and artillery, about 1,800 men, rode out the next morning up the south side of the Rappahannock, crossed over to Morrisville, and moved toward the Telegraph Road, where Stuart intended to disrupt Federal wagon trains rolling to supply Burnside. By this stage of the war, the Union high command had grown familiar with Stuart's long raids behind enemy lines, but had yet to devise a way to curtail them. This raid presented unique challenges to Burnside and his cavalry because Stuart divided his command into separate columns and sent them off in different directions. Fitz Lee was ordered to attack the Telegraph Road between Dumfries and Aquia and drive north toward Dumfries; Rooney Lee was directed to ride directly east toward Dumfries; and Wade Hampton was ordered to ride toward the Occoquan. Henry's section rode with Rooney Lee's column, while Breathed's section accompanied Fitz Lee's men.[11]

Rosser's Virginia cavalry led Fitz Lee's force. They captured a long column of large wagons laden with sutlers' stores, as well as 20 Union guards. Stuart interrogated these prisoners and learned the Union force at Dumfries consisted of three regiments of infantry, some cavalry, and artillery. Armed with this intelligence, he moved out again. By the time they reached Dumfries, the veteran Confederate troopers knew that the prospects for a fight were high. Colonels Rosser and James H. Drake, commander of the 1st Virginia Cavalry, were ordered to cross their regiments above the town. Lieutenant Colonels James H. Watts and William R. Carter, with detachments from the 2nd and the 3rd Virginia

Cavalry regiments, moved across Quantico Creek below Dumfries where the Telegraph Road Bridge was located. Rosser and Drake were ordered to charge the enemy in an attempt to distract the attention of the Federal garrison, enabling Watts and Carter to dash across the fords in the hopes of capturing of the town.[12]

A close appraisal of the situation, however, convinced Fitz Lee that a daylight assault would glean little even if it were successful, but would likely incur substantial casualties. Stuart agreed, realizing that storming Dumfries was not worth the effort. Lee instead skirmished with the enemy until darkness fell. His dismounted sharpshooters kept the Union infantry occupied, enabling Stuart to swing around with the rest of his troopers to the Brentsville Road. Breathed's two rifled pieces provided effective long range support for Fitz's efforts. The 5th Virginia Cavalry captured eleven prisoners without loss during the extended skirmishing. Other than some fresh horseflesh, twenty wagons, and some miscellaneous supplies, the raid gained little of substance at the cost of one killed, thirteen wounded, and a similar number of missing. Stuart fell back nine miles west of Dumfries, where he bivouacked for the night.[13]

On December 28, Stuart sent the guns to the rear of the Confederate column in order to facilitate its crossing of the Rappahannock.[14]

*   *   *

The cold and wet weather had turned the roads into rivers of mud, and the horse artillerymen happily established themselves in winter camp. They faced the daunting task of making sure the horses had sufficient fodder to get them through a long and what would prove to be a particularly harsh winter. They also had to recruit new men to fill depleted ranks. Promotions were due, and the batteries needed to be repaired and equipment replaced. The men also needed shelter for the winter. There was plenty of work to be done. On January 3, 1863, Breathed and his men were camped near Guinea's Depot, Virginia. A few days later the horse artillery moved to the Chancellorsville area and at the end of February to Culpeper Court House, where Fitz Lee's Brigade was camped.[15]

Breathed drew the thankless task of supplying the horse artillery. He made numerous requisition trips during the winter encampment in order to keep the animals fed. Although Pelham wanted to create additional horse batteries, Breathed had to settle for one new gun. His battery added a six-pounder Whitworth rifle imported from Great Britain. The rifle was a breech loader, lightweight, highly accurate, and had an extraordinary effective range of six miles.

While they were encamped that January a considerable snowstorm hit, leaving Breathed's troopers in desperate need of better shelter. The men huddled around campfires for warmth, making "cush" from bacon and cornbread. The winter elements took their toll, knocking men out of the ranks with fever and other diseases. The horses also suffered. On January 28, Breathed wrote a special requisition for one four-horse forage wagon, four horses, four sets of harnesses, one saddle, one wagon sheet, and two halters. On it, in his own hand, he added, "[T]he distance for me to obtain forage is so great, that it is impossible for me to supply my Horse[s] with present means of transportation." The horses had to be regularly moved to assure they had enough to eat. By February 8, the horse artillery was back at Hamilton's Crossing. Securing sufficient forage to keep the animals in fighting trim was a critical and difficult chore, and as each day passed, Breathed grew more anxious for the condition of his horses. If their needs were not meet, he would be unable to move his artillery far or well when the time came for active operations.[16]

A new officer was about to join the battery. Lieutenant Francis Halsey Wigfall, son of Confederate Senator Louis T. Wigfall, was transferred to Breathed's Battery after serving in two other mounted batteries. He assumed command of one of Breathed's sections. "Major John Pelham . . . will make application, after the most approved style, that I be ordered to report to him for duty, whenever I am ready to come," declared young Wigfall. "Breathed's battery is ordered up to Culpeper C. H. to join the brigade (General Fitz Lee's) and will probably be there until active operations begin in the spring." If there was any doubt whether the politician's son would perform his duties well, it was erased quickly that spring. Wigfall would serve Breathed with distinction and bring honor to the battery.[17]

Breathed had come a long way during 1862. He had developed into an effective soldier and leader of men, and had quickly mastered the science of artillery, drawing favorable notice from General Lee himself. He and his men had shared common dangers and hardships, which had served to create strong emotional and physical bonds within the battery.

They rode through the same dust and mud, and rain and stifling heat, and slept on the same hard ground. Each learned that discipline played an important role in how well any unit functioned when it mattered. "Capt. Jim Breathed used to go with us occasionally, not deeming himself of too great importance to go with the boys of his greatly loved battery," recalled Henry Matthews. "In camp, Breathed was one of the boys, jolly and companionable . . . protecting and guarding their interest with the most jealous care." Breathed rarely ate at his own mess, preferring instead to visit with his men. He was often found eating with whatever group had the best food. "He would often come to our mess, for he knew we were good foragers, and always had something to eat if there was anything in the land," Matthews remembered. "He would come in and sit down and say, 'Boys, I think I will dine with you today.' This occurred very often. It is needless to say that we were all very glad to have him, for who in that grand old battery did not love Jim Breathed."[18]

In addition to discipline, leadership played a key factor in determining a unit's effectiveness in battle, and Matthews and his fellow gunners had no doubt that Breathed filled that role admirably. "[The men] agreed that the two most important criteria for a good officer were concern for the welfare of his men and leadership by example—that is, personal courage and a willingness to do anything he asked his men to do," observed historian James M. McPherson, who could have been describing Breathed when he wrote this. Breathed cared for his men, and would not ask them to do anything he would not be willing to do. He never patronized his soldiers and did not attempt to ingratiate himself with high ranking officers by pitching his tent next to Jeb Stuart's. Breathed's conduct helped inspire loyalty and trust, and his men knew that if they found themselves in a tight spot, Breathed would be there with them, and would guide them back out again. His coolness and reckless bravery inspired complete confidence in his leadership. He would need all these resources when the spring sun dried the Virginia countryside and the armies moved out again.[19]

Despite his closeness with his men, Breathed did not become overly-familiar with them. He was one of them, but he was also their commander and would have to send them into places from which many would not return. "Breathed in camp and Breathed on the field were entirely two different people. In action he was the officer all over, commanding the

respect and instantaneous obedience of every man in the command,"
observed Matthews. He continued:

> 'He never had to speak twice, woe to that man who showed the
> *white feather*. He had better pack up and depart, for he would have
> to.' Indeed, most soldiers were more afraid of demonstrating
> cowardice on the field in front of their friends and families than of
> death. The soldier who skulked from combat could never again hold
> up his head again as a man among men. The motto 'death before
> dishonor' was widely accepted during the Civil War, and Breathed
> inspired his men through his conduct on the battlefield. As one
> young soldier explained, 'it is better to die the de[a]th of a brave
> Soldier than to liv[e] a cowards life.'[20]

*   *   *

The winter months of 1862-1863 witnessed more campaigning than
was generally conducted in cold climates by 19th century armies.
Although Virginia was not known for winters as harsh as those in New
England or even Pennsylvania, the second winter of the war was
unusually cold, snowy, and blustery. The cold (and dry) early days of
January prompted Burnside, who felt tremendous pressure to redeem
himself after the debacle at Fredericksburg, to launch an ill-advised
winter campaign. Instead of assaulting Lee's fortified position across the
river near Fredericksburg, the Union commander decided to march his
army west, cross the Rappahannock at several fords that did not require
pontoon bridges, and then attempt to outflank Lee from that direction.

The plan was rather good, but its potential for success depended on
the cooperation of the weather. Burnside set the Army of the Potomac in
motion on January 20, pulling out of camp at Falmouth and heading
upriver toward the fords. Burnside, however, seemed cursed by wretched
luck. The Virginia skies opened and turned the ground into a morass of
deep sticky mud. Dismayed but unwilling to admit yet another setback,
Burnside tried to press on, his men and animals slogging their way as best
they could. Animals and artillery pieces soon bogged down and his army
lost large numbers of men from injuries, illness from the cold and wet
weather, and desertion. The miserable Union soldiers quickly dubbed the
campaign "The Mud March." Even Burnside had to admit its failure, and
the humiliated and utterly demoralized army returned to Falmouth.

Most of the rank and file (as well as the politicians in Washington) realized that Burnside would have to go—but who should replace him? A cabal of senior officers led by Maj. Gen. Joseph Hooker, the army's senior subordinate, was fed up with Burnside. Together, they schemed to have the affable Rhode Islander removed. When Burnside learned of the plot against him he asked to have Hooker and his associates removed instead. When Lincoln rebuffed Burnside's request, it became obvious he no longer had the president's (or the army's) support. His request that he be relieved of command was granted. Lincoln's primary field army was in shambles from top to bottom, its morale low and its officer corps bitter and politically divided. Lincoln needed a man of action who could lift the army's sagging spirits and guide it into combat against the Army of Northern Virginia. He chose Hooker for the task. It was a selection Lincoln would ultimately come to regret. For Breathed, however, the choice of Hooker set in motion a chain of events that would eventually allow him to emerge from Pelham's long shadow and become a well-known and respected horse artillery commander in his own right.[21]

Hooker, commonly known as "Fighting Joe" as a result of a typographical error in a newspaper headline, had some unpleasant personality traits that had prevented him from taking command of the Army of the Potomac when McClellan had been relieved in the fall of 1862. Simply put, Joe Hooker was a braggart, a political schemer and manipulator, and frequently insubordinate. He was also imbued with the willingness to blame others for mistakes more justly laid at his own doorstep. Hooker was also fond of alcohol and camp followers, and his headquarters was considered by many to be a den of iniquity.

Despite these flaws, Hooker also had several admirable military qualities which the Army of the Potomac desperately needed after Burnside's leadership debacle. He was a competent administrator, a solid strategist, and a decent combat officer. Hooker cared about the welfare of his men, and saw to it that they were well fed, paid, housed, and received good medical attention. In an effort to raise morale, Hooker borrowed an idea from the late Union general Phil Kearny and instituted a unique badge for each corps. This increased unit pride and made shirking one's wartime duties more difficult. Hooker also set up an efficient combat intelligence operation that provided him with remarkably accurate order-of-battle information, which made it easier to pinpoint Lee's units. He also did away with Grand Divisions.

Union cavalry commander General George Stoneman and his staff.

One of the new commander's most important contributions to the army was the organization of its scattered mounted units into a single corps, with Maj. Gen. George Stoneman, a career horse soldier, in command. The new corps consisted of some 9,000 well-equipped troopers and a brigade of horse artillery. Stoneman had experienced and competent subordinates: Pleasonton, Averell, David M. Gregg, and John Buford. The Federal cavalry spent the winter reorganizing, training, and preparing for its new mission. By March of 1863, it was ready to demonstrate that it could hold its own against Stuart's vaunted troopers.[22]

The war was about to take a new turn.

Chapter 6

Spring 1863:
Victories Small and Large

While Hooker rebuilt the Army of the Potomac, General Lee tended to his own problems in advance of a spring that promised vigorous campaigning. Organizations were brought up to strength, promotions were announced, and equipment repaired. The Confederate side of the Rappahannock River from Banks Ford to Port Royal had been fortified. Between the beginning of February and the Ides of March, two feet of snow had fallen, making life for everyone difficult—especially for the cavalry, which was busy patrolling the banks of the Rappahannock and Rapidan rivers.

Still, the snow did not prevent the cavalry from raiding enemy lines of communication. With much of February behind them, Lee and Stuart were still unsure of the disposition of Hooker's army. The Army of the Potomac's picket line ended at Hartwood Church, roughly halfway between Fredericksburg and Kelly's Ford. It was time to probe across the river and see what the Federals were up to. Stuart assigned the task to Fitz Lee.[1]

With 400 hand-picked troopers and a two-gun section of Breathed's Battery, Lee rode out early on February 24. The Confederates rode through bitter cold accompanied by a nearly impassable six inches of fresh, slippery snow. After crossing the frozen Rappahannock River at

Kelly's Ford, about twenty miles northwest of Fredericksburg, the column passed through Morristown and moved as quickly as circumstances allowed to Hartwood Church, where Lee's troopers surprised and captured about 150 Union cavalry from Brig. Gen. William Woods Averell's Division with a loss of only about fourteen of his own men. Within half an hour Fitz Lee was heading back to the river. His take included five commissioned officers, horses, side arms, and associated equipment.[2]

Yet another successful raid had been performed, adding not only to the laurels of the Southern cavalry but to Fitz Lee himself, who was rapidly proving his value as a capable leader. He also had some of Stuart's sense of humor. Lee, who had been close friends with Averell since their cadet days at West Point, left the New Yorker a taunting note and a bag of Virginia tobacco. The note told Averell to leave Virginia, but also instructed, "if you won't go home, return my visit and bring me a sack of coffee." The angry and embarrassed Averell procured the sack of coffee and grimly set about planning a visit to his old friend. Lee would not have to wait long for the coffee: Averell had received instructions to attack Stuart's troopers at and around Kelly's Ford.[3]

The small but bold and humiliating raid at Hartwood Church proved difficult for Hooker to ignore. His cavalry had responded slowly, Lee had escaped unmolested, and Hooker was angry. The new commander planned to use the Warrenton Post Road to maneuver his army around Lee's left flank once the roads dried sufficiently to do so. If future reconnaissances-in-force, like the one Fitz Lee had just completed, were not discouraged, the spring offensive would have no chance of catching Lee by surprise. Hooker also believed it was time for his new cavalry corps to redeem itself in light of its abject failure at Hartwood Church, not to mention the cavalry's disappointments of the previous year.[4]

With 3,000 veteran troopers and a battery of horse artillery, Averell set out on March 16 to make a name for himself and prove the Army of the Potomac's horse-arm was capable of standing face-to-face with its Southern counterpart. Inexplicably, he detached nearly one-third of his command and ordered it to stay behind and picket his flank, reducing his effective combat strength as his command approached Kelly's Ford.[5]

After a cold bivouac at Morrisville, Averell moved out early on the morning of March 17 for Kelly's Ford. Fitz Lee, whose brigade was picketing the ford, counted only about 800 troopers available for action.

Averell, however, had lost the element of surprise. The day before, Lee received a telegram alerting him of a large Union cavalry presence at Morrisville. He guessed, rightly as it turned out, that the Federal cavalry was headed for Kelly's Ford, and made his dispositions accordingly. After bolstering the picket forces at the ford, he alerted Breathed that the enemy was probably approaching in force.

Averell's surprise visit left Fitz Lee and his troopers with their hands full that St. Patrick's Day. "My first intimation of their approach was in a telegram received at 11 A.M. on 16th, from headquarters Army of Northern Virginia," reported Lee. "At 6 P.M. scouts reported them at Morrisville, a little place 6 miles from Kelly's Ford. At 1 A.M. another report informed me that the enemy had encamped at that place, coming from three different directions."[6]

That same day, Breathed and a section of his gunners visited a small home near Brandy Station known today as "the Graffiti House." In 1863 it was owned by a Mr. Barber, the CEO of the Orange and Alexandria Railroad. The artillerists added their names to a hand-drawn scroll on the walls, proving they were only a few miles from Kelly's Ford. Pelham's name does not appear on the scroll. Earlier that day, the Alabama artilleryman had left for Orange Court House to visit one of his many female friends. Later that night word reached Pelham that Union cavalry was moving toward Kelly's Ford. He returned the next morning by train to Culpeper, where he met up with Stuart who had come to testify at the court-martial of one of his regimental colonels. With some difficulty, Pelham borrowed a horse and rode off toward Kelly's Ford, accompanying Stuart, Capt. Harry Gilmore, and Fitz Lee and his brigade of Virginians.[7]

Lee and his men had barricaded the river crossing with felled trees to slow the passage of any force trying to use the route to reach the southern bank, and his men had also dug rifle pits. However, where Averell would strike was still anyone's guess. Some information seemed to indicate that a road that crossed the Orange & Alexandria Railroad and led to Kelly's Ford was also vulnerable. Leaving his command north of Culpeper to respond to any development, Lee ordered some sixty troopers to picket the ford. Averell's crossing point was indeed the ford, and the impediments there proved wholly ineffective. The Union commander brushed them aside and forced the crossing before 7:30 A.M., capturing a number of pickets. "The report that enemy's attack was made at Kelly's

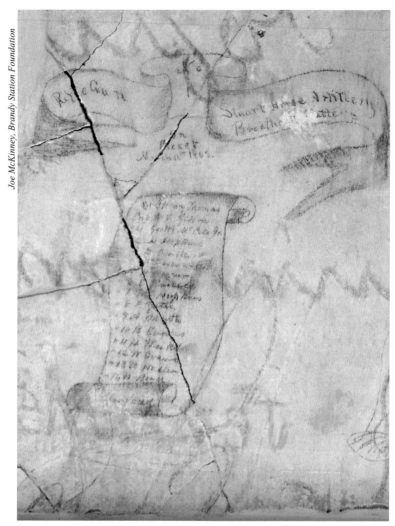

The Graffiti House "scroll" dated March 16, 1863, includes
16 names from the artillerists of Breathed's Battery.

never reached me; and the first intimation I received from that point was
at 7.30 A.M., to the effect that they had succeeded in crossing, capturing
25 of my sharpshooters, who were unable to reach their horses," reported
Fitz Lee. "I moved my command at once down the railroad, taking up a
position to await their approach, ordering my baggage wagons and
disabled horses to the rear, toward Rapidan Station. Some time elapsing,
and they not advancing, I determined to move upon them, and marched

Fitzhugh Lee's Confederate troopers in a charge at Kelly's Ford.

immediately for Kelly's." Celerity was required, for Averell was now on the wrong side of the river, and the railroad was open to destruction.[8]

Once word arrived that Averell had forced his way across the river at Kelly's Ford, Breathed's Battery received orders to follow Fitz Lee's column toward the crossing. "I do not think we ever traveled at a more rapid gait than on that occasion," recalled one of Breathed's gunners. "The distance from our camp to where we met the brigade at the Wheatley House is about 3½ miles. We made the distance in about 30 minutes, not more." The weather had warmed considerably, and the melted snow turned everything into a slippery morass. "Traveling at our pace," remembered Matthews, "[was] very dangerous."[9]

Unable to ascertain immediately the whereabouts of the enemy, Fitz Lee determined to move out and find them. With Stuart and Pelham at hand, Fitz Lee's men approached the ford from the northwest and ran into the Union troopers about one-half mile from the river. Averell's men held a strong and easily defended position sheltered by woods and a long stone fence that blocked the line of Lee's advance. Lee proposed an attack and Stuart agreed. Pelham, meanwhile, rode for the rear in search of Breathed and his guns. Unable to negotiate the fence and a ditch, the Confederate troopers wheeled to the left, taking point blank fire from the Federal troopers. The Virginians reformed under a steady oblique fire from both Union artillery and small arms. While Lee's charges rattled the Federals, they failed to dislodge them from their strong position along the stone wall. Unable to find a way through the fence, the cavalry was forced to give ground, falling back nearly one mile in the face of a surprisingly vigorous Union pursuit. There, Lee's men reformed and launched new attacks against the Federal cavalry. The enemy guns were also pushed forward and took position in front of a plot of swampy ground to the left of the northern-most road running away from the ford.[10]

The fighting was well underway by the time Breathed's lathered horses arrived on the battlefield. As the Southern cavalry was clattering about the stone fence in search of a gate to pass through, Breathed unlimbered his pieces on a patch of higher ground northwest of the ford in a clearing west of the Dean House. The guns immediately engaged Federal horse artillery in a counter-battery duel at a range of about 3,000 yards. "We had a battle royal holding our own," admitted Henry Matthews. From the perspective of time and subjectivity, Matthews believed it was Breathed's guns that "at last forc[ed] them from the field, driving the cannoneers from their guns, and if a regiment of cavalry had been available [it] would have captured the battery." It was not the gunfire that forced the retreat (though it helped), but Averell's own skittishness.[11]

Breathed's pieces pounded the enemy artillery while simultaneously wreaking havoc with the enemy cavalry. One round was particularly noteworthy. A shell from one of Breathed's guns struck Pvt. Johan George Segerer, Company G, 5th United States Cavalry in the shoulder before exploding, tearing the unfortunate man completely apart.[12]

Although Averell's force was significantly larger than the Confederates, Lee's bold tactics unnerved the Union commander. Without any reserves, Lee reformed his troopers for a final charge. The attack failed to drive Averell from the field, but it discouraged the New Yorker, who was not inclined toward aggressive behavior to begin with. There were no further Union attacks from Kelly's Ford that day.

Operating under the belief that Lee either was or would be soon receiving reinforcements, and with the pale winter sun dropping rapidly toward the horizon, Averell broke off the engagement and withdrew across Kelly's Ford. Lee, who had also received about as much battle as he could handle, let his old friend retire unmolested. In his wake Averell left a note and a sack of coffee. "Dear Fitz," he wrote. "Here's your coffee. Here's your visit. How did you like it?"[13]

That St. Patrick's Day engagement was memorable not for the sack of coffee and visit, but the loss of Maj. John Pelham, who fell early in the action mortally wounded before the stone wall. The officer had rashly joined in a cavalry charge against the dismounted Union troopers behind the wall. Pelham's final conversation may well have been with Breathed, whom he ordered to continue firing as he rode off to join in the attack. Exactly what happened when and how is in substantial dispute. What is certain is that a shell burst above him and a piece of shrapnel struck him in the back of the skull. Senseless, Pelham fell from his horse and was carried away in the nick of time; the fighting continued without him. He was taken to the Shackelford House in Culpeper, where he lingered until early the next morning before dying. He never spoke or regained consciousness. Stuart and many others wept over their fallen friend. Although Pelham had rashly participated in a cavalry charge, he was merely demonstrating yet again the valor and spirit he carried into every combat. This time, his amazing string of luck ran out, and it cost him his life. Pelham had left the battlefield to enter the realm of legend.

According to Lee, Averell left "a number of his dead and wounded on the field" and Lee captured 29 others in exchange for 11 killed, 88 wounded, and 34 captured. It was an expensive price to pay for the loss of the outstanding commander of the Stuart Horse Artillery. Everyone would have to elevate his performance to make up for the terrible loss.[14]

The day after the combat, Fitz Lee composed a general order congratulating his men on their winning effort. Breathed and his gunners earned their share of the plaudits. "Capt. Breathed and his brave artillerists have my sincere thanks," declared Lee. "They behaved, as they always do, with great gallantry." Breathed's losses, if any, were negligible. In his formal report dated March 23, 1863, Lee used the adjective "gallant" to describe Breathed. It was an apt description.[15]

When the battle ended, Breathed's fatigued gunners rode back to camp. As one would expect, a deep melancholy hung over them. Word of Pelham's mortal injury had passed quickly through the ranks. Breathed's response to Pelham's fall went unrecorded, but it is not difficult to guess how he must have reacted given his close relationship with him. They had

The Museum of the Confederacy

Major Robert F. Beckham.

served together from the formation of the Stuart Horse Artillery until Kelly's Ford. They had been good friends and comrades, and Breathed as much as anyone would have lamented his commander's death. That night, Breathed and Daniel Shanks visited the Shackelford House where the stricken gunner had been taken after his rescue from the field. The soldiers paid their last respects to their dead commander. The Pelham era was over.

The death of Pelham hit Stuart hard, and also forced him to make a difficult decision. He had to choose Pelham's successor as commander of the horse artillery battalion. Breathed was one of several candidates. Until Pelham received the assignment, Breathed had been Stuart's personal choice for command of the Stuart Horse Artillery. Breathed enjoyed a solid reputation with the men of the battalion, and had demonstrated outstanding leadership skills. However, his commission only dated to August 1862, meaning that he was one of the more junior battery commanders. Major Thomas H. Carter, a Virginia Military Institute graduate, was offered the position, but declined. Stuart next offered the command to Maj. Robert Franklin Beckham, a Culpeper native and one of Pelham's friends from West Point. It was a good choice. Beckham graduated from West Point in 1859, a respectable 6th out of 22. He had experience with artillery during the war's early months and as a gunnery drill master for the Jeff Davis Artillery, an Alabama outfit. After transferring to a staff assignment with Gen. Gustavus Smith in January of 1862, Beckham was elected captain of the same Alabama company two months later but declined, serving as an ordnance officer through 1863. Stuart needed the officer's expertise, and Beckham accepted the position on April 8, 1863. Filling Pelham's shoes would not be easy, and Beckham was fully aware of the awesome responsibility resting on his shoulders. How he would perform was anyone's guess. Beckham would soon have an opportunity to vindicate the wisdom or folly of Stuart's choice.[16]

* * *

The spring campaign season was about to begin. The roads were rapidly drying, the skies clearing, and the weather warming. The Army of the Potomac's cavalry corps numbered nearly 13,000 well-armed troopers on fresh horses, supported by ten batteries of horse artillery. Against them Stuart could field but three brigades of veteran cavalry under Fitz Lee, Rooney Lee, and Wade Hampton, supported by Beckham's three batteries of horse artillery under Breathed, William M. McGregor, and Marcellus N. Moorman. Time would tell whether the aggressive behavior demonstrated by the Union cavalry at Kelly's Ford was an anomaly, or whether the traditional dominance of Stuart's horse soldiers would reassert itself.

On April 12, Breathed's Battery was camped near Orange Court House. Although its members did not know it, Hooker was about three weeks away from launching his spring campaign. The move was essentially a modified version of Burnside's failed "Mud March." The Army of the Potomac, its ranks swelled to more than 130,000 men, would advance on two fronts. Major General John Sedgwick's VI Corps would remain opposite Fredericksburg with about one-third of the army and threaten it with capture while another third under Hooker crossed the Rappahannock at Banks' and United States' fords. Once across, Hooker planned to move quickly and turn Lee's flank in the vicinity of Chancellorsville. Lee could either fight there at a surprised disadvantage with a major Union force in his rear at Fredericksburg, or retreat as Hooker suspected he would. The remaining one-third of the army would act as a giant reserve, remaining north of the river ready to reinforce either wing. The army's cavalry was not going to sit idle during this operation. Hooker ordered Stoneman to take the entire cavalry corps, save a single brigade, on a grand raid deep into the Confederate rear in order to cut Lee's lines of communications and help prompt his withdrawal.

Hooker's operational plan looked promising—especially since two veteran divisions from Longstreet's Corps had been detached from the Southern army weeks earlier to forage in a large region around Suffolk, Virginia. Longstreet was besieging the Federal garrison at Suffolk while

Brigadier General David McM. Gregg.

LC

collecting tons of supplies that eventually helped make the June raid across the Potomac into Pennsylvania possible. The result was that Lee had only some 60,000 men available to confront Hooker—a striking 2-1 disadvantage. The Army of the Potomac moved out from its Falmouth camps on April 27, marching west toward the upper fords. They crossed the river the next day.

Unbeknownst to Breathed's artillerists, Stoneman received his orders to move as early as April 12. The cavalryman prepared his command for the rigorous assignment and left Morrisville, near Kelly's Ford, the following day. Heavy rains, however, quickly turned the country roads into ribbons of mud; Stoneman's troopers would not be going anywhere anytime soon.[17]

Once the rains stopped and the Rappahannock dropped to fordable levels, both infantry and cavalry moved out to execute Hooker's grand plan. Any element of surprise Stoneman might have enjoyed seemed lost, but instead of doing the prudent thing and canceling the raid, Hooker ordered him to move out. The Federal horse soldiers crossed the river with the main body of infantry and divided into two columns. The first, under Averell's command, moved west toward Gordonsville and the Orange & Alexandria Railroad to act as a diversion for the second column. This force was the main body under Brig. Gen. John Buford's command. Buford's task (Stoneman rode with him) was to ride behind Lee's army and cut the Richmond, Fredericksburg, & Potomac line. Unfortunately for Hooker, Stoneman's column accomplished little except for riding away from where they were most needed. Their self-imposed exile ended on May 8 near Yorktown on the Virginia peninsula.[18]

Averell's command, about 3,400 strong, immediately ran into Rooney Lee's troopers, who were supported by Stuart's Horse Artillery. Lee fell back in front of the enemy cavalry, skirmishing every yard of the distance until he finally formed a strong line of battle near the Rapidan River. From captured soldiers Averell learned that strong reinforcements were on the way, including infantry. The news prompted the always cautious Averell to become even more so. Although he could have smashed Lee, the Federal commander picked and prodded along the line until finally withdrawing. His losses were minimal: one killed and four wounded. Lee burned the bridge on the river and withdrew to safety. The hapless commander was later relieved of his duties by Hooker, who replaced him with Pleasonton.[19]

Breathed's role in the developing campaign began on April 28, when he alerted his men with the news that the enemy was on the move and trying to cross the Rappahannock. "We left camp Tuesday night the 28th at about eleven o'cl'k orders coming just after I had gone to bed," recalled Lieutenant Wigfall, one of Breathed's section commanders. "I was just falling asleep when Captain Breathed roused me to have my section hitched." With the Union cavalry on the move, and Rooney Lee moving to oppose them, Breathed rode with Fitz Lee beyond Brandy Station, where they bivouacked and remained in reserve to await developments. Wigfall remembered finding Breathed the next day shelling the woods in their front. "Capt. B had passed me on the way down. They had been firing on the rear of a column of infantry and on a wagon train," continued Wigfall, "I came up on the right with my two howitzers and opened fire also." As darkness fell, the battery limbered up and, with Hooker's men moving around the army's left, splashed south across the Rapidan River at Raccoon Ford. The men bivouacked for the night about two miles from the crossing.[20]

Stuart and his cavalry had to reach Lee's army, which meant riding south before turning east and then north—dangerously close to Hooker's marching infantry. The cavalry commander left some men behind to press and harass the Federals while he moved out with his main body, Fitz Lee's Brigade in the van. On the Germanna Plank Road near its intersection with the Orange Turnpike they encountered enemy infantry and a screen of protective cavalry. A regiment of Virginia cavalry engaged the 6th New York Cavalry for the right to possess a bridge over Wilderness Run, but was driven back when Union infantry arrived on the scene. Stuart quickly engaged the head of the infantry column with dismounted troopers and ordered Breathed to unlimber his guns and slow down the Federal advance. The engagement was brisk for a short time, and although the outcome was never in doubt and casualties minimal for both sides, Stuart managed to take prisoners from three separate Union corps. Here, finally, was more solid proof of Hooker's deep turning movement. Stuart made certain that this important information was communicated to the commanding general.[21]

Stuart had orders to report to General Lee's headquarters near Fredericksburg, and night found him well short of that place at Todd's

Tavern. Leaving his main command behind, Stuart left with his staff to join up with Lee. When the small party ran into some enemy cavalry probing the dark roads, Stuart withdrew and called up Rosser's 5th Virginia Cavalry, which quickly cleared a passage for Stuart to continue. Although the night was clear and the moon bright, the roads were narrow and confusing to navigate, and the woods dark. Before Rosser could withdraw, another Union cavalry group rode into his rear near the Alsop Farm. The riders belonged to Lt. Col. Duncan McVicar's 6th New York Cavalry, which Stuart had fought briefly earlier that same day. The Union commander was not pleased about his assignment to ride about in the dark unsupported in search of the enemy, and for good reason.

Without hesitation, Stuart recalled Rosser's regiment and ordered up Fitz Lee's entire brigade. The fight that developed was a confused affair that included pistol, sword, and carbine. "By the bright moonlight a series of charges routed and scattered this expedition," reported Stuart, "which had penetrated within a mile or two of Spotsylvania Court-House." The cavalry, remembered Lieutenant Wigfall of Breathed's Battery, had a "running fight with the Yankee cavalry on in front along the same road we were marching on. There we were marching along in the dark and our men drawing the Yankee cavalry out of the way to make room for us. We could hear them shouting and firing as they charged. Maj. Beckham has now three batteries with him—Moorman's, McGregor's, and our own." The wild affair left Lt. Col. McVicar dead, the victim of a bullet through the heart, and many of his men wounded and captured. The New Yorkers were lucky to escape without suffering additional losses. Fortunately for the Southerners, the way to Spotsylvania and Lee's army was now open.[22]

General Lee was unsure exactly what Hooker was up to, but by the first day of May he was convinced of the serious threat to his left flank and that the enemy hovering about in front of Fredericksburg was nothing but a demonstration. In a breathtaking display of boldness, Lee decided to split his army in the face of a superior enemy. Leaving behind Maj. Gen. Jubal Early and his division at Fredericksburg to watch Sedgwick, Lee moved the balance of his army west to meet Hooker's advance while the Army of the Potomac was still marching through the tangled thickets of the Wilderness. The brilliant, if risky, strategy, was launched on the premise that fighting Hooker in the woods would make it difficult for him to bring his superior numbers of both infantry and artillery to bare. To the surprise of men on both sides and to Lee's delight, Hooker fell back once the skirmishing began and settled down inside the Wilderness, turning the campaign's initiative over to Lee. Hooker fell back to such a strong position that it is difficult to believe his strategy had not been to get Lee on the move and invite an attack. Perhaps Lee's army would impale themselves on Hooker's well entrenched lines just as the Union forces had done at Fredericksburg. If that were Hooker's strategy, he should have paid more attention to how Lee had protected his flanks in that battle. Of course, Lee had cavalry at Fredericksburg, whereas Hooker had sent away virtually all of his on a raid the results of which would not meet expectations.

As Lee's infantry began arriving and skirmishing with the advance of Hooker's column, Stuart learned that artillery was needed to support the Southern infantry. Beckham had ordered Lieutenant Wigfall to leave one of his pieces at Spotsylvania Court House, and to join the rest of the battery at the front. Upon reaching Welford's Furnace on the Brock Road, one of Stuart's staff officers, Lt. Frank Robertson, galloped up with orders to hurry on, that the enemy was in full retreat. After marching about three miles, Wigfall's little column was turned back. "I gave the command Trot March and away we went. The young ladies were standing at the gate at Mr. Welford's and cheered us as we went by. I halted at the Furnace and remained there some time," remembered Wigfall.[23]

About 6:00 P.M., Stuart ordered Beckham to mass his guns and move forward from the Welford place to Catherine Furnace and beyond to support Brig. Gen. Ambrose Wright's Brigade of infantry. Beckham had six pieces available but moved forward with only four, one of which belonged to Breathed and was under the command of Lieutenant Wigfall.

Beckham advanced "with the view of driving back a line of the enemy's infantry from the heights, about 1,200 yards in our front, that General Wright might occupy the ground." The leader of the horse artillery was confident that just four guns would be sufficient because he did not believe the enemy had any artillery. He was wrong.[24]

Wigfall left an outstanding account of the action that followed, and remembered that he was personally called to the field by one of Wright's staff officers, who urged him to run his piece to the front as quickly as possible. The staffer told Wigfall "he had a most superb position for it." Getting there was not as easy as Wigfall would have liked. "I came along as fast as I could which was not very fast as the horses from hard marching and scarcely anything to eat were nearly broken down," he observed. "I found this magnificent position for Artillery in the woods on the side of a hill greatly sloping towards the enemy, and with one road leading to it and only wide enough for one carriage to pass and bordered on each side by a perfect chaparral through which it was difficult to force one's way on horseback."[25]

Wigfall unlimbered his gun and opened on the woods to his front with spherical case. "The very first shot burst beautifully but before I had fired more than two or three times the Yankee Artillery opened and Major Beckham ordered me to turn my attention to them. Just after I began firing, McGregor's battery came down and into position."[26]

Although his guns scattered the front line of enemy infantry, Beckham's gunfire immediately drew "a storm of shot and shell from eight or ten pieces of artillery," hidden by the rolling terrain. As Wigfall recalled, Beckham quickly turned his pieces against these batteries and a heavy exchange followed. "The 4 guns of the two batteries were soon hotly engaged in a fierce and bloody contest with the enemy's batteries. This unequal contest was very destructive to us, but we still held out," Matthews later wrote.[27]

In the excitement of battle, one of Wigfall's inexperienced men accidentally bent the priming wire before the powder charge was fully rammed in, disabling the piece by spiking it. "I had it pulled and hauled at until I found that it was impossible to pull it out and I then reported the fact to Major Beckham who ordered me to withdraw the piece," recounted an obviously disappointed Wigfall.[28]

None of the Confederates had any way of learning with certainty how effective their fire was that day, but Beckham believed the metal was launched with "some effect" because the enemy fire eventually "diminished" enough to convince him that some of the pieces had been forced to retire or were knocked out of action. The firing continued for about forty-five minutes until Beckham received instructions from Wright to withdraw. "I do not think that men have been often under a hotter fire than that to which we were here exposed," Beckham reported. The fact that Wigfall lost only one gun and two horses but not his life was rather amazing. While acting as a gunner, he "was shot through the neck. My overcoat which was on my saddle had the sleeve torn and two holes through the cape all I expect by the same shot. McGregor's Blakely rifle which was on my right had one or two men struck by fragments of shell, his light 12 pdr on my left had several men shot, one of them very seriously and the howitzer in the section left of the line had two men killed and several others struck—these were all that were engaged." Once he finally reached camp that night, Wigfall tried again to remove the bent priming wire. He finally succeeded the next morning by withdrawing the powder charge and straightening the primer with the gun's rammer. His diligence made it possible to use the gun that same day. The four pieces and their crews suffered heavily in the exchange, losing (according to Beckham) three killed and five wounded, damaged guns, and dead and wounded horses. According to Wigfall's account, the losses were much more severe than Beckham reported.[29]

When this engagement erupted, Jim Breathed took two rifled pieces and moved left a mile or so with Fitz Lee's troopers, where they "opened fire on the enemy on Talley's farm, about 1 ½ miles above the furnace," reported Beckham. "The enemy was within short range and in heavy force, but without artillery." Beckham's report confirms much of what Henry Matthews recalled of the engagement years later. "We advanced upon their column of infantry and artillery through a dense wood, advancing the guns by hand with great difficulty over stumps and roots of trees, at times being close enough to the enemy you almost see the color of their eyes," he wrote. "We used nothing but canister and shells would be of no service at such short range."[30]

The performance impressed the new commander of the Stuart Horse Artillery: "Breathed beyond doubt succeeded in doing them a great deal of damage. Citizens living near the point the next day represented their loss at more than 100 killed and wounded. No one hurt on our side."[31]

*   *   *

On the night of May 1, acting on Stuart's intelligence of the location and composition of Hooker's right column moving through the Wilderness, Lee and Jackson decided to implement one of the most audacious moves of the war. It was Fitz Lee who discovered that the Union right flank was "in the air," unanchored and unprotected. The entire right side of Hooker's army was susceptible to a flank attack. Lee decided to again divide his own smaller command (which was already in two pieces—Early was back at Fredericksburg watching Sedgwick), by sending Jackson and his corps, about 26,000 men, on a winding 17-mile flank march to crush and roll up the enemy's right flank. Lee would keep only the divisions of McLaws and Anderson to face all of Hooker's army at Chancellorsville. Their task would be to keep up a bold front in the face of heavily superior numbers.

The 1st, 2nd, and 3rd Virginia cavalry regiments spent May 2 screening the movement of Jackson's Corps, which had moved out early that morning. The march was carried off remarkably well given the fact that elements from the Union Third Corps spotted the flank movement early near Catherine Furnace and even opened fire on it. The information that the enemy was marching south on the Welford Furnace Road toward Todd's Tavern persuaded Hooker that a retreat was underway. The magnitude of his mistake would become apparent soon enough. With Fitz's Lee's cavalry scouting the route and flanks for Jackson, the Stuart Horse Artillery waited near the Orange Turnpike for the infantry to arrive. Jackson successfully completed the march late that afternoon and moved into position straddling the turnpike. About one-half mile distant was the exposed right flank of Maj. Gen. Oliver Howard's XI Corps.

Just before the attack went forward, Capt. John Esten Cooke, one of Stuart's staff officers, spotted Breathed standing under a tree chatting with Stuart. Cooke rode up and "shook hands with Breathed, whom he knew intimately." "Well, General," Cooke heard Breathed say in a low tone as he mounted his horse. "I understand I am to keep only a few yards behind the line of sharpshooters as they advance; but, if I see an opening, I'm going ahead." As Breathed rode away, Stuart responded, "Good. I know you'll do what you say, Breathed. Get everything ready."[32]

At 5:30 P.M., everything was in position and Jackson gave the order for his divisions to advance. Breathed and the first section of Johnston's Battery moved along the turnpike in the center of Jackson's front. Daniel Shanks and the second section moved immediately behind Breathed, with Moorman's behind that. Stonewall's flank attack was something no one who participated in it and lived ever forgot. Years later, Henry Matthews, who was riding with Breathed that early evening, recalled how he and his mates awaited the command of Stonewall Jackson to go forward, "[We] knew that immediately in our front, not far distant, was a Federal battery planted in the road ready to fire upon the approach of the rebs. The sight was not a pleasant one, to walk into the very jaws of a masked Battery. We did not object to standing in the open and

LC

Horse Artillery preparing to deploy under fire.

exchanging shots with any one Federal battery, but we certainly did object to walking into the jaws of death without being able to see the instruments of destruction."[33]

Jackson's infantry emerged from the thick woods driving turkeys, rabbits, and deer ahead of them. Without warning they slammed into the unsuspecting Howard's flank. Although pockets of the Union infantry stood tall and fought against overwhelming odds, the bulk of Howard's men broke and ran in utter panic. "In a few minutes we saw the rout—a confused mass of men, horses, wagons and guns streaming down the turnpike at top speed in a real panic," recalled a Southern artillerist.[34]

Stuart had ordered Beckham to make sure Breathed and his other commanders moved their guns down the Orange Turnpike just in the rear of the infantry skirmishers, "This we did not entirely succeed in doing," admitted Beckham, "owing to the narrow space in which the pieces had to be maneuvered and the obstructions encountered at various points along the road." As Beckham proudly pointed out in his after-action report, however, the guns "were able to keep up almost a continual fire upon the enemy from one or two guns from the very starting point up to the position where our lines halted for the night."[35]

Before the battle opened, Breathed advanced as far as he dared and unlimbered two pieces in the narrow road. The turnpike at this point was only wide enough for two guns, so no more could be squeezed in. Once the guns were deployed, Breathed crept forward to a spot just behind Jackson's skirmishers. He also had two more guns to his rear which he planned to leapfrog forward as they moved toward the Union army. Other pieces, including Moorman's Battery, were waiting behind him, ready and able to spring into action at a moment's notice. As the infantry tramped forward and the skirmishers opened fire, the opening blast of Breathed's pieces were the first notice many Union soldiers had that they were being attacked. Some mistakenly believed the artillery shots were some sort of signal that had nothing to do with a grand offensive assault.

Lieutenant Colonel Thomas H. Carter, with artillery assigned to Brig. Gen. Robert E. Rodes' Division, deployed his twenty pieces in an open field close to Maj. Gen. A. P. Hill's advancing battle line, where he enjoyed the opportunity to watch an exchange between Breathed and Rodes. When Breathed reported the status of the fight to the general, he asked the young artillerist, "Captain will those boys stand? Stand!" snarled Breathed, whose battle blood was now up. "———— ————, sir, when those boys leave their guns you will not have a man left in your division, and I am going to take them in with your skirmish line and show you d——n Tar Heels how to fight!"[36]

"From a high hill [the Barton House] on the right of the Plank road I had a splendid opportunity of witnessing the magnificent charge that soon followed," recalled one of Breathed's men, who watched "with pride our gallant Breathed with his two guns charging far in advance of the line of battle and pouring his destructive fire into the now startled enemy." Henry Matthews had a good view of the early stages of the attack. "Breathed, the fearless, during the advance was our guiding star, always near the guns, for the roar of the guns was music to him. We expected at every moment to see him fall amid the terrible fire that was hurled against us, but the God of Battles protected him, that thru the medium of the old 'Hornets' the world might give him praise and sing of his valor in verse and prose," he recalled.[37]

Major George Freaner, a cavalry staff officer and a close friend of Breathed's from Hagerstown, also had an excellent vantage point to watch the havoc wrought by Breathed's accurate advancing gunfire. "In the dense wilderness which fringed both sides of the road, the skirmishers could only proceed the forward line of battle a few rods and with the firing of their first shots almost, the whole line became engaged," wrote Freaner, whose continued description left little doubt of the effects of close-quarters artillery:

> The roar of musketry was fearful, the smoke soon became dense, but above it all, would be faintly heard and seen the rapid reports and flashing light of Breathed's guns. The attack was fearfully terrific, the rout sudden and complete. Down the road went Breathed at a tall gallop, men, horses and guns rushing pell mell over the first barricade—and closing up on the backs of the fugitives, he gave the command to unlimber and into them with double shots of canister. There was havoc then—bones were not broken, they were severed; flesh was not pierced, it was shredded; blood did not trickle, it left the victim in torrents.[38]

In spite of difficult terrain, the gunners pressed on. "Nothing stopped us. We moved on regardless of obstacles of all kinds that had been placed in the road," wrote Matthews, who always seemed to be in the thickest fighting. "The enemy were thrown into the wildest confusion by the first fire from [Rodes'] men. Breathed, with whip in hand, would help the drivers of the pieces to force the jaded horses across the trees and other obstructions that had been placed in our way, the cannoneers at the wheels, and everybody yelling in union. It was a sight long to be remembered and goes to show that nothing could keep the daring, reckless Breathed back. When he had determined to go forward obstacles of any kind could not do it." If his after-action report is any indication, Beckham agreed, noting how the guns moved forward frequently "under a perfect hail-storm of canister, but the men moved on steadily, apparently unconscious of any danger."[39]

Lieutenant Wigfall, who was also in the midst of the maelstrom, moved his piece up and unlimbered it, dismounted, and helped roll the piece by hand "to about six hundred yards of where the Yankees had two pieces on the Turnpike." With his howitzer behind the shallow brow of a hill, Wigfall walked forward to determine how far away the enemy guns were "in order to have the fuses cut correctly. We then opened and after firing two or three shots the Yankees replied." As the Federal infantry retreated, Wigfall and his gunners continued blasting away, advancing every time the Union line retreated. "We advanced in this way about a mile. We would fire a few shots, limber up move in a few hundred yards, unlimber, fire, and move in again," Wigfall later wrote. It was indeed, exhilarating work, he noted,

> but I was on foot and when my howitzer was halted and I was ordered by Captain Breathed to put horses to a rifle which the Yankees had been driven from and bring it on, I was pretty nearly exhausted. I put four horses to it and grounded a horse which one of the cannoneers was leading and moved on to where Captain Breathed was putting horses to one of his pieces and there got two more Yankee horses and dashed on as hard as I could go to where Colonel [Stapleton] Crutchfield [Jackson's chief of artillery] was putting two of the pieces at one of General Jackson's batteries in position to fire on the Yankees who had established a very heavy battery about eleven hundred yards in our front.[40]

Breathed deployed two of Johnston's guns on the road between Crutchfield's pieces, while Wigfall dropped trail a few feet to the right of the road under the cover of the woods. Wigfall, unfortunately, had run out of short-range fuses. Crutchfield told him not to worry about it and to use whatever he had on hand, since the enemy position was deep and long shots would strike Federals in the rear. "I then found that the Yankees had left no lanyard in the limber-chest and I was unable to get any from any of the other pieces, so Captain Breathed ordered me to move the piece to the right out of the range of fire," explained the lieutenant. "I moved it about sixty yards to the right of the road and came back to where Captain Breathed was."[41]

The carnage wrought by the devastating attack surprised even veterans like Henry Matthews:

> No one can imagine the complete rout and confusion of Hooker's troops. They seemed to have lost control over themselves, throwing away everything that they thought would lighten their load. Pile after pile of knapsacks were thrown along the road, blankets by the thousands were strewn in the wake of the fleeing Federals' guns of all kinds were scattered in every direction as if they were the cause of all their troubles. I saw two batteries of Federal artillery that had been abandoned in the panic—not a single man near the pieces. The horses had stampeded, running between the trees, and the guns were held fast as in a vise. Kitchen fires were in full blast, pots of cooking meat were suspended from rude camp cranes.[42]

The Confederate artillery continued firing even after the sun faded behind the horizon and blanketed the smoky wooded landscape in darkness. When it finally died away, counter-battery fire from Yankee gunners rained fitfully down on the Confederates until it, too, petered into silence. Barely able to stand because of exhaustion, Breathed ordered the battery to limber up and withdraw in search of a place for the men to bivouac for the night.[43]

Moorman's pieces had not fired a shot that memorable day, but Major Beckham's other gunners had more than made up for his absence. Breathed had performed admirably under very difficult circumstances, and Stuart did not fail to take notice of it. The cavalry chief's after-action report nearly gushed with praise for the young doctor-gunner he had helped recruit: "Breathed's services would have knighted him in any army where patents of nobility could be carried away from the cannon's mouth or from the point of the sabre." Beckham's report was also full of praise for the manner in which Breathed and his men worked their pieces. Breathed, he noted, "was ever ahead, choosing the best ground for his guns." Wigfall, observed Beckham, also deserved praise for his activity and skill in the way he handled his guns. The Stuart Horse Artillery losses "were 2 men killed—1 belonging to Breathed's, the other to McGregor's, battery—both as good soldiers as could be found in the Confederacy," lamented Beckham. "We had 5 horses disabled. Officers and men did their duty well."[44]

Even Stonewall Jackson noticed the valiant performance of Stuart's Horse Artillery. Old Jack was riding his horse when he spotted Major Beckham. He turned in the saddle and said, "Young man, I congratulate you and the brave men under you!"[45]

The attack against Hooker's right rolled up Howard's flank, folding back unit after unit upon one another until there was little any Union commander could do but fall back in search of a position to form a line of defense. By the time darkness brought the fighting to a close, Jackson had advanced nearly three miles and the XI Corps was finished as an effective force for the rest of the battle.

Unfortunately for the Confederates, the stunning triumph was also the last act of Jackson's equally stunning military career. That night, Jackson rode with his staff to reconnoiter the right side of the new Federal line west of the Chancellorsville crossroads. North Carolina infantrymen mistook the party for Union cavalry and opened fire, mortally wounding

Jackson, killing another, and injuring several more. The general lingered for one week before dying on May 10. A. P. Hill was injured shortly thereafter, and Jeb Stuart was given temporary command of Jackson's Corps.

Pushed into a tight knot around Chancellorsville, Hooker had a strong army enveloped by a much weaker one on May 3. A more ambitious or bold general might have gathered his muscle and launched his own attack, but Hooker was not that man. Stunned by a Southern shell, he spent much of the day recovering his senses while his army tried to repel attacks while falling back to anchor its flanks on the Rapidan River. The horse artillery did not take any active role in the fighting that day. The guns were placed in position to the left of the Plank Road, guarding against any attempts by the Union army to turn the Confederate flank from the direction of the Ely's Ford, where Averell's Cavalry Division had arrived on the night of May 2. "We remained here until ordered to join General Fitz Lee, and moved with his brigade toward Ely's Ford, near which place we stayed until we took up the march for Orange Court-House," reported Beckham.[46]

Although Breathed and his comrades could not know it, their active role in the campaign was over. While the cavalry remained active, Stuart's batteries were not offered another opportunity to engage the enemy. Hooker spent May 3-4 pondering how the tables had turned so quickly on him. If he was hoping for relief from John Sedgwick at Fredericksburg, he was disappointed. Although he was able to punch through Early's thin lines on Marye's Heights, Sedgwick was quickly outmatched when Lee deftly turned in his direction and came as close as possible to surrounding him without completely doing so. After a sharp fight at Salem Church on May 4, the Federal XI Corps slipped away across the Rappahannock River. That day and night Hooker did the same, retreating across the Rapidan fords even though entire divisions in his army had not fired a single round. The bloody Chancellorsville Campaign was over. The losses were staggering for both sides, with Hooker suffering more than 17,000 from all causes, and Lee some 13,000.

*   *   *

LC

The John Minor Botts home, where Stuart ordered a
review of his entire division.

Stuart's troopers, meanwhile, continued performing the important
duty of securing the fords of the Rappahannock River. Although the
death of Jackson depressed the entire army, everyone realized the
magnitude of the Chancellorsville victory and that the war, like it or not,
would continue. As a way of thanking his men for their outstanding
performance during the grueling campaign, on May 22 Stuart ordered a
review of his entire division. All three brigades (Hampton's, Fitz Lee's,
and Rooney Lee's, nearly 4,000 troopers) plus the horse artillery
participated in the event, which was held on the farm of John Minor
Botts, a vocal and ardent Unionist whose large property sat just outside of
Culpeper. To prepare for the grand review, Breathed and his comrades in
the horse artillery mended their battered harnesses, cleaned their
equipment, and did all within their power to get their accoutrements of
war back into operational order. Many of the gunners and troopers were
flirts of the first order, and they relished the fried chicken and other foods
brought to them by the local ladies who flocked from near and far to see
the event.

The review was an elaborate undertaking. The horse batteries rode at the head of the column, passing in review before stopping to fire a few volleys to kick off the event. Thousands of horsemen being put through their paces on the lush green fields and bright flowers of the Botts Farm was a sight to behold. Although these men had but recently passed through arduous campaigning, its ill effects were nowhere to be seen— men, guns, and horses glittered like new. The cavalry passed the review stand by squadrons, first at a walk, then at a gallop, offering an impressive demonstration of their outstanding horsemanship. The artillery went into battery and fired blank rounds while the cavalry charged past the reviewing stand. "This was a novelty to us as it was the first occasion on which we had ever been called upon to fire such a harmless thing as a blank cartridge," recalled Matthews. "The boys relished it very much, and voted the show a grand success."[47]

After the review, Breathed's men enjoyed a much-needed rest. "Reviews are very nice things for lookers on but far from pleasant for those concerned, especially if the weather be hot and dusty," observed Lieutenant Wigfall a few days later. Another review was scheduled for June 5, this time at Brandy Station. Two additional brigades of cavalry would add their horses to the event, for Grumble Jones' men had arrived from the Valley, and Beverly H. Robertson's from his duties in North Carolina. "We have been inactive now for nearly the month and I don't think it will continue much longer," wrote Wigfall in a letter home. "We have now five brigades of cavalry and five batteries of Horse Artillery and I expect on review [tomorrow] there will be nearly ten thousand men. It will be a grand display and I wish you could be here to see it." One thing made the reviews popular, even for a jaded soldier like the lieutenant. "Several young ladies also are coming up to witness the review tomorrow," he added, "and I suppose the whole country round will turn out to see it. There is to be a dance in town to-night and I shall probably go to it."[48]

The reviews were a clear sign to the men in the ranks that something big was in the making. Stuart's command was larger than it had ever been, with nearly 10,000 men and a full battalion of horse artillery—21 guns organized into five batteries. Chew's Battery had joined Stuart's command from the Valley. The third review in just a few weeks occurred on June 8 on the same field at Brandy Station. It was even more impressive than the June 5 affair, for General Lee, his staff, Longstreet, and others from his corps, including Maj. Gen. John B. Hood's entire infantry division, attended the review. "The Great Cavalry Chieftain of America [Stuart] and his cavalry were dressed in their splendid uniforms and they gathered in file and column in an open field. This time R. E. Lee was present for the Review," noted artilleryman George Neese, a member of Chew's Battery. General Lee, however, forbade galloping or firing. As one historian of the army put it, "the horses needed their flesh, the gunners their powder."[49]

Stuart's Horse Artillery battalion was now composed of five batteries: Chew's (Ashby Battery), Breathed's (1st Stuart Horse Artillery), Hart's (Washington, S.C. Battery), McGregor's (2nd Stuart Horse Artillery), and Moorman's (Lynchburg Artillery). (Another under Capt. William Griffin would join Beckham during the Gettysburg Campaign.) In essence, that meant that Stuart could field a battery for each of his six cavalry brigades in the upcoming campaign (including John Imboden's independent outfit). The artillery at the end of May (five batteries) numbered 18 officers and 519 present for duty, with a "paper strength" of 701 men, or about 107 effectives per battery. The battalion possessed 24 guns: three batteries of four guns each, and two with six. Beckham pushed to increase the four-gun batteries to an even half-dozen pieces each, but Lee was against it: there simply were not enough horses. Somehow, however, the resourceful major managed to achieve the notable goal.[50]

Beckham, Breathed, and the rest of the men in the horse artillery would need every gun, horse, and ounce of black powder they could muster—now more than ever.

Chapter 7

Screening Lee's Invasion of the North

Hooker's army remained on the north bank of the Rappahannock River while its commander wondered what Lee would do next. The concentration of Confederate cavalry in Culpeper County indicated a forthcoming raid. Desperate for information, on June 8 Hooker gave Brig. Gen. Alfred Pleasonton orders to take his entire command and destroy or disperse the enemy cavalry. Pleasonton had assumed command of the Union Cavalry Corps in mid-May after Stoneman went on medical leave. Pleasonton rode out with 12,000 cavalrymen and several batteries of horse artillery. By first light on June 9 they were poised to cross the Rappahannock River.

Pleasonton divided his command into two wings. Brigadier General John Buford commanded the right wing, and Brig. Gen. David Gregg the left. Buford's command, supported by a brigade of infantry, was to cross at Beverly Ford. Gregg's command, joined by the division led by Colonel Duffié, was to cross at Kelly's Ford. With Duffié's division (formerly Averell's command) covering the flank, the two columns would then move on Culpeper in a pincer movement.

The plan was solid but for one thing: it was based on a flawed premise. Pleasonton assumed the Confederate cavalry and horse artillery was much closer to Culpeper than to the river. In fact, on June 8 Beckham and the horse artillery were camped only about one mile from Beverly's

LC

Union cavalry commander John Buford.

Ford on the road leading to Brandy Station. Breathed's Battery was split, with Johnston and his guns joining Rooney Lee's Brigade near the Welford House. With Fitz Lee disabled by rheumatism, Col. Thomas T. Munford commanded the brigade, which was camped along Hazel River, a tributary of the Rappahannock. Lee's Brigade played little role in the drama that was about to unfold.[1]

Buford's cavalry splashed across the river at early dawn, scattering Confederate pickets. The men of Beckham's horse artillery were rudely awakened by the unmistakable sound of gunshots and thundering

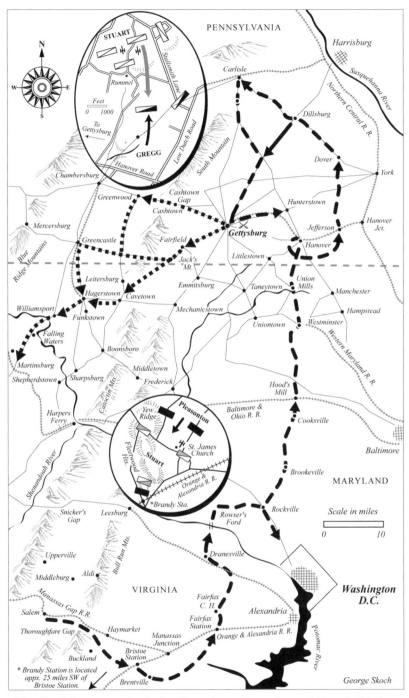

The Confederate cavalry in the Gettysburg Campaign and Brandy Station.

hooves, throwing the artillerists into disarray. Beckham quickly rallied his command and deployed his guns into line atop a commanding ridge near the wooden St. James Church. The men of the 6th Pennsylvania Cavalry made a desperate charge in an effort to capture Beckham's guns, but the Confederate gunners, supported by horsemen from Hampton's and Jones' brigades, fended off the determined Union cavalry, with many using their rammers and hand spikes to defend their guns.[2]

The largest cavalry battle of the war unfolded with no less than 23,000 Confederate and Union troopers and 3,000 Union infantry locked in mortal combat for nearly fourteen long and bloody hours. Charges and countercharges dashed back and forth across the countryside, sabers glinting in the bright spring sun, unfolding a spectacle unlike any ever seen on the North American continent. Breathed and his men joined in the fighting on that epic day.[3]

Johnston's section of Breathed's Battery had been deployed on the high ground of Yew Ridge, supporting Rooney Lee's Brigade. "A determined effort was made to capture this section but we made it too warm for them, by pouring shell into their ranks so rapidly that at last they were hurled back when almost up to the very muzzles of the guns," recalled gunner Henry Matthews. "They retired in the direction of Beverly's Ford leaving their dead and wounded on the field. W. H. F. Lee and Breathed following them."[4]

Dismounted troopers of the 9th Virginia Cavalry were heavily engaged with Buford's horse soldiers and some of his infantry near an L-shaped stone wall on the eastern slope of Yew Ridge. Johnston's guns were at each end of the Confederate battle line, firing to the east at Buford's advancing men. Union horse artillery dropped heavy and accurate fire into Johnston's guns. As the fighting intensified and Buford finally drove Lee's men from the stone wall and back up Yew Ridge, Breathed led Lieutenant Wigfall's section to Yew Ridge at a gallop, joining Johnston. As Stuart and Lee fell back to Stuart's headquarters atop Fleetwood Hill, Breathed's guns joined them, firing as they pulled back.[5]

While the fighting raged near St. James Church, Gregg's Union division arrived at Fleetwood Hill. Caught by surprise again, Stuart shifted his forces to meet the threat, leaving a force that included some of Beckham's guns to defend against Buford. The brigades of Jones and

Hampton galloped over to Fleetwood Hill to meet the arrival of Gregg's horsemen.

At this point Breathed rode onto the field. He noticed that the determined Federal attacks were pressing the 6th Virginia back toward Miller's Hill, near Fleetwood Hill. Acting on his own initiative, Breathed moved his section to support the 6th Virginia as it reached the base of the hill. "Breathed was in his second heaven, rushing from piece to piece, cheering the men and urging them to fire faster, if such a thing were possible directing the fire of the guns," commented Matthews. "The fire was so terrific that the enemy, who were pursuing the 6th, were compelled to retire in great confusion." Breathed galloped back and forth across the north end of Fleetwood Hill, determined to do whatever he could to shove the Union cavalry back across the Rappahannock River. [6]

At that moment, a determined charge by the 1st New Jersey Cavalry came roaring down the ridge. The Jerseymen struck McGregor's Battery in the unprotected flank, dashing between the guns and their caissons. "They were met by a determined resistance— hand to hand fight—from the cannoneers, who with pistol, sponge staff, trail hand-spike and anything in the shape of a weapon that they might possess fought so desperately that they did not succeed in getting a single one of our men, and we had determined never to let one of our guns fall into the hands of the enemy," proudly recalled a Confederate artillerist. [7]

After several hours of fluid fighting that lapped back and forth across the undulating terrain, Gregg was finally driven away from Fleetwood Hill. However, a final act remained to be played out in the drama between John Buford and Rooney Lee when Yew Ridge became the focus of the fighting. Buford's command, led by the Reserve Brigade, made a mounted charge up the ridge, briefly gaining the high ground overlooking Fleetwood Hill. Lee and Capt. Wesley Merritt, commander of the 2nd U.S. Cavalry, engaged in a personal saber duel on the slopes of high ground, with Merritt losing his hat and Lee getting a nasty saber wound to his head. Johnston's gunners, meanwhile, blasted away at the Federals, cutting down troopers as fast as they could load and fire. Breathed also opened on Buford's artillery, earning praise for his men's performance during the withdrawal of the Federal troopers and for helping to dislodge an entire brigade, supported by a battery. [8]

Late in the afternoon, Pleasonton finally ordered Buford to break off and withdraw. Buford did so rather casually, pulling his command back

LC

Captain Wesley Merritt, commander of the 2nd U.S. Cavalry.

across the Rappahannock River as Gregg's command, which had finally been joined by Duffié's division as the firing died out on Fleetwood Hill, also withdrew. Stuart, who had been caught by surprise and whose command had been handled rather roughly, was perfectly happy to let Pleasonton's troopers withdraw. The great Battle of Brandy Station was over.

The fourteen-hour engagement had been a spectacle beyond description. For the first time in the war, the Union cavalry had given as well as it had gotten against the vaunted Confederate horsemen. From that day forward until the final weeks of the war, the mounted arms of the two sides fought as equals on essentially even terms. Never again would the Confederate cavalry dominate its Northern counterpart. The tide had finally turned for the Federal troopers and against Stuart and his men.[9]

Breathed and his artillerists had performed valiantly in the narrow Confederate victory. "My guns did not get into the fight the other day until afternoon," declared Lieutenant Wigfall. "We had it all our own way, the Yankee artillery firing on us almost literally not at all. Johnston lost three men wounded out of his section in the morning." Although the gunners lost only a few men, more difficult trials and tribulations lay ahead.[10]

*   *   *

Brandy Station delayed the planned kick-off of Lee's second raid into the North by only one day. Instead of departing on June 9 as planned, the Army of Northern Virginia moved out on the 10th. In the wake of Jackson's untimely demise, the army had been completely re-organized. Instead of two corps there were now three. Lee deemed the original two corps too large for a single commander. Longstreet remained in command of the First Corps. Lt. Gen. Richard S. Ewell, finally recovered from a terrible combat wound suffered at Groveton, was promoted and given command of Jackson's Second Corps. The newly-promoted Lt. Gen. A. P. Hill was given command of the new Third Corps. How this new command structure would work remained to be seen. For the first time, Lee would have to fare without Stonewall Jackson.

Stuart's cavalry and horse artillery remained largely inactive until June 15, when they joined Longstreet's column to cover his right flank. Longstreet was headed for Snicker's Gap through the Blue Ridge Mountains with the cavalry brigades of Fitz Lee and Beverly H. Robertson, together with the batteries of Breathed, McGregor, and Chew.[11]

On June 16, Stuart crossed the Rappahannock River. The next day Col. Williams C. Wickham, with the 1st, 4th, and 5th Virginia, and Col. Thomas T. Munford, with the 2nd, and 3rd Virginia, accompanied by

Breathed's Battery, left Piedmont for Middleburg. They moved by way of Upperville in search of forage. The Confederates were heading toward the small town of Aldie via the Snickersville Turnpike, when the 1st and 4th Virginia and Breathed's Battery stopped to rest and water their horses. While they rested, Col. Thomas L. Rosser pushed his 5th Virginia on to Aldie.[12]

Although the Confederates did not know it, Pleasonton's active cavalry was searching for Lee's army, and a large force of Union cavalry was approaching Aldie on the same road. Wickham arrived at Aldie around 2:30 P. M., where he ran into the Federal troopers and triggered a sharp combat. After learning that Federal cavalry was in his front, "I at once placed the Fourth regiment in position to cover my left flank on the road from the Snickersville pike, and with the First regiment and two of Breathed's guns went forward to the support of Colonel Rosser, who, I found, had driven them back, [2nd New York Cavalry] but [had] been in turn compelled to give way a little, before a very large force," reported Wickham. "A few well directed shots from Breathed's guns checked the advance of the enemy upon this road (Colonel Douty at 5:30 P.M. on the Little River Turnpike), but not in time to save the gallant sharpshooters of the Fifth, who had, unfortunately, been pushed rather too far forward on ground where it was impossible for cavalry to aid them."[13]

With the 5th Virginia in serious jeopardy along the Little River Turnpike, Breathed hurried his guns to the front. He deployed them quickly and fired his pieces over heads of the cavalry and into the horse artillery of Capt. Alanson M. Randol's combined Batteries B and G, 1st U.S. Artillery. This counter-battery duel raged while charges and counter-charges were launched and repulsed and sabers slashed and stabbed in the warm afternoon sunlight. Judson Kilpatrick was forced to deploy his cavalry under a severe Confederate artillery fire. The 2nd New York Cavalry, which was still in column in the road, drew the attention of Breathed's gunners, whose well-placed shells forced Kilpatrick to withdraw the unit.

Skirmishers of the 1st Virginia advanced to support their beleaguered comrades of the 5th Virginia, but they took position too far to the rear to be effective. Kilpatrick unleashed two of his regiments against the 5th Virginia. Breathed's guns blasted away at them in response, but their ammunition was defective and many of the shells burst too soon, inflicting casualties on friendly riders. With friendly fire

Captain Alanson M. Randol, Batteries B and G, 1st U. S. Artillery.

over head and Union cavalry in their front and on their flank, Capt. Ruben Boston had no choice but to surrender men from the 5th Virginia. Seemingly satisfied with this result, Kilpatrick broke off the combat and withdrew toward Aldie. For the rest of the afternoon Breathed's two pieces and the skirmishers of the 1st Virginia fended off a few half-hearted Union probes as the focus of the fighting shifted to the north and west along the Snickersville Turnpike.[14]

The section of Breathed's gunners assigned to support Wickham had played a major role in the repulse of Kilpatrick's attacks. "Too much praise cannot be awarded to Captain Breathed and his brave men, who handled their guns with the utmost coolness, while their comrades were falling dead under the point-blank range of the enemy's carbines," reported Wickham. "This position I held until ordered to retire, bringing off all my killed and wounded."[15]

With his other section deployed behind on the Confederate left flank, Breathed's position remained virtually impenetrable to three determined charges by Union cavalry. "During all of this time there was only the small force on the left of the Snickersville road that had been stationed there by Col. Munford. Munford moved the 5th Virginia cavalry and the 4th Virginia under Col. Wickham to dismount as sharpshooters," recalled Henry Matthews. "With the 2 detachments of Breathed's battery, under Lt. P. P. Johnston, Munford had placed the remaining guns of the 1st Virginia cavalry on the Middleburg road." The Snickersville Turnpike curves at the point where it wraps around the corner of the Furr House, so that Breathed's gunners were able to inflict serious casualties on the charging men of the 1st Massachusetts Cavalry. Between Breathed's cannon fire and the determined work of Munford's horse soldiers, the 1st Massachusetts sustained 198 casualties in a very short period of time.[16]

Cavalry charges at Aldie, Virginia.

When the Bay Staters came around the curve in the road, they galloped right into the canister blasts of Breathed's two guns. With a stone wall on the right and a steep incline on the left, there was nowhere for them to go but straight down the road and into the teeth of the guns. "That gun used more canister on that occasion than was ever used by the entire section in any previous engagement," continued Matthews. The gunners poured volley after volley into the flanks of the Union horsemen as they charged down the narrow road in column of fours. Dismounted Confederate cavalrymen also poured their small-arms fire into the struggling mass of Bay Staters. All the while, the Confederate gunners were under fire from Randol's guns, prompting one of the Confederate artillerists to observe, "Time and time again the cannoneers had to cease firing and hug the ground so intense was the fire from Randol's battery."[17]

With no reinforcements within supporting distance to help Munford, Stuart instructed one of his staff officers, Lt. Frank Robertson, to "[g]o back and find Munford about Aldie, explain matters, and order him to fall back immediately and join me as best he can at Rector's Cross Roads tonight." At the end of the hard day's fighting, Pleasanton's troopers held Aldie Gap and had learned the whereabouts of Stuart's cavalry. Pleasonton able confirmed that there was no Southern infantry in the area. Still, he had paid dearly for the information in the running series of engagements.[18]

Emboldened by his success, Pleasonton continued pushing his cavalry farther out, hoping to find the whereabouts of the Army of Northern Virginia. He ordered Colonel Duffié, who had been returned to regimental command after his poor performance at Brandy Station, to march his 1st Rhode Island Cavalry to the town of Middleburg. By 9:30 A.M. on June 17, Duffié had his men in the saddle en route to Middleburg via Thoroughfare Gap. Pickets from Col. John Chambliss' Southern brigade delayed Duffié's passage of Thoroughfare Gap, prompting Stuart to strengthen his picket force. When Duffié's advance drove in the reinforced line, Stuart retreated to Middleburg via Rector's Crossroads.[19]

When he arrived at Middleburg, Duffié dismounted his men behind a stone fence and sent a staff officer to Kilpatrick in an effort to secure reinforcements. "Gen. Kilpatrick informed him that his brigade was so worn out that he could not send the reinforcements," reported Duffié, "but he would report the situation of our regiment to Gen. Gregg.

Returning, he said that Gen. Gregg had gone to state the facts to Gen. Pleasanton, and directed me to remain at Aldie until he had heard from Gen. Pleasanton." Duffié waited as directed, but did not receive any further orders. Pleasonton was essentially abandoning the Rhode Islanders to their fate. The brigades of Robertson and Chambliss arrived at Middleburg and reinforced Stuart. Their combined attack against Duffié routed the Rhode Islanders, dividing the regiment into pieces and scattering the men in every direction. Duffié and about 100 men eventually managed to escape after hiding from the enemy. Another 100 or so had been killed and wounded, and an equal number captured. "His regiment was almost exterminated, losing 20 officers and 200 men," remembered one Confederate. Although Duffié had been lucky to get any of his men out of the trap he was left in, explained one cavalry historian, it was not enough to save his career. Hooker promoted the colonel to brigadier general, but then fell under the "influence" of Pleasonton and essentially booted Duffié out of the Army of the Potomac.[20]

On June 18, determined Union probes drove Stuart's pickets back beyond the town of Middleburg. Stuart finally realized that a large force, composed of Pleasonton's cavalry, Brig. Gen. James Barnes' 1st Infantry Division, and three batteries of artillery, was in his front. Stuart had only two small brigades of cavalry and two batteries of horse artillery— Breathed's and Chew's—to cover the road to Union, Virginia. Early on June 19, Gregg's Union cavalry division attacked Stuart's position along the Upperville Road. Breathed's guns were deployed behind a stone wall in a hazardous position. They drew fire from Union horse artillery, whose shells sent stone rubble and shrapnel flying in all directions. The best the Southern gunners could do was keep their heads down and withstand the storm.[21]

Faced by Union cavalry and infantry, Stuart withdrew to the west toward Upperville. His troopers retired at their leisure without being harassed by the enemy. McGregor's and Moorman's men maintained a steady fire as they withdrew their guns. While one section retreated, the other section maintained a fire until the first section took up a new position and went into action. Thus the guns played a game of deadly leap-frog, permitting the artillerists to maintain an umbrella of protection even in retreat.

Unfortunately, Stuart and his command suffered a significant loss during the fighting at Middleburg. A Union bullet struck his favorite aide, Prussian Heros von Borcke, in the neck. Pieces of cloth lodged in his lungs and throat, making breathing painful and difficult. However, von Borcke was a strong man and survived a wound that would have killed many others—even though a doctor advised him the wound was fatal. "I have often watched him and wondered how he escaped the enemy's bullets. He was a very large man and dressed so conspicuously that he could not fail to draw the enemy's fire upon himself," recalled Henry Matthews. "He was very fond of the battery and when Harry Thomas or Joe Warrow would make a good shot he would manifest his approval in his genuine German way. When the Yankee would fall like quail from the fire of our guns it did not effect him in the least, but seemed to please him the more." The Prussian recovered slowly and never took up his sword again in this war. One of the more colorful figures to grace Stuart's headquarters, Heros von Borcke was on hand in May 1864 to keep Stuart company when that officer lay dying after the combat at Yellow Tavern. Von Borcke never forgot his time in service to the Confederacy; he flew a Confederate flag from his great house in Prussia long after the conflict had ended.[22]

After escorting A. P. Hill's Corps behind the Blue Ridge, Grumble Jones' Brigade arrived on June 19. Stuart stationed Jones at Union, with Chambliss in support, and placed Munford on the left to cover Snicker's Gap. Hampton was ordered to straddle the pike at Upperville. Robertson's Brigade was held in reserve because it had fought the Federals at Middleburg the day before. "Stuart had now 5 brigades of cavalry, but he had to divide them in such a way as to cover the three roads leading across the mountains," observed Matthews. "He still determined to act on the defensive, in consequence of the heavy force of infantry in his front." If Stuart had been hoping the fighting at Brandy Station had been a fluke, the recent engagements convinced him otherwise.[23]

*   *   *

On the morning of June 21 at 8:00 A.M., Pleasonton and his three cavalry divisions, horse artillery, and supporting infantry moved out of Middleburg. Buford's three brigades moved off to try to turn Stuart's left flank, while Gregg's three brigades and Col. Strong Vincent's 3rd Brigade, 1st Division of the V Infantry Corps headed straight for

Upperville. Stuart's Horse Artillery opened fire on the advancing Union horsemen, harassing their advance and buying time for Stuart to shift troops to meet Buford's flanking movement. The stakes were high: if Stuart failed, the active and diligent Union cavalry would locate the main body of Lee's army heading north down the Shenandoah Valley just on the other side of the Blue Ridge.[24]

Gregg had correctly judged that Stuart's movements were a bluff, and the Union cavalry would be fooled no more. "Buford tried to turn the Confederate left at Union," observed Matthews, "but finding the position so strong, he was compelled to make a direct attack upon Munford." Gregg's movement brought on a sharp engagement. However, Stuart ordered Hampton and Robertson not to permit themselves to become heavily engaged, and instructed Jones and Chambliss to retire toward Upperville. "In retiring from these positions Breathed always kept up the formation of sections, retiring in that way," recalled Matthews. "If we had limbered up as a battery, they would have made it so warm for us that we would not have been able to get in position; but with one section doing their best to knock them out they had no time to shell the ground that we expected to occupy."[25]

Using the impediment of deep and fast-flowing Goose Creek, Stuart was able to delay the relocation of the Federal cavalry. Two Confederate batteries and dismounted cavalrymen held the hill overlooking the handsome stone bridge across the swift waterway. Union cavalry and infantry held the high ground to the east of the bridge, which was built in 1802 as part of the Ashby Gap Turnpike, a privately funded road that played an important role in the country's western expansion. Chew's Battery and a section of Moorman's Battery engaged in a counter-battery duel with the Union horse artillery there, and before long were facing most of Buford's Division.[26]

Watching these developments, Grumble Jones sent the 11th Virginia Cavalry forward to contest the Union crossing. The Federal horse soldiers moved to the steep bank and forded the creek under heavy fire from the Confederate horse artillery. Major Charles J. Whiting, the commander of the Federal Reserve Brigade, hesitated before ordering his Regulars to charge. Two of Jones' Confederate regiments rushed to reach a stone wall before Buford's troopers, but men from the 2nd and 6th U.S. Cavalry reached it first.[27]

The pressure was too heavy to hold back, and the Union horse artillery batteries and Regular cavalry made their way across the creek and massed in front of the Confederate position. The enemy pressed on in the face of a steady artillery fire. The Confederates were forced to withdraw west toward the Trappe Road, which was lined by yet more stout stone walls.

While Buford and Jones slugged it out along the Trappe Road, Gregg's troopers and Vincent's infantry were heavily engaged with Robertson's North Carolinians. The Federals eventually drove Robertson back to a dominating ridge just to the east of the town of Upperville. The Confederates kept Buford's and Gregg's troopers at bay for nearly two hours, buying sufficient time for Stuart to concentrate his forces just to the east of Upperville. At Upperville, Stuart's command lost about 180 men, while Pleasonton suffered 209 from all causes. For all three running cavalry actions, Confederate losses totaled 510, and the Union's more than 600.[28]

Breathed's guns had been engaged for many days running, and the men were utterly exhausted. They had had little to eat, and had changed position so often that they had no time to cook rations. "From the 15th of June, when we left our camp on the John Minor Botts farm near Brandy Station, to the evening of the 21st of June, we had marched and fought every day," remembered Matthews. "The men and horses were in a deplorable condition, totally unfit for the great invasion of Maryland and Pennsylvania."[29]

The Stuart Horse Artillery's performance during the Aldie, Middleburg, and Upperville engagements impressed Munford, who praised them in his after-action report: "Capt. Breathed and his fighting battery did excellent service and are entitled to much credit and have my thanks for their spirited conduct in this engagement." Munford also reported that well-directed blasts from Breathed's guns at Aldie had hindered the Federal advance and enabled the 1st Virginia Cavalry to hold its ground for nearly the entire afternoon until Breathed's determined fire finally forced the Federals to withdraw. "Too much praise cannot be awarded Capt. Breathed and his brave men," declared Munford, "who handled their guns with the utmost coolness while their comrades were falling dead under the point blank range of the enemy's carbines."[30]

The unrelenting pressure of the Union attacks forced Stuart back to the mouth of Ashby's Gap, leaving the town of Upperville in the hands of the victorious Federals. This was the first true battlefield defeat suffered by the boastful Confederate cavalry, and it stung. However, Stuart only pulled back as far as he had to in order to reach infantry support; consequently, the Federal cavalry remained unable to find the main body of Lee's army. Stuart's cavalry and horse artillery had performed admirably in keeping Pleasonton's horsemen at bay, permitting Lee to advance into Pennsylvania largely unmolested.

Chapter 8

To Pennsylvania and Back Again

On June 23, Lee granted Stuart permission to move north with three brigades and "pass around" the Union army if he found that the Army of the Potomac was moving north—and if he believed the mountain passes in Virginia and Maryland could be held by two remaining brigades of cavalry. Lee expected the cavalry commander to cover the advance of the Confederate right flank, gathering supplies and information along the way, with the ultimate goal of establishing contact with Ewell's Corps in Pennsylvania. However, Lee's orders were a bit vague and probably gave Stuart too much discretion.

Stuart marched on June 23 with Hampton's, Fitz Lee's, and Chambliss' brigades, Breathed's Battery, and a section of McGregor's Battery. The column followed a route laid out by Capt. John S. Mosby, one of Stuart's favorite scouts. When the head of Stuart's force emerged from Glasscock's Gap near Haymarket, he found the entire Union Second Corps in front of him, and had to find a new route after a brief skirmish with the surprised Federal infantry that included participation by Breathed's gunners. Stuart broke off the engagement and marched to nearby Buckland, where he paused to make some important choices that would impact the entire campaign.[1]

With the enemy moving north and between his column and Lee's main army, Stuart had to find a route around the Army of the Potomac.

One of the many cavalry charges launched during the advance into
Pennsylvania, captured in a woodcut for the public.

He headed south and east on June 26 for Wolf Run Shoals on Bull Run,
and then passed through Fairfax Court House. As he soon learned, he had
come close to, but missed, the marching enemy army. Stuart arrived at
Dranesville at dusk on June 27. Knowing he had to cross the Potomac
River via Rowser's Ford, he ordered his command to make the arduous
crossing early on the morning of June 28, with the horse artillerists
emptying their limber chests in order to keep their ammunition dry. After
a brief rest, the column pushed on toward Rockville, Maryland.[2]

When Hampton's Brigade reached Rockville, it spotted a lengthy
Union wagon train that seemed ripe for the picking. Unable to resist
seizing nearly 150 new and well equipped wagons and their mule teams,
Hampton moved his troopers into position and ordered Lt. Thomas Lee,
2nd South Carolina Cavalry, to charge and capture the train. Union
troops fled in panic when the attack began, and one of the wagons
overturned, causing frantic mules to pile up on top of the overturned
vehicle, the mules desperately kicking and braying the entire time. The
Confederate troopers chased the teamsters for several miles before
bagging the entire train. Apparently giving little serious thought to the
fact that 150 wagons would seriously hinder his march, Stuart took the
entire train along with him into Pennsylvania. In hindsight, the only
bright spot was that the wagons were filled with high-grade fodder,

which Stuart's weary and famished horses desperately required. With the wagons tucked into his column Stuart rode into Rockville, where his men received a rousing welcome from pupils attending the local girl's seminary.[3]

Shortly after daylight on June 29 Stuart moved north, brushing off the Maryland militia in an unexpected skirmish. With Breathed's Battery in tow, Fitz Lee headed for the B & O Railroad, the critical line of supply and communication for the Army of the Potomac if it had to move into Maryland. General R. E. Lee had ordered Stuart to do all he could to disrupt the flow of supplies and communication with Washington, so Stuart sent Fitz Lee to tear up the B & O and to destroy the telegraph lines at Hood's Mill and Sykesville, and also to set fire to two small bridges. Lacking the proper equipment to do permanent damage to the rail line, Stuart did what he could and headed north toward Westminster, where he nearly captured Joe Hooker, who had been relieved of command of the Army of the Potomac on June 28 at his own request. With Fitz Lee's Brigade leading the way, the head of Stuart's column reached Westminster that afternoon. Chambliss guarded the flanks while Hampton drew the unhappy and dusty task of escorting the captured wagons.[4]

Stuart was unaware that approximately 100 troopers of Maj. Napoleon B. Knight's 1st Delaware Cavalry were guarding the important railhead of the Western Maryland Railroad, located in Westminster. Captain Charles Corbit, who was in command of the 1st Delaware because Major Knight was indisposed, did the unthinkable: he ordered his small band to charge Stuart's column! Corbit's attack crashed into the head of Fitz Lee's Virginians, forcing them back and triggering a desperate saber melee in the streets of the town. Two officers from the 4th Virginia Cavalry were killed in the affair. Most of Corbit's men were captured, but their bold effort slowed Stuart's advance for the rest of the afternoon, forcing him to proceed cautiously to avoid any more unpleasant surprises.[5]

Stuart spent the night in Westminster as his five-mile long column of cavalry moved north to Union Mills, Maryland. The rigors of the march were taking their toll on his command. "My boots were utterly worn out, my pantaloons were all one big hole as the Irishman would say, my coat was like a beggar's and my hat was actually falling to pieces in addition to lacking its crown which has allowed my hair, not cut since some time before leaving Culpeper, to protrude and gave a highly picturesque finish to my appearance," complained Lieutenant Wigfall. Breathed and his men arrived at Union Mills, only a few yards south of the Mason-Dixon Line, and bivouacked at the homestead of Andrew K. Shriver, a strong supporter of the Union cause. His brother William, who lived across the street, sympathized with the Confederate cause.[6]

Both Stuart's men and their horses were hungry and utterly exhausted. William Shriver's daughter, along with two of her friends, helped prepare food for some of the thousands of troopers. By the afternoon, "three hundred must have got their supper." The whole family pitched in and helped out with the monumental task of feeding large numbers of ravenous men. Stuart and his staff stayed in William Shriver's house, while Fitz Lee slept in Andrew Shriver's orchard.[7]

Always jovial, Stuart entertained the Shrivers by singing songs of the Southland, including his favorite ditty, "If you want to have some fun, jine the cav'ry." Sampson D. Sweeney, Stuart's orderly, played the banjo, and Mulatto Bob accompanied him on the bones. Because he was unfamiliar with the local road network, Stuart needed a knowledgeable local resident to lead his command into Pennsylvania. William's sixteen-year-old son Herbert volunteered to guide Stuart's column toward Hanover, Pennsylvania, a few miles northeast of Union Mills.[8]

* * *

Once Stuart and his troopers crossed the Mason-Dixon Line, they headed northeast toward Hanover. Stuart had no way of knowing that Brig. Gen. Judson Kilpatrick, who had recently been promoted to division command, was also headed for Hanover. Hampton's Brigade was in the rear of the wagon train, with Fitz Lee's Brigade and the horse artillery in the middle of the column. Chambliss' Brigade led the advance.

The two columns ran into each other on the outskirts of town when the head of Stuart's command caught up with the tail of Kilpatrick's division passing through Hanover. The encounter was a surprise to both combatants. "Hastening down the declivity with the order for Chambliss, I found him advancing rapidly in column of fours to charge the enemy, who were drawn up in the outskirts of the town," recalled Capt. John Esten Cooke, one of Stuart's aides. "Before he could issue the order it was rendered somewhat nugatory by the blue people in front. We had supposed their force to be small, but it was now seen to be heavy. They swarmed everywhere, right, left, and front; rapidly formed line of battle, and delivering a sharp volley at short range in the faces of the Confederates, made a gallant and headlong charge." Almost before either side was aware of it, combat was raging at Hanover.[9]

Brig. Gen. Elon J. Farnsworth, the commander of Kilpatrick's First Brigade, arrived on the scene with the 5th New York and 18th Pennsylvania cavalry regiments. Col. William H. Payne, the commander of the 2nd North Carolina Cavalry, led his regiment and the 13th Virginia in a mounted charge that led to hand-to-hand combat when they smashed into Farnsworth's Pennsylvanians.[10]

By 2:00 P.M., Breathed and Hampton appeared on the right of the Confederate line. The gunner unlimbered his guns in town at Mount Olivet Cemetery and began his deadly work as the determined Federal horse soldiers advanced against him. "Breathed replied by opening upon them with shell and canister," recounted Cooke. "The first shell burst in the line; the second near the first; and the third made it waver. A more rapid fire succeeded; everything depended upon these few moments, and then the [Federal] line was seen slowly retiring." As far as Cooke was concerned, the advance was "one of the finest sights I ever beheld." It was so well conducted that Stuart's aide worried that "Breathed's guns would never leave that field of tall rye where they were vomiting fire and smoke—under the command of this gallant [Captain] at least."[11]

After Farnsworth rallied his troops and drove Payne's Tar Heels from the town, Breathed pulled his guns back to a hill on the left on the road leading into Hanover. Henry Matthews, an artillerist with Breathed, picks up the story:

> We had not long to wait before the enemy threw out skirmishers, advancing through a wheat field outside of the town and to the right of the road. Immediately in front of these Yankee skirmishers was a stream running through the meadows having banks about ten feet high. We soon got the range of this stream and threw over shells in such a way that it was made very uncomfortable for these blue coats. Our position was a grand one. We could see the Yankees advance through the shocks of wheat and hesitate, and then we would shell them in earnest. It was not long before they hugged the mother earth and ceased firing altogether.[12]

As the fighting raged, Breathed continued firing, knocking men from their saddles. After a long day of fighting—the Confederates fended off at least six separate attacks—Stuart broke off the engagement and began withdrawing. Kilpatrick allowed the Confederates to go—especially since he was under orders not to bring on a general engagement. As for Stuart, finding Ewell's infantry was more urgent than ever because at least one large body of Union cavalry was in his front, and he had no way of knowing the dispositions of the enemy or what pieces of the Army of the Potomac were within striking distance. After some discussion, Stuart decided to send Fitz Lee's Brigade and the captured wagons through Jefferson to York, where Maj. Gen. Jubal A. Early's Division was reported to be. The wagon train hindered the men during that long night's march, "especially the 400 prisoners that we had with us since leaving Rockville and what we had picked up on the road," recalled one of the Southern soldiers. "Many of these prisoners were loaded into the wagons. The mules were weary—and so were we— and were suffering for the want of food and water, and frequently became stalled in the roads, thereby stopping the whole command. The drivers became negligent, and it was with the greatest difficulty that the train was kept in motion."[13]

On July 1, Stuart's column marched from Jefferson to Dover, and then on toward Carlisle after learning that Early had already abandoned York. Two of Ewell's three divisions were rumored to be operating in that vicinity. After leaving Hampton's Brigade and the wagon train at Dillsburg, Stuart headed in that direction hoping to find Ewell. His troopers desperately needed provisions, and there was a substantial U.S. Army base in Carlisle.

Stuart did not find Ewell in Carlisle, however, he did find two brigades of Union infantry drawn from the defenses of Harrisburg and commanded by Maj. Gen. William F. "Baldy" Smith. When Smith refused to surrender the town, Fitz Lee ordered Breathed to unlimber his guns and open fire. Captain Henry D. Landis' Philadelphia Battery answered. Breathed's gunners found the range of Landis' guns almost immediately, and the second shot took two fingers off the hand of one of the inexperienced Philadelphia artillerists. When Smith refused a second surrender demand, Breathed opened fire again, damaging a few buildings and scaring civilians. The shelling continued until nearly 3:00 A.M.[14]

Stuart, meanwhile, was growing increasingly worried. He had sent various staff officers in different directions to try to find Lee's army. Maj. Andrew R. Venable finally made contact when he located the Army of Northern Virginia at Gettysburg, where it was fighting a battle neither side had expected. Venable dashed back to Carlisle with orders for Stuart to hurry forward his command. Venable arrived well after midnight. Breathed lobbed a couple of parting shots at the town, and by 3:00 A.M. the entire Confederate column was on the road south, headed for South Mountain and the important village of Gettysburg. Stuart rode ahead and was the first to arrive.

The beleaguered column finally straggled into Gettysburg on the early afternoon of July 2, "with a grateful sense of relief, which words cannot express. No one except those who were on this expedition can imagine the condition of the men and horses," explained Matthews. Hampton's Brigade and the wagons arrived last after Hampton's troopers fought a spirited skirmish with Kilpatrick's troopers at Hunterstown, a few miles from Gettysburg.[15]

Although Stuart's exhausted command had already played a significant role in the campaign, primarily because of its absence, the hardest fighting was ahead of them.

*   *   *

Stuart reported to General Lee as soon as he reached Gettysburg. Although no firsthand accounts of that meeting have been found, several of Lee's staff officers suggested that Lee rebuked his cavalry chief for his protracted absence and lack of usable intelligence. Stuart may have confided the results of the meeting to aide Henry McClellan, who found the entire episode excruciatingly embarrassing. Lee ordered his errant general to ride to Ewell's exposed flank northeast of town and protect it.[16]

Much had happened during Stuart's self-imposed absence. While Lee's army had been moving north, Hooker had a falling out with President Lincoln and asked to be removed—and Lincoln did exactly that, replacing Hooker with Maj. Gen. George G. Meade. The careful professional assumed command on June 28, just three days before the armies found one another at Gettysburg, a small but important road hub in the southeastern part of the state. On July 1, Lee advanced in force toward the town, first from the west with A. P. Hill's Corps, and then from the north with Ewell's divisions, flanking and defeating two corps from Meade's army. Falling back through town, the Federals assumed a strong defensive line running from Culp's Hill on the north to lower Cemetery Ridge on the south—in effect a giant fishhook with strong natural obstacles and wide open fields of fire. When Stuart arrived on July 2, Lee was in the process of attacking Meade on his left with Longstreet's Corps (minus Pickett's Division, which was not yet up), an assault that was to be taken up, *en echelon*, by the right of Hill's Corps, then the center, and so forth until Ewell's men wrapped around Culp's Hill were also engaged. The idea was to get Meade to commit his forces early on his left or center, which would leave weak spots to be exploited. It was a difficult plan to implement, but one that very nearly succeeded.

On July 3, with Meade's army damaged but still holding its position, Lee decided to attack the Union right center on Cemetery Ridge. He would do it that afternoon with Pickett's fresh division and other troops pulled from Hill's Corps. Stuart's assignment was to ride into the rear of the Army of the Potomac and create confusion when the primary infantry attack broke through the center.

Augmented by elements of Brig. Gen. Albert G. Jenkins' Brigade, Stuart moved out with three brigades about 10:00 A.M. on July 3. He rode out the York Pike, but Union pickets had spotted the move and cavalry was shifted to block Stuart. To his dismay, he found two brigades of the enemy occupying a critical road intersection where the Hanover and Low Dutch roads converged about four miles east of the Gettysburg town square. The Low Dutch Road provided a direct route into the center of Meade's rear area, and if Stuart and his troopers could get there, they could wreak havoc on a grand scale. The cavalier ordered Chambliss and Jenkins (who would leave the field early because of a lack of ammunition) to dismount and deploy their men on the ground of the John Rummel Farm; Lee's and Hampton's brigades would remain mounted in a nearby stand of woods. Stuart hoped to draw the Federal troopers into a trap by using his dismounted troopers as bait, and then strike hard with his mounted brigades.

When he arrived on Cress Ridge, a dominating spine of ground overlooking the intersection of the Hanover and Low Dutch roads, Stuart did something that still puzzles historians to this day. He ordered four guns of his horse artillery to move out of the woods, and had each one fire a single shot, one in each compass direction. Union horse artillery promptly responded, and a counter-battery duel broke out. While some have speculated that the firing of the four shots was a signal to General Lee, there is no evidence to support this theory or to indicate that Stuart's efforts were in any way coordinated with the grand infantry assault that Lee had planned for the Union center.[17]

The departure of Breathed's and McGregor's batteries was delayed because they needed to resupply their caissons from the supply train. Breathed was not happy about the delay. "The way that Breathed flew around that morning cursing the ordnance officer for not having the ordnance on the ground, would have been shocking to a Sunday school convention," remembered Henry Matthews. "He swore up hill and down vale, and still the wagons did not make their appearance." Although some of the other batteries had already re-supplied, Breathed was impatient because "he did not want any other batteries to go into a fight while he waited for ammunition. At last the wagons came in sight and the 2 batteries began to refill their limbers, and caissons."[18]

Breathed was almost finished loading his limber chests when he heard artillery fire booming from the vicinity of Stuart's cavalry. He quickly mounted and galloped to the Cress Ridge with the battery following as fast as its beleaguered horses could haul the guns. "We took position on the right slope within sight of the Pennington battery and awaited orders to go into action," recalled Matthews. Within moments, a counter-battery duel broke out that lasted for most of the afternoon.[19]

Gregg had Col. John B. McIntosh's brigade from his division and Brig. Gen. George A. Custer's Michigan brigade of cavalry from Kilpatrick's division at his disposal, as well as Pennington's and Randol's batteries of horse artillery. Nothing of consequence occurred until about 3:00 P.M., when Gregg positioned McIntosh's men and two regiments of Custer's Brigade to assault the Rummel Farm position. The dismounted Federal troopers advanced and a vicious firefight developed at short range. Pennington, in particular, was a familiar adversary for Breathed's men and around 4:00 P.M. the Breathed Battery arrived on the field.[20]

After the fighting was well developed, Chambliss saw an opportunity and ordered portions of his brigade to draw sabers and charge. Gregg responded by sending Custer forward with the 7th Michigan Cavalry. The two forces crashed together violently, with Chambliss' men fighting for a time at close range before falling back. Realizing how close he had

George Armstrong Custer, one of the Union's celebrated cavalry officers.

come to shattering the thin Union line, Stuart ordered Hampton and Fitz Lee to charge from their positions in the woods northeast of the Rummel Farm. The two brigades drew sabers and slowly marched across the open fields, first at a walk, then a trot, and finally at a gallop. George A. Custer led the 1st Michigan Cavalry in a countercharge, and another collision of horses and men took place, this one larger and more intense than the earlier melee. Wade Hampton found himself in a saber duel with a Union trooper who raised his blade and delivered a blow that severely wounded Hampton. When additional Union troopers charged from the flanks, the weary Confederates fell back in disorder.[21]

An interesting indication of the extent to which James Breathed became legendary is contained in a book that Breathed's nephew, Henry P. Bridges wrote in the 1950s. At the time he heard the story, around 1900, Henry Bridges was a law student at the University of Maryland. The head of the University Law School was Judge Charles E. Phelps, a Union Civil War veteran who rose to the rank of general. According to the judge, as the battle unfolded Federal troopers captured one of the Confederate guns and dragged it back to the Union lines. Phelps recalled watching as Breathed rode out from the head of his battery to meet the charging Union horsemen. "Suddenly, the Union troops were dumbfounded to see a horseman, Breathed, from the Confederate ranks ride at full gallop into their midst. He leaped from his horse and into the saddle of the gun carriage and commenced to driving the horse and gun back to the Confederate lines. The troops shot at him, but his audacity had unnerved them." As if a phantom, Breathed had appeared and disappeared into the swirl of discharged black powder.[22]

According to Judge Phelps, Breathed made another dramatic appearance on the field, "Breathed rode out from the skirmish line challenging a Union major to a duel of honor. He fought from horseback in the duel to the death. . . . They fought furiously up and down the field and as they charged past each other slashing metal on metal, there was only one outcome, a winner and a loser. Their swords flashed and rang as steel clashed on steel. They slashed savagely at one another as they parried sabres." With a savage blow, Breathed knocked the mortally wounded officer from his saddle. Breathed's medical training was now displayed for all to see. "Breathed dismounted and gave the dying man medication to ease his pain. The dying man gave him a watch that had a picture of his sweetheart in the back of it," recalled the observer. "He asked Breathed to give it to the young lady when the war was over. The Union Major asked that he be remembered to his wife as a man who fought to his own death on the battlefield of glory. Breathed assured the dying Major that he would honor his final words as soon as the war ended." When the man died, Breathed closed his eyes, mounted his horse, and galloped back to his own battle line.[23]

As dramatic as this account is, Breathed' audacious rescue of the cannon did not happen at Gettysburg. Phelps was serving in the Union V Corps, which had been busy on Little Round Top the day before. It is highly unlikely that he was several miles farther east on July 3 and in position to witness the cavalry clash. Phelps may have (and probably did) witness Breathed save a field piece in almost identical circumstances ten months later on the Alsop Farm. Judge Phelps was not the type of person to invent stories. A former Congressman from Maryland, at the time of he wrote his recollections Phelps was also a noted jurist on the Baltimore bench, an insightful commentator on Shakespeare (whose works are still being reprinted today), and a distinguished professor of law at the University of Maryland. He was also a Civil War veteran who had served with the 7th Maryland (U.S.). Ironically, the same day Breathed actually rescued a gun at the Alsop Farm, Colonel Phelps was cited for his own brave actions in battle a short distance away at Laurel Hill. Phelps was promoted to brigadier general for his heroics and later awarded the Congressional Medal of Honor. There is also some doubt as to whether Phelps' account of Breathed's hand-to-hand combat with the Union major happened at Gettysburg. The details he provided of the combat closely resemble another well-document similar hand-to-hand action that occurred late in the war. Such was the nature of the "Breathed legend." Sifting through recollections to uncover factual accounts of some of the things Breathed was reputed to have done is often hard work, even when the memories come from otherwise unimpeachable sources like Judge Phelps.

Henry Matthews had a bird's eye view of the battle raging in front of him. "Breathed brought the battery into position, but could not fire because of the continual mix up of the blue and the grey in the plains below. For many minutes the fight raged, pistol and sabre being used freely," he wrote. "Neither force seemed willing to give way and held on tenaciously like two bull dogs. The fierce attack of the Federals was broken at last. Both forces withdrew to the lines held at the opening of the fight. Now was Breathed's opportunity and right glad did he avail himself to it."[24]

As the firing petered out, Stuart and his adjutant, Maj. Henry B. McClellan, rode their horses along the Rummel Farm property. The light was fading as they surveyed the battlefield. An occasional Federal artillery shell burst here and there, but the fighting was over. Stuart only pulled back when he was satisfied that the enemy was through for the day. The cavalier withdrew his command to the York Pike, leaving only a picket force behind him. Stuart was giving up the field. By this time Stuart was also well aware that Lee's effort to break through Meade's center had ended badly.

Casualties from the fight on what would become known as East Cavalry Field were moderately heavy on both sides. For the Confederates, who had failed to reach the rear of Meade's army, there was no gain whatsoever. Stuart suffered about 200 men killed, wounded, and captured, including the severely wounded Hampton, who would be out of action for weeks. Federal losses were slightly higher at 254. Breathed's Battery suffered heavily. Five men were killed and 13 wounded, and many horses had been struck down, according to the National Park Service plaque that marks the site at Gettysburg. "The men dropped to the ground in utter exhaustion after the darkness made it impossible for the cannoneers to fire any more rounds. Their gun had not moved one yard from their initial position until after nightfall," recalled Matthews. "They came into the battle tired and the immediate fight did nothing to reinvigorate their strength or their spirits, however, they knew they had done their duty." Although Breathed's guns had reached the field late that afternoon, their commander had played a conspicuous role in the fighting, first with the cavalry and then leading his battery. His actions earned the respect of his enemies. Years later, Lieutenant Pennington—Breathed's opponent on several fields and a fine horse artillerist in his own right— complimented the Southern gunner for the way in which he handled his battery. "I never knew Breathed, as we never got close enough for an introduction, but I knew the battery he commanded and can testify to its bulldog tenacity and conspicuous gallantry," Pennington recalled. "It was always, it seemed to me, the one most prominent horse battery on [the Confederate] side, and the men all knew it well. Its fine discipline and good marksmanship were, I have no doubt, due to and were a credit to its gallant commander."[26]

Lt. Carle A. Woodruff was a Union officer with the 2nd U.S. Artillery at Gettysburg. On July 24, less than three weeks after the fight at East Cavalry Field, his own gallantry on the field at Newbys Crossroads in Virginia would earn him a Medal of Honor. Like Pennington, Woodruff was also impressed by Breathed's courage and dedication to his craft. "I always knew when Breathed's Horse Battery was in my immediate front. This battery and Hart's battery, of South Carolina also of Stuart's Horse Artillery, I always dreaded meeting in action," wrote Woodruff. "Breathed's battery was undoubtedly well-disciplined, well instructed, and always ready for a fight—a foe to be respected," continued the old soldier in 1903. "That its personnel was composed of brave officers and brave soldiers devoted to the cause in which they were engaged goes without saying. Their conduct in action proved this." It would seem that James Breathed had by this time become a legend in both armies.[27]

* * *

By the night of July 3 General Lee realized he had no choice but to withdraw from Pennsylvania. His casualties had been horrendously high, and his supply situation made it impossible for him to remain stationary. Lee did not know the true extent of his losses, but as he would discover later that month, his army had suffered about 27,000 killed, wounded, and missing—nearly 5,000 of whom were dead—during the campaign. Meade's losses were similarly costly: about 23,000 from all causes, including more than 3,000 killed. The retreat began in earnest on July 4. It was Stuart's job to cover the withdrawal and keep the Federal horsemen at a distance. The most important goal was to get the army safely back across the Potomac River. Stuart instructed Fitz Lee, with Breathed's Battery as support, to serve as the army's rear guard as the long gray column of wagons and soldiers moved out the Cashtown Road toward Chambersburg. Lee had a seventeen-mile wagon train of wounded to transport back to Virginia, and everyone knew that protecting it would be a challenge. Uncertain of Lee's intentions severely injured himself, Meade did not pursue as vigorously as he might have until he was certain the Army of Northern Virginia was headed for the Potomac crossings. One reason for waiting was that Meade needed his cavalry to protect his supply route from Westminster, and he could not immediately spare troopers to chase down Lee's battered army.[28]

By July 5, Breathed was camped near Williamsport, not far from his family home. Heavy rains had raised the level of the Potomac River so high that it could no longer be safely forded, leaving the Confederates no choice but to wait until the river dropped enough for the army to cross. With a flooded river to his back and the Army of the Potomac in his front, Lee dug in his dangerously exposed divisions and waited. Many men on both sides expected another major engagement—especially since the Confederates appeared trapped against an unfordable river. However, there would be no Battle of Williamsport.[29]

The College of St. James lay just east of the Confederate defensive perimeter around Williamsport. (According to the map Gen. Meade submitted with his official report of the Battle of Gettysburg, the Confederate defensive works ran along the hills of the Breathed Farm at Bai-Yuka.) Once the army arrived, hordes of Southern soldiers flooded the grounds of the school. Reverend Kerfoot took as many precautions as he could to protect the property of the college. His efforts, however, were largely fruitless for it was all but impossible to prevent the soldiers from looting the local stores. One swarm of Confederates pillaged 100 pounds of butter from the College of St. James. By July 14, the grammar school had been completely looted and left in total disarray by Breathed's Confederate comrades. The threat of major combat on the college grounds only served to heighten Kerfoot's stress—especially when Southern batteries were deployed on the campus behind hedgerows in anticipation of a Federal assault.[30]

Breathed was not on the grounds of his alma mater during this time, though not for want of trying. His days were spent combating probing Union cavalry at Boonsboro, Beaver Creek, Funkstown, and near the old Sharpsburg battlefield. Stuart and his troopers did a masterful job shielding Lee's vulnerable army from the enemy horsemen, which in turn provided the general with sufficient time to assemble a formidable defensive position north of the river.[31]

Still, the lure of home, and family was too strong to resist. Sometime during the retreat Breathed attempted to pay Bai-Yuka a visit. He also tried to visit the College of St. James. When he was some distance away from the school, Reverend Kerfoot spotted Breathed and approached him, but so did a small contingent of Union cavalry, which forced Breathed to withdraw. The enemy also prevented him from visiting his home. As Breathed tried to approach Bai-Yuka one day he was evidently seen and recognized by one of the St. James' faculty with Union sympathies, who hurriedly reported the event to Union troops. According to Major George Freaner, Breathed's friend from Hagerstown and a cavalry staff officer, the subsequent unsuccessful pursuit of Breathed by the Federals chagrined the informing, "distinguished prelate, whose loyalty [to the Union cause] and other similar and redoubtable manifestations of cheap patriotism, have since been generously rewarded with an Episcopal hat. Breathed often laughed heartily when he thought of his former preceptor's first attempt to implement military strategy." [32]

With the Army of Northern Virginia fixed in a firm defensive position north of the Potomac, Meade did not want to make the same mistake Lee had made by attacking into strength. Unsure of the proper course of action, he held a council of war on the night of July 12 during which his generals voted 5-2 against any full-scale attack. Meade, however, feeling the pressure from Washington and appreciating the military and political fall-out should Lee escape unchallenged, spent the day of July 13 mulling his options and ordered a general assault all along his lines for the next morning. By the time the sun rose on July 14, however, the Confederate trenches were empty. Longstreet and Hill had crossed their corps at Falling Waters, while Ewell's troops slipped over at several other fords around Williamsport, Maryland. Once the infantry was across, the Confederate cavalry followed using the river fords. Lee was safely south of the Potomac.[33]

The night crossing was arduous. As Breathed's men made their way to the Potomac River fords, Northern cavalry and horse artillery approached. "They did not annoy us, as a battery on the other side of the river made it decidedly unpleasant for them and caused them to halt until we had crossed once again to Virginia soil," recalled Henry Matthews. "This had been the most exhausting campaign of the war to us."[34]

The men of the horse artillery were now given the job of guarding the Virginia side of the Potomac. On July 15, Breathed and his men were camped near Leesburg, Virginia. Lee's army remained in good spirits in spite of its rough handling at Gettysburg. Writing after the war, Matthews spoke of all the hardships they had faced as Southern soldiers:

> When I look back and recount the privations and severe strains that were forced upon our boyish frames—exposure to heat and cold, no shoes for many instances, days without food, wearing wet clothes in winter and summer for days at a time, I only wonder that a single man who was in that grand old battery is alive today. What a magnificent body of men composed the army of Northern Virginia. In its realm were the best men of the South, and for what? All for principle and honor, nothing for comfort and pleasure. I consider it a great privilege to have been a humble cannoneer in that half-starved, ragged army of Marse Robert, and that I rode with Stuart, Fitz Lee and the peerless Jim Breathed.[35]

July 16 found Breathed back in action and guarding the fords near Shepherdstown, in western Virginia (today's West Virginia). There, he encountered pickets of the 10th New York Cavalry. Breathed's and McGregor's men unlimbered their pieces and dropped shells across the river. The brief skirmish only served to highlight, at least for Lieutenant Wigfall, the rough condition of the battery. He was especially concerned about the lack of good horses and ammunition—two critical components for operating horse artillery successfully. "The battery is in very bad condition as regards horses and is out of ammunition," he complained.

"Two of the guns got some of the latter before we recrossed the river leaving the other two without and I was left with them and have consequently been in the rear ever since the cavalry fight near Boonsboro Md. on the 8th inst." As Wigfall noted, ordnance officers had been dispatched to Staunton and Richmond to seek out ammunition. Without a horse, lamented the lieutenant, he would be forced to travel to the capital with 'Company Q' [the common nickname for cavalrymen who had lost their mounts and were unable to locate replacements]." By July 25, Breathed's Battery had crossed the Blue Ridge Mountains at Thornton's Gap and reported to Culpeper Court House, where the bulk of the Army of Northern Virginia had gathered to rest and refit after its trying ordeal in Pennsylvania.[36]

After a few days of rest, Stuart's cavalry and its artillery component were back on familiar territory, spread out and watching the fords along the Rappahannock River. Breathed's three guns and a section of Moorman's Battery were sent toward Brandy Station behind Kelly's Ford. Their journey carried them through the Chancellorsville battlefield and they camped at Salem Church. They remained there until August 18. A few days later they returned to Fleetwood Hill, where Beckham rotated his fourteen guns on the hill as a strong picket outpost.[37]

Although the Army of Northern Virginia was quickly returning to fighting trim, there is evidence that Breathed was in poor spirits. He asked the Confederate Secretary of War to transfer him. "I am tired of my arm of service, and know that I can do better service in another arm of service," he implored. Williams Wickham, now a brigadier general in command of a brigade of cavalry, disapproved of Breathed's resignation request. "Capt. Breathed is the best man for the management of a battery of horse artillery that I ever saw," he wrote. Fitzhugh Lee also disapproved, writing, "Capt. Breathed is an excellent officer. He can do no better service in another arm of the service." Impressed by Breathed's reckless bravery, Jeb Stuart also refused, declaring that he would "never consent for Breathed to quit the Horse Artillery with which he has rendered such distinguished service, except for certain promotion, which he has well earned." Not surprisingly, Secretary of War Seddon rejected the resignation letter.[38]

Chapter 9

Bristoe, Mine Run, and the Charlottesville Raid

In September 1863, Confederate President Jefferson Davis summoned Robert E. Lee to Richmond for a planning session. Boiled down to its essence, the issue was whether to advance in the East against Meade, or go over to the defensive, detach reinforcements, and send them West to bolster Braxton Bragg's Army of Tennessee. Opposing Bragg was Maj. Gen. William S. Rosecrans' Army of the Cumberland, which was now occupying the important railroad and industrial center of Chattanooga. Davis decided the best decision was to send James Longstreet and the bulk of his corps to North Georgia, where it would reinforce Bragg. Longstreet was eager to make the move and saw the benefit of using the South's interior lines of communication to shuttle troops where they could best be utilized.[1]

As it turned out, Longstreet's men provided the hard luck Army of Tennessee with the manpower it needed to score its only decisive victory of the war. On September 19 and 20 in northwest Georgia, Bragg's army attacked and drove Rosecrans' men from the field at Chickamauga, chasing them all the way back to Chattanooga. The ramifications of that victory were felt as far away as Virginia, where Lee learned that Meade was detaching two of his own corps from the Army of the Potomac to reinforce Rosecrans at Chattanooga, which Bragg was now threatening

LC

The 1st Virginia Cavalry, part of Fitzhugh Lee's Division.

with capture. Even though he was missing a large segment of his own army, and what remained was in a weakened condition, Lee believed the time was right to move against Meade (who was camped north of Culpeper Court House) and force him back across the Potomac. The best way to turn him out (much like Hooker had tried to do with Lee) was to attack if possible while the armies were in motion. If he could force Meade north of the river for the winter, it would be easier to obtain food and forage, protect the railroads, and improve lines of communication and supply. Lee would also have more room to maneuver without exposing Richmond.[2]

Lee's Fall campaign began on the chilly morning of October 9 south of the Rapidan. A reorganized cavalry command screened the army's advance. Stuart now led a corps consisting of two divisions, one commanded by Fitz Lee and the other by Wade Hampton. Because Hampton was still recovering from his Gettysburg wounds, Stuart led the South Carolinian's division on the army's right—that closest to the enemy, while Lee's Division, along with Breathed's Battery, monitored the army's rear and watched fords on the Rapidan.[3]

Lee's infantry moved west and then crossed the river, heading northwest beyond Culpeper Court House and Brandy Station, and thus around the right flank of the Army of the Potomac. Once across the

Rappahannock River, Lee headed northeast toward Manassas. Meade, of course, could not sit still while his enemy positioned himself astride his line of communications, and so moved expeditiously to block the threat. It was a campaign of movement, picking, prodding, and shielding as the opponents maneuvered for advantage.

With the army behind him at Madison Court House, Stuart crossed the Robertson River and rode northeast toward James City on the road to Culpeper. Before him he drove Union pickets as far as Bethesda Church, where he encountered the 129th New York Infantry and some of Kilpatrick's cavalry. Gordon's Tar Heels attacked the Federals in front while some of Young's Georgians flanked them. Stuart pushed on to James City, where he found the main body of the Federal cavalry, supported by infantry and artillery. Knowing it was time for prudence, Stuart broke off the reconnaissance and withdrew. However, his probe had helped successfully screen Lee's infantry movements. That night, the Federals pulled out, leaving Stuart's command in sole possession of the field.[4]

As the infantry continued its northward advance, Col. Thomas Owen, in command of Wickham's Brigade of Virginians, splashed across the Rapidan at Raccoon Ford on October 11. He rode cautiously ahead until he found Union cavalry under Col. George H. Chapman and some artillery "in line of battle near Stringfellow's house." With him was Breathed's Battery, which was ordered into position. Owen ordered his men to charge Lt. Edward B. Williston's Battery D, 2nd U.S. Artillery, but the order was countermanded during the approach by Fitz Lee when it was learned the guns were more strongly supported than originally believed. Breathed, meanwhile, opened fire, "doing good execution," reported Owen.[5]

As the fighting developed, Union sharpshooters found the range, forcing Owen to dismount the 1st and 3rd Virginia regiments and deploy them behind a fence. His other two regiments, the 2nd and 4th Virginia, drew sabers and rallied near Breathed to protect his guns. When the enemy advanced, the 4th Virginia charged from the cover of thick woods and fended off the assault on the artillery, driving the Federals back. Owen charged anew with three regiments, leaving the 1st Virginia to support Breathed. The attack drove the enemy horsemen beyond Brandy Station and back toward Beverly Ford. Breathed's guns followed, harassing the Union retreat at every opportunity.[6]

LC

Horse artillery on the move.

Stuart, meanwhile, had reached Culpeper, where he learned Meade had retired beyond the Rappahannock River. Kilpatrick occupied the ground east of the county courthouse, and Stuart realized that it would be foolish to attack. He was determined to rendezvous with Fitz Lee at Brandy Station and occupy Fleetwood Hill. Their intention was to drive a wedge between Kilpatrick and Buford, whom Lee had driven away from Raccoon Ford. Stuart wisely withdrew from Kilpatrick's front and galloped toward the backroads and farm lanes for Brandy Station. That night the cavalry and Breathed's gunners camped on the familiar grounds of John Minor Botts' farm.[7]

The next morning, October 12, Owen marched past Brandy Station toward Miller's Hill to support the 2nd Virginia. Moving out at midnight, Owen advanced toward Jeffersonton while Lee, with Breathed's Battery, splashed across the Hazel River at Starke's Ford and headed for the Rappahannock. Stuart, with Hampton's Division and three batteries of horse artillery, rode northeast through Jeffersonton on the way to Warrenton Springs. Owen proceeded toward the Hedgeman River, with orders to cross at Fox's Ford. His 3rd Virginia crossed the river quickly

LC

The John Minor Botts family on the front porch of their home.

and easily and charged Union pickets on the far shore and seized the heights overlooking the ford. Breathed's guns spent the night there.[8]

On October 13, Owen moved his command northeast to Warrenton, probing to determine Meade's strength and disposition. Stuart ordered him to continue on and reconnoiter along the Orange and Alexandria Railroad in the direction of Catlett's Station. Outside Auburn, Owen ran headlong into massed Union troopers helping guard the critical Federal supply depot at Warrenton Junction. A brief firefight ensued, but it became obvious that continuing the fight would gain little. Breathed was not engaged. The cavalry camped near Catlett's Station that night.[9]

Unbeknownst to Stuart, he was heading into a trap. By the evening of October 13, the Union II Corps had surrounded his position in the Auburn area—though none of the Union high command seemed to realize this. Stuart arranged his men as best he could in the growing darkness and waited. The men of the Stuart Horse Artillery found shelter on top of a small hill that overlooked the Cedar River Ford close to the road where much of the Union army was positioned. "Yes, the men kept quiet as they had never done before, for they realized that even Stuart never before had been in such a tight place," remembered one of the artillerists. "But many times did we fear that we would be betrayed by the weary, hungry mules of the ordnance train. Men were stationed at the head of every team, but in spite of all precautions a discordant bray would every now and then fill the air. Never was the voice of a mule so harsh, though not without an admixture of the ludicrous. Those were anxious hours."[10]

Stuart had never been in a spot as tight as this one, and the normally unflappable cavalier was visibly alarmed. One soldier watched the general during those anxious hours: "This was the only occasion in which I have ever seen Stuart give outward manifestations of his deep concern. So close were we to the marching columns of the enemy that we could hear the voice of the men in conversation, and could distinguish between the passage of wagons and artillery by the noise of the wheels. Through the whole night and almost without interruption did we listen to the sound which [was] across from their camp." Somehow the Confederates had to find a way out, and many different schemes were considered. One idea entailed abandoning the guns and wagons and making a hell-for-leather mounted dash to freedom. "Stuart would not listen to a plan which involved the loss of a single gun or wheel," an artillerist reported. "Stuart still had hope that Gen. R. E. Lee would attack this column, in which case he was in the best position to inflict damage."[11]

The men spent a long and anxious night, fully expecting a fight in the morning. "As day began to dawn it was manifest that a collision of some kind was unavoidable." A large body of Union infantry lay between the cavalry and the ford. The Federal soldiers, blissfully unaware of the prize sitting in their midst, had stacked their arms and were cooking breakfast. The artillerists pushed their guns to just below the crest of the hill where they would command the entire campsite below and waited for orders to open fire. "As soon as it became light the infantry began to straggle in search of water, and some of them approached so near that they could not fail to recognize the Confederate States uniform," explained the gunner. A few shots rang out on the Warrenton side, announcing the beginning of the morning's festivities, and within a few minutes McGregor's, Chew's and Griffin's Batteries were raining shells and canister on the shocked enemy. "Never were men more completely surprised, ... Soon they recovered themselves and a regiment or more were moved up in line of battle, without skirmishers, directly upon our guns." Some of the infantry were men from Capt. Charles H. T. Collis' 114th Pennsylvania Infantry, a Zouave outfit known for its fancy uniforms and outstanding fighting ability. The artillerists fire quickly convinced them to fall back to safer ground, at least temporarily. Supporting the horse artillerists was Brig. Gen. Lunsford L. Lomax's cavalry, which protected the guns while the infantry threatened them with capture, and while enemy batteries "were pouring canister through the woods furiously."[12]

As the fighting developed it became obvious the guns were in some danger, and Stuart had the 1st North Carolina Cavalry charge the enemy battle line. Although a few enemy soldiers were captured, the effort was rather easily thrown back. Some of Stuart's scouts had managed to slip out the night before and reach army headquarters, and that morning some of Ewell's infantry had made their appearance on the Warrenton Turnpike within supporting distance of Stuart's beleaguered command. The appearance of infantry and daylight provided Stuart with the opportunity and distraction he needed to slip out of the tightening noose by riding quickly around the flank of the Federals. It had been a near-run affair that could have ended badly.

Things did not turn out so well for A. P. Hill's unfortunate infantry. Hill's troops were serving as the column's spearhead on October 14 when they ran into Gouverneur Warren's II Corps, the rear guard of Meade's army, at Bristoe Station along the Orange & Alexandria Railroad. Without taking time to deploy skirmishers and conduct a proper reconnaissance, Hill launched a rash attack into what he thought were retreating enemy troops. Warren was waiting for him and caught the Confederates in a terrible crossfire, cutting them down by the hundreds. One of the most famous quotes of the war followed when Hill and Lee rode over the field that afternoon, the former trying to explain to the latter just how he had made such a critical mistake. Lee listened coldly and answered, "Well, well, General, bury these poor men and let us say no more about it."[13]

Now fully alerted to the threat, Meade retreated quickly toward Manassas, with Stuart's cavalry in pursuit. The next day, October 15, Stuart's troopers found the Union army entrenched across Bull Run Creek. Colonel Owen dismounted his Virginians and skirmished with the Federals while Lomax's cavalry checked the fords and engaged in what he described as "heavy skirmishing," driving their Union counterparts back across Bull Run and into their breastworks. Stuart promptly ordered up his horse artillery to feel out the strength of the Union position. Breathed's three guns and one from Capt. Chew's Battery went into action, dropping trail and opening with shell. Union artillery promptly answered and a sharp counter-battery engagement broke out. Exposed to enfilading fire from the well-positioned batteries on the far side of Bull Run, Breathed's guns were hit hard during this engagement, one was disabled, and several men wounded. While directing the fire, Major Beckham's horse was shot. He was injured when the beast fell to the ground. Recognizing they were in a potentially precarious situation, Chew, now the senior artillerist on the field, ordered Breathed to limber his guns and retreat while Chew's single piece covered his withdrawal.[14]

After pulling back, Stuart and his horsemen camped near Manassas. The two armies spent October 16 eyeing one another until late that evening, when the Federals splashed their way across Bull Run. When Stuart learned the next morning that the Army of the Potomac seemed to be advancing from Groveton he moved to block it. Light skirmishing occupied much of the day with the Confederate cavalry ending their journey with a ride southeast on the Warrenton Turnpike toward Buckland.[15]

With Meade now in a strong position, Lee was unable to execute the plan he had envisioned. The campaign had failed to push Meade back to the north bank of the Potomac. Rather than compound the mistakes already made, Lee turned his army around and headed for the Rappahannock River. At Buckland, the Confederates seized an important ford and bridge, cutting off and capturing a number of the enemy in the process. On the morning of October 19, the cavalry rode toward Auburn by way of Bristoe Station and Catlett Station. A courier informed Colonel Owen that Stuart, in command of Hampton's Division, had been stalled on the Warrenton Turnpike, prompting Fitz Lee to ride to Stuart's assistance. The Union division opposing Stuart was led by his latest would-be nemesis, Judson Kilpatrick. Breathed deployed his guns on either side of the pike and opened fire, supporting Stuart's attack against the front of Kilpatrick's position and Lee's strike against the flank. Henry Matthews helped man the artillery that day, and, when Matthews later described the action, he quotes Lt. P. P. Johnston, of Breathed's Battery as saying, "battery was hotly engaged when Fitz Lee attacked Custer's brigade . . . . The battle was of the most obstinate character, Fitz Lee exerting himself to the utmost to push Custer into Broad [R]un, and Custer seeming to have no thought of retiring."[16]

Breathed's guns were once again pitted against Pennington's Union horse artillery. As usual, Pennington's Regulars served their guns effectively, wounding four men, including two of Breathed's lieutenants, and killing six horses. His accurate fire effectively crippled Breathed's effort to fight effectively, but the determined captain remained at his post and returned fire, refusing to give up the field.[17]

When it looked as though Breathed would have to retire, the sharp fighting ended without warning when, "a cloud arose on the road towards Warrenton, and as suddenly every thing in our front gave way," remembered Matthews. "The mounted men were ordered forward and I saw no more of the enemy." Kilpatrick's men, like they often had during an earlier time, broke and fled, triggering a vigorous pursuit that Stuart and his men later derisively referred to as the "Buckland Races."[18]

Once free from Pennington's debilitating fire, Breathed limbered up his pieces and followed the cavalry, exacting a small measure of revenge by joining the pursuit of the retreating Federals until darkness ended the matter. "Stuart handled Kilpatrick pretty badly that afternoon," observed one of Pennington's section commanders. After the fight ended, Fitz Lee rode up to Breathed and asked, "Breathed, did you develop the enemy? "Yes," replied Breathed, "[and] they enveloped us."[19]

*   *   *

On October 20, Stuart's command marched to the Rappahannock River by way of Auburn, crossing at Beverly's Ford. Lee's infantry was safely south of the river by the end of the day. Breathed camped at Orange Springs, where his exhausted command rested for a few days. By October 30 he had relocated to Welford's Farm. It was now time for worthy officers of the Stuart Horse Artillery to receive promotions richly deserved. "Under the first order of things it was pretty well understood that Moorman and Chew, the two senior Captains of the old battalion, were to be Chiefs of Artillery in their respective divisions," wrote gunner Halsey Wigfall. "Whether this new turn augurs favorably for Breathed's promotion or not, it certainly has that appearance to me." Wigfall was right; a bump in rank was finally coming Breathed's way. Within days

Brig. Gen. William N. Pendleton, the Army of Northern Virginia's chief of artillery, recommended him for promotion to major.[20]

While waiting for his promotion, Breathed relocated his command to Madison Mills where he purchased "one artillery horse for $350.00." Stuart planned another grand review of the cavalry on the John Minor Botts Farm outside Culpeper, and Breathed had to get his command in tip-top shape for the festive occasion. The review was held on November 5, the Southern cavalry dashing past Stuart and General Lee in grandiose style, Beckham's guns passing to the music of Hampton's divisional band. The recently promoted (September 28) Thomas L. Rosser, now a brigadier general in charge of Grumble Jones' old Laurel Brigade, together with Chew's Battery, missed the event. The general and battery were on a reconnaissance of Rappahannock County trying to ascertain Meade's intentions. Would he go into winter quarters or go over to the offensive as Burnside had done a year earlier?[21]

*   *   *

After the close of the Bristoe Campaign, the Army of Northern Virginia encamped on the Orange & Alexandria Railroad near Culpeper Court House. Most of the men assumed the year's campaigning was finally over. They were soon disabused of that notion. Stuart's cavalry spent the days picketing the familiar Rappahannock River fords. As everyone soon discovered, the Army of the Potomac was on the move, having marched out of its camps on November 7. Stuart's scouts detected the movement, but Meade's intentions were not immediately clear.[22]

Showing a dash and style often displayed by Lee's men, Meade's infantry crossed at Kelly's Ford and surprised and overran two infantry brigades stationed on the far side of the river at Rappahannock Station. The lightening attack captured some 1,800 men. Stuart's horse artillery deployed and set down a heavy field of fire that helped prevent enemy infantry from flanking the Confederate position near Fleetwood Hill. The horse artillerists made a determined stand under heavy fire until the cavalry, with Breathed's and McGregor's guns, cobbled together a defensive position another half a mile back, where the men held their position until nightfall on November 8. The attacks and crossings forced Lee to retire to the south bank of the Rapidan River. Stuart, as usual, remained behind to determine Meade's intentions.

The next morning, Breathed moved with some cavalry to cover the Confederate left on the Rixeyville Road, where he was later joined by Shoemaker's Battery. They opened fire on the Union forces before retiring themselves. At least for now, the immediate threat was over, but Meade's aggressive ambitions were not.[23]

Mine Run Campaign

One of General Lee's talents was his ability to anticipate enemy plans and react accordingly. This uncanny skill served him well in November 1863, when one false move could have placed his entire army in serious jeopardy. Lee had aligned his corps carefully behind the Rapidan, with Ewell's line stretching from Clark's Mountain to Mine Run and Hill's line from Orange Court House to Liberty Mills. (Longstreet was still on detached service in the Western Theater.) Stuart's cavalry patrolled the flanks and rear of the army. Reading Northern papers and studying intelligence reports, Lee correctly predicted that Meade would attempt to turn his right flank in the vicinity of Germanna Ford on the Rapidan River. By November 26, Lee's prediction had come true when Stuart's scouts reported to him that the Army of the Potomac was on the move. Lee ordered the Army of Northern Virginia to move to meet the threat, and by 3:00 A.M. on November 27 the army was on the march.

Lee's engineers found a strong defensive position atop a ridge overlooking a tributary of the Rapidan called Mine Run, just a handful of miles from the old Chancellorsville battlefield. As the advance elements of both armies skirmished around Locust Grove on the Orange Turnpike, an entire Confederate division was roughly handled and nearly cut off and destroyed late on November 27 at Payne's Farm when a Federal corps took the wrong road. The meeting engagement would be the only significant fighting of the campaign. The next day, Meade's army appeared in Lee's front and it looked to everyone as if a major battle was about to erupt. Confederate scouts reported that the Army of the Potomac was preparing for a massive frontal assault on Lee's position. In search of a vulnerable point in the lines the two armies stared each other down for three days while Meade studied his enemy. Finally, on December 1, he admitted that Lee's line was invulnerable and ordered a withdrawal

Germanna Ford on the Rapidan River, Virginia.

across the Rapidan. Lee was chafing a bit at the lost opportunity to strike a blow before winter. Consequently, he ordered an assault on the Union lines for December 2, only to find the Federals gone. "I am too old to command this army," declared a thoroughly frustrated Lee. "We should never have permitted those people to get away."[24]

*   *   *

On December 21 the horse artillery moved to Rio Hill, just to the north of Charlottesville, where the artillerists settled into winter quarters. Lee's infantry settled into camps along the Rapidan. The men of the horse artillery built comfortable huts with chimneys and canvas roofs and settled down for what they believed would be several months of peace and quiet. Each hut held at least six men, and the gunners enjoyed their well-deserved rest and the hospitality of the friendly local populace, who occasionally gave the grateful soldiers the luxury of a home-cooked meal. Their horses were likewise better provided for, even if they did not always get enough to eat.[25]

While Breathed enjoyed a peaceful winter, his brother Isaac had a much less pleasant experience. At age 16, Isaac had joined the 43rd Battalion of Virginia Cavalry on November 20, 1862. Its commander was

John Singleton Mosby, who became one of the most famous Confederate partisan leaders of the war. In the summer of 1863 Isaac had met General Lee who, upon learning that Jim Breathed was his brother, told him, "You may well be proud of being a brother of Captain Breathed's [for] he is one of the most gallant and bravest of Officers of my Army!"[26]

On December 12, Isaac was captured in northern Virginia by a party of enemy riders. Because he was not wearing a proper uniform, his captors believed he was a spy and sent him to Old Capitol Prison in Washington to await his fate. After three long months of captivity Isaac was freed and eventually decided to move west. In the years after the Civil War, he joined the United States Army and was stationed at Fort Laramie, Wyoming, where as a corporal he fought Indians and went on to have a long military career. [27]

Major Beckham had embarked on the Mine Run Campaign with the following batteries of horse artillery: Capt. James Breathed, Breathed's (Virginia) Battery; Capt. James F. Hart, Hart's (South Carolina) Battery; Capt. R. P. Chew, Chew's (Virginia) Battery; Capt. W. M. McGregor, McGregor's (Virginia) Battery and Capt. M. N. Moorman, Moorman's (Virginia) Battery. Most of these men and guns would be with the Army of Northern Virginia in some capacity when the Spring 1864 campaign opened, but Beckham would not. Beckham had been recommended for advancement in rank to Lieutenant Colonel, but the number of men in the horse artillery was too few to be commanded by someone of that rank, therefore, Beckham would have to leave. His leaving meant that the horse artillery would need a new commander, and Breathed was in the running to fill one of the slots.[28]

Like any military unit, Stuart's Horse Artillery had its own political issues, and Beckham's pending promotion and transfer (if the men knew of it at that time) would only have added fuel to the fire. Lieutenant Wigfall, the son of the prominent Southern politician, was acutely aware of the political considerations. "Gen. Stuart has recommended four of the Captains of the batteries for Majorities: Hart on his own application and to be assigned elsewhere and possibly Moorman. Breathed, and Chew are the other two," he informed his father a few days before Christmas. "General Stuart has made so many recommendations for promotion at different times and of different officers that it has come to be regarded as by no means an indication that an officer will be promoted [just] because he has General Stuart's recommendation."[29]

Tracking promotions in the Armies of the Confederacy can be a very tricky business. The recommendation for promotion would most frequently be made some months before the promotion. However, if the promotion was actually approved, the date of promotion frequently preceded the date of the approval and sometimes the date of the recommendation. This was particularly true in Stuart's command.

In time, the promotions for the horse artillerists came through. Beckham would be elevated to lieutenant colonel. Beckham was transferred (for a short time) to command a battalion of artillery attached to the I Corps. On February 16, 1864, Lt. Col. Beckham was transferred to the Army of Tennessee. The capable artillerist who had stamped his own style of leadership onto the horse artillery was slated to assume the more difficult position of chief-of-artillery for Stephen D. Lee's infantry corps. As he did in Virginia, Beckham distinguished himself during the long withdrawal to Atlanta and the battles around that important city before heading north with General John Bell Hood as part of his unfortunate invasion of Tennessee in late 1864. On November 29, 1864, the always gallant Beckham—young, handsome, and capable—would suffer a mortal head wound in an inconsequential exchange of gunfire at Columbia, Tennessee, linger for an agonizing six days, and then expire on the 5th of December.

The capable Lieutenant Wigfall was also transferred, for he desperately wanted a promotion and did not think one possible or likely while still serving in the Stuart Horse Artillery. Like his friend Beckham, he too traveled West and eventually achieved the rank of major as an aide-de-camp to Gen. Joseph E. Johnston. [30]

The question of Moorman's, Chew's, and Breathed's promotions were tied up with the question of who would be the next commander of the horse artillery. There was only room for one Major in the horse artillery at this time. However, before the question of command would be decided, another test of the officers and men of the Stuart Horse Artillery was in the offing.[31]

*   *   *

The horse artillerists settled into the monotony of their winter routine at Rio Hill. Finding adequate forage for their mounts was a constant challenge. When the army failed to provide sufficient forage, the artillerists were left to their own devices, frequently "requisitioning" forage from nearby farmers. "Many a night have we started out on an expedition in quest of forage (when graveyards yawn) to visit some unsuspecting Albemarle farmer in order that we might obtain some fodder, by any means, for our dear old horses," Henry Matthews fondly recalled. "And when in the morning our camp was visited by the aforesaid farmer, bent on finding the midnight marauders, we had been convulsed with laughter by [the] indignant manner in which Capt. Breathed would dismiss him, with the assurance that the men in his battery were all gentlemen, and did not do such naughty things. At the same time Bill, the horse of Breathed's, was quietly nibbling on some of that identical fodder." In order to maximize the available resources, Breathed sent some of his men to visit their homes and families.[32]

The unvaried routine of winter camp life was rudely interrupted on the only February 29 of the war, a cold day when Union cavalrymen unexpectedly appeared in front of Rio Hill. The energetic, if personally unlikable, Judson Kilpatrick had proposed a dangerous multi-pronged raid on Richmond intended to free Union prisoners of war being held at Belle Isle and Libby Prison. The plan was approved over the objections of Alfred Pleasonton, who thought it unworkable and dangerous. As a diversion, 500 hand-picked troopers under Brig. Gen. George A. Custer would raid into Albemarle County to cut the Virginia Central Railroad. It was hoped his thrust would confuse the Confederate high command as to the expedition's true purpose. Meade reluctantly approved the affair although he was skeptical about its prospects for success. The raid commenced on February 28, with Kilpatrick heading east toward Richmond with his division and Custer heading toward the Shenandoah Valley.[33]

Just after noon on February 29, Lt. James N. Cunningham of the 1st Virginia Cavalry galloped into camp with the unwelcome news that a large body of enemy cavalry was approaching. Cunningham had closely observed Custer's men and their movements, and had ridden directly to the Stuart Horse Artillery camp to report the danger. "Camp was at once notified and pickets sent forward to Rio Bridge, 1¼ miles north, but before they arrived the enemy had crossed and held the bridge," reported Capt. Marcellus N. Moorman.[34]

About the same time, another column was revealed. Union horsemen were headed for Cook's Ford, not far from Rio Bridge. Just who was issuing orders and who was obeying them in the surprised horse artillery camp depends upon who was writing their account. Moorman later stated that at the time he believed the whole command could not be assembled and moved effectively before the Union troopers arrived at the camp, so he instead ordered his guns to open fire while the rest of the guns limbered up and moved to a safer location. Whether Moorman issued orders or not, wandering horses were gathered up, hitched, and the guns were moved. In the event, the guns moved out quickly, except for four guns that remained in the camp. The rescued guns re-deployed on a hill above the campground while skirmishers armed with pistols went out to try and slow the Federal forces. These men soon came flying back to camp with a large body of enemy cavalry in their rear.[35]

Moorman related in his after action report how he left mounted men to support the four guns remaining in the camp, galloped off with Chew and Breathed to guard the flank. "Just at the moment when the enemy's columns which had crossed at Cook's Ford had reached and set fire to our camp, their right, which had crossed at Rio, made a charge just in time to receive and mistake the explosion of one of Captain Chew's caissons for the reopening of our guns, for they had just ceased firing at that point," he reported. Confused hand-to-hand combat broke out, prompting Chew and Breathed to rally their artillerists for a mounted charge. "They opened upon us two pieces of artillery, to which I made no reply," reported Moorman. "Much credit is due both to officers and men for their coolness, bravery, and self-sacrifice, leaving clothing, blankets, and all for their guns."[36]

The unexpectedly stout resistance of the artillerymen baffled Custer and his men. Spotting the mounted horse artillerists from a mile away, Custer believed that they were "a superior force of the enemy's cavalry, four batteries of artillery, in position, and a heavy force of infantry." However, there was no Confederate cavalry or infantry—Stuart Horse Artillery gunners were all that opposed Custer's horsemen this day when his men raided the Confederate artillerists cannon and camp. [37]

Captain Joseph P. Ash of the 5th U. S. Cavalry, with 65 men, were sent to find out what force lay in Custer's front. Ash's Regulars captured six caissons full of ammunition, two forges, and equipment, and destroyed the Confederate camp. Ash's efforts to interrogate his prisoners came to naught, and he decided that the prudent course would be to withdraw. Custer became convinced that his force was not strong enough to mount a counterattack with his back against the Rivanna River. Meanwhile, the Confederate artillerists steadily rained shot and shell on the Federal position.[38]

Breathed's part in the action was not small. "Breathed had been lounging like the rest, laughing and talking with the men. Peril made him suddenly king, and sabre in hand, he rushed to the guns, calling to his men to follow. Breathed wheeled a gun around, trained the piece to bear upon the Federal cavalry and drove home a charge," recalled an observer. When the Federals drew within fifty yards of his position, Breathed bellowed, "Men, you have fought around these guns in many battles! Your first and only duty is to die by them. Will you do it?" A chorus of elated voices rang out in support of Breathed, whose courage inspired the artillerymen to shred the oncoming Federal troopers with canister. Breathed was reportedly everywhere, and was impervious to the heavy fire of the Union artillery. Eventually the bravado of the Union troopers diminished. When Breathed called out the command "Mount!" twenty men followed his lead, armed themselves with sabers, clubs, and fence rails scavenged from camp fire sites.[39]

Stuart's staff officer, Capt. John Esten Cooke, left another account of the event. "Breathed seized the moment and jumped upon one of the hastily saddled horses. As the drivers disappeared, his own horse was shot under him, staggered, sunk, and rolled upon him," he wrote. "Breathed dragged himself from beneath the bleeding animal, rose to his feet, and rushing to the lead horses of the gun, leaped upon one of them, and struck them jointly with his sabre to force them on." After finding another mount, Breathed recovered his wits and "'roared out Charge!' and at the forefront of his men he led a headlong charge at the Federal cavalry." As enemy horsemen dashed in, one stopped at a caisson and shouted, "Ah, you dirty rebels, we've got your camp." Breathed, offended by the taunt, angrily retorted, "yes, you infernal scoundrels, you've got it; but you shall not hold it." With two of his gunners, Breathed opened fire upon the enemy horsemen with revolvers. The enemy replied with a volley of carbine fire. A burning caisson then exploded, that deafened all who heard the blast.[40]

Breathed led the charge all the way to Barboursville, and was pursuing the Federals for twenty-four hours and chasing them back across the Rivanna River. "While passing Barbourville one of the Federals stopped to get a drink of water at the house of a citizen. This concerned citizen asked the Federal 'What's the matter?' he replied 'We are retreating', the citizen then asked 'Who is after you?' and the reply was: 'Nobody but old Jim Breathed and his men, armed with fence rails.'" Chew, Breathed, and the proud artillerymen had routed an entire brigade of enemy cavalry. [41]

Considering all the claims that Moorman made as to his prowess on Rio Hill, and in light of the histrionic account of Breathed's gallantry left by the past and future novelist, John Esten Cooke, it is worthwhile to consider how the battle looked to George M. Neese, a gunner in Chew's Battery whose diary for that day reads as follows:

> February 29—To-day the Yankees attempted a raid on Charlottesville and the Virginia Central Railroad. A force of about twenty-five hundred cavalry [sic 1,500] and two pieces of artillery, all under the command of General Custer, advanced on the Earleysville road and came within one mile of our camp before we were apprised of their approach. They were then advancing rapidly, and we were wholly unprepared for any such winter surprise in this part of the country. However, we hurriedly mixed up a drastic dose and administered it under unfavorable and difficult circumstances, yet it eventually had the effect of saving Charlottesville from the hands of the marauders. The raiders rushed in so suddenly on our camp that we had no time for preparation, even for a forced leaving, consequently many of our company lost all their baggage, and some of the men even lost their blankets. Our artillery horses were scattered all over the fields and we had scarcely time to get our guns out before the Yanks were right on us; in fact we had to fire some of our pieces in park, before we had our horses hitched up, in order to check the oncoming raiders long enough to give us a little precious time to say good-bye to our winter quarters and get our guns moved to a more advantageous situation. As it was, we had to leave our caissons in the tender care of the enemy, and abandoned all baggage and kitchen utensils.
>
> By the time we had our horses hitched to the pieces and were ready to move, bluecoated horsemen were riding excitedly among our quarters, firing their pistols and brandishing their sabers, trying to play thunder in general with the horse artillery. We rapidly got our guns out and to a good position, and opened a rapid fire on our own camp, which was then full of Yankee cavalrymen destroying our winter home.
>
> Our artillery fire completely checked the raiders, and they did not proceed any farther in the direction of Charlottesville than our camp. We had no support whatever in the way of sharpshooters or

cavalry, and about two hundred horse artillerymen, including the lame, sick, and Company Q, with no sabers, very few pistols, and one old battle flag, with our guns successfully defended Charlottesville. . . . A little strategy seasoned with a large proportion of the finest kind of deception were the principal weapons and instruments with which the backbone was entirely and efficiently extracted from the great Custer's raid on destruction bent, without bloodshed on our side.

The undoing of General Custer's raid was accomplished in the following manner: We had sixteen guns in our battalion, all in position and ready for action after we got out of our camp. The guns in the artillery were served with as few men as possible, and Captains Breathed and Chew formed the remainder of the artillerymen into a newly composed regiment of cavalry, and drew them up in battle array just in rear of the artillery, with an old Confederate battle flag waving over the center of the pseudo cavalry line. There was not one rifle or carbine in the whole crew, a few pistols and one or two sabers composing all the dangerous arms; the rest of the men had sticks and clubs. Some of them had pieces of fence rails, and all sorts of representative sabers and carbines were on exhibition to make the command appear warlike, formidable, and dangerous. We kept up a rapid artillery fire until the enemy's cavalry begun to waver and retire toward the Rivanna. When they got beyond the range of our guns our motley cavalcade advanced and retired the enemy beyond the Rivanna. As a parting deception, with good effect, Captain Chew called out with a loud voice and commanding tone: "Tell Colonel Dulaney to bring up the Seventh Regiment." The Yankees heard it and struck for the safe side of the Rivanna. That ended the last act of the raid. Colonel Dulaney's regiment is at Mount Crawford in the Shenandoah Valley, but calling for it in the range of a Yankee's ear had the desired effect of discomfiting the doughty raiders at their last stand on our side of the Rivanna. The whole Yankee force retired beyond the Rivanna late this evening.[42]

The disparities between the Moorman, Cooke, and Neese accounts of the action at Rio Hill are indicative of how hard it is to establish details in confused cavalry actions. However, Stuart was sufficiently impressed with Breathed's conduct to acknowledge it in a letter. "I am sensible of the distinguished gallantry which you have always displayed when brought in contact with the enemy, and can also assure you of its appreciation by the commanding General. I feel confident that you will soon be promoted. Labor to get your battery in fighting and flying trim as soon as possible," wrote a grateful Stuart a few days later. "Your conduct in the late attempt of the enemy at Rio Mills to seize your guns was in keeping with heroism, which has distinguished your career as a soldier, and I regret that necessary absence from my headquarters prevented me from seeing you on your recent visit, and expressing to you in person, as I wished, my congratulations upon your achievement, as well as my high appreciation of your gallantry."[43]

The daring actions of Breathed, Chew, and Moorman did not go recognized by the local populace. On March 7, they received the thanks of the residents of Charlottesville. For this and other deeds of daring, the ladies of the town presented Breathed with a handsome new silk flag (which, if Neese's description of the old battle flag is correct, was sorely needed). "This community knowing the service you performed recently in turning the enemy back from their recent advance upon this place, have learned with great regret that you have not been promoted as you deserve to be, in the recent promotions among Stuart's Horse Artillery," read the letter transmitting the gift. "You did more to serve our town and neighborhood than any other person whom so ever and this fact is known to every person here. You were more than brave, you risked yourself for our safety; and you led the gallant men under your command." The letter declared, "This community at least will never forget you. We recognize in you the tune 'Griadia certain essin' which we have seen illustrated in few others. Now if you wish to transfer your efforts to another theatre where they will be better appreciated than in the Horse Artillery; if you will let your friends of Charlottesville and vicinity know this fact, there is no statement, regarding your value as man and officer, they will not make and must conscientiously make, to forward your wishes. As to me you may count on me as a friend forever."[44]

The new flag waved above the Stuart Horse Artillery guns until the sun rose over the field at Appomattox Court House.

Custer's raid into Albemarle County had accomplished nothing, and he had permitted Breathed and a few hundred cannoneers to run him off. The victorious horse artillerymen then moved their camp north of Gordonsville, where they could protect both the Virginia Central and Orange & Alexandria Railroads.[45]

*   *   *

Jefferson County Museum, Charles Town, WV

The flag presented by the women of Charlottesville, Virginia,
to the Stuart Horse Artillery.

On March 20, horse artillerists moved to the Bolling Haxall Farm, north of Gordonsville. A few days later, Stuart recommended Breathed for promotion to major. On March 24, Stuart wrote:

> I respectfully recommend that Captain James Breathed, Stuart Horse Artillery, be appointed Major and assigned to duty with the Horse Artillery of this command for the following reasons:
>
> First, the exhibition of extraordinary valor and skill on many occasions but especially on the 29th of February near Charlottesville where his guns unsupported, were mainly instrumental in checking and driving back a large column of the enemy's cavalry under General Custer, destined to cooperate in the diabolical scheme of Kilpatrick and Dahlgren.
>
> Second, because the Stuart Horse Artillery from the time of its inception under the 'gallant Pelham' has done more fighting than any other Artillery in this service. The Captains, however, have not been advanced in promotion with equal step with their comrades of the foot Artillery. The officers feel this is an unmerited slight, and in this particular case, where Captain Breathed has been so conspicuously daring, I feel justified in asking for his promotion on

special grounds, so bare equal dated with the appointments lately made in Artillery.

Third, Lt. Colonel Dearing assigned to command of the Horse Artillery, has command of a regiment of cavalry south of James River, and I was informed by him in February that he preferred it to such a command, but even if he accept, Gen. Johnson has recently applied for Artillery officers form this Army which will make vacancies of the general schedule justifying Captain Breathed's promotion under the law. This matter is surely the serious attention of the Department of War, and I respectfully solicit early action. Major Chew is the only field officer on duty with the battalion.

Judging by the contents of Stuart's recommendation for promotion for Breathed, Chew must have already received his Majority.[46]

It is not unlikely that the incidents at Rio Hill helped determine who would command the Stuart Horse Artillery. The Secretary of War also had plans for the leadership of the Stuart Horse Artillery; Lt. Col. James Dearing was assigned to lead the horse artillery. However, he declined to accept the assignment unless he was permitted to retain his present rank. When Stuart learned that Dearing had adopted such an attitude, he quickly moved to have the order canceled.

Lynchburg Battery commander Marcellus Moorman was a candidate for the position. Moorman, although senior to both Chew and Breathed, was never popular with the cavalry. Instead of being placed in command of the Stuart Horse Artillery, Moorman was promoted to major and offered a battalion of artillery in Ewell's II Corps.[47]

The transfer of Moorman left Stuart free to recommend Major Chew to fill the vacancy at the head of the horse artillery. General Lee agreed, and Chew assumed command of the battalion.[48]

Breathed, however, was not forgotten in the command shuffle. On April 7, General Lee recommended his promotion. On April 22, Breathed was made a major, with an effective date of February 27, 1864. He accepted the promotion on April 29 and reported to Stuart to assume command of his battery. (Hart would not be promoted to major until March 1865, when Pendleton reorganized the horse artillery.)[49]

The weather was warming and the roads were drying out. The spring campaigning season was calling.

Chapter 10

From the Wilderness
to Spotsylvania

The Army of Northern Virginia was reorganized over the winter of 1863-1864, including the Cavalry. Just before the Grant launched what would become known as the "Overland Campaign," the Cavalry of the Army of Northern Virginia was re-organized as follows:

Cavalry Corps: Maj. Gen. James E. B. Stuart

Hampton's Division
Maj. Gen. Wade Hampton

Young's Brigade: Brig. Gen. Pierce M. B. Young
7th Ga. Cav., Lt. Col. Joseph L. McAllister
Cobb's Legion, Col. Gilbert J. Wright
Phillips Legion, Capt. Hugh Buchanan
20th Ga. Cav. Bn., Lt. Col. John M. Millen
Jeff Davis Legion, Col. J. Frederick Waring

Rosser's Brigade, Brig. Gen. Thomas L. Rosser
7th Va. Cav., Lt. Col. Richard H. Dulany
11th Va. Cav., Col. Oliver R. Funsten, Sr.
12 Va. Cav., Lt. Col. Thomas B. Massie

35th Va. Cav. Bn., Lt. Col. Elijah Viers White
Dismounted Cavalry, Maj. Edward H. McDonald
Butler's Brigade: Brig. Gen. Matthew C. Butler
1st SC Cav., Col. John L. Black
2nd SC Cav., Col. Thomas J. Lipscomb
4th SC Cav., Col. Benjamin H. Rutledge
5th SC Cav., Col. John Dunovant
6th SC Cav., Col. Hugh K. Aiken

Fitzhugh Lee's Division
Maj. Gen. Fitzhugh Lee

Wickham's Brigade: Brig. Gen. Williams C. Wickham
1st Va. Cav., Lt. Col. William A Morgan
2nd Va. Cav., Col. Thomas T. Munford
3rd Va. Cav., Col. Thomas H. Owen
4th Va. Cav., Col. William H. F. Payne

Lomax's Brigade: Brig. Gen. Lunsford L. Lomax
5th Va. Cav., Col. Henry Clay Pate
6th Va. Cav., Lt. Col. John S. Green
15th Va. Cav., Col. Charles R. Collins
1st Md. Cav., Bn., Col. Bradley T. Johnson

Rooney Lee's Division
Maj. Gen. William H. F. "Rooney" Lee

Chambliss' Brigade: Brig. Gen. John R. Chambliss, Jr.
9th Va. Cav., Col. Richard L. T. Beale
10th Va. Cav., Col. J. Lucius Davis
13th Va. Cav., Col. Jefferson C. Phillips

Gordon's Brigade: Brig. Gen. James B. Gordon
1st NC Cav., Col. William H. Cheek
2nd NC Cav., Col. Clinton M. Andrews
3rd NC Cav., Col. John A. Baker
4th NC Cav., Col. Dennis D. Ferebee
5th NC Cav., Lt. Col. Stephan B. Evans
Gary's Command: Brig. Gen. Martin W. Gary
7th SC Cav., Lt. Col. Alexander C. Haskell
Hampton Legion (after 5/19/64), Lt. Col. R. B. Arnold

The Stuart Horse Artillery was organized as follows:

Horse Artillery: Maj. Roger Preston Chew
Breathed's Artillery Bn., Maj. James Breathed
1st Stuart Horse Artillery, Capt. Philip Preston Johnston
2nd Stuart Horse Artillery, Capt. William M. McGregor
Hart's Battery, Capt. James F. Hart
Chew's Battery, Capt. James W. Thomson
Lynchburg Artillery, Capt. John J. Shoemaker
2nd Baltimore Light Artillery, Capt. William H. Griffin

Breathed and Chew worked together well, and the new arrangement was promising. Stuart began 1864 optimistically, writing to his brother, "that he thinks the chances of the Confederacy are as good as they ever were if we learn from our mistakes and make the most of our resources."[1]

Even though the horse artillery batteries were assigned to the same battalion, the units were not stationed together when the Federal Spring offensive began. Chew and Breathed were just north of Gordonsville with Johnson's, McGregor's, Thomson's, and Shoemaker's Batteries. Hart's Battery was located at Milford Station, near Fredericksburg. Griffin's Battery, stationed near Hanover Junction, was still attached to the "Maryland Line." This geographic dispersal made command a challenge.[2]

This extremely competent and bold band of horse artillerists was about to face its greatest test to date. Ulysses S. Grant, who had enjoyed great success in the Western Theater, was brought east by President Lincoln, promoted to lieutenant general, and given command of all of the armies of the United States of America. Grant designed a plan for the spring campaign that would place unrelenting pressure on the armies of the Confederacy by launching coordinated attacks on every front, thereby preventing the Confederates from shifting their already thin resources to meet threats. Grant himself would maintain his headquarters with the Army of the Potomac, which would remain under the command of Maj. Gen. George G. Meade.

Grant's Spring campaign would try to advance on Richmond via the Wilderness, a densely tangled region of secondary growth that had been the site of much of the 1863 Battle of Chancellorsville. The Army of the Potomac broke its winter camp at the end of April and hit the road,

LC

Lieutenant General Ulysses S. Grant.

splashing across the Rapidan River at Germanna Ford. The Confederate horse artillery faced a heavy task in the coming campaign. It was outgunned by the Federal horse artillery, but good management and the courage of the individual soldiers who manned its guns gave Chew's and Breathed's gunners the ability to confront the enemy on a more equal footing. More than once, these intrepid artillerists stood alone against the Army of the Potomac that Spring.

Robert E. Lee, who was a tactical master, made brilliant use of the tangled terrain of the Wilderness to even the odds. The nature of the terrain prevented Grant from massing his forces, and ultimately enabled Lee to defeat Grant in the Wilderness even though his army was much smaller. The Wilderness was just the beginning of what proved to be the bloodiest and most demanding series of fights ever experienced by the soldiers of either side. James Breathed and his reliable cannoneers made their mark on this epic campaign.[3]

* * *

Politics also played a major role in the reorganization of the Army of Northern Virginia. Maryland units had suffered greatly during the Gettysburg Campaign, prompting the Confederate War Department to form the "Maryland Line" as a gesture to acknowledge the important role of Maryland in the Confederacy. Brig. Gen. Bradley T. Johnson would command the Maryland Line. The challenge lay in finding sufficient Maryland troops to fill the new unit's ranks.[4]

The high command of the Army of Northern Virginia scoured the ranks for soldiers who were native Marylanders, and Breathed's name came to the attention of the recruiters. Breathed, who was content with his present assignment, was not interested in a transfer into the Maryland Line—he was, after all, a native Virginian. In defiance of the command structure, the Maryland Line was to be under General P. G. T. Beauregard's command and assigned a defensive role east of Richmond. It was not a place for a horse artillery commander of Breathed's competence and fighting spirit to apply his talents.

Stuart promptly took steps to keep Breathed with his command. He asked that the men of Breathed's old Battery not have to transfer from the Stuart Horse Artillery. He said, "This battery as well as McGregor's was, during the first year of the war, organized under the auspices of the Governor of Virginia as a part of the State troops, and enlisted for the war, the officers receiving their commissions from the Governor of the State. Under the immortal Pelham it received large accessions by recruits from Maryland, and while Captain Breathed remained with it, 3 of its 4 officers were natives of that State," wrote Stuart. "Thus have these men, though enlisted for the war in a Virginia organization, been under officers from their own State, and this will continue to be the case, as the officer who succeeds Major Breathed in the command of this battery is also a native of Maryland." He also argued that the transfer of such an important command at the outset of a campaign would cripple the horse artillery with no corresponding gain to any other branch of the service. "I visited this battery yesterday, and find that many of the men are changing their opinions, and, desiring to remain in that company, are requesting that the order for their transfer be revoked," concluded Stuart.[5]

The movement of the Army of the Potomac toward the Rapidan River caused this discussion to become moot. Breathed's guns were soon needed for the coming campaign, and Breathed would play a major role in a string of Confederate victories, justifying Stuart's faith in him.

*   *   *

Grant's Spring 1864 campaign was unlike any yet seen in this brutal war. The traditional pattern had been for a Northern general to advance toward Richmond, suffer a repulse, and then fall back to lick his wounds. Grant, however, was not like the other Northern generals. He was determined to press on, no matter what. His object was Lee's Army of Northern Virginia, and not the Confederate capital at Richmond. "This was the opening of the grandest campaign of the war, and one in which General Lee showed himself the foremost and greatest of masters of war" remembered an officer of the 12th Virginia Cavalry. "The tactics of Grant were different from those of any of his predecessors...he did not retreat, but continued to hurl his broken columns against our [Confederate] impregnable lines, merely moving slowly by the left flank." Hence, the campaign—the bloodiest of the war—was more like a single running battle with a series of names than a series of separate major battles. Names like Wilderness, Spotsylvania, Yellow Tavern, North Anna, and Cold Harbor were burned into the public conscience.[6]

Grant took the field with 120,000 men of the Army of the Potomac and Maj. Gen. Ambrose E. Burnside's IX Corps, while General Lee had only 61,000 Confederates under arms. Lee's army had to contend with shortages of food, clothing, weapons, ammunition, forage, and horseflesh. Draft animals had to be used sparingly to conserve horseflesh. Thus, the odds were definitely stacked against Lee's army, which had only Lee's superb leadership and the plucky determination of the Confederate soldier as obvious advantages. Lee also had to keep his army between Grant and Richmond. General Lee wrote to one of his generals "I think every preparation should be made to meet the approaching storm, which will apparently burst on Virginia." Future historians would soon refer to the campaign as The Overland Campaign.[7]

In 1882, a Confederate soldier recalled, "Everybody remembers how we used to talk about 'one Confederate whipping a dozen Yankees.' Literally true sometimes, but, generally speaking, two to one made hard work for the boys." In addition, the ragged Confederate forces went into battle fired with religious fervor incited by a Great Revival then in full swing in the Confederate Army. One lieutenant of the 35th Virginia Cavalry was heard to say, "that whatever was foreordained, by the Almighty would be accomplished, and if we were intended to be killed there we couldn't help it." However, he also said, "on the other hand, if our time had not yet been fulfilled according to God's predestined plan, we were safe, although a thousand cannon should open their thunder upon us; and in this comfortable doctrine (under the circumstances) the Captain readily acquiesced, greatly to the gratification of Colonel [Elijah Viers] White, [who after the war became a minister in Leesburg, Virginia] who in religious opinion was an Old School Baptist." Lee's soldiers attended religious services with a frequency and piety seldom seen in the annals of warfare. Believing that they had God on their side, the Confederate soldiers unfurled their red battle flags and prepared to give battle. The only question was: where would Grant strike?[8]

* * *

By May 1, Stuart's diligent scouts had detected the movement of Grant's huge army. Hampton's troopers, responsible for picketing that sector, did what they could to hold back Grant's advance, and then retired to report to Stuart that the entire Army of the Potomac was on the move. Consequently, Stuart was able to provide General Lee with a steady flow of good intelligence in relation to the whereabouts and movements of the Army of the Potomac, which, in turn, gave Lee an opportunity to develop a strategy for stopping Grant.[9]

On May 4, cavalry scouts informed General Lee that the Union "Infantry, artillery, and cavalry are moving toward Germanna and Ely's fords. This army in motion toward Mine Run" in strength, with the Union army headed toward Chancellorsville. Lee's troops were massed to the south and west of Chancellorsville. However, Lee knew that if Grant could get his huge army into the open fields south and east of the Wilderness, the Army of Northern Virginia would be at a dangerous disadvantage. Lee realized that bringing Grant to battle in the tangled Wilderness would even the odds. The underbrush in the Wilderness was so thick that a soldier could stand in the middle of a road and barely see ten yards to his front; off-road visibility was much worse. The thick brush would make command and control of troops difficult, but the terrain definitely favored Lee's army. To make things worse, this particular year the Wilderness was bone dry, making it prone to fire.[10]

The majority of Stuart's Cavalry was to the east of Grant, too far away to quickly join forces with Lee. Only Rosser's Brigade (which Rosser had named the Laurel Brigade) and a few batteries of horse artillery were close enough to contest Grant's advance. Lee now ordered the rest of the cavalry and horse artillery to congregate to the east of Grant and to stall the Union forces until Lee's infantry, moving toward the Wilderness from the south and west, was able to meet and engage the enemy. "I heard to-day that the Yankee army is crossing the Rapidan in great force," recalled artillerist George Neese, a gunner in Thomson's Battery, "and that General Lee is on the march to meet it; if that is true, we will soon be in the middle of some bloody work. This evening at sunset we broke camp and are now marching to the front. Farewell, my peaceful cabin."[11]

On May 5, one of the Laurel Brigade troopers reported that the morning "opened calm and still, and there was no sign by which men could judge of the bloody day before them, for literally all was 'quiet along the lines,' but the quiet of the scene was oppressive in its extreme stillness, and the sun rolled like an immense ball of barely red hot iron, seeming to be almost touching the tops of the pine trees under which lay the "Laurel Brigade," unrefreshed by even the quiet repose of the past night." The troopers responded to "boots and saddles" as soon as their eyes opened and soon began to attack the Union flank. Rosser's Brigade moved out toward the Catharpin Road near Shady Grove Church, a few miles from Brig. Gen. James H. Wilson's Third Division of the Army of the Potomac's Cavalry Corps.[12]

Wilson's Division marched down the Orange Plank Road, turning east at Parker's Store and continuing until it reached the Catharpin Road. Rosser's skirmishers first clashed with Wilson's troopers at Craig's Meeting House, about a mile southwest of Shady Grove Church on the Catharpin Road. Wilson dismounted his troopers, who drove Rosser's skirmishers back. Wilson brought Pennington's excellent battery of horse artillery to bear, as well as Union artillerist Fitzhugh's Battery, giving Wilson twelve guns to his disposal. The advancing Army of the Potomac was now protected to the front and right flank. [13]

Responding, Chew and Breathed led Johnston's, Thomson's (formerly Chew's), and Shoemaker's Batteries into the Wilderness.

Brigadier General James H. Wilson, commander of the Union Third Cavalry Division.

LC

Chew quickly realized that the thick undergrowth would make it difficult to deploy all of his guns to advantage. Reacting to the threat to the brigade his guns had supported for so long, Chew took a section of two rifled guns of Thomson's Battery to reinforce Rosser, while Breathed and the other batteries remained at the Allman Farm on the Catharpin Road, awaiting orders.[14]

Rosser's men pushed forward into the withering fire of the twelve Union guns stationed close to Craig's Meeting House on the Catharpin Road. Shrapnel and canister were taking a toll among the Confederate troopers. Chew's two guns arrived at that moment. The Union "shrapnel shot exploded all around and over us, and the everlasting ping and thud of slugs, balls, and fragments of shell filled the air with horrid screams for an hour, and the death-dealing mixture tore and raked up the sod all around us like a raging storm of iron hail," recalled a private of Chew's Battery.[15]

Rosser's Confederate troopers charged headlong into the Union artillery. As the melee raged in the road, "Breathed rode up with the rest of the guns and pursued the retiring enemy with Rosser's troopers." Breathed unleashed the batteries of Johnston's, the rest of Thomson's, and one gun of Shoemaker's battery. Even with additional support from Breathed's guns, Rosser's horsemen continued to have a difficult time of it. "The field that we were in was covered with dry broom-sedge about two feet high, and the cowardly Yanks, although they had the best position and eight pieces to our two, attempted to drive us from the field by setting the dry broom-sedge on fire" remembered gunner Neese, "by shooting some kind of a something of the firework family at us, which, from its appearance as it came flying slowly and emitting a thick volume of inky black smoke, and blazing with glaring red fire, looked like a little bunch of hell. It ignited the grass, which burnt rapidly all over the field and right around, and even under our guns, but we stuck to our position and kept up our fire on the Yankee battery." Screams of wounded men unable to escape from the advancing flames filled the air.[16]

What happened next is a matter of dispute, or perhaps, perspective. About this time as "pistol and sabre were busy in slaughter, while the shrieks of the stricken and the shouts of the victors mingled with the roar of battle," Wilson learned that he could not retire by the same route he had used to get to the battlefield because Confederate troops now occupied the intersection of the Orange Plank Road and the Parker's Store Road. Wilson was unsure whether these Confederate troops were cavalry or infantry (in fact, it was A. P. Hill's entire Corps), but he knew he had lost contact with the Union army. Consequently, Wilson claimed that he retreated because he was separated from the main body of troopers, while Rosser's troops thought that they were driving Wilson's troopers from the field. Whichever caused the withdrawal, Wilson ordered his tired troopers to fall back to his reserves at Robertson's Run, where they found safety.[17]

LC

Earthworks along the Brock Road in the Wilderness.

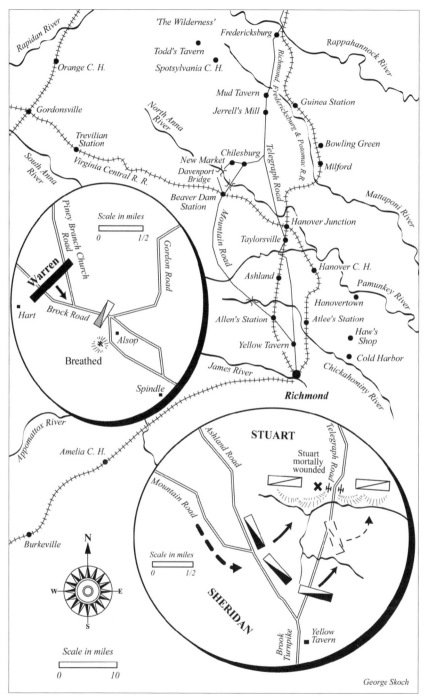

Stuart's Cavalry in the Overland Campaign
and the Battle of Yellow Tavern.

"About 2 o'clock General Rosser succeeded in driving the Yankees from their position, and at once pushed his brigade rapidly forward" remembered a trooper of White's Battalion. Rosser did not intend to allow Wilson to retire unmolested. His cavalry and Breathed's guns pursued Wilson up the Catharpin Road, past Shady Grove Church. Rosser's troopers finally carried the day, pushing Wilson back to Robertson's Run and cutting him off from the rest of the Union line. Rosser controlled the Catharpin Road, meaning that Wilson would have to find a way out through the back roads of the Wilderness. Things were looking very bleak for the Union horsemen. The tight Confederate noose also meant that none of the couriers sent by Wilson got through to Meade. Wilson eventually found a way out of the trap, just before Rosser hit the panicky Federal rear guard. [18]

Now worried about Wilson's whereabouts, Meade sent Brig. Gen. David M. Gregg's Second Cavalry Division to find Wilson. Gregg's Division advanced down the Brock Road to a location 2 miles south of Todd's Tavern, searching for Wilson. With Breathed's guns still blazing, it was not hard for Gregg to locate his quarry. As Wilson's exhausted and defeated troopers retired through Gregg's column, Gregg launched his own attack against Rosser along the Catharpin Road. Rosser was surprised by the arrival of a fresh division of cavalry, and his men thought they had found the Union infantry. The Confederate troopers had nearly run out of ammunition when they had to face off with Gregg's men. A concerned "Comanche" of the 35th Virginia, Captain Frank Myers, asked Lieutenant Colonel Elijah V. White, "Colonel, how can we fight those fellows with no ammunition? We'd as well have rocks as empty pistols." White's response was sure and swift, "What are our sabres for?" Gregg's attack blunted Rosser, who realized he was badly outnumbered. Consequently, he retired to high ground south of the Corbin Bridge. The opposing forces kept up a steady fire until nightfall brought the fighting to a halt. [19]

Gregg, a skilled and dependable cavalryman, sent a detachment down the Brock Road to cover his flank. Not far from Todd's Tavern, Gregg's cavalry ran into Wickham's Brigade of Fitz Lee's Division plus the guns of Hart's Battery. These troopers had moved west from Fredericksburg, and soon made their presence felt. After a sharp skirmish, both sides withdrew and prepared for the next day's action, setting the stage for another epic cavalry battle. [20]

However, the repulse of Wilson's Division cleared the Catharpin and Shady Grove Roads for use by the Army of Northern Virginia. They were headed for the important crossroads town of Spotsylvania Court House.

*   *   *

May 6 opened with the lines around Todd's Tavern pretty much as they had been when the fighting ended the night before. Both sides used the night to consolidate their forces. Custer's Michigan Brigade reinforced Gregg's Division.

Although Gregg had to be concerned about the Confederate cavalry in his front, he was more worried about finding Longstreet's infantry. Major General Winfield S. Hancock's II Corps, which composed the left wing of the Army of the Potomac, was exposed and somewhat up in the air, and Meade feared that Longstreet might suddenly materialize on Hancock's flank in a replay of the Chancellorsville debacle.[21]

The Confederate cavalry was intimately familiar with the lines of communication in the area. Stuart's horsemen had spent a great deal of time in this area over the past year, and his men knew the road network thoroughly. Consequently, Rosser suggested use of a byway connecting the Catharpin and Brock Roads that circumvented Todd's Tavern. This route carried the cavalry around the far left of the Union line. Custer, who was also familiar with this road, had picketed it. Rosser's advance drove Custer's pickets, and Rosser then charged headlong into Custer's Wolverines. Lieutenant Colonel White's 35th Battalion Virginia Cavalry crashed into Custer's line with their trademark war whoop, and the fight was on. One of Stuart's staff officers recalled that "the fight was renewed with great vigor, lasting all day, both sides fighting mostly on foot, and neither gaining a decisive advantage." White had his stallion shot out from under him. The Wolverines drove the Comanches back, where they rallied on a single gun of Thomson's Battery. Chew ordered up Shoemaker's Battery and the rest of Thomson's guns, and the rest of the day was spent firing into the woods at an unseen foe.[22]

On the morning of the 6th we moved with Gen. Rosser's brigade to Rowe's farm where Captain Shoemaker's entire battery was engaged for three hours under heavy fire from the enemy's batteries, and also from dismounted men in his front and flank," reported Breathed. "His losses were severe both in horses and men." The arrival of the additional horse artillery stabilized Rosser's line. Fitz Lee's Division then came up to reinforce Rosser. "We were with our old division, Fitz Lee's, and had some severe fighting in the Wilderness. We pushed our pieces by hand through the dense forest until at times we were in advance of the line of skirmishers," remembered Henry Matthews. "P. P. Johnston had been promoted to Captain. Breathed was with us that day. He seemed to forget that he was Major of the battalion and not Captain."[23]

The fighting eventually became so fierce as to persuade Hancock that Longstreet's infantry was present, not just dismounted cavalry. Blasts of canister drove back Gregg's troopers, prompting one of Rosser's troopers to describe this day's fighting as "the bloodiest day of the war." The combination of thick smoke from the guns and smoke from flames made it almost impossible for the contesting horsemen to see more than a few feet in front of them. "The hissing flames, the sharp, rattling, crashing roar of musketry, the deep bellowing of the artillery mingled with the yelling of charging, struggling, fighting war machines, the wailing moans of the wounded and the fainter groans of the dying, all loudly acclaimed the savagery of our boasted civilization and the enlightened barbarism of the nineteenth century," shuddered George Neese, remembering the horror of the blazing Wilderness. "Even the midday sun refused to look with anything but a faint red glimmer on the tragical scene that was being enacted in the tangled underbrush where the lords of creation were struggling and slaughtering each other like wild beasts in a jungle." The smoke blotted out the sun that rose up from around the dead. It was a morbid scene, and one could easily imagine the Grim Reaper walking from body to body as if to check on the predestined departure time of each man. The second day of the Battle of the Wilderness ended in much the same fashion as the first, with the armies staring at each other across fieldworks. More than 18,000 Union men had fallen in the line of duty and less than 10,000 Confederates were already casualties in this horrific battle.[24]

That night, Rosser and Chew pulled back and dug in on the Catharpin Road, south of the Po River. Fitz Lee had no way of knowing it, but his division was about to render the Army of Northern Virginia its greatest service in the war. Instead of withdrawing, Grant intended to press on.

*   *   *

Before describing what Fitzhugh Lee's Division, supported by Breathed with Johnston's and Hart's batteries, did on the 6th, 7th, and 8th, of May, it is useful to understand the nature of the terrain along the Brock Road between Todd's Tavern and the Alsop Farm. The novelist John Esten Cooke, who was also Stuart's inspector of artillery during this time, described the Brock Road in his novel *Mahun*, written shortly after the war:

> Do you know the Brock road, reader? and have you ever ridden over it on a lowering night? If so, you have experienced a peculiar sensation. It is impossible to imagine any thing more lugubrious than these strange thickets. In their depths the owl hoots, and the whippoorwill cries; the stunted trees, with their gnarled branches, are like fiends reaching out spectral arms to seize the wayfarer by the hair. Desolation reigns there, and you unconsciously place your hand on your pistol as you ride along, to be ready for some mysterious and unseen enemy.

The section of the Brock Road over which the cavalry actions were to be fought for much of the next three days was much as Cooke described it, a good setting for fictional intrigue, but hardly conducive to cavalry maneuver, let alone effective use of artillery. There were a few open areas on the byroads north of the Brock Road, and there were open areas on both sides of Piney Branch where it passed through the Stuart Farm, and a small field in front of the R. Lewis Farm. The rest of the terrain was as Cooke described it. If artillery were used, its effectiveness would be open to question, given the terrain.[25]

On May 6-8, Hart's Batteries of the Stuart Horse Artillery Battalion supported Fitz Lee's Division. Sometime after noon on May 6, but probably on the morning of May 7, Breathed, with Johnston's Battery, joined Fitz Lee's troopers on the Brock Road about three-quarters of a mile east of Todd's Tavern (probably on the eastern side of the small field where the Stuart Farm Road met the Brock Road). Remembered by trooper Alexander Hunter of the 4th Virginia Cavalry the arrival of Breathed and the horse artillery was:

> During a halt, while the men were wiping the perspiration from their faces, a sudden ripple ran down the line. 'Give way,' came the cry, 'Here comes Major Breathed, of Stuart's Horse Artillery!' and soon the rapid hoof-strokes of the horses and jingling of the equipments

were heard; and as the artillery passed along the road with the boy-major at its head, the sun burnt troops arose to a man and saluted him with the wild Rebel yell. It was a tribute that the oldest general would have been proud to receive, and I see again the gallant boy's face flushed to a deeper red as he lifted his cap and rode with bared head through the lines.

The mantle of the lamented Pelham, the greatest light artillerist of America, had fallen on Jim Breathed, the young Marylander. He was about twenty three years old, but like a boy of eighteen; he was muscular and athletic, with a fine head set well on his square shoulders; he was not what the ladies would term 'a handsome fellow' but his character was shown in his dark gray eyes, which flashed and gleamed in a very striking way when he was aroused. His voice was rich and rare, being low and deep. It would now be seen how Hunter's lavish praise was purchased.[26]

Breathed deployed his artillerists down a byroad near the Lewis House, with the 4th Virginia Cavalry in support. Breathed's men occupied a secure position, from where they engaged in warm work. The same trooper of the 4th Virginia observed;

> For the cavalrymen, securely placed in a ravine, it was a grand sight to watch the evolutions. It was Breathed's light battery, the crack guns of the Army of Northern Virginia; and the way they were handled by the men was a spectacle calculated to stir the most sluggish blood and make it run like quicksilver through the veins.

> The cannoneers were stripped to the waist, displaying their brawny arms and hairy chests. They swung the guns around as if steel and brass had lost their weight and were the playthings of the hour. In loading, the men would throw themselves unconsciously into attitudes and magnificent poses which, could a sculptor have caught, would have made his fame. The swelling muscles came out like whip-cords, denoting the hidden force of the frame; every position was an exponent of the strength of manhood in its rich youth, while each figure was thrown into bold relief against the flashes of fire which darted from the muzzles of the guns.

> The shells of the enemy burst all around, but by a wonderful chance did not explode in the midst of the battery, which formed, as it were, the hub of the wheel, rimmed round with fire. The rim was a cordon of danger to cross, yet when once crossed there was safety to be found within. Many soldiers, especially old artillerymen, often

observed this strange fact, a torrent of hail falling through the air, ploughing and tearing the earth to the right and left, in front and in rear, filling the air at a distance either way with bursting fragments, yet not hurting a man.[27]

Gregg's and Fitz Lee's troopers maneuvered for position, and Gregg eventually drove Lee's men back by overwhelming force. However, when Lee's men came under the protection of Breathed's guns on the Brock Road, they rallied. "At last the work [fighting the Union advance] became too warm even to hurrah or cheer; the men needed all the breath they had. It was hard, silent, deadly fighting. The combatants were in full view of each other whenever the purple smoke would drift away for a few moments," recalled one Virginia trooper. "The advance was irresistible through the woods to where our small reserve was stationed and breastworks thrown up for protection, and better than all, a section of Breathed's battery." Once the dismounted horse soldiers were safely behind the breastworks, and the safety of Breathed's two guns, the Confederate artillerists "sent the solid shot ploughing and crashing through the trees and right into their teeth. This stopped the advance, but did not cause their retreat at first, but in a few minutes the combined fire caused them to recede, and then our men advanced and ran against a fresh line and were broken to pieces." Trooper Hunter was quite adamant that "Nothing saved the regiment from a rout but those two guns of Breathed's battery. We drifted back."[28]

The same trooper later recounted that "About an hour before sundown [battle] came with vengeance. Two solid lines of bluecoats, both cavalry and infantry, struck us, and after a few minutes deadly work drove us back in disorder. We retreated to the woods and made a stout resistance there, but a front and flank attack sent us reeling out into the open and we went flying through the field, the hurrahs of the Federals rising high above the rattling of the guns." Things looked very bleak for Wickham's Brigade. At just the right moment, Breathed arrived to save the day. "All at once from the Spotsylvania turnpike there emerged a number of guns almost hid by the dust. Straight to the foe they advanced, dashing through the running cavalry as if they were stalks of corn. I heard a mounted officer who was trying to rally our men, say: 'My God, Jim Breathed must have gone mad.'"[29]

Phil Sheridan (left), August Kautz (center) and an unidentified "friend."

It did appear that way. No sane artillerist charged cavalry with his guns, but Breathed was determined. He was not considered to be an ordinary artillery commander. When his guns reached one hundred yards from the enemy line, he gave the command to halt, and "then four iron throats bellowed and the guns, loaded with grape and canister, poured their iron into the line of blue. In an instant it was stopped, and with a shout the flying cavalrymen turned right-about face and then the rebel yell was heard and we rushed forward," recalled one of Wickham's troopers. "It was a pretty fight, give and take. I happened to be near the guns and I saw Major Breathed standing there serene and cool as if on a parade. Lord! How he did work those guns. They flashed, they roared, and when the Federals charged he gave some orders and was silent. The scene was indelibly impressed on my memory." [30]

Breathed was a vision. "There stood Jim Breathed holding his horse by the bridle, his boyish face flushed, his eyes shining like fire; there stood the cannoneers with the lanyards in their hands, while prone on the earth without line or formation lay the cavalrymen. The shock came, and the blue line reeled back, broken and harmless," continued the cavalryman. "There was no soldier in the Army of Northern Virginia more popular than Jim Breathed was. The cavalrymen swore by him and would cheer him whenever his batteries passed by. Among all the Johnny Rebs—'those tattered sons of fortune'—there was no braver man, no truer soldier, no finer artilleryman than glorious Jim Breathed." [31]

That night, the battered Federal cavalry broke off the engagement and withdrew. And Jim Breathed's guns had demonstrated the power and effectiveness of horse artillery in the hands of a competent and aggressive commander, even when the ground was unsuited to artillery. [32]

*   *   *

The morning of May 7, the Union cavalry had received orders to go to and hold Spotsylvania Court House. Grant had the Army of the Potomac in motion, heading south and east toward Spotsylvania Court House, hoping to flank Robert E. Lee by moving around his right in an

effort to cut Lee off from Richmond. Maj. Gen. Philip H. Sheridan, the aggressive new commander of the Army of the Potomac's Cavalry Corps, was to seize the roads to Spotsylvania Court House and hold them, so that Lee could not use them. Gregg

Major General
Gouverneur K. Warren.

LC

was to pass through Todd's Tavern, turn down the Catharpin Road, cross Corbin's Bridge, proceed to Shady Grove Church, then take the Shady Grove Road to Spotsylvania. Merritt (temporarily commanding the division of Brig. Gen. Alfred T. A. Torbert, who was on medical leave) was to proceed through Todd's Tavern, go down the Brock Road, then take back roads to the Block House on the Shady Grove Road. Wilson was to move from the Alrich Plantation, take the Fredericksburg Road to Zion Church, and then move east and south in order to come into Spotsylvania from the north. Once the Union cavalry had secured the roads, Maj. Gen. Gouverneur K. Warren's V Corps, followed by Hancock's II Corps, were to proceed by way of the Brock Road to Spotsylvania, the most direct route.

However, when he could not find Sheridan, Meade jumped the chain of command and gave orders directly to the individual division commanders of the Cavalry Corps. Meade gave orders conflicting Sheridan's. He ordered Gregg to guard the Po River at and near Corbin's Bridge. He ordered Merritt to Spotsylvania to lead the way for Warren's infantry, and failed to give Wilson any orders at all. Wilson therefore had no way to know that cavalry, instead of infantry, would make contact with him at Spotsylvania Court House. The confusion meant that a critical opportunity for the Army of the Potomac to seize and hold Spotsylvania Court House was lost.[33]

When the sun rose on the morning of May 7, neither side controlled the important road intersection at Todd's Tavern. Fitz Lee moved first to fill that void. His men moved to the north and west of Todd's Tavern in a well-designed and well-executed delaying action intended to hinder the Army of the Potomac's advance. Breathed, with Johnston's Battery, probably held open ground along byroads to the north of the Brock Road, as described by trooper Hunter.

Back on the Catharpin Road, Capt. George Baylor, commander of Company B of the 12th Virginia Cavalry, Company B remembered, "our cavalry advanced and the fight was renewed with great vigor, and lasted until late in the afternoon, without decisive result, excepting the advance of our lines. There were several hand-to-hand conflict[s] during the day. Our brigade and the enemy's force in our front occupied elevations, with depressions between, about a half-mile apart." Baylor heard the guns dueling, but could not identify the source of the gunfire, as "the artillery on both sides were firing rapidly, when the enemy, moving two mounted regiments to their front, made a charge on our guns." Rosser responded by ordering a charge of White's "Comanches" (35th Virginia Cavalry Battalion) and the 12th Virginia, "the opposite forces met midway between the lines, and a hand-to-hand conflict ensued and the enemy were repulsed."[34]

While Lee and Grant played an intricate chess game, Lee held the upper hand. His army, although still outnumbered, had more than given as well as it had gotten, and it had inflicted heavy losses on Grant's army. A stalemate had developed, and Grant was determined to break it. The engagement at Todd's Tavern eventually involved two Union cavalry divisions and elements of three Confederate cavalry divisions. The engagement at Todd's Tavern marked the largest dismounted cavalry fight during the war. Fitz Lee's three-thousand and five-hundred men, reinforced by elements of Hampton's Division, including Rosser's Laurel Brigade, made for a stubborn Confederate stand. Hampton attacked along the Catharpin Road toward Todd's Tavern. Chew, with Thomson's and Shoemaker's batteries, supported Hampton's attack. By afternoon, the aggressive Federals had driven the stubborn Confederates away from Todd's Tavern to the east, but Fitz Lee's valiant delaying action bought Robert E. Lee's army an entire day to win the race for

Union V Corps commander Major General Gouverneur K. Warren
leading his men toward Breathed's four waiting guns.

Spotsylvania Court House. Darkness ended the fighting on May 7 with Sheridan's horsemen in tenuous possession of Todd's Tavern. However, Fitz Lee's dogged troopers still blocked the direct route to Spotsylvania Court House.[35]

*   *   *

Information gathered by Stuart's diligent scouts enabled Robert E. Lee to guess Grant's intentions, permitting Lee to take advantage of his well established interior lines of communication to win the race to Spotsylvania. Longstreet's Corps, was now commanded by Major General Richard H. Anderson. Longstreet was wounded at the Wilderness, had to get to Spotsylvania Court House before the Federals. Although Warren's infantry had the shorter route to march, his men had to fight their way through Fitz Lee's determined troopers supported by Breathed's guns, which slowed them down considerably.[36]

When Grant ordered Warren's V Corps to march, he was operating under the mistaken notion that Sheridan's cavalry had secured the Brock Road between the Wilderness and Spotsylvania Court House. Late on the night of the 7th, Grant and Meade learned that Sheridan had failed to secure the Brock Road. Consequently, Meade ordered Warren's and Sheridan's men to secure the Brock Road as soon as possible. At first light on the 8th, Warren's V Corps marched through Todd's Tavern and started down the Brock Road. They did not get far. Fitz Lee's troopers stopped Sheridan's cavalry with no advance. "Both our line and that of the enemy were formed in a dense wood so as to make it impossible to use artillery except at very short range," reported Breathed. "Satisfied that by placing guns immediately on our line of battle I could inflict great damage on the enemy I proposed it [to] Major General Fitz Lee, and he at once consented. I succeeded in getting one section in position and for a half hour sent charge after charge of canister and short range shell into the ranks of the enemy with great effect."[37]

Warren, who was anxious to learn the state of affairs, sought out Brig. Gen. Wesley Merritt, who had recently been ordered to clear the road of Confederates. Brig. Gen. Merritt sent Col. Alfred Gibbs' Brigade and the Reserve Brigade south, with the 1st U.S. Cavalry in the advanced position of the march. The fighting began before breakfast and continued for three hours before Merritt finally gave up on the idea of driving Fitz's

Priscilla Breathed Bridges

In 1893, the *Chicago Tribune* ran an article on Breathed's daring escape and depicted it with Breathed pulling the single gun from the field.

men off. Merritt deferred to Warren's infantry, which attacked about 7:00 A.M.

The Confederate cavalry really had no hope of fending off Warren's Corps as they had the Union cavalry, but they stood as long as they could. "This morning we went back to the same position we left at dusk yesterday evening, but the Yankees seem to be getting very uneasy in the Wilderness and are trying to back out or flank out, and in their maneuvering to-day they flanked around our right and compelled us to abandon our position," observed George Neese. Chew's stand permitted Breathed's Battery to move to the favorable position atop a knoll. "Consequently we fell back and moved to our right too, in order to intercept and if possible rebut their flanking advance. We pierced their flank and had a spirited little engagement early in the day, but the enemy proved too strong for our force, as their cavalry advanced in conjunction with their ever present infantry, and we had nothing but cavalry and our battery." Neese accurately described the intricate chess game being played by Grant and Lee in the Wilderness. "We retired about a mile and took a good commanding position at the Dobbins house, and awaited the approach of the huge wriggling war machine that was trying to extricate itself from the intricacies of the Wilderness by stealthily gliding around the bristling bayonets of General Lee' infantry."[38]

That morning, Fitz Lee ordered the 4 guns of Johnston's Battery under Breathed's command to hold the knoll at the Alsop House. Breathed placed the guns on the knoll north of the house, at the junction of the Brock and Gordon Roads, about three miles from Todd's Tavern. Breathed had fields of fire that commanded the nexus of two converging roads that met directly to in front of the Alsop House. Breathed's "mastery of the pieces was a spectacle calculated to stir the most sluggish blood and make it run like quicksilver through the veins," recalled Confederate cavalryman Alexander Hunter. Before long the Union infantry emerged in a line of battle from the woods along the Brock Road, the Confederate cavalry was in support of the guns. The Union's V Corps was marching right into the teeth of Breathed's guns, which were the only significant barriers standing between the bulk of the Army of the Potomac and Spotsylvania Court House.[39]

Fitz Lee's dogged cavalrymen contested every foot of ground as they moved to the rear down the Brock Road toward Spotsylvania Court House. Once the Union forces crossed the high ground at the Alsop Farm, only Laurel Hill stood in the way in this hour of crisis. The longer Breathed's guns could hold back Warren's infantry and Merritt's cavalrymen, the better the chance for Anderson to come up behind Laurel Hill and win the race to Spotsylvania Court House. Breathed and his gunners relentlessly blasted canister into the face of the advancing Union cavalrymen and infantry. Johnston's 4 guns gouged great holes in the ranks of the disoriented Union infantrymen. Meanwhile, Wilson's Union cavalry was circling in behind Fitz Lee and Breathed's guns by way of the northern approach to Spotsylvania Court House. If Wilson's horse soldiers swung west up the Brock Road, they could attack Breathed's guns from the rear. Things were getting tense. [40]

A minie-ball tore a gaping hole through Captain Johnston's shoulder when Hancock's II Corps flanked Breathed's position, forcing all but one of the 4 guns to retire. Union infantry demanded Breathed's surrender, but the gallant artillerist refused, and he did not abandon his lone gun. "We were obliged to abandon our position, as the enemy was flanking on our left with Hancock's Corps," reported Breathed. "I ordered Captain Johnston to put his guns in a position commanding an open field through which the enemy had to advance. Ten minutes afterward they emerged from the wood and seeing that we were supported by a small body of Cavalry at once charged the guns and although large gaps were made in their ranks first with shell and then with canister they continued to advance." Breathed continued, "I ordered three guns to retire after the enemy had charged to within a short distance and kept one gun in position. My support having given back, I was obliged to run the risk of losing one gun to save the other three. It was brought from the field with two horses, the other four having been killed. The loss to the battery during the day was severe, both in horses and men Captain Johnston being among the wounded during the charge on the guns when Lt. Shanks succeeded to the command of the battery." [41]

There were other witnesses to Breathed's actions this day. These accounts tended to show that Breathed's report of his actions understated his role a bit. Fitz Lee reported that Breathed's gunners ran low on ammunition, and they feared that the Federal infantry would capture them and their guns. Many of the artillerists ran, leaving Breathed alone to defend his remaining gun. A Union officer cried out, "Come on, men, get that gun!" and the race for the gun was on. Nearly two-thousand determined Union infantrymen moved toward Breathed and his lone gun. "I was sitting on my horse near Breathed and directed him to withdraw his gun, but he was so much elated with his success, that he begged to be allowed to give the enemy some more rounds," recounted Fitz Lee. "He fired until their line got so close that you could hear them calling out 'Surrender that gun, you rebel son of a bitch.'"[42]

Ignoring Lee's orders to abandon his gun, Breathed continued blasting away until the Union line of battle was within seventy-five yards of his position. Finally, Breathed jumped on his horse and tried to escape. The horse was shot from under him, and the mortally wounded horse fell upon Breathed. Breathed leapt from the fallen horse, attached the limber and caisson to the team of four horses behind the cover of trees to the rear of the cannon. He mounted the lead wheel horse, which was also shot from under him. Again, Breathed tumbled to the ground. He picked himself up, spotted the team's other lead horse, and jumped on its back. This third horse was also mortally wounded. The Union soldiers were bearing down on him; minie balls whizzed all around him. However, Breathed was determined to save his gun from capture, so he cut the leather traces from the dying horses and mounted a fourth animal, and pulled the gun to safety behind the Confederate line of battle. Legend has it that the fleeing Breathed put his thumb to his nose and jiggled his fingers in contempt for his hastily pursuing Union foes.[43]

"I knew the Confederate personally who, in the battle so bravely dismounted, cut the lead and carried the gun swiftly back. This was Major James Breathed, and he told me himself of this daring deed, to save our gun. He said he saw the driver was bewildered, the Yankees were so near but, without a moment of hesitancy, he severed the halter traces, while balls were flying in all around him," recounted one of Breathed's men years later. "Breathed humbly spoke of himself in this report. However, his action this day was to further his legendary image as one of the hardest artillery fighters the South ever produced. Outnumbered by thousands of men he held his ground until he had to escape or be captured."[44]

After Breathed's daring stand, he dashed off to another crisis point. Warren's infantry had pursued Lee's hard-pressed troopers back along the Brock Road to a low ridge south of the Spindle's Field, called Laurel Hill. However, the Federals had gotten there too late—Anderson's infantry had arrived just in the nick of time, complete with artillery support. The Southern infantry easily repulsed the Federals, driving them back. Despite numerous determined attacks over several days, the Federals were unable to drive Anderson's men from Laurel Hill. It remained firmly in Confederate hands throughout the Battle of Spotsylvania, which was now under way in earnest.[45]

* * *

Breathed's stand at the crossroads delayed Warren's infantry just long enough to permit Lee to win the race to Spotsylvania Court House. His lonely stand was unparalleled and earned the respect of the infantry and artillery of the Army of Northern Virginia. "I note here in passing, that this Spotsylvania business was a 'white day' for the cavalry. When the army came to know of what the cavalry had done, and how they had done it, there was a general outburst of admiration—the recognition that brave men give to the brave," recalled William Dame, a member of the Richmond Howitzers. Dame had arrived at Laurel Hill just after Breathed's stand. "Stuart and his men were written higher than ever on the honor roll, and the whole army was ready to take off its hat to salute the cavalry ... And, from that day, there was a marked change in the way the army thought and spoke of the cavalry; it took a distinctly different and higher position in the respect of the Army, for it had revealed itself in a new light; it had shown itself signally possessed of the quality, that the infantry and artillery naturally admired most of all others—obstinacy in fight."[46]

Prior to the stand on the Brock Road that day, the infantry and the mounted artillery were not accustomed to seeing cavalry and artillery standing and fighting with such tenacity as Breathed had done that day. "Upon the advance of the enemy, of course, we were accustomed to see cavalrymen hurrying in from the outposts to the rear, to report," continued Dame. "So the thoughtless infantry, not considering that this was 'part of the large and general plan,' got fixed in their minds an association between the two things,—the advance of the enemy, and, the rapid hurrying off to the rear of the cavalry, until they came to have the fixed idea, that the sight of the enemy always made a cavalryman 'hungry for solitude.'"[47]

All of that changed after Laurel Hill and Breathed's stand at the Alsop House. "Here had these gallants gotten down off their horses. They hadn't run anywhere at all; didn't want anybody else to come, and fight for them. They had jumped into about five or six times their number of the flower of the Federal infantry. They met them front to front, and muzzle to muzzle," explained Dame. "Of course they had to give back; but it was slowly, very slowly, and they made the enemy pay, in blood, for every step they gained. They had worried these Federals into a fever, and kept them fooling away nearly twenty-six hours of priceless time; and made Grant's plan fail, and made General Lee's plan succeed, and had secured the strong line for our defense." The hard-bitten Confederate infantry realized that they owed Stuart's cavalry and horse artillery a great debt that day. "Obstinacy, toughness, dogged refusal to be driven, was their test of manhood, and this test the cavalry had signally, and brilliantly met. Everybody was satisfied, the cavalry would do, they were 'all right'" Dame concluded. "And we all admired the cavalry; honored the cavalry; shouted for the cavalry, from that time!"[48]

Breathed's men hardly fought at all on May 9. The Confederate infantry relieved the horse artillery. Breathed's artillerists had moved to the extreme right of Lee's line. There they spent the rest of the day in peace, while they tried to regroup, reconstitute, and resupply. However, their respite would not last long. Word filtered in that Sheridan's cavalry had gone off on a raid in the direction of Richmond, which would climax at a place called Yellow Tavern.[49]

*   *   *

Even though he had lost the fight at the Wilderness and the race to Spotsylvania Court House, Grant still did not consider himself defeated. On May 11, he described his strategy. "We have now ended the 6th day of very hard fighting. The result up to this time is much in our favor. But our losses have been heavy as well as those of the enemy. We have lost to this time eleven general officers killed, wounded and missing, and probably twenty thousand men," wrote Grant. "I think the loss of the enemy must be greater-we have taken over four thousand prisoners in battle, whilst he has taken from us but few except a few stragglers. I am now sending back to Belle Plain all my wagons for a fresh supply of provisions and ammunition, and propose to fight it out on this line if it takes all summer."[50]

The "tremendous ordeal of fire which has made the Spottsylvania Wilderness famous for all time in the bloody history which marks the progress of the world from the days of old down to the present, and if ever hard, stubborn fighting deserved success, the army of Lee in those May days of 1864 earned it," recalled Captain Frank Myers of the 35th Virginia Cavalry, "for every day the same awful roar of battle rolled along the lines, and every night came the same encouraging reports of the enemy repulsed with heavy slaughter, until it was a given up point that soon Grant would stop his 'hammering,' for the good reason that the hammer was shivered to atoms on the solid anvil of Southern endurance and grit." However, Myers underestimated Grant's determination. Grant had no intention of letting the "Grey Fox" get away this time. The astonished Myers reported that instead of turning back, "the national butcher kept throwing his doomed legions upon the invincible veterans of Gen. Lee, and supplying, from the teeming millions of Yankeeland and Germany, the places of the slaughtered men in blue."[51]

For the first time, the Army of Northern Virginia faced a Union general who would no longer consider retreating or resting until the Confederacy was defeated. This time, Robert E. Lee would get no opportunity to rest and refit his army before it had to meet another "on to Richmond" thrust. Grant was determined to push Lee relentlessly, all the way to Richmond. It was to be a war of attrition, and the North had more men to feed into the meat grinder.

The question was, could Lee hold out?

Chapter 11

"Not War, But Murder,"
Yellow Tavern to Cold Harbor

T he Army of Northern Virginia and the Army of the Potomac faced off in front of Spotsylvania Court House in what became some of the bloodiest fighting in any war. While the armies were locked in mortal combat, the cavalry of both armies clashed at the gates of Richmond. In the process, the Confederate cavalry suffered a staggering blow.

Major General George G. Meade, the commander of the Army of the Potomac, and Major General Philip H. Sheridan, his chief of cavalry, engaged in a hot dispute over the best use of cavalry. Meade believed that the cavalry should protect his wagon trains and perform other defensive duties consistent with more traditional notions of the proper use of mounted soldiers. Sheridan, on the other hand, believed that massed cavalry could serve as an offensive weapon that could face off against Stuart's cavalry and also perform the more traditional roles of scouting, screening and reconnaissance. While engaged in a tempestuous argument over the misuse of the Federal cavalry at Todd's Tavern, Sheridan bragged to Meade that if he were allowed to command the entire cavalry independently, he could whip Stuart. Meade, offended by Sheridan's insubordination, reported the episode to Grant. When Meade got to the part about whipping Stuart, Grant said calmly, "Did Sheridan say that?

Well, he generally knows what he is talking about. Let him start right out and do it."[1]

By May 8, Sheridan was on the move with the entire Cavalry Corps in tow. By the next morning, word of the Union movement had reached Stuart, who set off in pursuit with two divisions—Sheridan could not be permitted to get around Lee's right flank. Stuart sent Wickham's Brigade to nip at Sheridan's heels while Stuart personally led the brigades of James B. Gordon and Lunsford L. Lomax off toward Richmond. Breathed rode along with Stuart, bringing two batteries of horse artillery with him.[2]

On May 11, 1864, the opposing forces came together on the Telegraph Road, about eight miles north of Richmond, near Yellow Tavern. The regimental surgeon of the 1st Virginia Cavalry of Wickham's Brigade had accompanied his unit into the field. "General Stuart had hastily thrown into line of march a few regiments of cavalry," he recalled, "with Breathed's battery and left Lee's army near Spotsylvania Court House and pressed toward Richmond to intercept Sheridan, then racing toward the Confederate capital with twelve thousand cavalry." In the desperate fight that developed at Yellow Tavern, Stuart was outnumbered by a ratio of thirty guns to ten guns and two to one in men.[3]

Stuart had arrived at the junction of the Telegraph and Mountain Roads, north of Yellow Tavern. Lomax's Virginians charged into Sheridan's horsemen and were repulsed, falling back to the main body of the Confederate cavalry. Wickham's Brigade was positioned on the right, near a wood, facing the Mountain Road, while Lomax's Brigade was drawn up on the Telegraph Road, with his left anchored on Yellow Tavern. Stuart's line of battle thus formed an obtuse angle. "On elevated ground, near Lomax's right, that is at the central was posted a battery of the 'Stuart horse artillery' under command of the bravest and best artillerist of the army, Major James Breathed a Marylander, well known for his dash and bulldog obstinacy," remembered John Esten Cooke. "Their dispositions were excellent to meet the attack of an enemy advancing by the mountain road, and as Stuart had sent Adjutant, Major McClellan, to Richmond to an advance of any force there it seemed probable that General Sheridan would be repulsed." [4]

"Wickham's brigade and Breathed's battery had a fierce struggle to hold their own, and fought desperately to do so," recalled Henry

Matthews. Chaos reigned, and Stuart's command lost all semblance of organization. Only the 1st Virginia Cavalry remained a coherent command, so Stuart ordered them to charge. "When we reached the road we met some of Breathed's men coming out of the engagement, many of them hatless and bleeding arm sabre cuts, while others were gesticulating wildly and crying aloud that they had lost their 'dear commander,' Major Breathed," reported Colonel William Morgan, the commander of the 1st Virginia. "As the squadron moved on to the next small hill, where the road curved to the left, we saw a lone horseman in full speed coming down the hill towards us, waving over his head a sabre broken in the middle, and as he arrived a mighty shout went up, for it was the Major, whom had just been believed dead and left upon the field."[5]

Here is how Breathed's brush with death came about that desperate day at Yellow Tavern. "Breathed! Take command of all the mounted men in the road and hold it against whatever comes," cried Stuart. "If this road is lost we are gone!"[6]

The artillerist saluted and immediately called for "the men to follow him [and they] charged the Union column. Breathed rode apparently careless of whether he was followed by his comrades. He was immediately surrounded and a hot sabre fight took place between himself and a swarm of bluecoats. A sabre blow nearly cut him out of the saddle, and he received a pistol shot in his side, but he cut down one Federal officer [and] killed another with his revolver." A nasty saber slash to the head that gushed blood and a glancing blow from a pistol knocked Breathed from the saddle. Breathed was terrified of being captured. "When consciousness returned and he realized his situation he determined to face and risk death. Near him a Federal officer-mounted upon his horse-within his reach (he a very active man) quickly sprang, caught him by the leg, dragged him to the ground, mounted his horse and in lightning speed, ran through the enemies lines," recounted his sister, Priscilla Breathed Bridges. "Blood streaming down upon his shoulders – if possible the next moment he was with his command, and heard the voices of his men – 'Breathed! Breathed! —is not dead!' At the same moment heard distinctly the voices of the Federal soldiers – 'Kill! Kill him!' he said of his narrow escape: deftly explained. The act so speedily done – caused purpose, and excitement, and before the Federal soldiers and Federal officers had time to recover – he was safe in the Confederate line."[7]

One of his gunners heard Breathed cry out, "Boys, I'm not dead yet!" as he galloped back to the safety of the Confederate lines, with his head wound gushing blood. He presented quite a sight, inspiring his men with his courage under fire. "We were descending the hill, and as he reached the front of our column, although bleeding continuous and with only a broken sabre took command, he wheeled into position in the first rank of the squadron and appealed to the always cool and fearless Morgan to charge and recapture his guns," remembered the same gunner. "When we reached the crest of the hill General Stuart rode up and gave to Colonel Morgan probably his last command on the field of battle, which was to make a counter charge upon a brigade of the enemy then charging down the road, and if possible hold them in check until he could withdraw over the bridge on the Chickahominy River."[8]

After the charge, Breathed ended working one of Captain Griffin's guns. While he worked the gun, a Union officer charged him, and they engaged in desperate hand-to-hand combat. Breathed killed the man, but guns of Griffin's Battery were lost. "The command was marching until the 11th when the fight at Yellow Tavern occurred," Breathed reported to Chew. "Captain Johnston's battery suffered but little as the fire of the enemy was concentrated upon the Balt. Light Artillery [Griffin's Battery] which had joined us on the 10th. This battery suffered severely losing many men and horses and two guns." Both Custer and Wilson were too much for Griffin's men to stave off.[9]

Stuart was not as fortunate as Breathed had been that day. As Sheridan's troopers drove the Confederate cavalry back, things became desperate. "Stuart was nearly in despair and was seen galloping about, shouting and waving his sabre in a desperate attempt to rally his men, but it was impossible," recounted Captain Cooke. "The field was a scene of the wildest disorder. Federals and Confederates were darting in every direction and one of the former, as he darted by Stuart, fired at him and shot him through the body." An unidentified Michigan cavalryman shot Stuart with his pistol at short range, striking Stuart in the right side. The bullet passed through his body and exited through his back, grazing a small Bible that he always carried, a gift from his mother.[10]

Stuart's famed plumed hat fell to the ground as he slumped over onto his saddle in anguish. His stunned troopers watched as the men of Company K of the 1st Virginia Cavalry dashed to his aid. The company commander caught Stuart before he toppled to the ground, prompting

Stuart to say, "Go back and do your duty as I have done mine, and our country will be safe!" As other troopers fell back in front of the furious Union assault, he called out, "Go back!' Go back! I'd rather die than be whipped!" There was bedlam all around as troopers cried out for a surgeon to come aid Stuart. The wound was mortal, and Stuart eventually became speechless as a result of blood loss and shock. He tried to direct the battle with hand signals, but soon that became too much for him. His stunned troopers and horse artillerists watched in shock as they realized that their beloved commander had been desperately wounded.[11]

With Stuart down, command of the field devolved upon Fitz Lee, who continued resisting the advances of the Federal cavalry. Fitz Lee left the field long enough to ensure that Stuart was taken to safety and then returned, but not before Stuart informed Lee that he had entrusted him with the battle. Stuart was loaded into an ambulance and moved toward the Chickahominy River. Some of Custer's Wolverines pursued the ambulance and threatened to capture its precious cargo. Although he was still covered with blood from his head wound, Breathed sprang into action and rallied nearby troopers to intercept the Wolverines bearing down on Stuart's ambulance. Breathed's quick thinking blunted the Federal pursuit and kept Stuart from falling into enemy hands. He was taken to the home of his brother-in-law, Dr. Charles Brewer, where he lingered for a day. The wound claimed Stuart's life on May 12. Robert E. Lee wept when he heard that Stuart had died, proclaiming, "He never brought me a false piece of information."[12]

His painful head wound kept Breathed out of action for a while as he recuperated. He also received careful, tender care, and was sent to Richmond with a few other casualties from the Battle of Yellow Tavern. When General Lee learned that Breathed had been wounded at Yellow Tavern, he praised the artillerist's heroism and skill.[13]

* * *

The dawn after Yellow Tavern, while Stuart lay dying and the cavalry continued its running battle with Sheridan, Grant struck Lee's Spotsylvania line at the tip of a large salient dubbed the "Mule Shoe." The massive pre-dawn attack broke through the front, captured large numbers of men and guns, and nearly split Lee's embattled army in two pieces. It took an entire day of fighting that stretched into the night time hours for General Lee to seal the breach and preserve the integrity of his Spotsylvania position.

By May 21, Grant became convinced through the lack of success of his probing attacks and the ineffective maneuvering of his various corps would not break Lee's line. Grant decided it was time once again to maneuver around the Confederate flank. The complicated moves of Grant's corps to try and flank Lee and Lee's moves to parry Grant would cover almost fifty miles in ten days, until booth armies were reassembled for the face-off at Cold Harbor. This ten-day period was characterized by numerous small engagements at various places along the roads and by-ways between Spotsylvania and Cold Harbor.

Before the next mention of Jim Breathed upon the battlefield, a word about the command structure of the Cavalry Corps of the Army of Northern Virginia. Although it was reported that Stuart had personally passed command to Fitz Lee at the Battle of Yellow Tavern, Robert E. Lee did not confirm that. In fact, Robert E. Lee would retain direct command over the Cavalry Corps for some time, until Maj. Gen. Hampton would finally receive command of it. During this period, the command situation at the Division level was quite unsettled. Rooney Lee had been elevated to Division command on April 23, 1864, when he returned to the Army of Northern Virginia after nine months as a Federal prisoner. Rooney Lee's Division would have two brigades, Brig. Gen. John R. Chambliss' Brigade (Rooney's command prior to his capture) and Brig. Gen. James B. Gordon's Brigade of North Carolinians. However, Gordon was mortally wounded on May 12. By seniority, Col. John A. Baker of the 3rd North Carolina Cavalry became commander of Gordon's Brigade, but that command was not physically with the main army until May 27. Thus, at the time Breathed is mentioned again in battle, Maj. Gen. Rooney Lee has direct command only over Chambliss' Brigade.

General Robert E. Lee anticipated that Grant would possibly side-step to the east during the latter stages of the Battle of Spotsylvania. Consequently, General Lee sent out several of his cavalry commands to scout the right flank and detect any such movement. Among these units was Chambliss' Brigade of Rooney Lee's Division. The various regiments and companies of Chambliss' Brigade were ordered to patrol the roads, bridges, and railroad to the east of Spotsylvania, as well as north towards Fredericksburg. If they encountered movement of the Union forces, they were to report it immediately.

A company of the 9th Virginia Cavalry was probing in the direction of Guinea Station, under the command of Lt. George W. Beale, when the Federal flanking movement began in earnest. After watching Hancock's and Warren's Federal Corps move toward Bowling Green, Beale's command turned west to rejoin the main body of Chambliss' Brigade. Beale recalled, "We reached the Telegraph Road, and were at a loss to know which direction to take, when two soldiers' forms moving side by side rode past us. One of the men with me proposed to get some information from them as to where W. H. F. Lee's [sic Chambliss] Brigade could be found. He quickly returned, saying: 'Why that was General Robert E. Lee!'" General Lee, accompanied by a single orderly, was riding through the dark night examining his army's dispositions as it prepared for another's day of what promised to be hard fighting against a determined adversary.[14]

Lee told the cavalrymen where they could find Rooney Lee's Brigade, and the horsemen and artillerymen joined the balance of the brigade, which was given the important task of holding back the Union infantry. The cavalry, accompanied by Breathed's Battery, marched through the thick woods until the artillerists found an open space where they could unlimber their guns. As the Federal infantry was moving quickly and had nearly caught up to the cavalrymen and gunners, by a road through the thick woods, the 9th and 10th Virginia Cavalry regiments deployed on either side of the battery, stubbornly contesting the advance of the Union infantry.

"The fire on this line became more and more rapid, and the shells from our battery flew faster and faster. I listened anxiously to the enemy's guns to be heard in our rear on the road over which we had passed, in which case, it being impossible to get the battery off through the woods, nothing could remain but to abandon it," remembered Lieutenant George W. Beale of the 9th Virginia Cavalry. "I felt sure Breathed must be in very deep concern for the escape of his guns, but on looking at him he appeared sitting composedly on his horse with one leg across the boot of his saddle and reading an open volume with an intentness that the roar of his guns did not seem to disturb in the smallest degree." Breathed leapfrogged his guns back over the road by which they had come, and then took an obscure road leading toward the west into a valley. The horse soldiers followed along behind, ascending a slope to high ground on the other side, with Breathed unlimbering his rear gun near a body of woods.[15]

"Looking to our left, three-quarters of a mile away, we could see a column of Federal infantry emerging from the timber from which we had escaped, and Breathed was bent on giving them a parting shot. His first shell struck the ground near the head of the column, and concealed the files where it struck for a moment with the dust and smoke of its explosion," recalled Lieutenant Beale. "The gap created was quickly closed up, and the column moved on. Other shots from our gun went wild, and a Federal battery having opened on us, we continued our course under the cover of the woods." This action occurred on the Littleton Flippo Farm on the banks of the Matta River.[16]

After this skirmish ended, Breathed's Battery relocated to Beaver Dam Station. By May 27, the Army of the Potomac had pulled out of its trenches along the North Anna River. General Lee was uncertain about Grant's intentions, so he summoned Hampton to find out. Lee sensed that something serious was afoot.

On May 28, Maj. Gen. Hampton, now acting commander of the Army of Northern Virginia's Cavalry Corps by virtue of seniority (though not officially appointed as such until August 11, 1864), met Sheridan's cavalry at Haw's Shop. Hampton's command was reinforced by part of a brigade of hard-fighting cavalry from his home state of South Carolina commanded by Brig. Gen. Matthew C. Butler, from whom much would be heard before the end of the war. Hampton and the Union cavalry slugged it out for nearly an entire day. Johnston's and Shoemaker's batteries were engaged that day. Breathed's gunners blasted away at the Union center while the dismounted Confederate cavalry fought. Late in the afternoon, Hampton, who had gone out that day to determine the whereabouts of the Union army, learned that Meade was crossing the Pamunkey River near Hanovertown. "The object of the reconnaissance having been accomplished," reported Hampton, "I ordered my command to withdraw." Veterans of both sides remembered Haw's Shop as the hardest cavalry fight of the war. [17]

On May 29, Sheridan and his cavalry struck out southwest toward Cold Harbor, a non-descript cluster of houses famous for being the site of the 1862 Battle of Gaines Mill during the Seven Days. If Sheridan could seize and hold the important road junctions at Cold Harbor, he would

LC

Federal troops building pontoon bridges across the North Anna River.

open the door to Richmond, only ten tantalizing miles away. On June 1, Fitz Lee's Division did what it could to protect the territory between the Confederate right flank and the Chickahominy River. Lee deployed his dismounted troopers at the important crossroads, determined to hold it at all costs. He placed Lomax's Brigade in a blocking position astride the road, covering the approaches from Old Church. Wickham's Brigade took position at a road intersection along the Bottoms Bridge Road, and Breathed unlimbered his guns where they could support the dismounted cavalrymen. Johnston's Battery, under Breathed's personal command, was only lightly engaged and suffered few losses while Fitz Lee's and Custer's troopers slugged it out. Just as it appeared that Sheridan's troopers would carry the day, Major General Robert F. Hoke's Infantry Division arrived. Hoke's men deployed into line of battle at the run, driving Sheridan's dismounted troopers from the road intersection, and regaining their position at the crucial crossroads at Cold Harbor.[18]

With Breathed's artillerists pounding away with their guns, the Southern infantry prepared hasty breastworks. Before long, both armies were in place and engaged in ghastly trench warfare that foreshadowed the horrors of World War I. On the afternoon of June 1, Connecticut Captain James Deane believed his men could charge and take the breastworks in his front. However, "fire which no human valor could withstand" erupted as one hundred and two Confederates attacked his left. "The air was filled with sulphurous smoke, and the shrieks and howls of more than two hundred and fifty mangled men rose above the yells of triumphant rebels and the roar of their musketry." The Confederate musketry devastated the ranks of the Connecticut troops, prompting their regimental commander to cry out, "About face!" just before he fell dead from multiple bullets. The colonel and fifty-two men lay dead, and another three hundred and thirty-three men were wounded or missing.[19]

Grant, who realized that he was fighting on the same ground where McClellan's campaign had bogged down two years earlier, was determined to make this the final struggle. He ordered a grand assault along his lines, hurling his infantry onto the stout Confederate breastworks. The uncoordinated attacks by the Army of the Potomac were easily repulsed. The Army of the Potomac suffered nearly 7,000 casualties, while Lee's army sustained less than 1,500. Grant later admitted in his Memoirs that the only order he ever regretted giving was for the final assault at Cold Harbor. "I have always regretted that the last assault at Cold Harbor was ever made." He went on to say, "At Cold Harbor no advantage whatever was gained to compensate for the heavy loss we sustained. Indeed, the advantages, other than those of relative losses, were on the Confederate side."[20]

The fighting continued on June 2, with Johnston's Battery on the army's right flank near Turkey Hill. Lieutenant Edmund H. Moorman's section of Shoemaker's Battery joined them there with Breathed in overall command. When the Federals brought up a battery and opened up on the Confederate infantry, Breathed turned his guns on the Union artillery in the hope of silencing them. A fierce counter-battery duel raged for an hour in which two of Johnston's men suffered frightful arm wounds that required amputation. The Union artillerists finally broke off and retired, pulling their pieces behind a hill.[21]

More fighting raged on June 3. Breathed reported:

> On the 3rd . . . Johnston's battery became very hotly engaged at Cold Harbor contending against the enemy batteries for three hours but nobly held its position until relieved by our infantry. His loss was not so heavy in men as in horses. At Turkey Ridge [an irregular rise at the end of Confederate line] one section of each battery [Shoemaker's and Johnston's] were warmly engaged for about

forty minutes by which time they had succeeded in driving from its position a six-gun battery trying to enfilade our infantry line.[22]

The next day, Fitz Lee ordered Lomax to picket Crouch's Ford with a regiment and two of Breathed's guns. That day, the enemy appeared in their front and taunted the artillerists at the river crossings until the fire of Breathed's guns drove them off. Grant's campaign had bogged down, and he realized that he would have to develop a new strategy because there was nowhere else for him to go if he was to defeat Lee's army.[23]

Both armies had suffered massive losses throughout the Overland Campaign. Both armies were exhausted and needed rest. Grant's army was closer to Richmond than it had been at the outset of the campaign, but those last ten miles proved to be an insurmountable hurdle. The Confederate cavalry, and Breathed's horse artillerists, had done yeoman work in resisting the advance of the Army of the Potomac. Wade Hampton was unofficially in command the Army of Northern Virginia's Cavalry Corps; Robert E. Lee officially held the command personally. As one of Fitz Lee's officers put it, "Sheridan had crossed the Pamunkey expecting to pave Grant's way to Richmond, only to run aground against 'Hampton's half fed, half armed, half mounted, ill-disciplined yet ubiquitous and resolute cavalry.'" They had performed admirably in spite of being outnumbered by a better-armed and better-mounted enemy. However, Grant was engaged in a war of attrition, and it remained to be seen whether the Confederacy could survive.[24]

By June 8, the horse artillery was in motion once again, pursuing Sheridan's raiders as they made their way across central Virginia. Sheridan had received orders to march with two divisions of cavalry to link up with the army of Major General David Hunter at Charlottesville, and then bring that army back to Petersburg, where the Army of the Potomac and the Army of the James would try to sever the Confederate capital from its last remaining major lines of supply from the deep south. Unforeseen events awaited them at an obscure stop on the Virginia Central Railroad in Louisa County called Trevilian Station.[25]

Chapter 12

Pursuing Sheridan's Raiders

After realizing that his campaign had bogged down along the Chickahominy River outside Richmond, Grant decided on a bold strategy. He would send Sheridan and two divisions of cavalry on a raid intended to link up with Maj. Gen. David Hunter's army in the Shenandoah Valley. This move, hoped Grant, would draw off the Confederate cavalry in pursuit and permit the Army of the Potomac to steal a march on Lee. Grant's intended to cross the James River and capture the critical railroad junction of Petersburg, Virginia, before Lee could react. The logistical hub south of the Southern capital was where the Weldon and South Side railroads came together. Without these rail lines supplying Richmond and Lee's army, neither could survive for long. If successful, Lee would have no choice but to come out from behind his entrenchments and fight on ground of Grant's choosing—or abandon Richmond.

Sheridan's column—Torbert's and Gregg's divisions, supported by horse artillery—left the Cold Harbor front on June 7. The plan was to march along the north bank of the North Anna River, cross at Carpenter's Ford, move on Gordonsville, destroy the junction of the Virginia Central and Orange and Alexandria Railroads, and proceed to Charlottesville, where they would link up with Hunter's army. Because of the hot dry weather, the Union cavalry would have to march slowly in order to

LC

Butler's horse artillery thundering into action.

conserve horseflesh. General Lee learned of their departure the next day, June 8. Correctly surmising that Sheridan was moving to link up with Hunter, Lee ordered the divisions of Hampton and Fitz Lee, along with their attached battalions of horse artillery, in pursuit. Hampton was in command of the expedition.[1]

Hampton and Lee moved out that morning. Hampton had the advantage of a shorter interior line of march that enabled him to get ahead of the unsuspecting Sheridan. Breathed, with Johnston's and Shoemaker's batteries, rode with Fitz Lee. Chew, in command of Hart's and Johnston's batteries, remained with Hampton's Division, which was now under the command of his senior brigadier, Matthew Butler. By the night of June 10, Hampton was astride Sheridan's route at Trevilian Station, an obscure stop on the critical Virginia Central Railroad about six miles west of Louisa Court House and sixty-five miles west of Richmond. Sheridan, who had failed to send out flankers or scouts, was unaware of Hampton's presence. On the night of June 10, Sheridan's troopers crossed the North Anna River at Carpenter's Ford not realizing that two full divisions of Rebel cavalry was waiting for him. Hampton camped near the depot and Fitz Lee camped in the town of Louisa. Sheridan camped around Clayton's Store about four miles north of Louisa on the Fredericksburg Stage Road.

The two commanders developed plans for June 11 that were nearly mirror images of one another. Sheridan intended to divide his command. Most of it would march down the Fredericksburg Stage Road toward the depot, where it would head west on the Gordonsville Road. Custer's Michigan brigade would take a different road to guard Sheridan's flank. The two columns would meet up at the depot before proceeding. Hampton's plan was to send Fitz Lee's Division north from Louisa along the Marquis Road, an old commerce route, while Hampton's Division advanced up the Fredericksburg Stage Road. The plan was for Lee and Hampton to unite at Clayton's Store, driving Sheridan's command back against the North Anna River. The stage was set for what would be the largest cavalry battle of the Civil War.[2]

Wickham's Brigade of Lee's Division sortied up the Marquis Road about 3:00 A.M. on June 11. After advancing a mile or so from Louisa they encountered pickets from Custer's 7th Michigan Cavalry and a heavy skirmish commenced. After about forty-five minutes, Wickham retired to Louisa. Fitz Lee's Division was several hours late, leaving Hampton's command to go it alone against a much larger Federal force.

After shaking free of Wickham, Custer moved out about 6:00 A.M. The rest of Torbert's First Division, with Merritt's Regulars in the lead, marched down the Fredericksburg Stage Road toward the depot. After advancing a mile they ran into Butler's South Carolina pickets and heavy dismounted fighting broke out. Unable to hold their ground, Hampton's command was pressed backward toward the depot when the sound of gunfire and chaos broke out in their rear. Custer's Brigade had found Hampton's entire wagon park and the lead horses of the Confederate troopers and soon captured the entire lot. Hampton responded by shifting troops to meet the threat and Tom Rosser's Laurel Brigade, which had been guarding Hampton's western flank, galloped to join the fighting. All too quickly Hampton had found himself fighting a two-front battle.

While Hampton was fighting, Fitz Lee's Division arrived from Louisa and pitched in, surrounding Custer's Wolverines and capturing Custer's personal baggage and effects, as well as his black cook Eliza. For four hours the fighting raged while a desperate Custer tried to extricate himself from the Confederate trap. Some of Lee's men briefly captured one of Pennington's guns during the affair, but a determined charge led by Custer himself recaptured the lost piece.

Fitz Lee ordered up Breathed's guns and a severe sharp counter-battery duel broke out. When Pennington found the range and his shells began dropping too close for comfort, Breathed's yelled out, "Move up closer, they have got the range, boys!" It was not the first time they had heard that order. His artillerists did as they were told, moving their guns around the battlefield like pawns on a chessboard, though they suffered several casualties in the process. Henry Matthews remembered how "Breathed threw double shots of canister in their ranks, the cavalry charging. The battery advanced with the cavalry, one section firing; while the other section advanced in a gallop to an advanced position." The combat was, continued the gunner, "an animated scene long to be remembered." Breathed's insistence on moving his pieces closer to the enemy was baffled them, remembered Matthews. Indeed, the "movement was so successful, that the enemy deeming it expedient for the good of the service, fell back in great confusion, leaving his dead and wounded on the field."[3]

After long hours of combat, some of Torbert's and Gregg's troopers finally cut their way through to Custer's encircled brigade, freeing the Wolverines from their trap. A determined charge by parts of the 1st and 7th Michigan Cavalry regiments drove back Lee's men and Breathed's gunners to the William Wood Farm, where Breathed redeployed and continued his duel with Pennington, who shifted his own pieces accordingly.[4]

The chaos on a fluid battlefield like Trevilian Station is impossible to describe, and even the participants had trouble grasping all that took place there. Although the combat featured galloping charges and counter-charges, much of the fighting was dismounted. When a determined assault by four Union brigades finally drove Hampton's men from the depot, Fitz Lee retired to Louisa and Hampton drew off to the west, taking up a position astride the Gordonsville Road about two miles distant, leaving Sheridan's exhausted command in control of the battlefield. Both sides suffered heavily in the long day of fighting. General Rosser had his leg broken by a Federal bullet during one of the day's last attacks.[5]

After Fitz Lee pulled back to Louisa, Hampton's men prepared a strong defensive position along the Virginia Central Railroad near the Ogg Farm about two miles from Trevilian Station. Inexplicably, Sheridan failed to send out scouts and was thus unaware that Hampton's men were still blocking his direct route to Gordonsville. Believing that he had driven the Confederates away, Sheridan spent the morning of June 12 evaluating his losses from the previous day's fight and resting his men and horses. Some of his troopers busied themselves tearing up track on the Virginia Central Railroad while others marched toward Louisa to search for forage. About 2:00 P.M., Torbert's First Division rode up the Gordonsville Road and stumbled into the Southern position. Using their Enfield rifles, Butler's dismounted troopers opened a fire so heavy the Federals believed they were facing infantry instead of dismounted cavalry. After several attacks failed to carry the line Torbert called off the effort.

Fitz Lee's troopers, meanwhile, were on a long ride around Torbert's flank. They arrived in position after the sixth Union assault had been repulsed. Breathed deployed his guns in a good position and Wickham's men took up a position well to the front. Lomax's Brigade, with Shoemaker's Battery in support, made another flanking move. While Lomax was moving into his position, Torbert launched his seventh failed assault. Sensing an opportunity, Lomax charged the Union flank, struck it hard, and began rolling it up. Seeing this, Hampton ordered an assault of his own all along the line and within a few minutes the Federal cavalry was streaming from the field in a wild rout. "I ordered Lieutenant Phelps to report to you [Chew] with one gun. The others I got in position on the enemy's right so as to enfilade their dismounted line and at 5 P.M. opened upon them first with canister and then with short range shell," reported Breathed. "They stood but a short time, [we] having inflicted very heavy loss upon them. In this engagement Captain Shoemaker's battery sustained the heaviest loss."[6]

Low on ammunition and with heavy losses, and realizing that he had no way of achieving his objectives for the raid, Sheridan believed that he had no alternative but to break off the engagement and retire. By midnight, his command had re-crossed the North Anna River at Carpenter's Ford and was heading back toward Spotsylvania Court House. Sheridan stayed on the north bank of the North Anna River, while Hampton paralleled his movements along the south side of the river.

Lieutenant Colonel
George W. Covode,
commander of the 4th
Pennsylvania Cavalry.

LC

Hampton repeatedly offered battle, but Sheridan assiduously declined. By June 19, the Federals had reached White House Landing on the Pamunkey River, which had served as Grant's main supply depot during the Overland Campaign. The next day, with Chew in overall command (supported by Breathed's guns of Johnston's, Shoemaker's, Thomson's and Hart's Batteries), Fitz Lee's troopers attacked Sheridan's pickets. However, heavy fire from Union gunboats drove the horse soldiers off. Sheridan, now burdened by the garrison from White House Landing and a lengthy wagon train, was headed for the James River to join the rest of the Army of the Potomac. "From the 13th to the 19th the command was marching. On the 20th we opened fire on the enemy's entrenchments near the White House with slight loss," reported Breathed. "On the 21st we marched to Bottom's Bridge where we encamped until the 23rd."[7]

On June 24, most of Sheridan's column, including the wagon train and the infantry, crossed the James River. Sheridan had left David Gregg's Division behind as a rear guard. Gregg held a position near Samaria Church, about twenty miles southeast of Richmond. Sensing an opportunity, Hampton, now reinforced by Brig. Gen. Martin W. Gary's independent cavalry brigade, pounced on Gregg's isolated division. Hampton launched frontal and flanking attacks and heavy fighting ensued. During this fighting, Breathed himself led a cavalry charge, much as Pelham had done at Kelly's Ford fifteen months earlier. He soon found himself engaged in a saber duel with Lt. Col. George W. Covode, the commander of the 4th Pennsylvania Cavalry and the son of an influential Pennsylvania Congressman. Breathed severely wounded the Pennsylvanian, who died a short time later.[8]

"When Fitz Lee was ordered to assault the enemy's works Breathed was placed in the centre. As soon as the command forward was given, the first section of Breathed's battery [with Johnston in command] went in action, while the second section went forward in a gallop and took position; then the first section would do likewise," recalled Henry Matthews. "All of these movements were made under a terrific fire from Pennington's battery [sic. as well as Randol's and Dennison's batteries] and the cavalry. The last position we occupied was so close to the enemy's works that we could look into the muzzles of their artillery." [9]

Hampton finally broke off the pursuit of Gregg's shattered division when his troopers met heavy fire from Col. Thomas C. Devin's Brigade. Col. Devin and his troopers had the task of guarding the James River crossing near Charles City Court House, permitting the balance of Sheridan's command to cross to the safety of the south bank of the James River. The long raid had finally ended, seventeen days after it began. On June 26, Hampton crossed and moved on to join the Army of Northern Virginia at Petersburg. However, plenty of hard work still lay ahead for Hampton's weary troopers and horse artillerists.[10]

Although Sheridan had failed to accomplish virtually all of his

objectives for the raid, the rest of Grant's master plan worked well—at least for a while. With the Confederate cavalry distracted, the Army of the Potomac stole a march across the James River on June 13 and moved on Petersburg. Lee failed to detect the move for some time. Only a brilliant

Colonel
Thomas C. Devin.

LC

defensive stand by a scratch force under Gen. P. G. T. Beauregard and poor execution by Grant's subordinates, primarily Maj. Gen. William "Baldy" Smith, prevented Petersburg from being captured. However, when Lee was finally convinced that Grant had indeed left his front and stole a march on him, he shifted much of the Army of Northern Virginia below the river to meet the threat, reinforce Petersburg, and save the city from capture. Entrenchments were quickly thrown up by both sides, and a stalemate around the rail hub ensued.

On June 21, Grant ordered another cavalry raid, even though Sheridan and the other two divisions had not made it back to the Army of the Potomac. He instructed Brig. Gens. James H. Wilson and August V. Kautz, who commanded the small cavalry division assigned to the Army of the James, to destroy the main rail arteries in and outside of Petersburg, the Weldon and Southside Railroads. Departing on June 22, the Wilson-Kautz raid had no opposition for the first several days because Hampton was still off chasing Sheridan's raiders. However, once Sheridan crossed the James, Hampton was free to go after Wilson and Kautz. On June 25, a scant force of Confederates led by home guards and convalescents repulsed Wilson and Kautz at the Staunton River Bridge in Southside, Virginia. After the repulse, Wilson began making his way back toward Petersburg.[11]

With all three divisions of the Army of Northern Virginia Cavalry Corps and two independent brigades, Hampton went after the Federals with a vengeance. On June 28, the main body of Hampton's Cavalry Corps got to Stony Creek Depot on the Weldon Railroad before Wilson and Kautz. In addition to his strong cavalry force, Hampton also had two brigades of infantry under the command of Maj. Gen. William Mahone, so he outnumbered Wilson and Kautz by more than a two-to-one ratio. That morning, a fierce fight erupted between Hampton and Wilson that continued all day. Wilson commented that, "with alternating charge and countercharge till nearly midnight without either side gaining any substantial advantage." That night, Wilson broke off the inconclusive battle and withdrew toward Reams Station.[12]

When Hampton tried to resume the fight at Stony Creek Depot the next morning, he found the enemy gone. Hampton pursued. Wilson and Kautz were now deployed in this area, and Hampton was determined to destroy the isolated division. He ordered Chambliss' Brigade to attack, and the Virginia horse soldiers crashed into Brig. Gen. George

Chapman's command on the right flank, while Rosser's and Butler's Brigades fought the rest of Wilson's command and Kautz's Division, when it arrived to reinforce Wilson. Kautz ran into both Fitz Lee's cavalry and Mahone's infantry, and a heavy fight ensued.

"The fire of their artillery becoming very hot I directed Major Chew to place two guns (all I had) under Captain Graham, where they could respond," reported Hampton after the raid concluded. "These guns were well served and rendered me great assistance . . . the enemy retreating in confusion and leaving their dead and wounded on the ground. They were followed closely for two miles, when, finding that they had taken the road to Reams' Station, I moved by Stony Creek Depot, in order to get on the Halifax road to intercept them, should they attempt to cross below Reams." According to Hampton, they followed the enemy for four miles, "capturing a large number and scattering the rest. The force of the enemy was entirely broken and the fragments were seeking safety in flight in all directions. They scattered through the woods, and night coming on the pursuit had to cease. . . . I had not heard one word of the result of the fight at Reams' Station, nor did I know the position of Maj. Gen. Fitz Lee or of the enemy."[13]

"We captured 806 prisoners, together with 127 negroes—slaves. My loss was 2 killed, 18 wounded, and 2 missing," claimed Hampton. Wilson and Kautz lost all thirteen pieces of their artillery and all of their rolling stock, including their ambulances and wagons, together with nearly 1,000 prisoners.[14]

Wilson and Kautz, completely outnumbered, had been soundly routed at Reams Station. With three brigades of cavalry, two brigades of infantry, and Cayce's Battery (under command of Capt. William Pegram), and the entire battalion of horse artillery, the Confederates surrounded the Federals. "In this affair, Pegram, Chew, and Breathed were in their glory, and in no engagement of the war did the Horse Artillery display greater dash, notwithstanding the preceding weeks of constant marching and fighting," observed Jennings Cropper Wise, the chronicler of the history of the artillery of the Army of Northern Virginia.[15]

Breathed's guns had lagged behind. His horses were worn out, and they could not keep up with the fast-moving cavalry. The gunners often got ahead of the teams pulling their cannon, and they often acted as cavalry in those instances instead of waiting for the guns to come up. This would cost Breathed dearly. With his guns trailing behind, Breathed rode with Fitz Lee's cavalry that day. Breathed was again caught up in the excitement and led a charge with the 6th Virginia Cavalry. A Union trooper's pistol ball struck him in abdomen, knocking him from his horse. Henry Matthews saw Breathed fall:

> The horse artillery did not have much chance to distinguish itself on this occasion, but individual members of Breathed's [Johnston's] Battery when they found it impossible to keep up with the flying Yankees followed with the cavalry and were in at the death. I was one of those individuals who took advantage of the situation to join the cavalry pro tem. Breathed, when he found his artillery could not be of any use, placed the artillery near Stony Creek, joining his fortunes with the 6th Virginia Cavalry, who were always glad to see him, continuing with them until he was shot down at the head of the regiment. His wound was a very severe one, being hit in the stomach by a pistol ball. . . .

Matthews also related an eye-witness account of Breathed's wounding. According to E. H. O'Brien,

> he and Corporal Al Hopkins rode on after the cavalry, as did the others. We had not seen Breathed up to this time, but knew he would give a good account of himself when we did see him. After galloping down the road a mile or two we saw a small group standing near the road. On reaching them we discovered our much loved Breathed lying on the ground severely wounded, his old battery around him as if to receive his dying benediction. His sufferings were intense and as we gazed on our hero we thought his hours were few: that but [in] a short time his soul would go to meet his commanders, Gen. J. E. B. Stuart and the gallant Pelham. As we bent over him he said, "Boys, they have got me this time." [16]

After examining the wound and determining that it was not mortal, Surgeon Leigh assured Breathed, "by good care and nursing he would be able to worry the Yankees a good many times yet." Fortunately, the pistol ball had settled in the walls of the stomach, consequently, he would not die of peritonitis. As a physician, Breathed well knew the consequences of being shot in the gut, and hearing the surgeon's diagnosis must have eased him immensely. If the ball had entered the abdominal cavity, infection would have set in and the wound would almost certainly have been mortal. Thankfully, the attending doctor determined that the ball had not entered this cavity. Dr. Leigh summoned an ambulance to carry Breathed from the battlefield. Delirious with pain, the artillerist ordered O'Brien and Hopkins to retrieve their guns, which had been captured by the Federal cavalry early in the engagement. Breathed's order heartened the Confederate artillerymen, who set spurs to their horses and charged the enemy. They not only managed to recaptured their lost pieces, but also turn them on the fleeing Federal horse soldiers.[17]

An ugly incidence occurred once Breathed was taken from the field; Henry Matthews recounted the circumstances: "After Major Breathed was carried in the ambulance to the home of Mrs. Malone, he was placed in a bed on the first floor and everything was done for his comfort that the doctor's limited resources would permit." The next evening, however, "Dr. Bill Murray (the battery Surgeon) and myself went over to see how he was getting along. Mrs. Malone met us at the door in the most cordial manner telling us that Major Breathed had just shot a Negro who had insulted her, and that the Negro was lying to the left of the door steps. Thinking perhaps she had made a mistake, we went to the left entrance of the porch and discovered the dead Negro. Asking Mrs. Malone for the particulars, she stated that the Negro had come to her house with a Negro woman, had taken possession of one of her rooms and in the most insulting manner had ordered her to get something for them to eat at once, saying that he was going out and when he returned he wanted the meal to be ready. Breathed, who heard every word, crawled out of bed, got his pistol and fired, killing the Negro instantly."[18]

The dead man was a slave who had been freed by Union cavalrymen in the vicinity of Reams Station. He was one of 127 who ran for freedom when the Confederates attacked. Henry Matthews claimed the freed slaves had been promised a "mule and 40 acres and a white man to pull the plow." Matthews described the killing as "justified," and Breathed was never punished for it.[19]

No one will ever know what words were exchanged when the black man entered the house uninvited. Whatever he said was enough to spur Breathed to action in spite of his severe wound. The man likely had no idea Breathed was in the next room, or that the grievously wounded major would defend the honor of his host in such a manner.

In 1903, George Cary Eggleston, a veteran of the 1st Virginia Cavalry, published a novel of the Civil War titled *The Master of Warlock*, which helps to explain why a gentleman such as Breathed would kill a man in cold blood. Although fiction, the code of honor that governed many Southern men was indeed a real one:

> [T]he men were free, as soon as a halt was called, to move about among the feminine throng, greeting their acquaintances when they had any, and being cheerily greeted by strangers, in utter disregard of those conventions with which womanhood elsewhere than in Virginia surrounds itself. There womanhood had always felt itself free, because it had always felt itself under the protection of all there was of manhood in the land. No woman in that time and country was ever in danger of affront, for the reason that no man dared affront her, lest he encounter vengeance, swift, sure, and relentless, at the hands of the first other man who might hear of the circumstance.

Under this strict code, Breathed would have been required to defend Mrs. Malone's honor if it were threatened. Apparently the man did just that, and Breathed shot him dead.[20]

Revenge for a perceived insult and injury was an important component of the masculine code of honor, even though revenge was at odds with Christian ethics. However, many men were able to set aside this code of ethics during the Civil War and reconcile Christianity and vengeance. No man embodied this seeming contradiction more than did Lt. Gen. Thomas J. "Stonewall" Jackson, who was a devout Presbyterian Christian who firmly believed that killing the enemy was akin to a religious crusade.[21]

When Breathed finally reached Richmond his former mentor, Dr. Macgill, was probably the attending physician. Dr. Macgill had been appointed a surgeon for the Army of Northern Virginia, and he was on duty in Richmond at this time. The attending surgeon would have removed the pistol ball and stitched the wound. He would have also prescribed the opiate laudanum to ease the major's suffering. On July 11, Breathed went on medical leave. He spent all of July and part of August in the hospital recuperating. His absence, however, was keenly felt in the Army of Northern Virginia.

On July 7, Robert E. Lee penned a note to the injured artillerist. "I heard with great regret that you were wounded and incapacitated for active duty. I beg to tender you my sympathy, and to express the hope that the army will not long be deprived of your valuable services," wrote the sympathetic army leader. "The reports I have received from your superior officers of your gallantry and good conduct in action on several occasions, have given me great satisfaction, and while they increase my concern for your personal suffering, render me more anxious that your health will soon permit you to resume a command that you have exercised with so much credit to yourself and advantage to the service."[22]

The loss of their second-in-command left the men of the Stuart Horse Artillery deeply concerned as Breathed convalesced in Richmond. The future of the horse artillery was uncertain, and the morale of the artillerists was low. Matthews described the mood of the horse artillerists at this time: "There was a great deal of dissatisfaction in the battery at that time. Owing to the unpopularity of P. P. Johnston, who succeeded Breathed as Captain, many members of the battery did not go with it to the Valley, but were transferred to the Maryland [L]ine. I have always regretted the charge [in which Breathed was severely wounded], for I loved the old battery and its grand association dearly. We should have staid [sic] in the battery and held up its unequalled reputation for Breathed's sake at least, but, unfortunately, we did not at that time look at it in that light." For Matthews, and many of the old veterans of the "Breathed Battery," the transfer of command to Johnston marked the end of the old unit: "If Johnston had been in possession of a particle of manhood knowing that the greater part of the men did not want him as command, why, he would have resigned or asked to be transferred to another battery where the men did not know him as well as we did. He staid [sic]—and the result is known he lost the very best men he had. It was a sad day when I turned my back on the dear old battery." [23]

The fate of his men may well have embittered Breathed. One of the few recorded conversations Breathed engaged in after the war was with Matthews in the Fountain Inn in Baltimore. "Major Breathed . . . told me that the day the boys left the battery was the saddest day he passed through in the war," recorded Matthews.[24]

However, the war was far from over for Breathed. In August, the remaining men of the horse artillery were transferred to meet a new and ominous threat in the Shenandoah Valley. A powerful 45,000-man army under the command of Phil Sheridan was threatening the breadbasket of the Confederacy.[25]

Chapter 13

The Last Great Stand of the
Stuart Horse Artillery

As the Army of the Potomac began tightening its stranglehold on Richmond and Petersburg, General Lee realized that unless he took a bold step, the outcome of the war would simply be a matter of time—a lengthy siege that would cripple his army, followed by capitulation. He could not hope to win a determined and protracted war of attrition. Remembering the havoc created by Jackson's operations in the Shenandoah Valley in 1862, Lee decided to roll the dice and gamble again. He decided to send the II Army Corps, now commanded by the newly-promoted Lt. Gen. Jubal A. Early (who had replaced the disabled Ewell) to the Valley. Lee's hope was that Early would create chaos sufficient to force Grant to break off the siege or at least respond in kind, sending off a large portion of his own command to contend with Early. With about 17,000 men, Early's command marched on June 13 toward Lynchburg, where he would parry the thrust of Major General Hunter's army, which was rapidly closing in on that important railroad and supply center.

On June 14 Early's army marched along the route of the Virginia Central Railroad, passing through the Trevilian Station battlefield, and arrived at Charlottesville, where they boarded trains for Lynchburg. On June 16 the Confederate infantry disembarked at Lynchburg, in time to repulse Hunter's army. Hunter pulled back into West Virginia, thus effectively removing himself from the war for a month. The retreat of Hunter's army cleared the Shenandoah Valley of significant Union forces, permitting Early, now reinforced by the division of Maj. Gen. John C. Breckinridge, to advance down the Valley, cross the Potomac River, and threaten Washington, D.C. After a hard-fought day-long battle at Monocacy Junction on July 6, Early was at the outskirts of Washington by July 12. His little army drew up in front of Fort Stevens, located in Silver Spring, Maryland, and prepared to attack the next day. President Abraham Lincoln himself personally observed some of the skirmishing at Fort Stevens on July 11, recklessly exposing himself to fire by Early's men.

However, Grant, responding to the cries of panic emanating from the national Capitol, had sent the VI Corps, under command of Maj. Gen. Horatio G. Wright, to defend the city. The Federal infantrymen boarded trains and went to Washington (one division actually arrived in time to fight at Monocacy on July 6), and the other two divisions arrived just in time to force Early to call off his planned assault on Fort Stevens on July 13. After a brief demonstration, Early withdrew and retired across the Potomac, taking up a position near Winchester, waiting for the Federals to come and get him. Wright proved himself unequal to the task of independent command, and a vigorous debate broke out as to who should lead the Union army being cobbled together to fend off Early. The Union high command wanted to retain Hunter as the department commander while giving Major General Philip H. Sheridan the command of the troops in the field. Hunter declined, so Sheridan was given overall command of the Middle Military District over the objections of Secretary of War Stanton, who believed that Sheridan was too young to hold such a high command.

The War Department pulled together an army of 45,000 men for Sheridan, consisting of the VI, VIII, and XIX Corps of infantry, two divisions of Sheridan's Cavalry Corps of the Army of the Potomac, and assigned to the Middle Military District Brig. Gen. William W. Averell's Independent Cavalry Division. Early's army would be outnumbered by more than two-to-one. His little army would have to hold back Sheridan's onslaught.

Worried about the state of affairs in the Shenandoah Valley, Robert E. Lee sent Maj. Gen. Joseph B. Kershaw's Division of Longstreet's

LC

Sheridan's Federal troops rampaging through the
Shenandoah Valley in the summer of 1864.

Corps and Fitz Lee's Cavalry Division to reinforce Early. The infantry
was to wait at Culpeper Court House until they were needed, while Fitz
Lee's cavalry joined Early's army at Winchester. The Shenandoah
Valley was the breadbasket of the Confederacy, and Early had to defend
it while also keeping Sheridan at bay. With the addition of Kershaw's
foot soldiers and Fitz Lee's horsemen, Early now mustered 23,000 men
of all branches for service against Sheridan's Army of the Shenandoah,
as his army was soon dubbed.[1]

On July 28, Breathed's men left Richmond, crossed the James River,
and bivouacked near Ream's Station. Breathed had returned to duty even
though he was still recovering from his severe combat wound, reporting
that, "Having been wounded on the 29th June I did not join my command
until the 5th August [when I] was released from . . . convalescence in
Richmond." Accompanying Fitz Lee's Division, Breathed's Batteries
were headed for Early's army at Winchester, which was a critical supply
center for the Confederate army. On August 10, Fitz Lee's Division
marched, with Johnston's and Shoemaker's Batteries in tow, and with
Breathed back at his post. The cavalry arrived at Front Royal on August
14.[2]

On August 16, Johnston's Battery supported Wickham's Cavalry
Brigade in fighting at Front Royal. Colonel Thomas C. Devin's Brigade
of Merritt's Cavalry Division had established his picket line on high
ground on the North Fork of the Shenandoah River at a place called
Guard Hill. Confederate infantry of Brig. Gen. William T. Wofford's
Brigade drove in Devin's pickets in spirited action. Johnston deployed

Captain James M. Robertson's Federal horse artillery.

his four guns on Guard Hill, and was raining shrapnel and canister on Devin's 4th and 5th New York Cavalry when Custer's Michigan Brigade arrived and turned the tables. When the Wolverines charged, they drove Wickham's troopers back to the banks of the river.[3]

Johnston took up a new position and opened fire with his four guns. "The enemy by incredible exertion, succeeded in placing his guns upon the almost perpendicular crests," remarked Devin, "and during the whole action kept an incessant rain of shot and shell upon our line, but fortunately with slight effect." Devin brought his own horse artillery to bear, and the encounter evolved into an artillery brawl. In an engagement marked by poor fighting by the depleted Confederate cavalry, Johnston's Battery showed it could still offer the fierce and effective resistance.[4]

On August 17, Merritt and the Union cavalry retired toward Berryville. Merritt's horsemen bloodied the Confederate cavalry that day, but the still-feisty Southern horsemen knew that more heavy work awaited them. On August 21, Breathed, who had regained a measure of his old strength and vigor, pushed on toward Berryville. There, his command attacked the Federal horse artillery on the Berryville Pike. "Both batteries did splendid firing," he proudly reported. "Near Berryville the enemy was posted behind a strong work but by the well directed shots of Sgt. [John] Herly of Shoemaker's Battery they were forced to leave it in a short time. The batteries did not suffer much either in men or horses." The precise fire of Shoemaker's artillerymen almost drove Col. Charles Russell Lowell's reserve brigade all the way back to Berryville. Throughout the Valley Campaign of 1864, however, the Union cavalry would prove to be a very battle-worthy opponent.[5]

On the morning of August 26, Breathed placed two of Johnston's guns on the Virginia side of the Potomac River overlooking the town of Williamsport, Maryland. "The enemy was strongly posted behind the canal with their flag planted on the bank. The General Commanding directed me to try and drive them from their position which was done in about forty minutes Sgt. Smith [Barney] shooting down their flag," reported Breathed. Rarely did he fail to accomplish his objectives.[6]

While en route to Winchester, Breathed and Lt. Col. Pendleton stopped by Williamsport to visit the family homestead of Bai-Yuka. Judge Breathed was involved in the arrest of his neighbors, who worked for the nearby College of St. James. Dr. Kerfoot, the College's headmaster, and Rev. Professor Coit had been arrested by Early. Major Henry Kyd Douglas, who was Breathed's friend, remembered the occasion. "Before I was in bed in my tent, Mr. John W. Breathed, father of Captain [Major] Jim Breathed, than whom no more gallant officer ever commanded a Confederate battery—whom Dr. Kerfoot had sent for—was at my tent, urging me to see General Early in behalf of the two prisoners," recalled Kyd Douglas. "At early dawn the next morning, General Early and Lt. Col. Pendleton of his staff rode into our Headquarters and Mr. Breathed was at hand." Kyd Douglas accompanied them to the Rectory and made a personal appeal for Kerfoot's release. Judge Breathed made an earnest appeal, but Early seemed unwilling to budge. "He called Dr. Kerfoot and Mr. Coit into the parlor and seated himself at a table. He then told the two gentlemen that he had ordered their arrest in retaliation for the arrest of the Reverend Dr. Andrew H. H. Boyd of Winchester, who was then sick in prison at Wheeling, Hunter's favorite Bastille."[7]

Early finally relented and agreed to release the two men, but only if Boyd was also released. With the understanding that they would travel to Washington to gain Boyd's unconditional release Early released them. Early gave them three weeks to accomplish this objective. If they failed, they were to present themselves as prisoners of war in Richmond. Unfortunately, this sort of tit-for-tat exchange happened all too often during the Civil War. Although Judge Breathed was a strong Southern sympathizer, he was also loyal to his friends and neighbors. Kerfoot and Coit succeeded: Boyd was released upon their appeal, and the two men returned to the College of St. James, their ordeal over without a trip to Richmond.[8]

The horse artillery battalion, under Breathed's command, headed to Smithfield, West Virginia, where they remained until August 28. On August 27, Johnston and his battery were ordered to report to Maj. Gen. Lunsford L. Lomax, who had been promoted to division command. Johnston supported Lomax's advance to the banks of the Opequon Creek, where a skirmish with some Union artillery occurred. After forty minutes of heavy and accurate firing, Johnston and his gunners had driven off a pesky Union battery. "The battery was highly complimented by General Early, Breckinridge & Lomax," proudly reported Breathed.[9]

From the end of August until September 2, the armies remained rather quiet while Early and Sheridan skirmished lightly and evaluated their options. The horse artillery scouted and supported the cavalry. Breathed's gunners—Johnston's and Shoemaker's batteries—were attached to Rosser's Division, who had returned to duty from his Trevilian Station wound with a fresh promotion. Although he was still recovering from his stomach wound, Breathed remained at his post to lead his men. "We arrived at Front Royal on the 14th [September] where we remained until the 16th," he reported. "On the 17th marched to Winchester and remained in that vicinity until the 20th."[10]

* * *

The Third Battle of Winchester marked the beginning of the end for the Confederate presence in the Valley. After more than a month of inactivity, Sheridan finally was ready to move. Implementing a plan designed by Sheridan's chief lieutenant, Maj. Gen. George Crook, Sheridan's cavalry advanced from the north on the morning of September 19 while his infantry attacked from the northeast and east. Fitz Lee's two brigades—Wickham's, now commanded by Col. Thomas T. Munford, and Payne's—moved out early to meet the enemy horse north of Winchester. Breathed unlimbered his six guns on the north bank of Red Bud Run not far from the Hackwood Farm to support Maj. Gen. John B. Gordon's infantry division, which held the left flank of Early's small

A depiction of the fighting at Third Winchester.

army. The fighting commenced early in the morning and lasted most of the day. The morning phase ended about 11:00 A.M., with Breathed's gunners involved for the entire time.[11]

After a brief lull, the fighting resumed in earnest about 11:40 A.M., when Union Generals Cuvier Grover's and William Dwight's four infantry brigades of the XIX Corps attacked near Breathed's position. The Southern front was shaped like a large inverted "L," and the wave of attackers struck the joint of the bent Confederate line. As the Federals emerged from thick woods, remembered one of them, "it was one of the most beautiful of early autumn days; the air was cool and mellow, the sun shed a tempered warmth and the whole face of nature smiled in the harvest-time." Blasts of flying metal—both bullets and canister from Gordon's infantry and his supporting artillery—shattered the idyllic Valley scene.

When Breathed joined in with his six guns, firing case and canister shot obliquely into the advancing enemy. Before long, the Northern infantry and Averell's dismounted cavalry began to waver under the barrage of fire. "Our men were falling very fast," recalled a New York infantryman. Fitz Lee was badly wounded in the leg during this fighting and had to leave the field, leaving Wickham in command.[12]

A deep gully called "Ash Hollow" lay a short distance from the Confederate right flank. Sheridan's infantry gathered in this hollow and used its shelter to rally and reorganize while pieces of hot metal flew over their heads like bees buzzing around a hive. About noon, Ricketts' division of the Union VI Corps, along with Grover's division of the XIX Corps, attacked directly from the east, just to the left of the earlier Union attack. "The handling of the six guns of horse artillery was simply magnificent. Strange enough, the enemy's guns did not respond to these Confederate guns," reported Munford. "Our cannoneers made their battery roar, sending their death-dealing messengers with a precision and constancy that made the earth around them seem to tremble, while their shot and shell made lanes in this mass of the enemy moving obliquely to their right to attack Evans' brigade." Breathed's artillery blasted the ranks of the Union infantry. "See how cheerfully [the horse artillery] go in. How rapidly they load, fire and reload" a Confederate soldier noticed. "They stand six and twelve feet apart, calling to each other, laughing, shooting, and cheering, but advancing." The Union artillery did not return counter-battery fire, which enabled Breathed's men to load and fire in an uninterrupted sequence. When Grover's soldiers retreated, Breathed was able to train his guns on a second clump of trees and another body of Union soldiers. "The first Rebel shell killed Colonel Samuel R. Per, Lee's horse; the second the major's horse, the third, exploding above the ranks, caused some casualties. One fragment struck a corporal, literally demolishing him," remembered one observer. Breathed's guns were inflicting significant damage, but the Union soldiers' discipline and training steadied them. The enemy closed up ranks and pressed on, stepping over and around their dead and wounded comrades. "They had the best of range on us, and I tell you that the ground fairly worked under our feet," remembered a Union soldier of the advance. "There is one great mystery that is how we ever so many of us got off alive."[13]

Constant pressure on the Confederate front slowly drove it south and west on the Valley Pike toward Winchester. Exhausted, confused, and suffering heavy losses, Early's infantry began to buckle under the strain. Late in the afternoon, a five-brigade cavalry charge by the Union horsemen of Averell and Merritt shattered the left end of Early's line and sent the Confederates "whirling through Winchester," as one of Sheridan's staff officers described it. Early's shattered army fled in a wild rout. "Late in the day the right was still steady, but the left was becoming more and more critical," reported Munford. "The enemy's cavalry in driving back Fitzhugh Lee's small force dashed through the infantry brigade sent to his support and captured many of its men. Our left still receding, the center became more and more salient, and had also to be gradually drawn back."[14]

The Confederates became disorganized as the melee turned into a large scale rout. With Fitz Lee down and Robert Rodes, one of the finest infantry division commanders of the army killed, the army fled as fast as it could. "The bands playing national airs, presented in the sunlight one moving mass of glittering sabers," reported George A. Custer. "This, combined with the various and bright-colored banners and battle-flags, intermingled here and there with the plain blue uniforms of the troops, furnished one of the most inspiring as well as imposing scenes of martial grandeur ever witnessed upon a battle-field. No encouragement was required to inspirit either man or horse."[15]

With wounded men crying out in agony, and with the dead scattered all around, the battlefield presented a ghastly sight. Early ordered Munford to move his brigade of Virginians from Early's far right to his far left, near the so-called Star Fort. Munford's four regiments arrived just as the great Federal cavalry charge crashed upon them. After repulsing the first attacks by Averell's horsemen, Shoemaker deployed two of his guns and opened fire on the Union cavalry, wreaking havoc on their charge. Eventually, the weight of Averell's Division drove Payne's and Munford's troopers from the Star Fort, with Shoemaker's guns staying behind to cover their retreat. The gunners worked with great effect, firing rapidly and covering Munford's retreat until the Union horse artillery finally found the range and began dropping shells into the Fort amid the Confederate cannon. Munford finally ordered the men to withdraw from the fort. It was uncertain as to where Breathed himself was during the retreat from Star Fort, but one can be assured he was engaged somewhere on the battlefield. [16]

Captain John Shoemaker, whose guns were in Star Fort, later wrote, "My battery remained on the hill, shelling the enemy, until Sheridan's entire army came into view on the plateau in front of Winchester and fired on us with all their artillery from our left and front. The sight of

30,000 troops drawn up in line of battle with their glistening arms was a grand and impressive spectacle, but the flashing of all their artillery and the storm of shells thrown at us were more persuasive, and we had to bid them a very hasty—Good afternoon."[17]

One of the artillerists was decapitated by accurate Federal artillery fire. The men strapped the unfortunate victim to their caisson and brought his body off the field. However, Breathed's gunners had performed admirably under some very difficult circumstances. "Breathed's guns, of the Horse Artillery, were operating with good effect from point to point, as occasion offered," praised Pendleton in his after-action report. Resistance by Lomax's cavalry and the horse artillery blunted the pursuit of Wilson's cavalry division, allowing Early's army to escape. The falling darkness proved to be the "savior" of the retreat, ending the Third Battle of Winchester. Both sides were ready for a rest after the exhausting day of fighting.[18]

Early fell back to a position south of Winchester, where he rallied his scattered forces. At first light the next morning, Breathed marched, with Shoemaker's two guns leading the way, followed by Munford's and Lomax's troopers. They fell all the way back through Newtown to Front Royal, blocking Sheridan from having access to the mouth of the Luray Valley. The bulk of Early's army assumed a position along the crest of Fisher's Hill, a stout defensive position astride the Valley Pike, which was anchored on the Shenandoah River on one side and Little North Mountain on the other. Although the position was thinly held, it could not be taken by direct assault. Once again employing a battle plan designed by Crook, Sheridan attacked Early's flank and rolled it up, driving the Confederates from Fisher's Hill in a panic. Early was forced to fall back again, but Sheridan did not follow up because the Southern cavalry had tied up his horsemen in the Luray Valley.[19]

The next day, September 22, Breathed accompanied Munford's troopers, including Johnston's Battery, to Milford, south of Overall's Run, where they took up a strong defensive position on a crest above the Run. Wilson's dismounted troopers assaulted the Confederate right flank, but ran into the teeth of the still viable remnant of the Stuart Horse Artillery. "Torbert, running out his artillery, commenced a furious shelling, which our battery [Johnston's] answered with vigor. His men demonstrated heavily in front of Payne, whose men were at the bridge, and they moved up in our front as if they intended to assault my lines," reported Munford. Payne fended off these attacks. However, Munford began to suspect that something was afoot, so he sent out scouts to determine whether Wilson was moving on his flank. The scout reported back that a large Union force—perhaps a brigade—was moving on the flank. Munford was worried, as his line was already stretched too thin by dismounting his men; the very act of dismounting cavalry reduced effective strength by one-quarter, as every fourth man had to hold his horse and the horses of three others at the ready. "I was in conversation with Major Breathed when this information was brought me" reported Munford. "I asked him if he felt safe with his battery, if he moved the squadron in his front and over whose heads his guns were firing?"[20]

"If Billy (Col. Payne) can hold that bridge—and it looks like he is going to do it—I'll put a pile of canister near my guns, and all h—l will never move me from this position," responded Breathed. "I'll make a horizontal shot turn in full blast for them to come through; you need not be afraid of my guns." Breathed's determined artillerists drove off Wilson's flanking probes, and Munford was able to withdraw his command safely. "Unfortunately Torbert did not succeed in driving Wickham's cavalry from its strong defensive position at Millford," remembered Munford, "and hence the portion of Sheridan's plan which contemplated cutting off the enemy's retreat by seizing the pike at New Market was not carried out."[21]

On September 27, Wickham's Division, accompanied by a section of Johnston's Battery, led the infantry divisions of Maj. Gen. John B. Gordon and Stephen D. Ramseur across the South Fork of the Shenandoah River at Patterson's Mill and pounced on Sheridan's camps there. Munford unlimbered two of Johnston's guns and then shifted his troopers into a position where he could launch an assault. Wickham arrived and ordered the guns to open fire. Johnston's artillerists opened up with a heavy and accurate fire. Wickham then learned that Wilson's Division and Col. Charles Russell Lowell's Reserve Brigade of Merritt's Division were near Waynesboro, destroying an iron railroad bridge over the South Fork of the Shenandoah. Wickham sent Munford's Brigade and Johnston's guns to deal with them, and promised that Brig. Gen. John Pegram's infantry division would support them.

Johnston opened fire on the Union troopers, breaking up the bridge destruction party. However, Early had no choice but to withdraw farther south, leaving most of the fertile Valley in Sheridan's hands. Sheridan was about to implement a scorched earth policy that would leave the beautiful Valley a wasteland, depriving the Confederacy of desperately needed provisions. Sheridan began a week long campaign of destruction called "The Burning." Provisions were destroyed and homesteads put to the torch. Many families were left destitute as their crops and homes were burned.[22]

On October 1, Breathed's command consisted of Johnston's, Shoemaker's, and Thomson's batteries. Chew commanded Graham's, Hart's, and McGregor's Batteries. On October 2, Johnston's Battery skirmished with Union troops moving up the Valley while Shoemaker's Battery was sent through Brown's Gap. On October 7, it was reported by Sheridan that "the burning" was going splendidly, "In moving back to this point the whole country from the Blue Ridge to the North Mountains has been made untenable for a rebel army." Sheridan then boasted about the destruction of the Valley. "I have destroyed over 2,000 barns, filled with wheat, hay and farming implements; over seventy mills filled with flour and wheat; have driven in front of the army over 4,000 head of stock, and have killed and issued to the troops not less than 3,000 sheep. This destruction embraces the Luray Valley and Little Fort Valley as well as the main valley. A large number of horses have been obtained, a proper estimate of which I cannot now make. Lieutenant J. R. Meigs, my engineer officer, was murdered beyond Harrisonburg, near Dayton. For this atrocious act, all the houses within an area of five miles were burned."[23]

Early told a different story of the lieutenant's death. "Three of our cavalry scouts in their uniforms and with arms, got around his lines near a little town called Dayton, and encountered Lieut. Meigs, a Federal engineer officer, with two soldiers," he recounted. "These parties came upon each other suddenly, and Lieut. Meigs was ordered to surrender by one of our scouts, to which he replied by shooting and wounding the scout, who in his turn fired and killed the Lieutenant. One of the men with Lieutenant Meigs was captured and the other escaped."[24]

* * *

On October 8 the army had moved up the Valley to the small village of New Market. "Early halted the infantry, but pushed his cavalry to the front some twenty-five or more miles from any support, Rosser, with the brigades of Wickham, Paine and his own on the back road;" remembered a Maryland Cavalier, "Lomax, with Johnson's and Jackson's brigades, on the turnpike. At this time these two last commands did not aggregate more than 1000 or 1200 men at the outside." Relating the evening's strategy discussion with Lomax, Rosser reported that, "he had driven the enemy before him and would advance again at early dawn. Lomax stated Early's orders were to keep on." Even though the Confederate cavalry was isolated, far in front of any Confederate infantry support, Early had ordered the attack.[25]

On October 9 at Tom's Brook, the Confederate cavalry suffered its worst defeat of the war. Considering that they were outnumbered 10,000 to 4,000, this outcome came as no great surprise. Rosser's Division had been sent to the Valley to reinforce the beleaguered forces trying to hold back Sheridan's hordes. Most of Rosser's men were from the Valley, and the destruction of their homes and farms infuriated them. "We called on Rosser at the Willow Pump one evening, and he very jocularly enquired why we had been permitting the federal cavalry to misuse us so terribly, stating on the Petersburg lines our people were virtually having their own way, and he would now show us how it ought to be done," remembered a Maryland cavalryman of Rosser's overconfidence. "I recall a very pertinent reminder that came before us that night." Local newspapers, desperate for good news, quickly dubbed Rosser "the Savior of the Valley," much to his later consternation. His troopers had doggedly clung to Sheridan's column while it burned the beautiful Valley, but to no avail. Rosser took up a position atop a low ridge astride the Back Road, at the base of Little North Mountain. Sheridan, infuriated by Rosser's dogging his column, ordered Torbert, his cavalry commander, to go out, attack Rosser, and either whip the Confederates or be whipped himself.[26]

George Custer, now commanding Wilson's Third Division, attacked Rosser's position on the morning of October 9. "We met in a position where the turnpike was closed in on either side by hills or woodland, and without hesitation charged the enemy, who gave way, and we followed for some distance, until striking the open country we deployed and went into position." recalled the Maryland horse soldier.

> This movement, while necessary and the proper thing under the circumstances, now proved to be the occasion of our undoing, for, as we reached the highland, the mist of the Valley cleared up and

our weakness was at once made apparent to our adversaries, who immediately moved to the attack. This attack we withstood for some time; in fact, the men behaved better than we looked for; but in less than an hour's time it became evident we were being over-matched, and our lines began to give away.

Breathed's guns were deployed atop the ridge, overlooking Tom's Brook.[27]

Breathed's old adversary, Alexander C. M. Pennington, now commanded a brigade of cavalry in Custer's division. Pennington's New Jersey troopers clashed with the 4th Virginia Cavalry on Mt. Olive. Before long, the Union horse artillery opened on Breathed's guns, and a counter-battery duel broke out. Unable to dislodge Rosser with frontal attacks, Custer instead decided to flank the position. Caught in the confusion, one Confederate artillerist said to his commander, "Captain, if you will only get your runaway cavalrymen out of the road I will let into them." However, the artillerist's efforts were to no avail. Custer and his troopers soon found the end of Payne's line and overlapped his flank, rolling it up and driving the Southern horsemen in a rout. As the panicked cavalrymen fled, Breathed's guns were left exposed and all of Johnston's and Thomson's cannon were captured. Rosser unsuccessfully tried to make a stand two miles to the south, but Custer's victorious horsemen overwhelmed them, capturing the rest of Breathed's guns. The day had been an unmitigated disaster, and Breathed had to endure the humiliation of losing nearly all of his guns.[28]

Thomson's Battery also suffered humiliating losses that day. Thomson's guns were taken during the headlong flight from the battlefield, losing fourteen men and nearly losing their battle flag in the process. "The worst day in the history of the Confederate horse artillery saw eleven guns with most of the ordnance wagons, forges, and ambulances captured. Sixty-three men were casualties, almost all of them prisoners," recalled Charles McVicar of Thomson's Battery. "Johnston's Battery, too, became a battery on paper. With all its guns and most of its equipment captured, it would be quite some time before it could again take a field." Because the Confederacy could not replace these losses, most of the horse artillerists were sent back to Petersburg to join the Army of Northern Virginia in the siege lines. Only five guns remained as part of the horse artillery after October 9.[29]

Early vented his disgust in his report to General Lee. "This is very distressing to me, and God knows I have done all in my power to avert the disasters which have befallen this command," he declared, "but the fact is that the enemy's cavalry is so much superior to ours, both in numbers and equipments, and the country is so favorable to the operations of cavalry, that it is impossible for ours to compete with his." Confederate John Newton suggested that after the Tom's Brook drubbing, Rosser's horsemen should remove the laurel as their hat emblem and replace it with a gourd vine. Instead of saving the Valley, these men had taken an unprecedented drubbing at the hands of Sheridan's horsemen.[30]

On October 12, the remaining men of the horse artillery encamped at New Market before rejoining Rosser's Division. What remained of Johnston's, Shoemaker's, and Thomson's Batteries waited for supplies and for the arrival of replacement guns. Twenty-four horses and a section of guns were sent to Staunton. The Battalion was slowly being reborn, and Early's army was on the move again. Breathed's reconstituted artillery force now consisted of Johnston's, Shoemaker's and Thomson's Batteries. The Confederates spent October 15 and 16 marching to Mount Solon, where they camped until October 28. They missed the violent Battle of Cedar Creek on October 19, the last major engagement of the Valley Campaign.[31]

The horse artillery did not engage the Federals at all in November. Breathed, meanwhile, accompanied Rosser and his division on a raid into West Virginia.[32]

* * *

With Breathed now riding with Rosser, the rest of the Stuart Horse Artillery Battalion was put under Chew's direct command. Most of the batteries were mere shadows of what they had once been. There were few horses and cannon with which to replace losses, and there were few men available, either. "After our misfortune at Woodstock or Tom's Brook, in October, 1864, losing part of our guns, we moved in the vicinity of Staunton, feeling the loss of our guns and being laughed at by our comrades in the cavalry" remembered one of Chew's artillerymen. "The men of the battery talked of making independent raids and trying to recapture their guns, or gain new laurels, but they had not long wait," said Private Brady, as General Rosser was preparing for a daring raid.[33]

New Creek, West Virginia, was an important supply depot along the Baltimore & Ohio Railroad. Brevet Maj. Gen. Benjamin F. Kelley commanded the Union garrison at Hancock, Maryland, not far from New Creek. Rosser's Division was on a raid into New Creek, heading for the Union depot there. On December 7, Kelley reported, "Upon being advised, on the 27th, of the presence of the enemy in large force in the valley, and of the result of Lieutenant Colonel Fleming's operations, I felt assured that the enemy would follow up the advantage he had gained by attacking New Creek or Cumberland, or both, and at once to guard against the possibility of a surprise, telegraphed to Colonel Latham, at New Creek, advising him of my belief, and ordering him to take measures for the defense of the post. To this dispatch, at midnight, Colonel Latham replied that, he was prepared for them."[34]

The depot at New Creek was well fortified and was held by 700 men of all arms, but primarily consisting of dismounted cavalry. Three pieces of Battery L, 1st Illinois Light Artillery and another four pieces at the depot supported this garrison command. Even though Rosser's Division consisted of 2,000 men and outnumbered Kelley's command by nearly three-to-one, it should not have been easy to drive off Kelley's men. Rosser left strong detachments at Moorefield and Claysville and marched down the valley. About 11:30 A.M. on November 28 the force arrived at the depot and captured Kelley's pickets. Payne's men then charged the Federal breastworks and captured the artillery without meeting any real resistance.

Breathed rode with the 5th Virginia Cavalry. A brave Union officer, believed to have been Lt. John McAfee, tended his guns as the Confederates bore down on them. As he prepared to unleash a blast of canister, Breathed burst from the ranks, charged McAfee, and ran him through with a saber before the Federal officer could pull the lanyard on his cannon. "The officers and men were apparently in their quarters and the horses in the stables, and 'confusion worse confounded' at once ensued. No successful attempt was made to rally the men, and the Government buildings and property were in a few minutes in rebel hands," reported Kelley. "These buildings were at once fired, and the property therein collected destroyed, together with several houses and considerable merchandise, and other effects owned by private parties."[35]

Rosser detached some troops and sent them to Piedmont, five miles west of New Creek, and still on the Baltimore and Ohio Railroad. This task force, commanded by a major named McDonald, was to capture the small garrison at Piedmont, and destroy the engine and machine shops. McDonald failed. The small garrison of thirty-five West Virginians confronted the Confederate horsemen, and repulsed them after a savage firefight. McDonald's task force then rejoined the main body of Rosser's Division at New Creek before the entire force marched up the Valley to Brock's Gap.[36]

Rosser's successful raid on New Creek Depot resulted in the capture of $123,382 of Union supplies and 450 prisoners. Because New Creek Depot was the only station west of Harpers Ferry on the Baltimore & Ohio, the raid severed the critical Union supply artery. Breathed brought a few new 12-pound brass rifles back with him, one wagon, some horses, and other miscellaneous spoils. The bold raid had generally been a success for Rosser.[37]

The men settled into comfortable winter quarters near Waynesboro with the tattered remnants of Early's army. However, each time the men thought that they had established their winter quarters, Union pressure forced Breathed to move them. After a final skirmish on December 20 and 21, Breathed ordered his men into their permanent winter encampment. None of them realized that the Confederacy had only a few months of life left to it.[38]

The Stuart Horse Artillery's last Valley Campaign had been an unmitigated disaster. The Tom's Brook fiasco had left many of the battalions without sufficient horses, guns, and, in some cases, officers to field an effective fighting force. Under the leadership of Chew and Breathed the horse artillery had performed well. Would the outcome have been different if so many of the experienced Marylanders of the old Breathed Battery had not transferred to other units?

Chapter 14

The Final Days of the Confederacy

On January 2, 1865, Pvt. William J. Black, of Shoemaker's Company, encountered Breathed in camp, near Mt. Solon, Virginia (about 10 miles southwest of Harrisonburg), observing that Breathed "went down today and when he came back reported that if Shoemaker's and Thomson's battery could each take 40 government [horses] we might stand a chance to be disbanded. Lieutenants Carter and Phelps each sent up a proposition to take the requisite number and Major Breathed approved and forwarded with pleasure." Thus, most of the men of the Stuart Horse Artillery were disbanded for the winter with their commander's consent so they could go home and take care of their horses until the Spring campaigning season began. There was no other way to care for horses over that winter than to disperse them across the South, wherever fodder could be gotten.[1]

Breathed was still attached to Rosser's Division headquarters at Waynesboro. By mid-January, Breathed again needed new men to replenish unit strengths, because the Battalion basically existed on paper only. The majority of his men returned home with the understanding that they might be called back up in the spring. Although Rosser believed that Breathed was "one of the most noted officers in the Confederacy for fighting qualities," Breathed could not effectively engage the enemy without his horse artillery at full strength. Instead, Pendleton suggested that Breathed assume command of one of the five battalions of two batteries each. Chew was promoted to lieutenant colonel and remained in overall command of the Stuart Horse Artillery Battalion.[2]

On March 1, Sheridan's two divisions of cavalry departed from their winter camp in Winchester and marched up the Shenandoah Valley. Grant had ordered Sheridan to march up the Valley, destroy or disperse the remnants of Early's army (which included Rosser's Division) at Waynesboro, destroy the James River canals and locks, and then, depending on the weather, either return to Winchester, or move on to join Maj. Gen. William T. Sherman's army in North Carolina. With Custer's Third Division leading the charge, the guns of the Staunton Artillery, under the command of Capt. John H. McClanahan, made a final stand. Although the Staunton Artillery had remained independent of the Stuart Horse Artillery, necessity would force it to become part of McGregor's Battalion very soon. However, Early's entire command numbered only about 1,500 men, and the Federals outnumbered them by nearly ten-to-one. Sheridan crashed into Early's flank and rolled it up, routing the Southerners. Early barely escaped capture as he fled the Union juggernaut. McClanahan's Battery lost all of its guns, and Sheridan took virtually Early's entire command prisoner. The Confederate Valley army ceased to exist; Sheridan, at long last, had absolute control over the Shenandoah Valley. Instead of returning to Winchester or marching to North Carolina, Sheridan instead marched overland to Petersburg and rejoined the Army of the Potomac.

Grant had been besieging the crucial railroad town, and had been gradually extending his lines to the south and west, extending Robert E. Lee's lines to their breaking point. Grant kept probing the Confederate lines for weaknesses, and continued extending west, knowing that sooner or later, he would find a weak point in Lee's lines and would shatter them. Once that happened, Petersburg would fall. When Petersburg fell, Richmond would fall too, and Lee would either have to come out and fight on ground of Grant's choosing, or he would have to try to flee. The end game finally appeared at hand.

In mid-March, Pendleton made a final attempt to re-equip the Stuart Horse Artillery Battalions. The problem, of course, remained finding sufficient guns and horses to mount the entire command. "Major Mason, of General Fitz Lee's staff, has called to see me in reference to equipping the battalions of two batteries of horse artillery under Major Breathed to serve with Gen. Fitz Lee's division of cavalry, and I have again to request that if you find it consistent with the general service of your department you authorize Major Mason to operate as among your agents in obtaining horses by purchase or impressment in such districts as may be agreed upon between him and yourself," wrote Col. A. H. Cole, the Confederate superintendent of field transportation. "While it is essential not unduly to reduce the working power of the farmers and not harshly to interfere with their rights, it is of the first importance to equip our artillery for an early campaign and especially to have our horse artillery ready for the conflict with the enemy's cavalry, which may be anticipated almost any day."[3]

On March 20, Pendleton ordered Chew to reorganize Breathed's Battalion by comprising it of Shoemaker's Battery and Griffin's Battery. The two batteries would serve with Fitz Lee's Division. "You will cause the several commanders to direct their energies to the thorough preparation of their respective commands for efficient service in the campaign soon to open and apply your own efforts to the same end. There is no time to be lost," instructed Pendleton. "Although horses cannot yet be called in because of insufficient forage, there are many elements of equipments and organization to be attended to at once. It is essential to get each command ready for service, so that however early or unexpectedly the enemy may advance the horse artillery battalion may on short notice repair to operate with their proper divisions." Supplies were hard to come by, and Breathed had to call up his furloughed men to man the guns for the upcoming spring campaign.[4]

Being the stubborn fighter that he was, Breathed refused to openly admit that the Confederacy was doomed. Still diligently doing his duty, he wanted to clarify the question of his rank in the Army of Northern Virginia before the spring campaign began. "I was told by Lieutenant Colonel Chew that General Pendleton had sent in my recommendation for Lieutenant Colonel of Artillery," he wrote to his friend John Esten Cooke, who was serving on Pendleton's staff. "Let me know by return mail if he has or not." Breathed was due to leave for Lynchburg to see to the refitting of his men, and he wanted to have this issue resolved before doing so. Although the war was about to end, Breathed had finally been recommended for a well-deserved promotion to lieutenant colonel. Unfortunately, the Confederate Senate would never get the chance to confirm it, so the promotion remained unofficial.[5]

The cavalry corps of the Army of Northern Virginia was reorganized during the last full month of the war in the Eastern Theater. To counter the threat from Sherman in South Carolina, Wade Hampton took his division south. Hart's Battalion went with him. The organization of the Confederate Cavalry left to confront Grant was as follows:

Cavalry Corps: Maj. Gen. Fitzhugh Lee

Rooney Lee's Division: Maj. Gen. William H. F. "Rooney" Lee

Barringer's Brigade, Brig. Gen. Rufus Barringer
Roberts' Brigade, Brig. Gen. William P. Roberts
Beale's Brigade, Brig. Gen. Richard L. T. Beale

Fitzhugh Lee's Division: Col. Thomas Munford

Wickham's Brigade, Col. Thomas T. Munford
Payne's Brigade, Brig. Gen. William H. F. Payne
Gary's Brigade, Brig. Gen. Martin W. Gary

Rosser's Division: Maj. Gen. Thomas L. Rosser

Rosser's Brigade, Brig. Gen. James Dearing
McCausland Brigade, Brig. Gen. John McCausland

With Hart's Battalion gone, the Horse Artillery was organized as follows:

Horse Artillery Command: Lt. Col. Roger Preston Chew

Breathed's Battalion, Maj. James Breathed
McGregor's Battalion, Maj. William M. McGregor
Johnston's Battalion, Maj. Philip P. Johnston
Thomson's Battalion, Maj. James W. Thomson

Each horse artillery battalion was to consist of two batteries with two guns per battery. This all looked very well on paper, but the men and the horses were scattered all over Virginia and the guns were still difficult to come by. [6]

Breathed suffered two personal losses in mid-March. On March 21 and 22, Breathed's grandmother, Kitty Jones Lyles Breathed, and his aunt, Elizabeth Breathed Snodgrass, died at Bai-Yuka a scant ten hours apart. However, his duty prevented him from attending the funerals. Word of these losses undoubtedly reached him, and it must have sapped his morale and saddened him. However, duty was duty, and Breathed had his duty to perform.[7]

Breathed reported for duty in Petersburg, where on April 1, 1865, seven guns of Lt. Col. William T. Poague's Battalion took position on the right of the Confederate line. The rest of his guns soon followed and were in place by dawn, out of sight of Union forces. The next morning, after Sheridan turned Lee's right flank by smashing through the line at Five Forks, Grant ordered a general assault all along the Union lines at Petersburg. This massed attack broke the line, forcing Poague's gunners to try to stem the tidal wave sweeping down on the city. His guns made a stand that bought time for some of the Confederate cavalry to escape westward. "Three pieces with Major Brander were placed on the north side of the Appomattox, so as to annoy the left flank of the enemy and prevent the Federals from crossing," reported Pendleton. "On the line and to the right of the Cox road were placed four pieces of the horse artillery under Lt. Col. Chew and Maj. Breathed. By 12 PM the enemy had by this time fully established his line from Fort Gregg to the Appomattox River."[8]

The collapse of Lee's distant right flank at Five Forks was the result of a large scale flanking operation under Phil Sheridan. He had marched toward Five Forks with nearly 10,000 well-equipped veteran horsemen. On March 29, his troopers clashed with Fitz Lee's Division at Sutherland's Station on the Weldon Railroad. During the engagement Col. Payne was shot from his saddle. Desperately short of experienced cavalry officers, Fitz Lee assigned Breathed to command of Payne's Brigade. It was a reasonable choice, because the artillerist's courageous battlefield record and familiar figure gave him the credibility he needed with the veteran cavalrymen. [9]

High Bridge

The once-vaunted Confederate horse artillery had fallen into a sad state of combat readiness. Only a few batteries could be fielded because of depleted manpower and equipment. The Army of Northern Virginia's cavalry corps was almost as badly depleted. Rooney Lee's Division, for example, consisted of eight regiments. Early in the war it would have numbered 8,000 men at full strength. By the end of March 1865, fewer than 2,000 officers and men were still in the ranks. Replacement soldiers, horses, ammunition, and equipment were in scarce supply, and neither the cavalry nor the horse artillery could function without the necessary supplies.[10]

The last remaining Confederate supply line, the South Side Railroad, lay beyond Grant's reach to the west of Petersburg. Richmond was evacuated after Grant broke through on April 2, and Lee's army was now fleeing west toward Lynchburg in the hope of linking up with General Joseph E. Johnston's army in North Carolina. It was a thin, desperate

High Bridge on the Southside Railroad, and the wagon bridge (lower right), the final escape route for the Army of Northern Virginia.

hope, but any hope was better than the prospect of surrender. The army followed the course of the Appomattox River as it withdrew. A large railroad span known as High Bridge carried the line over the river near Farmville, Virginia. There were actually two spans—the taller railroad bridge, and a lower bridge that carried foot and wagon traffic.

By April 6, the armies were in the vicinity of High Bridge. The day before, Lt. Gen. James Longstreet, who had returned to duty late the previous fall after his crippling Wilderness wound, had learned a Union "bridge burning party" was operating near High Bridge. Two regiments of Federal infantry and a squadron of cavalry had been sent to destroy the structure, and Longstreet was determined to defend the critical rail crossing. Its destruction would make it very difficult for Lee to continue retreating. Longstreet sent the cavalry commands of Rosser, Dearing, and John McCausland to locate the Union force and prevent it from destroying the bridge.

The terrain was clear of trees, but ravines and hilltops presented a challenge for the Confederates, who would have to try to stop the Union infantry. The cavalry pursued the bridge burners for an hour between noon and 1:00 P.M., and finally caught up to them at the Sandy River. Rosser dismounted Munford's and McCausland's brigades near the Farmville Road, while Dearing and Breathed were sent to attack the Union left flank. Because his regiments were so depleted, Fitz Lee had assigned Lt. Col. Chew to command the 3rd Virginia Cavalry while Breathed led the 8th Virginia Cavalry. Breathed and his brigade ran headlong into a column of about eighty members of the 4th Massachusetts Cavalry.[11]

On Rosser's order, Breathed and his troopers charged. At the same moment, two mounted Union officers galloped out from behind the Union lines. Breathed repeated the order to "charge," and dashed ahead, hoping his troopers would follow suit. Rosser left a detailed account of what happened next:

> Three mounted men [were] desperately fighting. There was no one near them. With pistol in hand, I rode directly towards them, but, before getting near enough to recognize them, one fell, or rather seemed pushed from his horse, but as soon as he touched the ground two quick shots from his pistol brought both of his assailants down lifeless, by the side of him, one, indeed, falling across him and to my surprise I recognized Major Breathed as he arose with face and

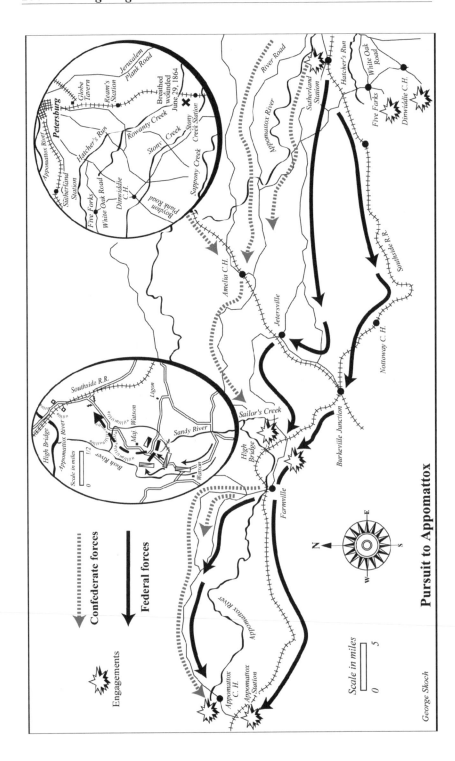

Pursuit to Appomattox

Confederate forces

Federal forces

Engagements

Scale in miles
0   5

George Skoch

body dripping with blood received from the thrusts and cuts of the sabres of his victims.

Rosser continued:

> Breathed had been detained in the rear and had not overtaken me when the fight begun, and, hearing the firing attempted to join me when he encountered two Captains and a sergeant of the enemy who ordered him to surrender, Breathed killed the sergeant, and the two Captains closed on him with their sabres and crowded him so closely that he could not use his pistol except to parry their quick blows until thrown to the ground. By some means one of Breathed's boots had been pulled off in the tussle, and drawing that on again, and without even mopping the blood from his face, and without apparent concern, he remounted his horse and dashed into the thickest of the fight.

Breathed had been ordered to take control of the "dismounted line and to charge the enemy." When he gave the order to charge, the Confederate troopers did not respond to his battle cry, so he dashed out ahead alone, knowing that "the entire engagement depended upon the promptness with which his order was obeyed."[12]

The "Breathed legend" rose to new levels following this medieval-style personal combat. There are at least three accounts of this fight, all from eye-witnesses, but none agree on all of the particulars. One account has Breathed fighting a single Union officer in a saber duel, while another has him shooting a Union officer while a Confederate sergeant ran out and shot the other enemy combatant. The third account claims there was another Confederate officer with Breathed during the encounter. Because each of these writers was an eye-witness, and none of them agree as to the details of the combat.

Breathed routinely sent personal artifacts to the families of his victims. According to the diary of Priscilla Bridges, "To the wives of the Union officers Breathed killed [in this incident] he sent the swords, rings, and papers, and writings to them and reported that their husbands had 'died as brave and noble soldiers.' The pistol he kept, and at the close of the war he presented it to one of the officer's wifes [sic]." After this personal duel, Munford's troopers charged through the woods, scattering the Union infantry and sending them running toward the bridges that they had come to burn. However, the small yet resilient band of Union

The brothers Hodges. George Foster Hodges (left) and William Townsend Hodges (on horseback), from an oil on canvas, 1866. Neither Harvard graduate survived the war. George, an adjutant with the 18th Massachusetts Volunteers; died of illness in 1862; Captain William Hodges was killed by Breathed in the fighting at High Bridge on April 6, 1865.

troopers, who created confusion in the melee, stymied Rosser. Once Rosser's troopers recovered from the confusion, they regrouped and countercharged, driving off the pesky Federal horsemen, who ended up surrendering to him.[13]

Fitz Lee's men captured nearly 800 of the Union soldiers and killed their commanding general. However, Gen. Dearing, Maj. James Thomson, the courageous artillerist, and Col. Ruben Boston, commander of one of Rosser's Brigades, were all killed (Dearing being mortally wounded) in this engagement. "The enemy's force proved to be a picked body of infantry and a squadron of cavalry, which, placed under this staff officer, had for its object the destruction of the High Bridge over the Appomattox, in our rear," reported Lee. However, the success came with a very heavy price in the form of the three irreplaceable officers who fell in combat that day. "The splendid gallantry of these three officers had been tested on many fields, and their conspicuous valor was universally known," Lee continued. "The genial and dashing Thomson was killed leading cavalry, his guns not being present." Breathed was lucky that he did not share the fate of Dearing, Boston, and Thomson with his daring and lonely charge.[14]

Why would Breathed engage in such reckless and heroic conduct with the Confederacy so obviously doomed? The brave though reckless behavior was not unusual conduct for Breathed, whose entire military career was studded with just this sort of bravery and careless disregard for his own safety. It would have been out of character for Breathed to shy away from a fight—even with the end in sight.

Major Thomson frequently pitched into a cavalry brawl when the opportunity presented itself. Although he had already been wounded in the arm, Thomson tenaciously rode into the melee. Warned that it was suicidal to do so, Thomson reportedly replied, "[I do] not wish to survive the Confederacy." When he learned that Dearing had fallen, Thomson could watch no longer. With his horse next to Rosser's, he reached over and drew Rosser's saber from its scabbard and spurred his horse into the thick of the fight. He spotted a white flag of surrender being raised by some Union soldiers, and gave a holler of joy. At that moment two Federal bullets struck him, one in the neck and the other in the torso. His faithful artillerists drew around him as he drew his last breath. Breathed, who had served with Thomson for nearly four years, lamented that "with ten thousand such men as Jimmie Thomson, I could whip Grant's Army."[15]

* * *

By April 9, Sheridan's hard-marching cavalry had gotten across Lee's line of retreat at Appomattox Court House. Grant demanded the Army of Northern Virginia's surrender, but Lee declined, figuring that he would make one final attempt to break out. That morning, Lee asked Gen. Gordon to attack Sheridan's lines in an attempt to break through the dismounted cavalryman. If they did, they might be able to reach desperately needed supplies and pull away from Grant. Gordon attacked and drove in the Union cavalry pickets.

However, Maj. Gen. E. O. C. Ord's Army of the James had arrived on the field. The cavalrymen opened their ranks, and the Confederates could see long lines of Union infantry in their front. Cut off and in danger of being surrounded, and with his army desperately low on supplies, Lee bowed to the inevitable. He sent out a flag of truce and asked to meet with Grant. In Wilmer McLean's handsome home, Lee surrendered the Army of Northern Virginia on generous and honorable terms.

Fitz Lee, however, was not prepared to surrender. Breathed was outside the Army of Northern Virginia lines with Tom Munford when word of the surrender came. Munford told a story that symbolized that the armies were now at peace. "Captain Buck Trent, the Quartermaster of my regiment, lived very close to Appomattox Court House and that morning as we had been forming, ready to move out, he had ridden up and handed me a canteen filled with fine old peach brandy," remembered Munford. Captain Trent believed "the Yankees would take it all anyhow, if he left it at home." Munford accepted the large canteen and soon thereafter he and some of his men ran into a few Federals. One of the enemy officers asked Munford if he knew of a spring near by. "No," Munford replied, "[but] here's some old peach brandy a friend of mine gave me this morning—if you could make that do?" Munford reported that the officer told him, "Well . . . it is not often soldiers meet under such circumstances. I believe I could." Munford gave the thirsty officer the canteen and then said, "Gentlemen you are welcome!" The canteen made its way from soldier to soldier. "It was quite a large circle to begin with," Munford recalled, "but it continued to enlarge at a rate that was amazing. I would scarcely have

The McLean house, where General Lee surrendered his Army of Northern Virginia to General Grant on April 9, 1865.

believed there were so many officers in the whole Union Army—and so amazingly thirsty! When my canteen returned to me it was more like a powder horn than a flask of brandy; the aroma was there but the fluid was gone."[16]

Breathed was with Munford during the reconciliatory canteen sharing, which represented as well as any event that the end had indeed arrived. Still, the two men were incredulous. "We turned our backs upon it and I may say that it is literally true we 'never surrendered,'" recalled Munford. "I overtook the main body of my troops about two miles further up the road and had a conference with my officers who, upon being informed that I could obtain no satisfaction from the Federals, agreed with me to move to Lynchburg. But the Command had already halted at a crossroads, one leading to the ferry over [the] James River and the other to Campbell Court House and Lynchburg. I have understood that most of Payne's brigade, [Breathed commander of the 8th Virginia] took the James River road as the Horse Artillery and part of our wagons had gone that way."[17]

The troopers reached Lynchburg on the night of April 9, returning to the place where so many of them had begun the war four years earlier. The next morning the Confederate cavalry disbanded on the very spot they had formed in the heady days of 1861. On April 13, a detachment of Union cavalry sent to capture Munford left a note at his Lynchburg home. Instead of surrendering, the Confederate cavalry simply melted away. Although the war had ended, Munford, Breathed, and the horsemen who followed them had a difficult time coming to grips with the surrender of the Army of Northern Virginia. It was time for the man of war to return to being a man of medicine.[18]

Chapter 15

Home, in Body

J ames Breathed made his peace with the Federal government in Winchester on April 24, 1865, when he took the oath of allegiance: "I will not take up arms against The United States Government until I am regularly exchanged. And that if I am permitted to remain at my home I will conduct myself as a good and peaceable citizen, and will respect the laws in force where I reside and will do nothing to the determinant of, or in opposition of the United States Government." The 26-year-old veteran who had sacrificed everything for the Confederate Cause for four long years was finally free to go home and resume his life.[1]

Breathed traveled to his sister Priscilla's home in Hancock, Maryland. He did not make his boyhood home at Bai-Yuka his new residence, although his family still lived there. Priscilla and her husband, Robert Bridges, a wealthy entrepreneur, offered James a place to stay. However, there is no historical record why James went to Hancock. Perhaps there was more of a need for doctors there than in the vicinity of Hagerstown. What is known with more certainty is that Breathed was "penniless and [his] possessions consisted of a pistol, a saber and the clothes on his back."[2]

Priscilla and Robert were also victims of the war. Stonewall Jackson's forces (including Chew's Ashby Battery) had shelled their hometown early in the war during his ill-fated Winter 1861 campaign.

The warm and spacious home of Priscilla and Robert Bridges in Hancock, Maryland. It was here, with the Bridges and their growing family, that the former Confederate major and doctor spent the rest of his life.

Even this home bore the memories, if not the actual scars, of the recent conflict. The emotional pain of fighting for the losing side was not the only anguish Breathed was experiencing. His wounds had never fully healed and caused him considerable pain. Priscilla's children, however, helped cheer their uncle: Ann McGill (1863), Robert Willis (1865), John Breathed (1866) and eventually Helen Mar (1869). Still, the pain was often crippling. As a doctor, Breathed knew how to self-administer laudanum. Although the drug brought him some temporary relief, his need for it may have addicted him to the opiate. He had beaten the odds and survived a stomach wound, but its lingering agony never left him.

Like many combat veterans, Breathed appeared emotionally shaken when he returned from the war. Still, he did his best to keep in contact with his friends and establish some semblance of a normal civilian life. "I was very sorry that your note reached me too late," he wrote to his friend and mentor Dr. Macgill in October 1865. "George Freaner is not well, looks badly. . . . I think I will be in Richmond before long— love to all."[3]

Freaner and Breathed had fought side-by-side on many fields, and remained close after the war. George, who was an 1853 graduate of Dickinson College, returned to his law practice in Hagerstown after the war. Although he appeared hale and hearty, he suffered lingering health problems brought about by the hardships of military service. The two remained close for the rest of Breathed's short life.[4]

Breathed was slow to reopen his medical practice. In all likelihood he simply needed time to let the memories of battle fade away before he resumed his duties as a healer of the sick. It took some time, for he rarely spoke with others about it. "My brother seldom ever mentioned his war history," recalled Priscilla. Despite a warm reception from the people of Hancock (many of whom were Southern sympathizers), Breathed found the adjustment to civilian life anything but easy. Even his relationship with Miss Mollie did not hold the spark for him that it had before the war. Love could not heal his wounds, and their reunion did not lead to the long-anticipated marriage both had been expecting.[5]

Although in the 1860s there was no name for it, Breathed may have suffered from what today we call Post-Traumatic Stress Disorder. Many soldiers suffered the results of combat fatigue after just a short time on the front lines. Breathed had served for the entire war. "Although [soldiers] exhibited some of the symptoms of what was called shell shock in World War I, combat exhaustion or battle fatigue in World War II," wrote one historian, "all of them continued to function as combat soldiers. But they were changed forever by their experiences."[6]

Murderous combat, exposure, and fatigue, as well as the constant threat of chronic disease, challenged the endurance of even the hardiest soldiers. This was as true in 1865 as it was in 1965. By the middle of the 20th Century, however, the medical profession had advanced far enough to be able to recognize and treat psychological disorders. Breathed was part of a generation of soldiers who were expected to keep their nightmares and unpleasant memories to themselves; anything else was viewed as a sign of weakness. Breathed followed this postwar code and would have known no other way to live with his emotional scars. However, silence was rarely the best way to deal with combat fatigue. Emotional detachment is a typical symptom of Post-Traumatic Stress Disorder, which may help explain why Breathed was unable to reestablish his relationship with Miss Mollie Macgill. Breathed also exhibited clear signs of substance abuse. The vibrant young man who had sat next to Jeb Stuart on a train bound for war in 1861 was no more.

A full year passed before James was ready to resume his medical practice. In 1866, he resumed his participation in the Washington County Medical Society. He converted a room in the Bridges' home into an office and, in May of 1868, Robert Bridges lent his brother-in-law $1,200 to get back on his feet. The doctor was ready to heal himself and resume healing other people in the process.[7]

Breathed periodically ventured north of the Mason Dixon Line, where some residents resented veterans of the Army of Northern Virginia. He understood this reaction; after all, he had once been the enemy. The former Confederate could only struggle with the ironies that ruled his life. He was a doctor who chose fighting and death during the war, but in peacetime he was the ex-Rebel who ventured into the North to deliver children and fight sickness.[8]

Breathed's medical rounds took him into Pennsylvania. "Some of the stay-at-homes living there notified him that if he came into Pennsylvania they would kill him. They didn't fully appreciate the temperament of the man or they would not have indulged in such idle talk," wrote Henry Matthews nearly forty years later. "Those threats made against him virtually forced him into forbidden territory, and go he did, spurning with contempt the low bred hirelings that had tried to intimidate him, and for years—up to the time of his death—went in and out across the line, penetrating the State of Pennsylvania for miles, fearful of no one except himself. He found friends [there] that stood by him when adversity overtook him." Directly north of Hancock was Fulton County, Pennsylvania, where Breathed routinely practiced. As a sign of their respect for his aid in delivering children, some of his patients named their offspring for him. Although he never married, the former major's name lived on through subsequent generations.[9]

Breathed continued practicing medicine until he died on February 14, 1870. He was just 32 years old. The cause of his death remains unknown. He had been wounded several times during the war, and the effects of those injuries, coupled with his laudanum addiction probably fatally weakened his constitution. "Dr. James Breathed committed suicide by taking Morphinal," wrote a local Hancock merchant. "Sad news for this community." Whether drugs played a role in his death or

St. Thomas Episcopal Church, Hancock, Maryland, the humble final resting place of James Breathed, overlooks his home state of Virginia.

whether the merchant was using the word "suicide" in the literal sense will likely never be determined.[10]

More than 1,000,000 Americans died in the Civil War or shortly afterward from the effects of wounds and disease. Medical complications from lingering injuries meant that many men continued to "give the last full-measure" for many years. According to writer Shelby Foote, the "Butcher's bill [was] no less than 1,094,453 for both sides, in and out of more than 10,000 military actions, including 76 full-scale battles, 310 engagements, 6,337 skirmishes, and numerous sieges, raids, expeditions, and the like."[11]

Men across the South mourned his passing. Even Robert E. Lee eulogized Breathed to the major's father, writing, "With an army of Breatheds, I could have conquered the world."[12]

By 1885, James' younger brother, Corporal Isaac Breathed, was a member of Company B, 7th Infantry Regiment, which was stationed out on the frontier battling Indians. Three years later Isaac wrote to his nephew, Robert Willis Bridges, from his post at Fort Laramie, Wyoming:

Jim and myself were very devoted to each other, in fact, I believe that I loved him more than I did myself, and I have every reason to believe that my feelings were fully reciprocated. As a soldier, he had no superior, I saw him upon many a hard fought field, and I have always thought he was, without exception, the most recklessly brave man in the Army of Northern Va. or any other army, for that matter, for the Army Northern Va. was composed of the best material that was stepped into a fire of battle. No other Army in the world has accomplished what they did, under similar circumstances.

Isaac also recalled an encounter he had a week after Gettysburg:

> I was riding up a road, alone toward Hagerstown when approaching a farm house a little off the road with a yard in front, I noticed quite a group of [Confederate] Officers sitting around a map which was spread out upon the grass, and a tall fine looking officer pacing up and down the yard, apparently in deep meditation, who when I got about opposite to the gate hailed me and asked how far down the road I had been, I saluted and answered "about three miles, Sir!"
>   "Did, you see anything of the enemies position?"
>   "Yes! Sir!, I exchanged shots with them!"
>   The man then asked "How old are you?"
>   "Seventeen years of age, Sir!"
>   "What is your name?"
>   "Breathed!"
>   "Are you related to Captain Breathed?"
>   "Yes! Sir! A brother!"
> He reached over the gate and grasped my hand and said, "You may well be proud of being a brother of Captain Breathed's [for] he is one of the most gallant and bravest of Officers of my Army! You are very young yet please be careful of yourself [and] never expose yourself unnecessarily."

The officer was none other than Gen. Robert E. Lee, and the officers sitting around the map were his trusted lieutenants, Gens. Longstreet, Ewell, A. P. Hill, and last, but not least, Gen. J.E.B. Stuart, his indefatigable Cavalry leader.[13]

*   *   *

The memories of Breathed faded as the years passed, but references to the gallant artillery officer continued to come up among those who knew him. During the Spanish-American War in 1898, Fitzhugh Lee found himself in the unusual position of wearing the blue uniform of a major general in the United State Army. James Macgill, a "Confederate

The Confederate Veteran "Breathed Camp" in Pulaski, Virginia. *Wilderness Road Regional Museum, Newbern, Virginia*

Veteran General," (a cousin of the major's who had also served at Gettysburg) had organized "The Breathed Camp" of Confederate veterans from Pulaski, Virginia. When the camp sent along their praise of Fitz Lee, the former cavalry general spotted the all-too-familiar name of James Breathed and in a flash a flood of memories washed over him. "This officer [was] directly under my command during the war, 1861 to '65, and I can bear personal testimony to his conspicuous daring, as well as to his splendid service in the Confederate Army," Fitz Lee wrote to the *Baltimore Sun* newspaper. "Should I, for any reason, go to the field again, and get in the saddle once more, no one would I rather have by my side, were he living, than the gallant Breathed, and I know that any camp bearing his name will ever be ready to go into battle at the first note of the bugle."[14]

Henry Matthews was probably the last of Breathed's contemporaries to assess the man. Writing in 1908, the old soldier compared Breathed to his mentor, John Pelham. "It would be a difficult matter for me, who served under both of them, to say who was the greater Artillery Officer of the two. Pelham was possessed of some attributes that Breathed did not possess and [conversely] so with Breathed," explained Matthews. "They were both fearless and courageous to a very high degree. Pelham was dashing and at the same time cautious. Breathed was reckless and not at all cautious—he would take his battery in places that would make your hair stand on end, depending on the bull dog fighting qualities of his men to bring him out safely, for example on the 9th of June 1863 and 7th of May 1864."[15]

Matthews continued: "Breathed was a military genius in the handling of Horse Artillery—as was also Pelham. The two are matchless and stand out—prominent figures in that grand galaxy of distinguished officers—especially in the A.[rmy] of N.[orthern] Va. Breathed would have made a magnificent Cavalry Officer. When his battery was not actively engaged he could always be found at the head of some cavalry regiment, especially the 4th Va. Cavalry when commanded by General W. H. Payne [William Henry Fitzhugh Payne] and later with his brigade. This healer also possessed a genius for war that exceeded that of many Confederate generals."[16]

Many others felt the same way about him. Stuart's former ordnance officer, John Esten Cooke, praised Breathed, proclaiming, "Napoleon would have made him [Breathed] a Marshall."[17]

James Breathed was buried on the north bank of the Potomac River in Hancock, Maryland. He sleeps on a high hill overlooking the state of his birth and the hills of his birthplace in Berkeley Springs, Virginia (now West Virginia). He was laid to rest by a few of his surviving brothers in arms, and was mourned by a large assemblage of friends and relatives at the Saint Thomas Episcopal Church. Reflecting at the grave of his old commander, Matthews wrote:

> We laid him to rest in his cold, narrow bed,
> And gazed on the marble we placed o'er his head
> As the proudest of tributes our hearts could pay:
> 'He never disgraced the dear jacket of gray.'[18]

*   *   *

During the early years of the 20th Century Robert Bridges, the chief editor of *Scribner's Magazine* in New York City, asked Priscilla to send him Breathed's wartime papers. The novelist Thomas Nelson Page, told Priscilla that James' life contained the "romance of the South" and wished to write about him. The papers, however, remained with Priscilla, probably because of her advanced age and deteriorating condition. Neither Robert nor the famous novelist ever wrote about Breathed. Perhaps another war got in the way.[19]

Chapter 16

Assessing James Breathed

Accordinng to a staff officer who served under Gens. Joe Johnston, Thomas Jackson, and Robert E. Lee, "There were other commands in which Marylanders so largely predominated that they might properly be claimed as Maryland organizations, such as Breathed's Horse Artillery, in which they were fully ninety percent, and no command made a more glorious record in the war." However, he continued, "all this should be made the subject of a carefully prepared historical paper." I hope this biography of James Breathed has helped to fill that void.[1]

In 1902, former Confederate cavalry brigade commander Col. William H. Payne was a resident of the Maryland Line Confederate Soldier's Home in Pikesville, Maryland. According to correspondence from Payne to Henry Matthews, James Breathed "hated Yankees" and fought for the "love of the Cause and the independence of his country." Breathed, according to Payne, did not fight for constitutional or States' Rights. Rather, his enemy was the Union infantryman, cavalier, artilleryman, and the officers who commanded them. Breathed's very survival depended upon his abhorrence of his enemy.[2]

War gives a man license to hate his foe. The human desire to live dictates this. When it is kill or be killed, human instinct and adrenaline take over and can morph a gentle person—even a doctor—into a warrior.

Breathed may or may not have truly hated his enemy; we will never know because he never left an account of his reasons for going to war. Like most soldiers in every war, however, he at the least detested his opponents. If he did not, he could not have so easily killed them. The educated Episcopalian and doctor, wrote cavalryman William H. Payne after the war, "entered a battle . . . to kill. He never shed any tears nor canted in melee mouthed philanthropy but yet to unarmed and helpless [he] was chivalry itself."[3]

Unencumbered by the structures of formal military training, the man who followed a Southern code of chivalry developed his own unique style of command. Relentless in his efforts to defeat the enemy, he exhibited conspicuous gallantry and accomplishments on so many fields that his actions separated him from the pack of other battery commanders—inside and outside the cavalry arm. Breathed's handling of field artillery and accurate fire became recognizable to his enemies. Alexander C. M. Pennington, the leader of a celebrated Union battery of the horse artillery, both looked forward to and dreaded his many encounters with Breathed. The Union gunner respected his abilities and knew that opposing the Southern gunner was a very dangerous proposition. "Breathed's battery needs no encomium," declared Henry Matthews in 1904. "If the survivors of Breathed's and Pennington's batteries could get together today, what a swapping of yarns there would be."[4]

"The famous Stuart Horse Artillery," wrote Stuart's colorful Prussian staff officer Major Heros von Borcke, "was made up of volunteers of many nationalities. . . . [who] distinguished themselves on every field of battle, and established such an enviable character for daring and good conduct that the body was soon regarded as a corps d'elite by the whole army, and it came to be considered an honour to be one of them." The major continued: "I have often seen men serving their pieces in the hottest of the fight, laughing, singing, and joking each other, utterly regardless of the destruction which cannon-shot and musket-ball were making in their ranks."[5]

According to Jennings Cropper Wise, the historian of Robert E. Lee's artillery arm, the men and officers who made up the horse artillery were men of "strong traits of character which typified the arm. [Pelham], Crutchfield, Walker, Alexander, Carter, Pegram, Chew, Caskie, McIntosh, Haskell, Breathed, McGraw, McCabe, Cutshaw, Thomson,

Latimer, Carpenter, Poague, and many others were the very embodiment of all that was skillful, courageous, gallant, each possessing a peculiar individualism developed to the highest degree." Wise concluded, "From the sentiments and character of these men were developed the élan and the morale which gave to their arm that distinctive mien so characteristic of the Field Artillery."[6]

The Stuart Horse Artillery attained such lofty heights through the efforts of a few outstanding leaders: Pelham, Chew, and Breathed. John Pelham is much better known today than either Chew or the subject of this book. The blond gunner remains the man most closely associated with the leadership of the Stuart Horse Artillery, not only because he was a daring and skillful artillerist, but because he was handsome, young, and a martyr for his cause. A member of Stuart's inner circle, Pelham often pitched his tent next to Stuart's. Eulogies for Pelham came easily. Breathed, however, personally stamped the Stuart Horse Artillery with many of its late-war qualities exhibited during the rigorous 1864-1865 campaigns. In the minds of the Confederate veterans who knew him best, Breathed was no less of a legend than Pelham. The Stuart Horse Artillery produced many other brave men, including Beckham, Chew, Henry, Thomson, Hart, and McGregor. Each in his own way stood out as an exceptional leader.

While history remembers Pelham fondly, it has largely forgotten James Breathed, a quiet man who did not seek the limelight either during or after the war. Breathed could have served in the Army Medical Corps and avoided many of the hardships suffered by the average soldier, but he chose not to do so. Instead, he pitched his tent in the field next to his cannoneers. He faced death with his men and shared the same food and privations. After the war, Breathed returned to his kin and eventually resumed the practice of medicine in a small Maryland town. The war interrupted his courtship of Miss Mollie Macgill, and he refused to speak much about his service or write about it once peace arrived. When he finally became the doctor he had originally set out to become, his wounds and a drug addiction prevented the career he would otherwise have enjoyed.

Today, we remember Breathed not for his medical skills but because he was an exemplary combat leader. He was able to motivate his men to do almost anything he asked. In return, his men loved and respected him. "The boys, of course, were all pleased at his promotion, but were fearful that he might be sent to some battalion of artillery in which we were not members," recalled Henry Matthews when Breathed was promoted in the spring of 1864. "So, when the news came that Breathed would be our Major, there was great rejoicing over the good news. Pandemonium broke loose in shouts and demonstrations. To have lost Breathed at this stage of our arduous campaign would certainly [have] been a calamity." The enduring loyalty the men felt toward their commander long survived the war:

> No one outside of the old battery can fully understand that strong bond of love that existed between Breathed and the boys. There was not a man in the battery that would not have gone into the very jaws of death itself at Breathed's command. He guarded their interests in the most jealous manner, even more carefully than he did his own. His only thought was how to advance or improve the condition of the boys. No one can dream how he loved his dashing battery. I remember on one occasion we were sitting around our camp-fire with Breathed in our midst. I noticed that his eye gleamed around that little group of true and tried veterans. At last he raised his head and said, 'Boys, I was just thinking as I have been sitting here that I would rather command you old ragged rebels than be in command of Longstreet's corps.' And he meant every word he uttered.

Matthews concluded:

> We looked upon each other as brothers, and woe be unto any man, be he officer or private, who attempted to annoy us in any way, Breathed would pounce upon them like a hawk upon a sparrow. And let me say here while on this subject, that I never tire of Breathed; that there are some men who imagine themselves oracles of Confederate History, and who have taken upon themselves the self-imposed task of criticizing soldiers who, in their faithful service on the firing line, seldom visited Richmond; that the warriors of Gen. Winder's Provost Marshal's Office and the defenses of Richmond never had the opportunity of meeting those bronzed and brave soldiers, so, in their narrow and perverted vision, come instantly to the conclusion that they did not exist, but were only myths of some dreamer or rainbow character who had created men like the very earthy Breathed to highly color the picture and to please the belligerent taste of their readers.
>   Let me say to them—and when I say them, I mean men who fought, died, and bled for their Southland behind a desk in one of the Departments in Richmond, some of whom live in Baltimore

today, and have the assurance and impudence to pass on a Confederate soldier's record, rating him good, bad, or indifferent as they in their prejudice seem fit. Major James Breathed of horse artillery imperishable fame was the most real myth that ever existed. He was intense in the flesh, an instrument of destruction that hurled death and disaster among his enemy on every battlefield in which the Army of Northern Virginia participated. He was as well known on the Federal side as among Confederate soldiers.[7]

No matter how fierce Breathed may have been on the battlefield, he never forgot his heritage. He was born a Virginian and was raised in a strong Maryland family; he had the cause of the South deeply seated in his heart and soul. He genuinely loved the "band of brothers" he served with throughout the war.

The fact that Breathed had no military training did not prevent him from becoming an outstanding gunnery officer. Obviously he was an intelligent man, and he used his intelligence and dedication to learn everything he could about artillery. Given his reputation as a fierce warrior, it is ironic to think of Breathed as a humanitarian. However, his use of his medical training on the battlefield to help both friend and foe is well documented.

Applying King Louis XIV's word about Marshal Villars, Tom Munford described Breathed and the horse artillery: "'Where the guns are playing he is sure to rise from the earth at the very spot,' so it was true of Breathed and also of Chew and McGregor, P. P. Johnston, Thomas and Carter, who were sustained with glorious courage by that splendid body of horse artillery." Munford continued, "The saddle was the home of the Southern gentleman, his predilections were ever to ride rather than walk, and the ranks of our Cavalry were largely made up of the chivalry of the South." As Napoleon put it, in order for Breathed "to be a good Soldier [he] must first be converted into a machine." The machine Breathed became was comfortable in the saddle for days on end, and was at home "where the guns were at play."[8]

Breathed's tactics with the Stuart Horse Artillery evolved over time on the school of the battlefield. Since Breathed left no treatise on his tactics, they can only be inferred. Obviously he had an instinct for handling his pieces and often aimed his own guns by eye. The war taught him many things, and he proved to be a quick study. Jeb Stuart's first ride around McClellan, as well as his experiences in the Second Manassas

Campaign, taught Breathed that horse artillery should be employed close to the front of a column; otherwise, it would not reach a battlefield in time to join the fighting. The poor quality of the Confederate fuses taught him that firing with shell from the rear was as likely to kill friend as foe. Sharpsburg, known in Confederate circles as "Artillery Hell," taught the young artillerist the value of possessing high ground and using it effectively against heavy odds. Pelham's effective and creative use of field guns at Fredericksburg was an eye-opener for many officers. The fight taught Breathed that the skillful and aggressive deployment of artillery could even the odds on the battlefield. An isolated battery, well-hidden and effectively served, could not only remain in the thick of combat but inflict disproportionate punishment on a numerically superior enemy. Chancellorsville demonstrated the effectiveness of Breathed's tactics when he leap-frogged his guns forward with the leading elements of Jackson's flank attack, winning in the event effusive and enthusiastic praise from the doomed infantry commander.[9]

By the time the Gettysburg Campaign began Breathed had fully mastered his trade with the Stuart Horse Artillery. At Spotsylvania Court House in May 1864, Breathed's handful of guns denied an entire Union army corps the use of a crucial road. Pinned down in the Richmond-Petersburg trenches later that summer rendered the Confederate horse artillery largely ineffective by denying it the ability to move about a battlefield with alacrity. By the time the Fall 1864 Valley Campaign was underway, the Confederate cavalry was so depleted that even though the horse artillery could move, it had little impact on the outcome of the campaign.

"Men are to be judged by what they have done under the circumstances in which they are placed, and it is but idle to speculate upon what they might have affected under other and different conditions," declared Tom Munford. "The officer who stops to deliberate, and falters in sight of an enemy in action, will rarely win in the fight, the critical passes, victory is turned to defeat." Breathed's instincts routinely steered him toward the right place at the right time. He rarely let an opportunity slip past him on the battlefield, even though he never had a day of formal military training. By the time 1865 rolled around, the cannon he commanded had become an extension of his own being.[10]

In November of 1888 George Trust, who had served in Breathed's Battery asked a rhetorical question: "Now, I ask shall the fame of this great man die?" He was fondly remembering his former commander. "Breathed! His was a restless spirit, never content unless striking for the land and cause he loved so well. We, who followed his sable plume, will ever remember his clarion-like voice above the shock and din of battle," Trust declared. "Of the long list of brave and gallant heroes that Maryland has produced, the name of Breathed stands second to none. More than one defeat was turned into victory by the intrepid Breathed. Oft did the thunder of Breathed's guns inspire with fresh courage our brigade (Fitzhugh Lee's) when opposed to overwhelming numbers." It was a fitting eulogy for a gifted artillerist.[11]

*   *   *

"Breathed, Breathed, what a name is thine! How justly are thy praises sung by comrades and the erstwhile foe alike," recalled Jennings Cropper Wise. "It was you of whom Wade Hampton wrote, 'A braver and more gallant soldier never lived'; whom Fitz Lee characterized as 'one of the bravest and best soldiers the Confederacy produced'; of whom Wickham said, 'Capt. Breathed is the best man for the management of a battery of horse artillery that I have ever known'; whom Rosser declared to be 'one of the most noted officers in the Confederacy for fighting qualities,' and whom Munford claimed to be 'as brave an officer and as hard a fighter as appeared in the war.' … Stuart's opinion of Breathed is amply testified to by the following letter he wrote to Lee concerning him [Breathed]: 'I will never consent for Capt. Breathed to quit the Horse Artillery, with which he has rendered such distinguished service, except for certain promotion, which he has well earned.'"[12]

In 1908, on the seventieth anniversary of Breathed's birth, Matthews paid tribute to the great warrior and leader:

> On the birth of that magnificent soldier, that matchless, peerless Confederate Horse Artillery officer, Major James Breathed whose name is still a household word among the hills and dales of the Southland. I do not think that the deeds of valor and the sterling characteristics of such a splendid soldier and true Southern gentlemen can be written about or talked of too often. The memory of such a man as Breathed should indeed be an inspiration to the youth of the land to emulate his example and to make for themselves and posterity a name that shall go down through the ages of the

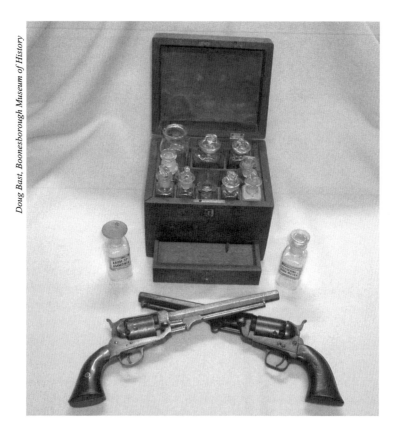

Doug Bast, Boonesborough Museum of History

Dr. Breathed's apothecary kit and typical Confederate pistols.

book of life. This sentiment; A man who was one of nature's nobleman, without a blemish: a man who possessed all of the qualifications that goes to make a man 'for he was a man indeed.'
. . . . As simplicity was the cardinal virtue of the soldier and in keeping with that idea his last resting place is simple and unpretentious in every way. It can be truthfully said, 'We shall never look on his like again.' This tribute is from one who knew him and followed him blindly and lovingly.[13]

Perhaps the finest compliment of all was one made by Robert E. Lee himself. "If my soldiers had all been such as your son," the general told Judge Breathed, "we would never have been a subjugated people."[14]

Postscript

L ike most combat veterans, many ex-Confederates continued to relive and remember the war for the rest of their lives. Dr. Macgill's son, Colonel James Macgill, who had joined the army at age sixteen, started a Camp of Confederate Veterans in Pulaski County, Virginia. Young Macgill had first married a niece of J.E.B. Stuart; after she died, he married a daughter of Lt. Gen. A. P. Hill. Macgill named his camp after James Breathed.

Many years later Macgill approached Priscilla about moving Breathed's grave to Hagerstown, Maryland. Priscilla declined, saying that it was too "'Northern a place' to lay to rest a man who had fought with so many Virginians." By 1900, the Breathed Camp of Confederate Veterans numbered 170 members. They celebrated their fallen hero and received complimentary letters from many former Confederate officers who had served with Breathed.[1]

In 1872, Judge John W. Breathed decided to move to the famous "Dungeness Plantation" on the James River outside Richmond. The plantation was one of the best known in Virginia, and its founder was a direct descendant of Thomas Jefferson. When the judge could not pay anything other than the down payment, Robert Bridges, a successful businessman and the husband of the judge's daughter Priscilla, bought the 1,000-acre plantation for $18,000. The Judge lived there and managed the plantation until 1876, when Robert Bridges sold it. By that time the Judge had already sold Bai-Yuka, so he needed another place to live. Judge Breathed moved to Lynchburg, Virginia, where he served as mayor of the city and lived out the remainder of his life. He greatly enjoyed visits with his eighteen children. He died in 1893.[2]

James Breathed's brother, John W. Breathed, Jr., a member of the 35th Virginia Battalion, ended his military career with Lee's surrender. He moved to Dungeness and helped his father manage the property.

Isaac Breathed, who had served in the 43rd Battalion, Virginia Cavalry (Mosby's Raiders), chose a career in the military. By July 16, 1885, he was a corporal in Company B, 7th Infantry Regiment. Isaac was stationed at Fort Laramie in Wyoming, where he fought Sioux Indians. He transferred to the 17th Infantry and was stationed in Russell, Wyoming, in 1893, where he acted as an Indian scout and sharpshooter under General Nelson Miles. Two of his brothers—Francis (Frank) and Edward—also served in the postwar United States Army in the far West. Isaac received his honorable discharge in 1894, when he was 43.[3]

James Breathed's fiancée, Mollie Macgill, never married her soldier beau, probably because of changes to his personality resulting from his service in the war. On October 30, 1911, Priscilla Bridges wrote to Breathed's old comrade, Roger Preston Chew that a certain woman "his lady-love Miss Macgill," was in possession of James' letters and papers.[4]

Mollie continued to carry a torch for her dashing major and did not marry until November 13, 1889, when she was 50 years old. Her husband, family friend Henry Rosenberg, was a leading citizen of Galveston, Texas, and the first president of the Santa Fe Railroad. The Swiss native was known as the "Texas Philanthropist," and was also an artillerist during the Civil War. Mollie actively participated in the Daughters of the Confederacy on a national level, turning down the presidency of the organization several times.[5]

By 1898, James' sister Priscilla had custody of Breathed's wartime artifacts, including his pistol, sword, personal articles, commissions as first lieutenant and major, letters from Generals Stuart and Lee, and his resignation letter. She lent these items to The Museum of The Confederacy in Richmond, Virginia.[6]

In 1912, Priscilla copied many of Breathed's papers and sent them to Lt. Col. R. Preston Chew. "You requested my brother, James Breathed's record," she wrote. "Though very poorly copied by me— being an old lady of seventy years of age I cannot hold my pen steadily, you will please pardon—I have marked the data of real facts & dates copied from his commissions & letters. The other papers have been written since the Civil War—by his commanders & Superior Officers. Also letters copied from Federal officers who were on the opposite side witnessing Breathed's fighting, written to me, or put in print." Breathed's sister continued:

> The paper copies, I think, are authentic. I have many others & some I have destroyed I felt were false. My brother James during his life never talked of his war history nor I did not know of his gallantry only through others. Just before his death, the lady whom he loved from childhood [Miss "Mollie"] & was engaged to [illegible]. He came out of war poor & lived to self & lonely, to have been shamed by this bothered him. She married sometime afterward another & I have sent her all letters written to Maj. Breathed during the war & many other prized belongings of his. His pistol & sword were also sent & I sent all to Richmond, VA. The papers I enclose to you are 'copies' word for word. I hope you can read & use. I will make one positive request. After you cull from the sent papers, will you kindly return them to me. I have been requested to send this data to New York. I find at my age—it is too much for me to collect & write them over again. After they serve you, I will ask you to return [them] & I can have them written or type written, as I do not intend to remove the original ones from the Confederate Museum. Thanking you again for past favors,
>
> I am yours Sincerely,
>
> Priscilla Breathed Bridges

[PS] I have a large book, I prize greatly. It has much in it to interest a Confederate soldier. Also many other tributes in it of my brother, I have not copied because I find those men who belonged to [his] command were so in love with him make large statements that may not be facts or actual. Therefore I only copied from the Superiors.[7]

In 1937, Priscilla's daughter, Priscilla Bridges Carmichael, asked that The Museum of the Confederacy return James Breathed's artifacts. It did so. Sadly, these items were subsequently lost through Priscilla Carmichael's estate sale.[8]

Appendix

Long after the war ended, Henry Matthews wrote to many prominent ex-Confederates who had fought with Breathed to ask them about their recollections of the artillerist. Below are a smattering of the letters he received in reply.

*   *   *

Charlottesville, VA. Jan. 30, 1902

H. H. Matthews quartermaster
Confederate Soldier's Home
Pikesville, MD

My Dear Sir
It is no trouble to give in a few words my opinion of Jim Breathed. As we were accustomed to call him. He was a super artillery officer, intelligent, active, vigorous. Fearless on all occasions. His place in the war picture was always near the flash of the guns, in every fight with a courage that could not be surpassed.
I am very truly yours,

Fitz Lee[1]

*   *   *

Washington, DC
February 9, 1903

My dear Matthews:

. . . . The history of my brigade could not be told without bringing in Breathed's battery. He was the closest fighter I have ever known and the most constant. On one occasion (near Spotsylvania C. H.) saw him under fire from a brigade bring off a piece with two horses [all] the others being killed and cut loose on this occasion he had no support excepting a small squadron of the 6th Virginia cavalry. Then again at Trevilian Station. He ran his battery close upon Sheridan's right flank and added much to his defeat. It was on this occasion, in my hearing, when a shot would strike near or in the battery he would give the order 'They have our range, move up closer.' I will only mention one more instance, Wilson's raid to Reams Station. You may recollect we moved marching faster than the artillery, but much to my surprise I found Breathed leading one of my regiments. On this occasion I saw him use the saber and continued to use it until shot down. There is nothing I can say that would add to Breathed's fame, but I cannot resist in telling some things I saw.

Your comrade,

L. L. Lomax[2]

*   *   *

May 22, 1902

H. H. Matthews
Pikesville, Md.

Dear Sir:

You have been correctly informed in supposing that I knew Major Breathed well. I was more than acquainted with him. We were intimate friends and I can say to you now what I have often said to others—that he was the finest artillery officer that I met during the war. If any distinction can be drawn as to the valor of Confederate soldiers I would give the palm to Jim Breathed. He was a born soldier and an intense passionate patriot. I think he really enjoyed and exulted in battle. He had more of the 'Gaudia Cataminis'—the rapture of battle ascribed to Attila—than any man I knew. The sound of his guns and the shone of conflict excited him to madness. He fought artillery as if it was a side-arm. He considered any distance except muzzle to muzzle as being too far off.

His military commands when his guns were barking were not according to the tactics, but they were expressive in the extreme. His conduct and his language at the battle of Winchester of Sept. 19, 1864, are vividly impressed upon me. The movements of an attacking column of Yankees exposed a large mass of them to his fire. His shots actually seemed to cut a swath through them and at one time seemed to sever the line, parting it like a broken cable. The only orders I remember to have heard him give on that day—and they are not to be found in the tactics or taught in the Sunday Schools—was 'bust hell into them —- —- —-!' When he saw the effect of his shots he would give a shout of exultation like that of Achilles from the ramparts. When his horses; of the condition of the roads, or the character of the expedition prevented his going with his guns, he and a number of his men, notably Captain Tuck Carter and Jim Thompson, volunteered to accompany some cavalry brigade and I am proud of the fact that it was to mine that he was most frequently attached.

I recollect seeing him at Bridgewater [a little village near Dayton and not far from Harrisonburg] when I was particularly struck and captivated by his valor. We had driven the Yankees across the river and had pursued them for some distance on the other side. There was but one ford and our men in pressing had crossed that, but returning they took the straight road. (If you were there you remember the scene). They had run into a 'hornet's nest' on the other side of the river and had to get back the best way they could. In returning some of them had either forgotten there was no bridge there or never knew it. They took the straight road, and in their eagerness to recross they plunged immediately into the waters below. Fortunately the water was "neither deep enough to drown our shallow enough to injure their horses. Amongst them was Jim Breathed. When he rode up to report to me he was very bloody. Lifting his hand with his sword in it he told me with great exultation and triumph that it was Yankee blood, and that he had 'thrusted' three of them through and through. You will recall that in the rapture of battle his grammar and his English was not always accounting to the rules of the pedagogue. I was afterward informed that he had, in fact, killed three Yankees. Breathed died fortunately in some respect. He could not have comprehended the present state of affairs. He fought the Yankees because he hated them. When he entered a battle it was to kill. He never shed any tears nor canted in melee mouthed philanthropy but yet to unarmed and helpless [he] was chivalry itself. He fought for the independence of his country and caring more for constitution liberty than he did for the multiplication table or the rule of three.

He would have thought it an insult to his dead comrades to dream in a nightmare that we were rightfully beaten and that they had died for a foolish cause.

Breathed's reputation is of course confined to his own division, via Stuart-Fitz Lee's. The rank he achieved and the deeds he performed are well known. You will recall that the cavalry at that time made no reports; they had neither the opportunity, the time, nor the material. consequently the career of that unrivaled division is unwritten and its heroes have died unknown.

I wish I had time to say more about our noble comrade. I could talk for hours about him and his battery. If I should ever have the good fortune at meeting you I will tell you other incidents in his gallant career which will interest you and raise him still higher in your estimation. I hope this letter will reach you in time to be of some service. It indicated hurriedly, probably imperfectly. My address is 1939 T Street, N. W., Washington, D.C. where I will always be glad to see you whenever you are in the city.

Very truly your friend and comrade,

William H. Payne[3]

*   *   *

Uniontown, Alabama
Feb. 12, 1902
Oakland Plantation.

Comrade H. H. Matthews, Pikesville, MD:

Your letter of the 6th was forwarded to me out here where I generally spend my winters on the plantation. You ask me in your letter to give you 'my opinion of Major Breathed and his fighting battery.' There never was in the Army of Northern Virginia a better battery, or in any other army one that did better service. All military organizations for better or worse—are under the influence of its immediate commander. Breathed was not only a brave, skillful and dashing flying artillery officer, but had in an imminent degree the qualifications to make him a cavalry leader of great dash. He was a soldier from instinct—a volunteer full of love for the cause, he espoused with his whole heart. He believed in firing low with leveled guns, double shotted with cannister and grape. He loved to push his guns right up. I believed that the cavalry was support enough for him as he was their support. He believed that his men had as much as should be expected of them—to fight their guns and not to be 'pestered' with any other side arms than a pistol—and his idea was to always use his guns for all they were worth in a pursuit and to keep them near enough to the rear guard to take advantage of every position when he could surprise and play upon the enemy's advance. 'Guns were there to fight and not for show' was his maxim, and there was a feeling always of 'esprit de corps' between the cavalry and the horse artillery—as the French have it—'we'll all go down together.' I fell akin to all the old soldiers of the horse artillery. It was by all odds the most distinguished arm in our service and their splendid work gave zest and added always to the [illegible] to which they belonged.

With my best wishes and my love to any and all of my comrades.

Yours sincerely,

Thomas T. Munford[4]

Notes

Preface

1. Frank Breathed, "In Memoriam-Maj. James Breathed, by his brother, Frank Breathed, Petersburg, W. VA." in *Confederate Veteran* (Nashville, TN.: November 1908), v 16, no. 11, 575. (hereinafter "*CV*"). The governor was Claiborne Jackson, and the Confederate general was John S. Marmaduke.

2. Alexander Hunter, *Johnny Reb & Billy Yank* (New York: Smithmark Publishers, 1996), 534.

3. James M. McPherson, *For Cause and Comrades* (New York: Oxford University Press, 1997), 61.

4. McPherson, *For Cause and Comrades*, 21 and 6.

Chapter 1

1. John McGill, *The Macgill-McGill Family of Maryland* (Washington, D.C.: Self Published, 1948), 122.

2. Thomas J. Scharf, *History of Western Maryland*, 2 vols. (Westminster, MD.: Family Line Publications, 1995), v 2, 1259.

3. McGill, *The Macgill-McGill Family of Maryland*, 122.

4. Advancement Office Staff, ed., *Saint James School Alumni Directory, 2003* (Purchase, NY.: Bernard C. Harris Publishing Company, Inc., 2003), v.

5. Reverend Charles R. McGinley, *They Continued Steadfastly in the Apostles' Teaching and Fellowship* (Hagerstown, MD.: The Printing Place, 1986), 75.

6. *ibid.*, 32; Walter B. McKinley, *The Story of Saint Mark's Episcopal Church* (Self Published, 1949), 12.

7. Richard R. Duncan, "The College of St. James and the Civil War: A Causality of the War," in *Historical Magazine of the Protestant Episcopal Church, The Church Historical Society*, Vol. 39, No. 3 (Austin, TX: The Church Historical Society, September, 1970), 265; David Hein, *A Student's View of The College Of St. James On The Eve Of The Civil War, The Letters of W. Wilkins Davis (1842-1866)*, in *Studies in American Religion,* 30 vols. (Lewistown, NY.: The Edwin Mellen Press, 1988), v 30, 11.

8. Scharf, *History of Western Maryland*, 2: 1240; Duncan, "The College of St. James and the Civil War: A Causality of the War," 265.

9. Priscilla Breathed Bridges, Diary, 1865-1920, Author's Collection. (many of the articles and materials in this Diary have been cut and pasted into the "Diary" without references to the primary source, meaning that a more detailed reference is not available. (hereinafter "Bridges Diary").

10. Duncan, "The College of St. James and the Civil War," 266; Hein, "A Student's View," 73 and 71; Scharf, *History of Western Maryland,* 2, 1259.

11. Duncan, "The College of St. James and the Civil War," 266.

12. Hein, "A Student's View," 55-56.

13. *ibid.*, 60-61; *Register of the College of St. James*, (Williamsport, MD.: 1858), 21.

14. Hein, "A Student's View," Reverend Joseph H. Coit, "Recollections," in *Studies in American Religion,* 30 vols. (Lewistown, NY.: The Edwin Mellen Press, 1988), V 30, 63-64.

15. Hein, "A Student's View," 64-65.

16. *ibid.*,70; Coit, "Recollections," 338.

17. Hein, "A Student's View," 72-73.

18. *ibid.*, 87 and 89

19. *ibid.*, 90 and 92; Sir Charles Bell's book *The Hand, its Mechanism and Vital Endowments, as Evincing Design* was first published in 1833 in London as the fourth of the famous Bridgewater Treaties. It subsequently went through many editions and was published in Philadelphia, Utrecht, Stuttgart, and New York. The volumes in this series appeared, ironically, during the period of young Charles Darwin's voyage on the naval vessel H.M.S. *Beagle.* All the treatises

were subtitled *On the Power, Wisdom and Goodness of God as Manifested in the Creation.* Their point was to demonstrate, along the lines of the natural theology of Joseph Butler (1692-1752) and William Paley (1743-1805), the reasonableness of Christianity; the Bridgewater books tried to supply scientific evidence for a teleological argument for God's existence. The orderliness and design of the world were held to reveal divine purpose. Of course, on Darwin's view, the natural process of biological development contained no hint of intelligence or purpose, let alone any proof of divine benevolence. Darwin's writing's, which were just starting to appear at the time William Wilkins Davis was a student at St. James's, soon overwhelmed the testimony of men like Bell; or, to put it more accurately, treaties such as Bell's came to be read in the light of Darwinism and were found to include valuable details corroborative of evolutionary theory. See Gordon Gordon-Taylor and E.W. Walls, *Sir Charles Bell: His Life and Times* (Edinburgh and London, 1958), 163-165.

20. Hein, "A Student's View," 100; Duncan, "The College of St. James and the Civil War," 271.

21. Hein, "A Student's View," 119 and 120.

22. *ibid.*, 126 and 129.

23. *ibid.*, 129 and 137.

24. Scharf, *History of Western Maryland*, 2, 1259.

25. *United States, 1860 Census.* Washington County, Williamsport District Maryland, Schedule 2, July 16, Page 6, line # 33; McGill, *The Macgill-McGill Family of Maryland,* 122.

26. Scharf, *History of Western Maryland*, 2, 1259.

27. McGill, *The Macgill-McGill Family of Maryland,* 217.

28. *ibid.*, 217.

29. Bridges Diary.

30. Peggy O'Rourke-Trott, *Centuries of Leadership, 1800-1900-2000, Deans of the University of Maryland School of Medicine* (Baltimore, MD.: University of Maryland School of Medicine, 2000), 1.

31. Dean T. Eric, Jr., *Shook Over Hell: Post-Traumatic Stress, Vietnam and the Civil War* (Cambridge, MA.: Harvard University Press, 1997), 52.

32. O'Rourke-Trott, *Centuries of Leadership*, 10.

33. University of Maryland, Office of the School of Medicine, *University of Maryland Fifty-Third Annual Circular, Session 1860-61 and Catalogue of Matriculates* (Baltimore, MD.: Sherwood, 1860), Introduction.

34. *ibid.*, 5-6.

35. Doctor James Breathed, "An Inaugural Dissertation on Pneumonia to the Provost Regents and Faculty of Physic of the University of Maryland For the

Degree of Doctor of Medicine" (Historical and Special Collection of the Health Sciences and Human Services Library, University of Maryland, Baltimore, MD.: May, 1860), 1-20.

36. *ibid*.

37. M. W. Hazlewood and W. Watson, eds., "Major Breathed, of the Stuart Horse Artillery, by A Comrade," in *The Old Dominion*, Vol. 5, No. 1 (January 15, 1871), 37-48 (hereinafter "Hazlewood and Watson"); *United States, 1860 Census*. Rush Township, Missouri, Schedule 1, June 12, Page 19, line # 39; McGill, *The Macgill-McGill Family of Maryland*, 123.

38. Preston Filbert, *The Half Not Told, the Civil War in a frontier town.* (Mechanicsburg, PA: Stackpole, 2001), 1-4.

39. *ibid*, 4-10.

40. Fact Sheet-University of Maryland, School of Medicine. Under Dean George Warner Miltenberger named Dean of School of Medicine (1855-1869). Courtesy Alumni Affairs Office, University of Maryland, (Baltimore, MD.).

41. Filbert, *The Half Not Told, 14*.

Chapter 2

1. Stephen F. Lang, *The Complete Idiot's Guide to The Confederacy* (Indianapolis, IN.: Alpha Books, 2003), 54.

2. *ibid*.

3. *Galveston (Texas) Daily News,* May 30, 1917, 2; Hazlewood and Watson, 37.

4. McPherson, *For Cause and Comrades*, 6; Hazlewood and Watson, 38.

5. McPherson, *For Cause and Comrades* 13 and 21.

6. Hazlewood and Watson, 38; Robert J. Driver, Jr. *1st Virginia Cavalry* (Lynchburg, VA.; H. E. Howard, 1991), 3.

7. John W. Thomason, Jr., *JEB Stuart* (New York: Konecky & Konecky, 1958), 97.

8. Driver, *1st Virginia Cavalry*, 6.

9. *ibid.,* 6.

10. James Breathed consolidated service records, National Archives, M226, R 336 (hereinafter "C.S.R.").

11. C.S.R. M226, R336; Driver, *1st Virginia Cavalry*, 12. [Corporal Compton wrote: "Was aroused very early by the sound of the bugle, and received orders to saddle up, which was quickly done."]

12. Don Troiani, *Civil War* (Norwalk, CT.: The Eastern Press, 1995), 8.

13. *ibid.,* 8-9.

14. McPherson, *For Cause and Comrades*, 141.

15. In fact, Stuart had Jones court-martialed in September 1863, and, instead of being convicted, Jones was sent away from the Army of Northern Virginia to assume command of the cavalry forces defending the Shenandoah Valley. Jones was killed in action at the Battle of Piedmont, June 5, 1864.

16. Laura Lee Davidson, "The Services of the Women of Maryland to the Confederate States," in Personal Narratives Vertical File, Enoch Pratt Public Library, (Baltimore, MD.); McGill, *The Macgill-McGill Family of Maryland*, 217.

17. *ibid.*, 124; November 4, 1861, Priscilla Williams Breathed, James' sister, married Robert Bridges of Hancock, Maryland.

18. C.S.R., M226, R336.

19. Reverend Henry H. Tucker, D. D., Sermon, November 15, 1861, "God in the War," Mercer University Collection (Macon, GA.).

20. David Cardell, "A Horse Battery," *CV*, (January-December 1919), 27, 1, 1-7.

21. *ibid.*

22. *ibid.*

23. Jennings Cropper Wise, "The Boy Gunners of Lee," *Southern Historical Society Papers*, (Richmond, VA.: December 1, 1916), 42, 158-159. (hereinafter "*SHSP*").

24. John E. Divine, *35th Battalion Virginia Cavalry* (Lynchburg, VA.: H. E. Howard, 1985), 4.

25. Bridges Diary.

26. C.S.R., M226, R336; C.S.R., M331, R195, Frame 203-204; McPherson, *For Cause and Comrades*, 46.

27. H. H. Matthews, "Pelham-Breathed Battery," in *St. Mary's (Maryland) Beacon,* (Lexington Park, MD.: 1904-1905), Articles 1-27 and Appendix. Article 1. (hereinafter Matthews, *St. Mary's (Maryland) Beacon,* Article and #); McPherson, *For Cause and Comrades*, 59. Note concerning quotations taken from Matthews' articles from the St. Mary's Beacon, all quotations used in this book were transcribed from microfilm. Unfortunately, that microfilm had deteriorated over time. The author has made his best efforts to transcribe the text as accurately as possible. In some instances, however, the legibility of the microfilm was so poor that some of the text is illegible. In other instances, the legibility was marginal, in which case the author was compelled to interpolate a word or two, based on the implications of context and grammar, that was not as legible as he would have preferred. In no case was illegible text used or construed by the author.

28. Matthews, *St. Mary's (Maryland) Beacon,* Article 1.

29. *ibid.,* Article 1.

30. *ibid.,* Article 1.

31. *ibid.,* Article 1.

32. McPherson, *For Cause and Comrades,* 5.

33. *The War of the Rebellion: A Compilation of the Official Records of the Union and Confederate Armies,* 128 vols. (Washington, D.C.: United States Government Publishing Office, 1880-1901), vol. 11, pt. 1, 575. (hereinafter *"OR"*). All references are to Series 1 unless otherwise noted.

34. *ibid.*

35. Douglas Southall Freeman, *Lee's Lieutenants: A Study in Command.* (New York: Charles Scribner's Sons, 1942), vol. 1, 145.

Chapter 3

1. Stephen W. Sears, *To the Gates of Richmond-The Peninsula Campaign* (New York: Ticknor & Fields, 1992), 151 and 168; Wise, *The Long Arm of Lee,* (Lynchburg, VA.: J. P. Bell Company, 1915, in 2 vols.) v. 1, 206.

2. *OR* 11, pt. 3, 590.

3. Longacre, Edward. *Lee's Cavalrymen* (Mechanicsburg, PA.: Stackpole, 2002), 86.

4. The basic facts of the "Ride Around McClellan" presented below are drawn from the following sources (except where noted): Douglas Southall Freeman, *Lee's Lieutenant's,* edited by Stephen W. Sears, 1-Volume Abridgement (New York: Simon & Schuster, Inc., 1998), 150; Sears, *To the Gates of Richmond,* 169; *OR* 11, pt. 1, 1036 and 1044-1045; Robert J. Trout, *Galloping Thunder The Stuart Horse Artillery Battalion* (Mechanicsburg, PA.: Stackpole Books, 2002), 60. An outstanding account of Stuart's ride is Edwin C. Bearss, "Into the Very Jaws of the Enemy: Jeb Stuart's Ride Around McClellan," 71-143, in William Miller, ed., *The Peninsula Campaign: Yorktown to the Seven Days*, Vol. 1 (Campbell, CA: Savas Woodbury, 1995).

5. *OR* 11, pt. 1, 1020, 1036.

6. *ibid.,* 1036.

7. *ibid.,* 1037.

8. Longacre, *Lee's Cavalrymen,* 88.

9. *OR* 11, pt. 1, 1020, 1037-1038.; Matthews, *St. Mary's (Maryland) Beacon,* Article 2.

10. Matthews, *St. Mary's (Maryland) Beacon,* Article 2; *ibid.,* Article 2.

11. *OR* 11, pt. 1, 1037; McPherson, *For Cause and Comrades,* 84-85.

12. In 1861, the War Department completely reorganized the Federal government's mounted forces. These units were re-numbered and re-designated according to their seniority of service. Thus, the oldest unit, the 1st Dragoons, became the 1st U. S. Cavalry, the 2nd Dragoons became the 2nd U. S. Cavalry, the Regiment of Mounted Rifles became the 3rd U. S. Cavalry, the 1st Cavalry became the 4th U. S. Cavalry, and the 2nd Cavalry, which was the prior unit of Robert E. Lee and his nephew Fitzhugh, was re-designated as the 5th U. S. Cavalry. A new regiment formed with the war's outbreak in 1861, originally designated the 3rd Cavalry, was soon re-named as the 6th U. S. Cavalry; *OR* 11, pt. 1, 1037.

13. *OR* 11, pt. 1, 1037-1038; *ibid.*, 1037-1038.

14. *ibid.*, 1038.

15. *ibid.*, 1038.

16. *OR* 11, pt. 1, 1038.

17. *ibid.*, 1038; Sears, *To the Gates of Richmond*, 170.

18. Matthews, *St. Mary's (Maryland) Beacon,* Article 2; *ibid.,* Article 2.

19. Trout, *Galloping Thunder,* 60; Matthews, *St. Mary's (Maryland) Beacon,* Article 2; *ibid.*, Article 2; *OR* 11, pt. 1, 1038.

20. Robert H. Moore, II, *The 1st and 2nd Stuart Horse Artillery* (Lynchburg, VA.: H.E. Howard, 1985), 15.

21. *OR* 11, pt. 1, 1045.

22. *ibid.*, 1039; Sears, *To the Gates of Richmond*, 172; Emory M. Thomas, *Bold Dragoon: The Life of J.E.B. Stuart* (Norman, OK.: University of Oklahoma Press, 1999), 122; Bearss, "Jeb Stuart," 122.

23. Quoted in Samuel L. Gracey, *Annals of the Sixth Cavalry* (Philadelphia, E. H. Butler & Co., 1868), 51-52.

24. Bearss, "Jeb Stuart," 122-124; *OR* 11, pt. 1, 1039.

25. *OR* 11, pt. 1, 1039, 1042.

26. *ibid.*; Matthews, *St. Mary's (Maryland) Beacon,* Article 2.

27. Trout, *Galloping Thunder,* 61; Sears, *To the Gates of Richmond,* 174; *OR* 11, pt. 2, 514; Matthews, *St. Mary's (Maryland) Beacon,* Article 3.

28. *OR* 11, pt. 2, 514.

29. Matthews, *St. Mary's (Maryland) Beacon,* Article 3; *ibid.*, Article 3.

30. *OR* 11, pt. 2, 514-515; Matthews, *St. Mary's (Maryland) Beacon,* Article 3.

31. *ibid.*, 515-516; Sears, *To the Gates of Richmond*, 255-256; Matthews, *St. Mary's (Maryland) Beacon,* Article 3.

32. *OR* 11, pt. 2, 516; Sears, *To the Gates of Richmond*, 210.

33. *OR* 11, pt. 2, 516-517; Matthews, *St. Mary's (Maryland) Beacon,* Article 3.

34. William Woods Hassler, *Colonel John Pelham: Lee's Boy Artillerist* (Chapel Hill, NC.: University of North Carolina Press, 1960), 41-42

35. *ibid*, 41-42; *OR* 11, pt. 2, 517-518.

36. *OR* 11, pt. 2, 529.

37. David G. Martin, *The Peninsula Campaign, March - July 1862* (Conshohocken, PA.: Combined Books, Inc., 1992), 219.

38. Thomas, *Bold Dragoon*, 136; Sears, *To the Gates of Richmond*, 311, 314, 319-321, 335, and 344; Martin, *The Peninsula Campaign, March-July 1862*, 226.

39. Edward G. Longacre, *Lincoln's Cavalry* (Mechanicsburg, PA.: Stackpole Books, 2000), 94.

40. Matthews, *St. Mary's (Maryland) Beacon,* Article 3, pt. 2. According to Martin's report in *OR* 11, pt. 2, 530, the only artillery with him was one gun commanded by Lieutenant Shaw; Stuart's report also mentions only one gun under Pelham went out, and then Martin moved with Shaw's gun to join them. The reports are silent as to Breathed's involvement in this matter.

41. Edward Porter Alexander, *Military Memoirs of a Confederate* (New York: Da Capo Press, Inc., 1993), 168.

42. *OR* 11, pt. 2, 519-520; Sears, *To the Gates of Richmond*, 340; Moore, *The 1st and 2nd Stuart Horse Artillery*, 20; Freeman, *Lee's Lieutenant's*, 272; Wise, *The Long Arm of Lee*, 1, 233; Alexander, *Military Memoirs of a Confederate*, 169.

43. *OR* 11, pt. 2, 521.

44. McClellan, *I Rode with JEB Stuart*, (Bloomington, IN.: Da Capo Press, 1994), pp 86-91.

45. Thomason. *JEB Stuart*, pp. 214-215.

46. Most of the data for the following bio-sketches are gleaned from Robert J Trout, *'The Hoss', Officer Biographies and Rosters of the Stuart Horse Artillery Battalion*. n.p.: JebFlo Press, 2003.

47. Trout. *Galloping Thunder*. 71-77.

48. Longacre. *Lee's Cavalrymen*. 106-107.

49. Trout. *Galloping Thunder*. 75.

50. *ibid*, 75.

51. Longacre, *Lee's Cavalrymen*, 108; McClellan, *I Rode With JEB Stuart*, 88-89.

52. Thomason, *JEB Stuart*, 221-223.

53. George W. Shreve, "Reminiscences in the History of the Stuart Horse Artillery, C.S.A." in *Chew Papers-Manuscript Collection* (Charles Town, WV.), #53, 2.

54. Bridges, Diary, *Richmond Times-Dispatch.*

55. Freeman, *R.E. Lee,* (New York: Charles Scribner's and Sons, 1934) vol. 2, 309-310; Longacre, *Lee's Cavalrymen,* 121-122.

56. Trout, *Galloping Thunder,* 83-84.

57. *ibid,* 84.

58. *OR* 12, pt. 2, 753.

59. Matthews, *St. Mary's (Maryland) Beacon,* Article 4.

60. *OR* 12, pt. 2, 754.

61. Matthews, *St. Mary's (Maryland) Beacon,* Article 4; Wise, *The Long Arm of Lee,* 1, 262; *OR* 12, pt. 2, 755.

62. *OR* 12, pt. 2, 755.

63. *Philadelphia Weekly Times,* October 7, 1882.

64. *OR* 12, pt. 2, 755.

Chapter 4

1. Douglas Southall Freeman, *R.E. Lee,* v. 2, 350 ff.

2. *ibid.* 350-351.

3. *ibid.* 352 ff.

4. Richard Townshend Dodson, "With Stuart in Maryland, Operations of the Stuart Horse Artillery in The Sharpsburg Campaign," as transcribed and presented to the author by Robert J. Trout.

5. Trout, *Galloping Thunder,* 89.

6. Heros Von Borcke, *Memoirs of the Confederate War For Independence* (Nashville, TN.: J. S. Sanders & Company, 1999), 135.

7. Burke Davis, *Jeb Stuart, the Last Cavalier* (New York: Bonanza Books, 1957), 195-196.

8. Edward G. Longacre, *Gentleman and Soldier, A Biography of Wade Hampton III* (Nashville, TN.: Rutledge Hill Press, 2003), 82-83.

9. Richard Townshend Dodson, "With Stuart in Maryland, Operations of the Stuart Horse Artillery in The Sharpsburg Campaign."

10. *ibid.*

11. Longacre, *Lee's Cavalrymen,* 130-131.

12. *ibid.* 131.

13. Joseph L. Harsh, *Taken at the Flood* (Kent, OH.: Kent State University Press, 1999), 152; Douglas Southall Freeman, *R.E. Lee,* v 2, 247.

14. Matthews, *St. Mary's (Maryland) Beacon,* Article 5.

15. O.R. 19, pt. 1, 435-436; Trout, *Galloping Thunder,* 98-99.

16. Lawrence R. Laboda, *From Selma To Appomattox, The History Of The Jeff Davis Artillery* (New York: Oxford University Press, 1994), 45-46.

17. Trout, *Galloping Thunder,* 99; Francis E. Heitman, *Historical Register and Dictionary of the United States Army,* 2 vols. (Washington, D.C.: U. S. Government Printing Office, 1904), vol. 2. Also present at Sharpsburg was future Breathed artilleryman Capt. Llyod Beall, 2nd U.S. Artillery Regular Army who was dismissed September 12, before the Battle of Sharpsburg, due to his own refusal to fight against the Confederacy. He did not fight in this day for either side.

18. Matthews, *St. Mary's (Maryland) Beacon,* Article 5.

19. *ibid.,* Article 5.

20. *ibid.,* Article 5.

21. Harsh, *Taken At The Flood,* 364; Wise, *The Long Arm of Lee,* 1, 296.

22. Hazelwood and Watson, 38.

23. Matthews, *St. Mary's (Maryland) Beacon,* Article 5.

24. Hazelwood and Watson, 38; Ted Alexander, "Antietam, the Bloodiest Day," in *North & South Magazine,* (October 2002), 5, 7, 78-89; Matthews, *St. Mary's (Maryland) Beacon,* Article 5.

25. Matthews, *St. Mary's (Maryland) Beacon,* Article 5.

26. *ibid.,* Article 5.

27. Trout, *Galloping Thunder,* 103; Hazelwood and Watson, 38.

28. *ibid.*

29. Duncan, "The College of St. James and the Civil War: A Causality of the War," 269.

30. *ibid.,* 275.

31. *ibid.,* 279, McGill. *The Macgill-McGill Family of Maryland.* 124.

32. *ibid.,* 272-73.

33. Kathleen A. Ernst, *Too Afraid To Cry* (Mechanicsburg, PA.: Stackpole Books, 1999), 168.

34. Longacre, *Lincoln's Cavalry,* 106.

35. C.S.R., M226, R336.

36. Trout, *Galloping Thunder,* 110-111.

37. Trout, *Galloping Thunder,* 111.

38. Matthews, *St. Mary's (Maryland) Beacon,* Article 6.

39. Thomason, Jr., *JEB Stuart,* 293; Trout, *Galloping Thunder,* 114; John McGill, *The Macgill-McGill Family of Maryland,* 123; Bridges, Priscilla Breathed: Letter, Receipt for goods received given to Confederate Memorial

Literary Society, Richmond, Virginia, in 1898 by Priscilla Breathed Bridges. Loan retrieved by Pricilla Williams Carmichael, August 4, 1937 from Museum of the Confederacy, Richmond, Virginia.

40. *OR* 19, pt. 2, 55; Matthews, *St. Mary's (Maryland) Beacon,* Article 6.

41. Trout, *Galloping Thunder*, 115-16. One of the things that complicates writing a biography of James Breathed is "The Breathed Legend." Again and again the accounts written after the war attribute deeds and honors to James Breathed that either should have been shared with others or did not happen at the time or place where they are remembered. This raid has a minor, but illustrative example. When Richard Dodson, Sgt. Maj. of the Stuart Horse Artillery, recalled this raid, he remembered that Breathed commanded the four guns, whereas Robert Trout has proved that both Breathed and Hart shared command. We will note other instances of "The Breathed Legend" deviating form the documented facts. Jim Breathed was the type of man of whom legends are made.

42. Matthews, *St. Mary's (Maryland) Beacon,* Article 6.

43. General Wickham, C.S.A., "Autobiographical," in Wickham Papers (Virginia Historical Society, Richmond, VA.)(hereinafter "*Wickham Memoir*").

44. John W. Thompson, IV, *Horses, Hostages, and Apple Cider, J.E.B. Stuart's 1862 Pennsylvania Raid* (Mercersburg, PA.: Mercersburg Printing, 2002), 65-68. The last laugh was on Stuart, however. The railroad bridge was not iron, but wood, and could have been easily burned; the towns folk were just bluffing.

45. Matthews, *St. Mary's (Maryland) Beacon,* Article 6.

46. *Wickham Memoir*; Matthews, *St. Mary's (Maryland) Beacon,* Article 6.

47. *ibid.*, Article 6.

48. Blackford, *War Years with Jeb Stuart*, (Baton Rouge: Louisiana University Press, 1993) 172.

49. Matthews, *St. Mary's (Maryland) Beacon,* Article 6.

50. *Wickham Memoir*

51. *ibid.*

52. *ibid.*

53. Longacre. *Lee's Cavalrymen*. 151 ff.

54. Trout, *Galloping Thunder*, 121; Matthews, *St. Mary's (Maryland) Beacon,* Article 7.

55. Longacre. *Lee's Cavalrymen*, 152 ff; Freeman, *R.E. Lee*. Vol. 2, 425 ff; Trout. Galloping Thunder. 125 ff.

56. Margaret A. Vogtsberger, ed., *The Dulanys of Melbourne, A Family in Mosby's Confederacy* (Rockbridge, VA.: Rockbridge Publishing Co., 1995), 51.

57. Trout, *Galloping Thunder*, 125.

58. Grease heel is an affliction of horses that left them lame, and usually results from insufficient grooming. Grease heel is a dermatological condition that usually arises from too much prolonged exposure to mud and water. It can be treated, but it is hard on the horses; Matthews, *St. Mary's (Maryland) Beacon,* Article 7.

59. Matthews, *St. Mary's (Maryland) Beacon,* Article 7; Trout, *Galloping Thunder,* 126; Richard Townshend Dodson, "With Stuart in Maryland, Stuart's Daring Raid," as transcribed by Robert J. Trout.

60. Matthews, *St. Mary's (Maryland) Beacon,* Article 7; Trout, *Galloping Thunder,* 127; *OR* 19, pt. 2, 142.

61. Matthews, *St. Mary's (Maryland) Beacon,* Article 7

62. Matthews, *St. Mary's (Maryland) Beacon,* Article 7; *OR* 19, pt. 2, 142

63. Matthews, *St. Mary's (Maryland) Beacon,* Article 7

64. *ibid,*. Article 7.

65. *ibid.,* Article 7.

66. Trout, *Galloping Thunder,* 128; Matthews, *St. Mary's (Maryland) Beacon,* Article 7; *OR* 19, pt. 2, 142

67. *ibid.,* Article 7; *OR* 19, pt. 2, 142-143.

68. Thomas J. C. Williams, *History Washington County, Maryland From the Earliest Settlements to the Present Time,* 2 vols. (Westminster, MD.: Family Line Publications, 1992), 2, 1014.

69. Hunter, *Johnny Reb and Billy Yank,* 220.

70. Longacre. *Lee's Cavalrymen.* 157-158, Trout. *Galloping Thunder.* 135, McDonald. *History of the Laurel Brigade.* 105-106.

71. Trout. *The Hoss.* 144-148.

72. Trout, *Galloping Thunder,* 135; *OR* 19, pt. 2, 143.

73. C.S.R., M226, R336.

Chapter 5

1. Henry Wager Halleck. *The Project Gutenberg EBook of Elements of Military Art and Science.* Release Date: July 1, 2005 [EBook #16170], http://www.gutenberg.org/dirs/1/6/1/7/16170/16170-h/16170-h.htm.

2. Douglas Southall Freeman, *R. E. Lee,* v 2, 441; Trout, *Galloping Thunder,* 144-145.

3. *ibid,* 144 ff; Frank O'Reilly, *Battle of Fredericksburg Historical Research,* Illustrated by John Dove, Revised and Produced by Steve Stanley, Maps # 1-5. Maps place Breathed's Battery at this location.

4 Freeman, *Lee's Lieutenants,* 2, 349-351.

5. Trout, *Galloping Thunder,* 145-147.

6. Hassler, *Pelham*, 148; Trout, *Galloping Thunder,* 145-147; Freeman, *Lee's Lieutenants*, 2, 349-351.

7. Shreve. "Reminiscences in the History of the Stuart Horse Artillery, C.S.A.," #53, 2.

8. O'Reilly, *Battle of Fredericksburg Historical Research*, Illustrated by John Dove, Revised and Produced by Steve Stanley, Maps # 1-5. Maps place Breathed's Battery at this location.

9. Shreve, "Reminiscences in the History of the Stuart Horse Artillery, C.S.A.," #53, 2.

10. Trout, *Galloping Thunder,* 148.

11. *ibid.*, 150-152.

12. *OR* 21, 738-739.

13. *ibid.*, 738-739.

14. *ibid.*, 739; Trout, *Galloping Thunder,* 150-52. Trout raises a question in a footnote in this section: given the amount of time involved, how could Breathed have expended all his ammunition while Henry did not? Trout postulates that Breathed must have been much more heavily engaged, which is a logical surmise if one assumes all of Breathed's battery was engaged. However, if Breathed had only brought his section of rifled guns, then the ammunition available for them would have been limited, and, therefore, more easily exhausted. Since the horse artillery was having trouble keeping up with Fitz Lee's troopers during this raid, it is not unlikely that Breathed was "traveling light."

15. C.S.R., M226, R336.

16. *ibid.; ibid.*

17. *The Wigfall Family Papers*, Private Family Collection of Marty Martin, Great Granddaughter of Halsey Wigfall, (hereinafter "*The Wigfall Family Papers*); Trout, *Galloping Thunder,* 155-156.

18. McPherson, *For Cause and Comrades*, 58; Matthews, *St. Mary's (Maryland) Beacon,* Article 8.

19. McPherson, *For Cause and Comrades*, 53.

20. Matthews, *St. Mary's (Maryland) Beacon,* Article 8; White feather was an old sign of cowardice that originated from the belief that if the tail of a cock rooster contained a white feather, that cock would not be a good fighter. McPherson, *For Cause and Comrades*, 77-78.

21. Bruce Catton, *Glory Road*, (New York: Doubleday & Company, Inc., 1952), 63-110. Obviously, a detailed discussion of these events strays far beyond the scope of this book. For a detailed examination of the formation of the

Army of the Potomac's Cavalry Corps, see Eric J. Wittenberg, *The Union Cavalry Comes of Age: Hartwood Church to Brandy Station, 1863* (Dulles, VA.: Potomac Books, 2003).

22. Catton, *Glory Road,* 111-154; Longacre, *Lincoln's Cavalrymen,* 124-129.

Chapter 6

1. Stephen W. Sears, *Chancellorsville* (New York: Houghton Mifflin, 1996), 49.

2. Wittenberg, *The Union Cavalry Comes of Age,* 49-57.

3. Matthews, *St. Mary's (Maryland) Beacon,* Article 8; Edward G. Longacre, *Fitz Lee: A Military Biography of Major General Fitzhugh Lee, C.S.A.* (Cambridge, MA.: Da Capo Press, 2005), 96-97.

4. Wittenberg, *The Union Cavalry Comes of Age,* 57-65.

5. The author must note at this point that it is not his belief that the Battle of Kelly's Ford or Kellyville, has yet been definitively described. Virtually all the sources I have consulted disagree with each other, often significantly. The account that follows is based on a general consensus of various accounts by H. H. Matthews, Harry Gilmore, W. W. Blackford, H. B. McClellan, Douglas Southall Freeman, Edward Longacre, Stephen W. Sears, Robert Trout, the *OR,* and especially Eric J. Wittenberg, who has done a remarkably fine job of sifting the available evidence and making sense of it. If some of the details do not bear too much scrutiny, that is because the sources are at odds, with no one source clearly in the right. I will try to make the story as accurate as possible, consistent with a biography of James Breathed.

6. *OR* 25, pt. 1, 60-61.

7. Matthews, *St. Mary's (Maryland) Beacon,* Article 8; As regards the Graffiti House scroll, the author recently participated in efforts to have it returned to its original location, where it stands at the time of publication; Trout, *Galloping Thunder,* 177-78.

8. *OR* 25, pt. 1, 61.

9. Matthews, *St. Mary's (Maryland) Beacon,* Article 8.

10. *OR* 25, pt. 1, 60-63; Sears, *Chancellorsville,* 83-89.

11. Matthews, *St. Mary's (Maryland) Beacon,* Article 8.

12. E.S. Gilman to the parent's of Johan George Segerer, March 20, 1863, in Private Collection of David Bridges, (Arlington, Virginia).

13. *OR* 25, pt. 1, 50; Sears, *Chancellorsville,* 83-89.

14. Matthews, *St. Mary's (Maryland) Beacon,* Article 8.

15. *OR* 25, pt. 1, 63, 64.

16. Trout, *Galloping Thunder*, 183; Robert J. Trout, "The Stuart Horse Artillery Battalion can stand with that of any artillery organization in any army, Northern or Southern," in *North & South Magazine* (September 2000), 3, 7, 80-84.

17. Wittenberg, *The Union Cavalry Comes of Age*, 111-138.

18. *ibid.*

19. *ibid.*

20. *The Wigfall Family Papers.*

21. Wittenberg, *The Union Cavalry Comes of Age*, 143-159.

22. *ibid,* Sears, *Chancellorsville*, 177; *The Wigfall Family Papers*; *OR* 25, pt. 1, 1047, 1049.

23. *OR* 25, pt. 1, 1047, 1049.

24. *ibid.*

25. *The Wigfall Family Papers.*

26. *ibid.*

27. The Wigfall Family Papers; *OR* 25, pt. 1, 1049; Matthews, *St. Mary's (Maryland) Beacon,* Article 9, pt. 2.

28. *ibid.*

29. *ibid.; OR* 25, pt. 1, 1049. The canvas bag of gun powder was rammed down the barrel and then a long needle like wire punctured the canvas so that when the primer was pulled by the lanyard the spark went down the primed hole and exploded the gun powder exposed by the prick.

30. Matthews, *St. Mary's (Maryland) Beacon,* Article 9, pt. 2; *OR* 25, pt. 1, 1049.

31. Trout, *Galloping Thunder,* 202-203, 205; Matthews, *St. Mary's (Maryland) Beacon,* Article 9, pt. 2; *OR* 25, pt. 1, 1049.

32. Sears, *Chancellorsville*, 244-245; John Esten Cooke, *Surry of Eagle's Nest* (New York: G. W. Dillingham Co., Publishers, 1866), 462. Cooke reported that these were his actual words, despite the fact that the book is a work of fiction.

33. *OR* 25, pt. 1, 1049; Matthews, *St. Mary's (Maryland) Beacon,* Article 9, pt. 2.

34. F. M. Colston, "What I Saw of the Battle of Chancellorsville," in *F. M. Colston Papers*, Virginia Historical Society, (Richmond, Virginia).

35. *OR* 25, pt. 1, 1049.

36. *OR* 25, pt. 1, 1049; Ernest B. Furguson, *Chancellorsville, 1863: The Souls of the Brave* (New York: Vintage Books, 1993), 169, 175; Matthews, *St. Mary's (Maryland) Beacon,* Appendix.

37. Colston, "What I Saw of the Battle of Chancellorsville," 1-7; Matthews, *St. Mary's (Maryland) Beacon,* Article 9, pt. 2.

38. Bridges, Diary.

39. Matthews, *St. Mary's (Maryland) Beacon,* Article 9, pt. 2.

40. *The Wigfall Family Papers.*

41. *ibid.*

42. Matthews, *St. Mary's (Maryland) Beacon,* Article 9, pt. 2.

43. *The Wigfall Family Papers.*

44. *OR* 25, pt. 1, 1050; Hazelwood and Watson, 40.

45. Matthews, *St. Mary's (Maryland) Beacon,* Article 9, pt. 2.

46. *OR* 25, pt. 1, 1050.

47. Freeman, *Lee's Lieutenants*, 3, 3-4; Hunter, *Johnny Reb and Billy Yank*, 434; Trout, *Galloping Thunder*, 212; Matthews, *St. Mary's (Maryland) Beacon,* Article 10, pt. 1.

48. *The Wigfall Family Papers.*

49. Trout, *Galloping Thunder*, 215 and 220; Wise, *The Long Arm of Lee*, v. 2, 577; Freeman, *Lee's Lieutenants*, v 3, 4.

50. Wise, *The Long Army of Lee*, v. 2, 578.

Chapter 7

1. Trout, *Galloping Thunder*, 223.

2. Wise, *The Long Arm of Lee*, 2, 586.

3. Possibly matched by the up and coming Trevilian Station Battle.

4. Matthews, *St. Mary's (Maryland) Beacon,* Article 10, pt. 1.

5. Trout, *Galloping Thunder*, 226.

6. Matthews, *St. Mary's (Maryland) Beacon,* Article 10, pt. 2.

7. *ibid.*, Article 10, pt. 2.

8. Longacre, *Lincoln's Cavalry*, 157; On the northern end of the Fleetwood Hill; Trout, *Galloping Thunder*, 230-231.

9. Robertson's Brigade was only engaged very briefly at Kelly's Ford and then withdrew. Robertson's men hardly fired a shot, and suffered no casualties in this sanguinary engagement. Only Fitz Lee's 4th Virginia Cavalry was engaged, and that was very late in the battle.

10. *The Wigfall Family Papers.*

11. Matthews, *St. Mary's (Maryland) Beacon,* Article 11.

12. Trout, *Galloping Thunder*, 255-257.

13. Matthews, *St. Mary's (Maryland) Beacon,* Article 11; W. C. Wickham, "Colonel W. C. Wickham's Report of an Engagement near Aldie, 17th, 1863,"

SHSP (1881), 9, 79-80; Gregg's 2nd Division was composed of Gen. Kilpatrick's Brigade, 2nd New Jersey, 1st Mass., 6th Ohio, 4th New York and the 1st Maine Cavalry, with Randol's Battery of horse artillery;.

14. Trout, *Galloping Thunder*, 257-258.

15. Wickham, "Wickham's Report," 79-80.

16. Matthews, *St. Mary's (Maryland) Beacon,* Article 11; *OR* 27, pt. 2, 739-741; see monument at stone wall, Snickersville Turnpike, Aldie, Virginia, for the verification that the 1st Massachusetts Cavalry sustained 198 casualties.

17. Mathews, *St. Mary's (Maryland) Beacon*, Article 11; Robert F. O'Neill, *The Cavalry Battles of Aldie, Middleburg and Upperville*, (Lynchburg, VA.: H. E. Howard, 1993), 50.

18. *ibid.*, 63-65.

19. *ibid.*, 68.

20. Matthews, *St. Mary's (Maryland) Beacon,* Article 11; Edward G. Longacre, *The Cavalry at Gettysburg* (Lincoln, NB.: University of Nebraska Press, 1986), 247.

21. *ibid.*; Thomason, *JEB Stuart*, 417.

22. Matthews, *St. Mary's (Maryland) Beacon,* Article 11.

23. Thomason, *JEB Stuart,* 418-419; Matthews, *St. Mary's (Maryland) Beacon,* Article 11.

24. *ibid.*, Article 11.

25. *ibid.*, Article 11.

26. *ibid.*, Article 11.

27. O'Neill, *The Cavalry Battles of Aldie, Middleburg and Upperville*, 111.

28. Fauquier and Loudoun Garden Club. *Save The Bridge Fund* (Upperville, Virginia); Mark Boatner, *The Civil War Dictionary* (New York, Vintage, 1959), 862.

29. Matthews, *St. Mary's (Maryland) Beacon,* Article 11.

30. *ibid.*, Article 11; *OR* 27, pt.2, 741.

Chapter 8

1. Jeffery D. Wert, *Gettysburg Day Three* (New York: Simon & Schuster, 2001), 24; Trout, *Galloping Thunder*, 279.

2. Matthews, *St. Mary's (Maryland) Beacon,* Article 12; Trout, *Galloping Thunder*, 279-280.

3. Frederic Shriver Klein, *Just South of Gettysburg* (Westminster, MD.: Historical Society of Carroll County, 2000), 41; Davis, *JEB Stuart, The Last Cavalier*, 328.

4. Klein, *Just South of Gettysburg*, 41-42.

5. *ibid.*, 42.

6. *ibid.*, 178; *The Wigfall Family Papers*. Maria Shriver and Pam Shriver, the former championship tennis player, are both related to the Shrivers of Union Mills.

7. *ibid.*, 178.

8. *ibid.*, 178; See Internet website www.nps.gov/apco/sweeney2.htm, for reference to Sweeney.

9. John Esten Cooke, *The Wearing of the Gray* (Baton Rouge, LA.: Louisiana State University Press, 1997), 240.

10. Trout, *Galloping Thunder*, 281.

11. Trout, *Galloping Thunder*, 282; Cooke, *The Wearing of the Gray*, 241-242.

12. Matthews, *St. Mary's (Maryland) Beacon,* Article 12.

13. *ibid.*, Article 12.

14. Trout, *Galloping Thunder*, 283.

15. Matthews, *St. Mary's (Maryland) Beacon,* Article 12.

16. Edward G. Longacre, *Lee's Cavalrymen,* 215-216.

17. *ibid.*, 337-338.

18. *ibid.*, 217; Matthews, *St. Mary's (Maryland) Beacon,* Article 12.

19. Matthews, *St. Mary's (Maryland) Beacon,* Article 12.

20. Trout, *Galloping Thunder*, 291; Davis, *JEB Stuart, The Last Cavalier,* 337.

21. Longacre, *Lee's Cavalrymen*, 222; Davis, *JEB Stuart, The Last Cavalier*, 340.

22. Henry P. Bridges, *The Woodmont Story* (New York: A. S. Barnes and Company, 1953), 23.

23. *ibid.*, 22-23; Williams, *History of Washington County*, 1, 336; Bridges, *The Woodmont Story,* 23.

24. Matthews, *St. Mary's (Maryland) Beacon,* Article 12.

25. McClellan, who was Stuart's very capable adjutant; Davis, *JEB Stuart, The Last Cavalier*, 340; See Breathed cannon and sign post on East Cavalry Battlefield at Gettysburg National Park, Gettysburg, PA. for casualties to Breathed Battery; Matthews, *St. Mary's (Maryland) Beacon,* Article 12; C. S. R., M324, R336-337.

26. Bridges, Diary, *New York Times*; Matthews, *St. Mary's (Maryland) Beacon,* Appendix.

27. *ibid.*, Appendix.

28. Trout, *Galloping Thunder*, 299-300; Stephen Sears, *Gettysburg* (New York, 2003), 496-498.

29. Longacre, *The Cavalry at Gettysburg*, 247; Longacre, *Lee's Cavalrymen*, 217.

30. On September 1, 1863, the perils of war forced the College of St. James to suspend its work.

31. Wise, *The Long Arm of Lee*, 2, 701, Atlas to Accompany the *OR*, Plate XLII, 5.

32. Bridges, Diary. From the Freaner quote, it is evident that the informer was assumed to be Rev. Kerfoot, Headmaster of the College of St. James. However, such an action would be a little out of character for Kerfoot, who eventually became Bishop of Pittsburg, in which position he was one of the most ardent supporters for amicable reunion of the Episcopal clergy after the war. The more likely informer would have been Rev. Joseph Howland Coit, instructor at St. James. Coit's diary shows that he was both a Union sympathizer and not on good terms with the Breatheds during the time of the Gettysburg Campaign. Roger S. Keller,. *Crossroads of War: Washington County, Maryland in the Civil War*. (Shippensburg, PA.: Burd Street Press, 1997) 171-181.

33. Longacre, *The Cavalry at Gettysburg*, 247; Longacre, *Lee's Cavalrymen*, 217.

34. Matthews, *St. Mary's (Maryland) Beacon,* Article 13, pt. 1.

35. *ibid.*, Article 13, pt. 2.

36. *The Wigfall Family Papers*; *OR* 27, pt. 3, 1049.

37. C.S.R., M226, R336.

38. Private Collection of David Bridges.

Chapter 9

1. Douglas Southall Freeman, *Robert E. Lee Abridgement*, 349-350.

2. *ibid.*, 350.

3. Longacre, *Lee's Cavalrymen*, 254; Trout, *Galloping Thunder*, 365; *OR* 29, pt. 1, 470; Matthews, *St. Mary's (Maryland) Beacon,* Article 13, pt. 2.

4. *OR* 29, pt. 1, 471; Longacre, *Lee's Cavalrymen*, 255; Matthews, *St. Mary's (Maryland) Beacon,* Article 13, pt. 2.

5. *OR* 29, 471.

6. Trout, *Galloping Thunder,* 369; *OR* 29, pt. 1, 471-472.

7. *OR* 29, 471-472.

8. *ibid.*, 471; Trout, *Galloping Thunder,* 372.

9. *The Wigfall Family Papers*; *OR* 29, pt. 1, 472; Matthews, *St. Mary's (Maryland) Beacon,* Article 13, pt. 2.

10. *ibid.*, Article 14.

11. *ibid.,* Article 14.

12. *ibid.*, Article 14

13. *ibid.*; *OR* 29, 1, 461, 463; Freeman, *Lee's Lieutenants*, vol. 3, 242-247.

14. Trout, *Galloping Thunder*, 375.

15. *OR* 29, pt. 1, 472-473.

16. Matthews, *St. Mary's (Maryland) Beacon*, Article 14.

17. *ibid.*, Article 14.

18. *ibid.*, 473; Matthews, *St. Mary's (Maryland) Beacon,* Article 14.

19. Trout, *Galloping Thunder*, 377; Matthews, *St. Mary's (Maryland) Beacon,* Article 14.

20. *The Wigfall Family Papers*; C.S.R., M226, R336.

21. *ibid.*

22. Matthews, *St. Mary's (Maryland) Beacon,* Article 15; Freeman, *Lee,* 354.

23. Trout, *Galloping Thunder*, 388; John Shoemaker, *Shoemaker's Battery* (Gaithersburg, MD.: Butternut Press, 1983), 60.

24. Freeman*, Lee*, 355; Matthews, *St. Mary's (Maryland) Beacon,* Article 15; *ibid.*, Article 15; Freeman, *R. E. Lee*, 356-357.

25. Trout, Galloping Thunder, 396-397.

26. Bridges, Diary.

27. *ibid.*

28. *OR* 29, pt. 1, 821.

29. *The Wigfall Family Papers*

30. Trout, *Galloping Thunder*, 441.

31. *ibid*; *OR* 29, pt. 2, 839.

32. Matthews, *St. Mary's (Maryland) Beacon,* Article 15.

33. Hazelwood and Watson, 41.

34. *OR* 33, pt. 4, 167-168.

35. *ibid.*; Trout, *Galloping Thunder*, 443-445.

36. *ibid.*

37. *OR* 33, 162.

38. *ibid.*, 162; Trout, *Galloping Thunder*, 443; *OR* 33, 162.

39. Bridges Diary.

40. *ibid.*; *Richmond Times Dispatch.*

41. *ibid.*

42. Neese, *Three Years in the Confederate Horse Artillery* (New York, Neale Publishing Company, 1911) Entry for February 29, 1864. Dulany's name is misspelled in the original.

43. Major General J.E.B. Stuart to Captain James Breathed, March 21, 1864, copy of letter, (David Bridges Private Collection).

44. Matthews, *St. Mary's (Maryland) Beacon,* Article 15; Bridges, Diary.

45. Roger Preston Chew, *Roger Preston Chew Papers*, Jefferson County Museum (Charles Town, WV.).

46. C.S.R., M226, R336; *ibid*; Adele H. Mitchell, ed., *The Letters of Major General James E. B. Stuart* (Middleburg, VA.: Stuart-Mosby Historical Society, 1990), 170.

47. Trout, *Galloping Thunder*, 454.

48. *OR* 33, 1264.

49. C.S.R., M226, R336., Trout, *Galloping Thunder*, 630.

Chapter 10

1. Wise, *The Long Arm of Lee*, 2, 740 and 917; Trout, *Galloping Thunder*, 455; Thomason, *JEB Stuart*, 483.; F. Ray Sibley Jr., *The Confederate Order of Battle, the Army of Northern Virginia*, (Shippensburg, PA.: White Mane, 1996) 75-76.

2. Trout, *Galloping Thunder*, 461 and 529.

3. Longacre, *Lee's Cavalry*, 280.

4. *OR* S 4, 1, 953-954.

5. *ibid*; *OR* 36, pt. 2, 948-949.

6. George Baylor, *Bull Run To Bull Run; OR Four Years In The Army of Northern Virginia* (Richmond, VA.: B. F. Publishing Company, 1900), Chapter 14 (facsimile in digital format).

7. Longacre, *Lee's Cavalry*, 276; Trout, *Galloping*, 456; *OR* 33, 1267.

8. Carlton McCarthy, *Detailed Minutiae of Soldier Life in the Army of Northern Virginia, 1861-1865* (Richmond, VA.: Carlton Press, 1882), 10; William W. Bennet, *A Narrative of The Great Revival which Prevailed in the Southern Army* (Harrisonburg, VA.: Sprinkle Publications, 1989); Reverend J. Williams Jones, *Christ in the Camp or Religion in the Confederate Army* (Atlanta, GA.: Martin & Hoit, 1904); Frank M. Myers, *The Comanches: A History of White's Battalion, Virginia Cavalry* (Baltimore, MD.: Kelly, Piet & Co., 1871), Chapter 15 in digital format.

9. Gordon C. Rhea, *The Battle Of The Wilderness May 5-6, 1864* (Baton Rouge, LA.: Louisiana State University Press, 1994), 80.

10. *ibid.*, 85 and 89-90; Longacre, *Lincoln's Cavalry*, 256.

11. George M. Neese, *Three Years In The Confederate Horse Artillery* Chapter 19 in digital format.

12. Myers, *The Comanches*, Chapter 15 in digital format.

13. Rhea, *The Battle Of The Wilderness*, 112; Longacre, *Lincoln's Cavalrymen*, 257; Baylor, *Bull Run To Bull Run; OR Four Years In The Army of Northern Virginia*, Chapter 14 in digital format; George Neese reported the Union artillerists had eight guns deployed.

14. Trout, *Galloping Thunder*, 458; Major James Breathed to Major R. P. Chew, September, 14, 1864, in the Edwin L. Halsey Papers #2447, Southern Historical Collection, Wilson Library, University of North Carolina at Chapel Hill, (Chapel Hill, NC.). (hereinafter *"ELHP"*); Rhea, *The Battle Of The Wilderness*, 113.

15. Trout, *Galloping Thunder*, 460; Neese, *Three Years In The Confederate Horse Artillery*, 259-260.

16. *ibid.*

17. William M. McDonald, *A History of the Laurel Brigade, Originally Ashby's Cavalry* (Baltimore, MD.: Sun Job Printing Office, 1907), 226; Rhea, *The Battle Of The Wilderness*, 114-115; *OR* 36, pt. 1, 897.

18. Myers, *The Comanches*, Chapter 15 in digital format; Longacre, *Lee's Cavalry*, 278; Rhea, *The Battle Of The Wilderness*, 115.

19. *ibid.*, 115; *ELHP*; Myers, *The Comanches*, Chapter 15 in digital format.

20. Trout, *Galloping Thunder*, 461.

21. Longacre, *Lee's Cavalry*, 279.

22. Baylor, *Bull Run To Bull Run*, Chapter 14 in digital format; Longacre, *Lee's Cavalrymen*, 279 and 280.

23. ELHP; Matthews, *St. Mary's (Maryland) Beacon*, Article 16, pt.1.

24. Rhea, *The Battle Of The Wilderness* 348; Neese, *Three Years In The Confederate Horse Artillery*, Chapter 20 in digital format; Longacre, *Lee's Cavalrymen*, 280.

25. John Esten Cooke, *Mohun* (New York: G. W. Dillingham, Co., 1868), 171.; *Atlas to Accompany the OR*, Plate XCVI, 3.

26. Fitzhugh Lee to Stuart, 11:15 A.M., May 6, 1864, in Fitzhugh Lee Papers, Alderman Library, University of Virginia (Charlottesville, VA.); Hunter, *Johnny Reb and Billy Yank*, 40 and 533-534. While Breathed is generally considered to have joined Fitzhugh Lee on the 7th, there is substantial evidence that Breathed may actually have arrived on the 6th. Rosser's fight was over when Fitzhugh Lee wrote his letter to Stuart on May 6th at 11:15 A.M. Lee places himself ¾ of a mile east of Todd's Tavern, permitting Breathed and

Johnston to come by way of the Catharpin Road, Shady Grove Road, and a back road that connects Shady Grove Road with the Brock Road at the Lewis Farm. There is corroboration of this from one of Breathed's men. Therefore, if Hunter's recollections are accurate, all the actions that Hunter personally witnessed involving Breathed's Batteries later that same day would have placed Breathed in significant action most of the rest of the 6th. From Hunter's narrative, it is clear he was wounded late on the 6th, was taken to Spotsylvania Court House on the 7th, and was there on the morning of the 8th in time to see Wilson's troopers take the Court House, only to be driven off by the advance of Anderson's first divisions later on the 8th. Therefore, the action Hunter witnessed relating to Breathed and his batteries could only have taken place on the 6th. Opposing this is Chew's report wherein he states that he ordered Breathed to join Fitz Lee on May 7.

27. Hunter clearly places the cavalry supporting Breathed's guns in a ravine, although Breathed would have worked his batteries up on the road. The only ravine that Hunter could have been referring to between Todd's Tavern and the Alsop Farm was on a byroad north of the Lewis Farm. Fitzhugh Lee's May 6 letter states that Union fire came from north of Todd's Tavern. There were no other roads available. This action had to be before 2 P.M., when Randolph orders the 4th Virginia Cavalry to retire; Hunter, *Johnny Reb and Billy Yank*, 536-537.

28. *ibid.*, 544-545.

29. Bridges, *Diary*.

30. *ibid.*

31. *ibid.*

32. Chew, *Roger Preston Chew Papers*.

33. Longacre, *Lee's Cavalry*, 280; Longacre, *Lincoln's Cavalrymen*, 261.

34. Fitzhugh Lee to Stuart, 8:30 A.M., May 7, 1864, Fitzhugh Lee Papers; Baylor, *Bull Run To Bull Run*, Chapter 14 in digital format.

35. Fitzhugh Lee to Stuart, 8:30 A.M., May 7, 1864, Fitzhugh Lee Papers.

36. Longacre, *Lee's Cavalry*, 280; Rhea, *The Battle Of The Wilderness*, 430-439; Gordon C. Rhea, *The Battles for Spotsylvania Court House and the Road to Yellow Tavern May 7-12, 1864* 43-44.

37. ELHP.

38. Rhea, *The Battles for Spotsylvania Court House*, 45; Neese, *Three Years In The Confederate Horse Artillery*, Chapter 20 in digital format.

39. This is the same position where Fitz Lee's cavalry had fought the 6th New York Cavalry on the night of April 30, 1863; Trout, *Galloping Thunder*, 464; Hunter, *Johnny Reb and Billy Yank*, 538.

40. Rhea, *The Battles for Spotsylvania Court House*, 48.

41. One of the charges was led by Col. Charles Phelps' Maryland Brigade. The colonel was wounded. After the war, he became a Congressman from Baltimore, and, eventually, a Baltimore City judge, and Law Professor of Breathed's nephew, Henry Powell Bridges; Rhea, *The Battles for Spotsylvania Court House*, 48-49; Three other men with Breathed were also wounded before the gun was removed from the field; ELHP.

42. Jed Hotchkiss, In *Confederate Military History*, ed. Clement Evans (Atlanta, GA.: 1899), also Library of Congress *The Jed Hotchkiss Papers*, MSS 17, 917, R59, F307; Chew, *Roger Preston Chew Papers*.

43. Private Collection of David Bridges; Rhea, *The Battles for Spotsylvania Court House*, 49.

44. Bridges, Diary, *Richmond Times Dispatch*.

45. Rhea, *The Battles for Spotsylvania Court House* 49; Trout, *Galloping Thunder*, 466.

46. William Meade Dame, *From the Rapidan to Richmond and the Spotsylvania Campaign* (Baltimore, MD.: Green-Lucas, 1920), 100, 102 and 105-107.

47. *ibid.*, 100, 102 and 105-107; Myers, *The Comanches*, Chapter 15 in digital format.

48. Dame, *From the Rapidan to Richmond*, 100, 102 and 105-107.

49. Trout, *Galloping Thunder*, 466.

50. Ulysses S. Grant, *Ulysses S. Grant Personal Memoirs* (New York: Penguin Books, 1999), 445.

51. Myers, *The Comanches*, Chapter 15 in digital format.

Chapter 11

1. Horace Porter, *Campaigning with Grant* (New York: Century Co., 1897), 84-85.

2. Trout, *Galloping Thunder*, 467; Rhea, *The Battles for Spotsylvania Court House*, 120.

3. Bridges Diary; Trout, *Galloping Thunder*, 468.

4. *OR* 36, pt. 1, 1045; Trout, *Galloping Thunder*, 468; Bridges, Diary, *John Esten Cooke*.

5. Matthews, *St. Mary's (Maryland) Beacon,* Article 16, pt. 2; Bridges, Diary.

6. *ibid.*

7. *ibid.*

8. *ibid.*; Bridges Diary, *Baltimore Sun Newspaper*.

9. Trout, *Galloping Thunder*, 470; ELHP.

10. Bridges Diary, *John Esten Cooke.*

11.Bridges Diary; Longacre, *Lee's Cavalrymen*, 288.

12. Longacre, *Lee's Cavalrymen*, 289.

13. Matthews, *St. Mary's (Maryland) Beacon*, Article 17, pt. 1; *ibid.*, Article 17, pt. 1.

14. G. W. Beale, *A Lieutenant of Cavalry In Lee's Army* (Baltimore, MD.: Butternut and Blue, 1994), 105.

15. *ibid.*, 105.

16. *ibid.*, 105; Rhea and Trout have both conjectured that Beale saw McGregor, and not Breathed, as Beale states in his memoirs. Their reasoning is that Breathed was supposed to be with Fitz Lee at that time, near Atlee's Station. However, after three years of service together, it is not likely that Beale would mistake McGregor for Breathed. In addition, the action at the Flippo Farm described by Beale took place on May 22nd at about 3:00 P.M. If Breathed was supposed to be at Atlee's at this time, why did he not leave with Fitz Lee when Lee received orders from Richmond on the morning of the 23rd to attack black Union troops at Wilson's Wharf, on the James? One of the reasons Fitz Lee listed for failing to take Wilson's Wharf was that he had no artillery, making it highly unlikely that Breathed was with him on either the 23rd or 24th. Therefore, when Beale stated that he saw Breathed at the Flippo Farm, he was probably correct. In addition, Richard Townshend Dodson, in "With Stuart in Maryland, Stuart's Daring Raid," states that McGregor lost a leg at Aldie on November 1, 1862, which is indicated also by Heros von Borcke. If Dodson is right, McGregor could hardly have been seated on his horse in the casual manner described by Beale. However, there is still some uncertainty as to when Jim Breathed was recovered enough from his wounds at Yellow Tavern to take the field again, so the matter is not entirely settled. If Beale mistook someone else for Breathed that day on the Flippo Farm, it would be another instance of the "Breathed Legend" in operation.

17. Longacre, *Lee's Cavalrymen*, 295; Gordon C. Rhea, *Cold Harbor Grant and Lee, May 26-June 3, 1864* (Baton Rouge, LA.: Louisiana State University Press, 2002), 163.

18. Longacre, *Lee's Cavalrymen*, 296.

19. Ernest B. Furgurson, *Not War But Murder, Cold Harbor 1864* (New York: Alfred A. Knopf, 2000), 102.

20. Grant, *Personal Memoirs*, 477.

21. Trout, *Galloping Thunder*, 490.

22. ELHP.

23. *OR* 51, pt. 2, 986; Wise, *The Long Arm of Lee*, 2, 825.

24. Longacre, *Lee's Cavalrymen*, 297.

25. *OR* 36, pt. 1, 1051.

Chapter 12

1. For a detailed discussion of the background and force structures of the opposing commands that took part in the Trevilian Raid, see Eric J. Wittenberg, *Glory Enough for All: Sheridan's Second Raid and the Battle of Trevilian Station* (Dulles, VA.: Brassey's, 2001), 1-35.

2. Trout, *Galloping Thunder*, 494; Walbrook D. Swank, *Battle of Trevilian Station* (Shippensburg, PA.: Burd Street Press, 1994), 5; *OR* 36, pt. 1, 1095.

3. Trout, *Galloping Thunder*, 495; Swank, *Battle of Trevilian Station*, 10; Matthews, *St. Mary's (Maryland) Beacon,* Article 17, pt. 1.

4. Trout, *Galloping Thunder*, 498; Wittenberg, *Glory Enough for All, Sheridan's Second Raid, The Battle Trevilian Station*, 286.

5. Matthews, *St. Mary's (Maryland) Beacon,* Article 17, pt. 1.

6. Swank, *Battle of Trevilian Station*, 10; Trout, *Galloping Thunder*, 502-503; ELHP.

7. Trout, *Galloping Thunder*, 503; ELHP.

8. Wittenberg, *Glory Enough for All*, 286. In the work just cited on pages 284-285 Eric Wittenberg raises some interesting points surrounding the death of Col. Covode. Wittenberg presents convincing evidence that Col. Covode did not die from the saber wounds he received in the battle, but rather from a bullet wound in the back. There is not enough evidence to conclusively prove that Breathed killed Covode, but in the confused nature of the battle it is possible that anyone from either army could have fired the fatal shot.

9. Matthews, *St. Mary's (Maryland) Beacon,* Article 17, pt. 1; *OR* 36, pt.1, 855-856.

10. Trout, *Galloping Thunder*, 506.

11. The specifics of the Wilson-Kautz Raid stray far beyond the scope of this book. For the only detailed examination of the Wilson-Kautz Raid, see Greg Eanes, *"Destroy the Junction": The Wilson-Kautz Raid and the Battle for the Staunton River Bridge, June 21, 1864-July 1, 1864* (Lynchburg, VA.: H. E. Howard Co., 1999).

12. *OR* 40, pt.1, 808-809; Longacre, *Lee's Cavalrymen*, 307.

13. *OR* 40, pt. 1, 808-809.

14. *ibid.*

15. Wise, *The Long Arm of Lee*, 2, 843.

16. Matthews, *St. Mary's (Maryland) Beacon,* Article 17, pt. 2.

17. *ibid.,* Article 17, pt. 2.

18. *ibid.,* Article 17, pt. 2.

19. *ibid.,* Article 17, pt. 2.

20. George Cary Eggleston, *The Master of Warlock* (Boston, MA.: Lothrop Publishing Company, 1903), 123-124.

21. McPherson, *For Cause and Comrades*, 71.

22. C.S.R., M226, R336; Hazlewood and Watson, 45.

23. Matthews, *St. Mary's (Maryland) Beacon,* Article 17, pt. 2.

24. *ibid.,* Article 17, pt. 2.

25. *ibid.,* Article 17, pt. 2.

Chapter 13

1. Longacre, *Lincoln's Cavalrymen,* 301.

2. ELHP; *OR* 42, pt. 1, 858; Trout, *Galloping Thunder*, 513-514.

3. *ibid.,* 580.

4. *OR* 43, pt. 1, 473.

5. *ibid;* ELHP; Trout, *Galloping Thunder*, 583.

6. ELHP.

7. Henry Kyd Douglas, *I Rode With Stonewall* (Greenwich, CT.: Fawcett Publication, 1961), 292.

8. Scharf, *History of Western Maryland*, 2, 1241.

9. ELHP.

10. C.S.R., M226, R336; ELHP.

11. Trout, *Galloping Thunder*, 588.

12. *OR* 43, pt.1 610; F. H. Buffum, *A Memorial of The Great Rebellion: Being A History Of The Fourteenth Regiment New-Hampshire Volunteers, Covering Its Three Years Of Service, With Original Sketches Of Army Life, 1861-1865* (Boston, MA.: Rand, Avery, & Company, 1882), 209, 225; Roger U. Delauter and Brandon H. Beck, *The Third Battle of Winchester* (Lynchburg, VA.: H. E. Howard, 1997), 38; Longacre, *Lee's Cavalrymen*, 312.

13. Trout, *Galloping Thunder*, 590; T. T. Munford, "Paper # 1, Reminiscences of Cavalry Operations: Battle of Winchester, 19th September '64," *SHSP*, 12 (1884), 10-12, 448; Philip Van Doren Stern, *Soldier Life in the Union and Confederate Armies* (Bloomington, IN.: Indiana University Press, 1961), 337; Jeffery D. Wert, *from Winchester to Cedar* Creek *The Shenandoah Campaign of 1864* (Mechanicsburg, PA.: Stackpole Books, 1997), 61.

14. Buffum, *A Memorial*, 210; Munford, "Paper # 1, Reminiscences of Cavalry Operations: Battle of Winchester, 19th September '64," *SHSP*, 10-12, 457-459.

15. *OR* 43, pt. 1, 456.

16. Delauter and Beck, *The Third Battle of Winchester*, 69.

17. Shoemaker, *Shoemaker's Battery*, (Gaithersburg, MD.: Butternut Press, 1983) 80.

18. Delauter and Beck, *The Third Battle of Winchester*, 70; *OR* 42, pt. 1, 862-863.

19. Wise, *The Long Arm of Lee*, 2, 888; Trout, *Galloping Thunder*, 594.

20. Thomas. T. Munford, "Paper # 1, Reminiscences of Cavalry Operations: Battle of Winchester, 19th September '64," *SHSP*, 12, 455.

21. Thomas. T. Munford, "Paper # 2, Reminiscences of Cavalry Operations: Battle of Winchester, 19th September '64," *SHSP* 12 (1884), 178.

22. Munford, "Paper # 1, Reminiscences of Cavalry Operations: Battle of Winchester, 19th September '64," *SHS*P, 12, 457-458.

23. Baylor, *Bull Run To Bull Run*, in digital format.

24. Jubal Anderson Early, *A Memoir of The Last Years of the War for Independence in the Confederate States of America, containing An account of the operation of his commands in the years 1864 and 1865* (New Orleans, LA.: Blelock & Co., 1867), 81.

25. Unknown Maryland Cavalier, *Personal Reminiscences of a Maryland Soldier in the War Between The States* (Baltimore, MD.: Self-published, 1898), in digital format.

26. *ibid.*

27. *ibid.*

28. Moore, *The 1st and 2nd Stuart Horse* Artillery, 118; Trout, *Galloping Thunder*, 607; Unknown Maryland Cavalier, *Personal Reminiscences of a Maryland Soldier*, in digital format; Baylor, *Bull Run To Bull Run*, in digital format.

29. Trout, *Galloping Thunder*, 608; Ada Bradshaw, ed., Diary, June 1863-December 1864, *Civil War Diary of Charles McVicar, Horse Artillery* (Winchester, VA.: Winchester-Frederick County Historical Society).

30. Early, *A Memoir of The Last Years of the War for Independence in the Confederate States of America*, 81.

31. Trout, *Galloping Thunder,* 610-614.

32. *ibid.*, 610-614.

33. C.S.R., M226, R336; Lewis Brady, "Notice of Chew's Battery," *SHSP* (1888), 16, 215.

34. *OR* 43, pt. 1, 656.

35. Fritz Haselberger, "General Rosser's Raid on the New Creek Depot," in *West Virginia History*, (January 1965), 26, 2, 99; *OR* 43, pt. 1, 656.

36. *ibid.*, 656.

37. *ibid.*, 656.

38. Trout, *Galloping Thunder*, 619.

Chapter 14

1. William J. Black, Diary, Manuscript No. 015, Virginia Military Institute Archives, (Lexington, VA.).

2. Matthews, *St. Mary's (Maryland) Beacon,* Appendix; Trout, *Galloping Thunder*, 625.

3. *OR* 46, pt. 3, 1331.

4. Robert J. Trout, "The Stuart Horse Artillery Battalion can stand with that of any artillery organization in any army, Northern or Southern," in *North & South* (September 2000), 3, 7, 75-84.

5. *Charles Macgill Papers, 1803-1865*, Perkins Library, Duke University (Durham, NC.).

6. *OR* 36, pt. 3, 1327-1328; Sibley, *Confederate Order of Battle*, 195-196; Trout, *Galloping Thunder*, 630.

7. McGill, *The Macgill-McGill Family of Maryland*, 99; Bridges, Diary.

8. *OR* 46, pt. 2, 1280.

9. Thomas T. Munford, "The Last Days of Fitz Lee's Cavalry Division," Manuscript Collection, MSS: 1M7237:1, Virginia Historical Society, (Richmond, Virginia), 54; Trout, *Galloping Thunder*, 640.

10. Edward G. Longacre, *The Cavalry At Appomattox* (Mechanicsburg, PA.: Stackpole Books, 2003), 5.

11. *ibid.*, 142.

12. Bridges, Diary; Hazlewood and Watson. 46.

References to other accounts of Breathed's fight at High Bridge; Myers, *The Comanches*, Chapter 20. "On reaching the top of the hill, and finding himself in command of the brigade, Col. [Elijah Viers] White [Commander of the 35th Virginia Cavalry] halted, to reform his scattered line, preparatory to charging again upon the Yankees, who were rallying at a corner of woods about a quarter of a mile away, but while thus engaged, a small party of the enemy's cavalry...appeared, and two of them attacked the gallant Maj. Breathed, of the Stuart Horse Artillery, who had ridden alone, some distance beyond the Confederate line, and a desperate conflict took place, in full view of both parties, wherein nothing but the sabre was used. In a short time the Major knocked one of his foes from his horse, and was almost instantly knocked down himself by the remaining one, but just as the Yankee had wheeled his horse, and was leaning over with his sabre in tierce [i.e., lined up for a direct thrust] to dispatch the prostrate Major, one of White's men approached, and with a pistol shot brought the Yankee to the ground, when Breathed sprang up with his sabre still in his hand, exclaiming, 'Oh! damn you! I've got you now,' and killed him. ...This seemed to convince the Yankees that they could do nothing with such men, and they again retreated";

OR 46, pt. 1, 1302; Fitzhugh Lee reported, "Gen. Rosser, in command of his own, and my old division, under Munford, proceeded to Rice's Station, on the South Side road, where learning that a force had been detached from the Federal left, confronting Longstreet at that point, to open on his rear, moved at once to counteract their purpose. The enemy were overtaken and attacked on the road toward and in the vicinity of High Bridge.";

R. Preston, Chew, "Defense of High Bridge, Near Farmville," CV (August, 1908), v 16, 8, 394-395; Chew described the sabre fight as follows, "Immediately after the enemy retired Major James Breathed, of the Horse Artillery, and a Companion, riding out in front of our lines [Confederate], were challenged by two Federal horsemen, who galloped forward from their ranks and attacked them. A desperate fight with sabers followed. Lieutenant W. B. Conrad, of the 12th Virginia Cavalry, happened to be near, and observing Breathed's antagonist, a very expert swordsmen, gaining some advantage, galloped forward and, using his pistol, put a bullet through his head. [some believed the courier Scruggs shot him dead: [Hazlewood and Watson, 47.] Then turning his attention to the other two men, who were engaged in a fierce fight, he [Breathed] fired two bullets into the Federal soldier and stretched him on the ground. Major Breathed, one of the most gallant officers in the army, greatly distinguished himself as an artillery officer, and often, leaving his battery when not in action, was seen boldly leading cavalry charges. On this occasion he would probably have been killed save for Conrad's timely arrival";

George A. Hundley, "Beginning and Ending: Reminiscences of the First and Last Days of the War," SHSP, (1895), 23, 294.

13. Bridges, Diary; Hodges' portrait, by William Sharp, was donated to Harvard University's Portrait Collection by his daughter in 1935, Harvard University Art Museum.

14. Longacre, The Cavalry At Appomattox, 144; OR 46, pt. 1, 1302-1303.

15. Robert J. Trout, The Hoss, 25; Wise, The Long Arm of Lee, 2, 936-937.

16. Munford, Last Days of Fitz Lee's Cavalry Division, 22.

17. *ibid.*, 23.

18. *ibid.*, 23.

Chapter 15

1. C.S.R., M226, R336.

2. Bridges, Diary.

3. *Charles Macgill Papers, 1803-1865*, Perkins Library, Duke University Library, (Durham, NC.).

4. Matthews, *St. Mary's (Maryland) Beacon*, Article 17, pt. 2.

5. Chew, *Roger Preston Chew Papers.*

6. McPherson, *For Cause and Comrades*, 43-44.

7. Scharf, *History of Western Maryland*, 2, 1133; Bridges, Diary (also see Washington County Courthouse records in Hagerstown, Maryland, under "At the request of Robert Bridges the following Mortgage was recorded May 12, 1868.").

8. McGill, *The Macgill-McGill Family of Maryland,* 124.

9. H. H. Matthews, "A Maryland Confederate Matchless for Hard Fighting and Bravery, Recollections of Major James Breathed," *SHSP*, (December-January 1902), 30, 346-348; At the time of this writing, the descendants of one such family from Fulton County, Pennsylvania includes cousins Breathed Lynch and Breathed Glen Garland. Complements of veterinarian/mayor Dr. Murphy of Hancock, Maryland. It should also be noted that the name of Breathed was no stranger to Fulton County., Pa. The 1830 Census and the 1840 Census both list Breatheds (Renny and John respectively) in Bedford County; since Fulton County was formed from Bedford County in 1850, it is possible that a number of local families would have had Breathed relations.

10. James Ripley Smith, *Diary for 1870*, Hancock Historical Society (Hancock, MD.).

11. Shelby Foote, *The Civil War, Red River to Appomattox* (New York: Vintage Books, 1986), 1040.

12. Wise, *The Long Arm of Lee*, vol. 2, 796.

13. H. L. Chipman, *Certificate of Promotion In the United States Army*, July 16, 1885; Bridges, Diary.

14. Bridges, Diary, *Baltimore Sun*.

15. H. H. Matthews to Colonel Norborne, April 10, 1908, in Museum of the Confederacy Collection, Eleanor S. Brockenbrough Library, Richmond, Virginia.

16. H. H. Matthews to Colonel Norborne; also see McGill, *The Macgill-McGill Family of Maryland*, 124.

17.; Cooke, *Mohun*, 145,

18. Breathed, "In Memoriam-Maj. James Breathed, by his brother, Frank Breathed, Petersburg, W. VA." *CV*, 575.

19. Chew, *Roger Preston Chew Papers*. The question of what happened to the Stuart Horse Artillery papers is still unsolved. It is unclear that Breathed ever brought them home, since he was not the last commander of the unit. The last commander was Daniel Shanks. If Shanks got the papers, he would probably have brought them home to Maryland's Western Shore counties of St. Mary's and Charles, where the Shanks family were prominent. This raises the interesting speculation that H. H. Matthews published his long account of Jim Breathed's war experiences in the St. Mary's Beacon because that was a condition of gaining access to those important papers. If that is true, it would also explain the numerous references by Matthews to Daniel Shanks bravery out of proportion to mentions of other equally brave officers of the horse artillery of similar rank.

Chapter 16

1. John Gill, *Recollections of a Maryland Confederate Soldier* (Baltimore, MD.: Sun Printing Office, 1904), 414.

2. Matthews, *St. Mary's (Maryland) Beacon,* Appendix.

3. *ibid.*, Appendix.

4. *ibid.,* Article 13, pt. 1.

5. Von Borcke, *Memoirs of the Confederate War For Independence*, 235-236.

6. Wise, *The Long Arm of Lee*, 1, 440.

7. Matthews, *St. Mary's (Maryland) Beacon,* Article 16, pt. 1.

8. Munford, *Last Days of Fitz Lee's Cavalry Division*, 10 and 12; McPherson, *For Cause and Comrades*, 47.

9. Scharf, *History of Western Maryland*, 1242.

10. Munford, *Last Days of Fitz Lee's Cavalry Division*, 19-23.

11. George Trust, *St. Mary's (Maryland) Beacon,* (St. Mary's County, Maryland, November 15, 1888), 49, 4.

12. Wise, *The Long Arm of Lee*, 2, 794.

13. *Richmond Times Dispatch*, (Richmond, VA.: February 16, 1908).

15. Hazlewood and Watson, 47.

Postscript

1. Bridges, Diary.

2. Goochland County Deed Book, (Goochland County, VA.: February 21, 1872), 42 and 113; Scharf, *History of Washington County Maryland,* 1, 365.

3. Chipman, *Certificate of Promotion in the United States Army*, July 16, 1885; Bridges, Diary.

4. Chew, *Roger Preston Chew Papers.*

5. *Galveston (Texas) Daily News*, (Galveston, Texas, May 30, 1917), 2.

6. Bridges, Priscilla Breathed: Letter, Receipt for goods received. Given to Confederate Memorial Literary Society, Richmond, Virginia, in 1898 by Priscilla Breathed Bridges. Loan retrieved by Pricilla Williams Carmichael, August 4, 1937, daughter of Priscilla Breathed Bridges acted after her mother's death to retrieve from Museum of the Confederacy, Richmond, Virginia, all of Major James Breathed's articles. They have subsequently been lost in estate sales, unfortunately.

7. Chew, *Roger Preston Chew Papers.*

8. Bridges, Priscilla Breathed: Letter, Receipt for goods received. Given to Confederate Memorial Literary Society, Richmond, Virginia, in 1898.

Appendix

1. Matthews, *St. Mary's (Maryland) Beacon,* Appendix.

2. *ibid.*, Appendix.

3. *ibid.*, Appendix.

4. *ibid.*, Appendix.

Bibliography

Primary **Sources**

Newspapers

Baltimore Sun
Galveston Daily News
Jacksonville Republican
New York Times
Philadelphia Weekly Times
Richmond Enquirer
Richmond Times
Richmond Times-Dispatch
St. Mary's Beacon

Manuscript Sources

David P. Bridges Collection, Arlington, Virginia

Various correspondence
Priscilla Breathed Bridges scrapbooks

Jefferson County Museum, Charles Town, West Virginia

Roger Preston Chew Papers
George W. Shreve, "Reminiscences in the History of the Stuart Horse Artillery"

Special Collections, Perkins Library, Duke University, Durham, North Carolina

Charles Macgill Papers 1803-1865

Southern Historical Collection, Wilson Library, University of North Carolina at Chapel Hill, Chapel Hill, North Carolina

Edwin L. Halsey Papers #2447

Goochland County Land Record, Goochland County, Virginia

Deed Books for 1872

Hancock Historical Society, Hancock, Maryland

James Ripley Smith Diary

Manuscripts Division, Library of Congress, Washington, D. C.

Jedediah Hotchkiss Papers

Marty Martin Collection, North Carolina

Halsey Wigfall Correspondence

Special Collections, Mercer University, Macon, Georgia

Rev. Henry H. Tucker, D. D., "God In the War"

National Archives and Records Administration, Washington, D. C.

Lloyd Beall Papers, Drawer #266, Microfilm Roll 336
James Breathed Papers, Drawer #226, Microfilm Roll 226
   Consolidated Service Records, RG 393
U. S. Census Reports for 1860
U. S. Census Reports for 1860. Washington Co., Williamsport
   District Maryland
U. S. Census Reports for 1860. Rush Township, Missouri

Historical and Special Collection of the Health Sciences and Human Services Library, University of Maryland, Baltimore, Maryland

James Breathed, Degree of Doctor, Vol. 1860
Fact Sheet-University of Maryland, School of Medicine. Under
   Dean George Warner Miltenberger named Dean of School of
   Medicine (1855-1869). Alumni Affairs Office

Enoch Pratt Library, Baltimore, Maryland

Laura Lee Davidson Papers, Personal Narratives Vertical File

South Carolina Library, University of South Carolina, Columbia, South Carolina

Wade Hampton Papers

Alderman Library, University of Virginia, Charlottesville, Virginia

Robert T. Hubbard Memoirs
Fitzhugh Lee Papers
Thomas L. Rosser Papers

Virginia Historical Society, Richmond, Virginia

F. M. Colston Papers
Thomas T. Munford, "Last Days of Fitz Lee's Cavalry Division,"
MSS:1M7237:1

Williams C. Wickham Papers

Archives, Virginia Military Institute, Lexington, Virginia

William J. Black Diary

Published Sources

Alexander, Edward Porter. *Military Memoirs of a Confederate.* New York: Da Capo Press, 1993.

Baylor, George. *Bull Run To Bull Run; OR Four Years In The Army of Northern Virginia.* Richmond: B. F. Publishing Company, 1900.

Beale, George W. *A Lieutenant of Cavalry In Lee's Army.* Reprint: Baltimore: Butternut and Blue, 1994.

Blackford, William W. *War Years with Jeb Stuart.* Baton Rouge: Louisiana State University Press. 1993.

Bradshaw, Ada Bruce. Despe, ed. *Civil War Diary of Charles William McVicar, Horse Artillery.* Hampton, VA.: 1977.

Brady, Lewis. "Notice of Chew's Battery." *Southern Historical Society Papers.* 16 (1888): 215.

Breathed, Frank. "In Memoriam-Maj. James Breathed, by his brother, Frank Breathed, Petersburg, W. VA." *Confederate Veteran.* (November 1908): v 16, no. 11, 575.

Buffum, F. H. *A Memorial of The Great Rebellion: Being A History Of The Fourteenth Regiment New-Hampshire Volunteers, Covering Its Three Years Of Service, With Original Sketches Of Army Life, 1861-1865.* Boston: Rand, Avery, & Company, 1882.

Cardell, David. "A Horse Battery." *Confederate Veteran.* (January-December 1919): 27, 1, 1-7.

Chew, R. Preston. "Defense of High Bridge, Near Farmville." *Confederate Veteran.* (August, 1908), v 16, no. 8, 394-395.

Coit, Joseph Howland. "Recollections," Vol. 30, 63-64, *Studies in American Religion*, 30 vols. Lewistown, NY.: The Edwin Mellen Press, 1988.

Cooke, John Esten. *Mohun.* New York, NY.: G. W. Dillingham Co. Publishers, 1868.

———. *Surry of Eagle's Nest.* New York: G. W. Dillingham Co. Publishers, 1866.

——. *The Wearing of the Gray*. Baton Rouge: Louisiana State University Press. 1997.

Dodson, Richard Townshend. "With Stuart in Maryland, Operations of the Stuart Horse Artillery in The Sharpsburg Campaign." As transcribed by Robert J. Trout.

——. "With Stuart in Maryland, Stuart's Daring Raid.," As transcribed by Robert J. Trout.

Douglas, Henry Kyd. *I Rode With Stonewall*. Greenwich, CT.: Fawcett Publications, 1961.

Early, Jubal Anderson. *A Memoir of The Last Years of the War for Independence in the Confederate States of America, containing An account of the operation of his commands in the years 1864 and 1865*. New Orleans: Blelock & Co., 1867.

Gill, John. *Recollections of a Maryland Confederate Soldier*. Baltimore: Sun Printing Office, 1904.

Gracey, Samuel L. *Annals of the Sixth Pennsylvania Cavalry*. Philadelphia: E. H. Butler Co., 1868.

Grant, Ulysses S. *Personal Memoirs of Ulysses S. Grant*. New York: Penguin Group, 1999.

Halleck, Henry Wager. *The Project Gutenberg EBook of Elements of Military Art and Science*. Release Date: July 1, 2005 [EBook #16170], http://www.gutenberg.org/dirs/1/6/1/7/16170/16170-h/16170-h.htm.

Hazlewood, M. W. & Watson, W. eds. "Major Breathed, of the Stuart Horse Artillery." *The Old Dominion*. Richmond: Vol. 5, No. 1 (1871).

Hein, David. "A Student's View of the College of St. James on the Eve of the Civil War: The Letters of W. Wilkins Davis (1842-1866)," *Studies in American Religion*. Lewiston, PA.: Vol. 30 (1988).

Hundley, George A. "Beginning and Ending: Reminiscences of the First and Last Days of the War." *Southern Historical Society Papers*. (1895), 23, 294.

Hunter, Alexander. *Johnny Reb & Billy Yank*. New York: Smithmark, 1996.

Kennedy, John Pendleton. *Swallow Barn; or, A Sojourn in the Old Dominion*. New York: George P. Putnam, 1851.

Matthews, H. H. "A Maryland Confederate Matchless for Hard Fighting and Bravery, Recollections of Major James Breathed." *Southern Historical Society Papers*. (December-January 1902), 30, 346-348

Matthews, H. H. "Articles I-XXVII and Appendix," *St. Mary's Beacon*, 1904-05.

McCarthy, Carlton. *Detailed Minutiae of Soldier Life in the Army of Northern Virginia, 1861-1865*. Richmond: Carlton Press, 1882.

McClellan, Henry B. *I Rode with Jeb Stuart, The Life and Campaigns of Major General J.E.B. Stuart*. Bloomington, IN.: Da Capo Press, 1994.

McDonald, William M. *A History of the Laurel Brigade, Originally Ashby's Cavalry*. Baltimore: Sun Job Printing Office, 1907.

Mitchell, Adele H., ed. *The Letters of Major General James E. B. Stuart*. Richmond: Stuart-Mosby Historical Society, 1990.

Moore, Edward A. *The Story of a Cannoneer Under Stonewall Jackson*. New York: Neale Publishing Co., 1907.

Munford, Thomas T. "Paper # 1, Reminiscences of Cavalry Operations: Battle of Winchester, 19th September '64." *Southern Historical Society Papers*. 12 (1884).

Munford, Thomas T. "Paper # 2, Reminiscences of Cavalry Operations: Battle of Winchester, 19th September '64." *Southern Historical Society Papers*. 12 (1884).

Myers, Frank M. *The Comanches: A History of White's Battalion, Virginia Cavalry*. Baltimore: Kelly, Piet & Co. Publishers, 1871.

Neese, George M. *Three Years In The Confederate Horse Artillery*. New York: The Neale Publishing Co., 1911.

Porter, Horace. *Campaigning with Grant*. New York: Century Co., 1897.

Shoemaker, John. *Shoemaker's Battery*. Gaithersburg, MD.: Butternut Press, 1983.

Smith, James Ripley. *Diary for 1870*. Hancock, MD., Hancock Historical Society, n.d.

Stiles, Robert. *Four Years Under Marse Robert*. New York, Washington: The Neale Publishing Co., 1904.

Taylor, Walter H. *Four Years with General Lee*. Bloomington, IN.: Indiana University Press. 1962.

The War of the Rebellion: A Compilation of the Official Records of the Union and Confederate Armies. 128 volumes in 3 series. Washington: United States Government Printing Office, 1880-1901.

Trust, George. *St. Mary's (Maryland) Beacon,* (November 15, 1888), 49, 4.

University of Maryland, Office of the School of Medicine. University of Maryland Annual Circular, School of Medicine, Session 1860-'61, Session 1860-61 and Catalogue of Matriculates. Baltimore: Sherwood & Co., 1860.

Unknown Maryland Cavalier. *Personal Reminiscences of a Maryland Soldier in the War Between The States*. Baltimore: Self-published, 1898.

Vogtsberger, Margaret A., ed. *The Dulanys of Welbourne: A Family in Mosby's Confederacy.* Rockbridge, VA.: Rockbridge Publishing Co., 1995.

Von Borcke, Heros. *Memoirs of the Confederate War For Independence.* Nashville: J.S. Sanders & Company, 1999.

Wickham, W. C. "Colonel W. C. Wickham's Report of an Engagement near Aldie, 17th, 1863." *Southern Historical Society Papers.* (1881), 9, 79-80.

Secondary Sources

Advancement Office Staff, ed. *Saint James School Alumni Directory, 2003.* Purchase, New York: 2003.

Alexander, Ted. "Antietam: The Bloodiest Day." *North & South* Vol. 5, No. 7 (October 2002): Tollhouse, CA.: North & South, Inc.

Bearss, Edwin C. "Into the Very Jaws of the Enemy: Jeb Stuart's Ride Around McClellan," in William Miller, ed., *The Peninsula Campaign: Yorktown to the Seven Days.* Campbell, CA: Savas Woodbury, 1995.

Bennet, William W. *A Narrative of The Great Revival which Prevailed in the Southern Army.* Harrisonburg, VA.: Sprinkle Publications, 1989.

Boatner, Mark. *The Civil War Dictionary.* New York, Vintage, 1959.

Bridges, Henry P. *The Woodmont Story.* New York: A. S. Barnes and Co., 1953.

Catton, Bruce. *Glory Road.* Garden City, New York: Doubleday, 1962.

Cordell, Eugene Fauntleroy. *The Medical Annals of Maryland, 1799-1899.* Baltimore: Williams & Wilkins Co. 1903.

Dame, William Meade. *From the Rapidan to Richmond and the Spotsylvania Campaign.* Baltimore: Green-Lucas, 1920.

Davis, Burke. *Jeb Stuart, the Last Cavalier.* New York: Bonanza Books, 1957.

Delauter, Roger U. & Beck, Brandon H. *The Third Battle of Winchester.* Lynchburg, VA.: H. E. Howard, 1997.

Divine, John E. *35th Battalion Virginia Cavalry.* Lynchburg, VA.: H.E. Howard, 1985.

Donald, David Herbert. *Lincoln.* New York: Touchstone, 1996.

Driver, Robert J., Jr. *1st Virginia Cavalry.* Lynchburg, Va.: H. E. Howard, 1991.

Duncan, Richard R. "The College of St. James and the Civil War: A Casualty of the War," *Historical Magazine of the Protestant Episcopal Church.* (1970): Austin, TX.: The Church Historical Society.

Eanes, Greg. *"Destroy the Junction": The Wilson-Kautz Raid and the Battle for the Staunton River Bridge, June 21, 1864-July 1, 1864.* Lynchburg, VA.: H. E. Howard Co., 1999.

Eggleston, George Cary. *The Master of Warlock.* Boston: Lothrop Publishing Co., 1903.

Eric, Dean T., Jr. *Shook Over Hell: Post-Traumatic Stress, Vietnam and the Civil War.* Cambridge, MA.: Harvard University Press, 1997.

Ernst, Kathleen A. *Too Afraid To Cry.* Mechanicsburg, PA,: Stackpole Books, 1999.

Fauquier and Loudoun Garden Club. *Save The Bridge Fund.* Upperville, Virginia. n.d.

Filbert, Preston. *The Half Not Told, the Civil War in a frontier town.* Mechanicsburg, PA: Stackpole, 2001.

Foote, Shelby, *The Civil War: Red River to Appomattox.* New York: Vintage Books, 1986.

Freeman, Douglas Southall. *Lee's Lieutenants: A Study in Command.* 3 vols. New York: Charles Scribner's & Sons, 1942.

——. *R.E. Lee.* New York. Scribners, 1934.

——. *Robert E. Lee: An Abridgement.* New York: Simon & Schuster, 1991.

Furguson, Ernest B. *Chancellorsville, 1863-The Souls of the Brave.* New York: Vintage Books, 1993.

——. *Not War But Murder, Cold Harbor 1864.* New York: Alfred A. Knopf, 2000.

Harsh, Joseph L. *Taken At The Flood.* Kent, OH.: The Kent State University Press, 1999.

Haselberger, Fritz. "General Rosser's Raid on the New Creek Depot," *West Virginia History*, Vol. 26, No. 2 (January, 1965).

Hassler, William Woods. *Colonel John Pelham: Lee's Boy Artillerist.* Chapel Hill, NC.: University of North Carolina Press, 1960.

Heitman, Francis E. *Historical Register and Dictionary of the U. S. Army.* 2 vols. Washington: U. S. Government Printing Office, 1903.

Henry, Robert S. *First With The Most: Nathan Bedford Forrest.* New York: Mallard Press, 1991.

Jones, Reverend J. Williams. *Christ in the Camp or Religion in the Confederate Army.* Atlanta: Martin & Hoit, 1904.

Keller, Roger S. *Crossroads of War: Washington County, Maryland in the Civil War*. Shippensburg, PA.: Burd Street Press, 1997.

Klein, Frederic Shriver. *Just South of Gettysburg*. Westminster, MD.: Historical Society of Carroll County, 2000.

Laboda, Lawrence R. *From Selma To Appomattox*. New York: Oxford University Press, 1994.

Lang, Stephen F. *The Complete Idiot's Guide to The Confederacy*. Indianapolis: Alpha Books, 2003.

Longacre, Edward G. *The Cavalry at Gettysburg*. Lincoln, NB.: University of Nebraska Press, 1986.

———. *Fitz Lee: A Military Biography of Major General Fitzhugh Lee, C.S.A.* Cambridge, MA.: De Capo Press, 2005.

———. *Gentleman and Soldier, A Biography of Wade Hampton III.* Nashville: Rutledge Hill Press, 2003.

———. *Lee's Cavalrymen*. Mechanicsburg, PA.: Stackpole Books, 2002.

———. *Lincoln's Cavalry*. Mechanicsburg, PA.: Stackpole Books, 2000.

———. *The Cavalry At Appomattox*. Mechanicsburg, PA.: Stackpole Books, 2003.

Martin, David G. *The Peninsula Campaign, March - July 1862*. Conshohocken, PA.: Combined Books, 1992.

McGill, John. *The Macgill-McGill Family of Maryland*. Washington: Self Published, 1948.

McGinley, Rev. Charles R. *They Continued Steadfastly in the Apostles' Teaching and Fellowship*. Hagerstown, MD.: The Printing Place, 1986.

McKinley, Walter B. *The Story of Saint Mark's Episcopal Church*. Self Published, 1949.

McPherson, James M. *Battle Cry of Freedom: The Civil War Era*. New York: Oxford University Press, 1988.

———. *For Cause and Comrades*. New York: Oxford University Press, 1997.

Moore, Robert H. II. *The 1st and 2nd Stuart Horse Artillery*. Lynchburg, VA: H. E. Howard, 1985.

O'Neil, Robert F. Jr. *The Cavalry Battles of Aldie, Middleburg and Upperville: Small but Important Riots*. Lynchburg, VA.: H. E. Howard, 1993.

O'Reilly, Frank. Battle of Fredericksburg Historical Research, Illustrated by John Dove, Revised and Produced by Steve Stanley, Maps # 1-5.

O'Rourke-Trott, Peggy. *Centuries of Leadership, 1800-1900-2000, Deans of the University of Maryland School of Medicine.* Baltimore: University of Maryland School of Medicine, 2000.

Rhea, Gordon C. *Cold Harbor: Grant and Lee, May 26-June 3, 1864.* Baton Rouge: Louisiana State Press, 2002.

——. *The Battles for Spotsylvania Court House and the Road to Yellow Tavern, May 7-12, 1864.* Baton Rogue: Louisiana State University Press. 1997.

——. *The Battles Of The Wilderness, May 5-6, 1864.* Baton Rouge: Louisiana State University Press. 1994.

Scharf, Thomas J. *History of Western Maryland.* 2 vols. Westminster, MD.: Family Line Publications, 1995.

Sears, Stephen W. *Chancellorsville.* New York: Houghton-Mifflin,1996.

——. *To the Gates of Richmond-The Peninsula Campaign.* New York: Ticknor & Fields, 1992.

Sibley, F. Ray Jr. *The Confederate Order of Battle, the Army of Northern Virginia.* Shippensburg, Pa.: White Mane, 1996.

Stern, Philip Van Doren. *Soldier Life in the Union and Confederate Armies.* Bloomington, IN.: Indiana University Press, 1961.

Swank, Walbrook D. *Battle of Trevilian Station.* Shippensburg, PA.: Burd Street Press. 1994.

Thomas, Emory M. *Bold Dragoon: The Life of J.E.B. Stuart.* Norman, OK.: University of Oklahoma Press, 1999.

Thomason, Jr., John W. *JEB Stuart.* New York: Konecky & Konecky. 1958.

Thompson, IV, John W. *Horses, Hostages, and Apple Cider, J.E.B. Stuart's 1862 Pennsylvania Raid*, Mercersburg, PA.: Mercersburg Printing, 2002.

Troiani, Don. *Civil War.* Norwalk, CT.: The Eastern Press, 1995.

Trout, Robert J. *Galloping Thunder: The Stuart Horse Artillery Battalion.* Mechanicsburg, PA.: Stackpole Books, 2002.

——. "The Stuart Horse Artillery Battalion Can Stand With That of Any Artillery Organization in any Army, Northern or Southern," *North & South*, Vol. 3, No. 7 (2000): Tollhouse, CA.: North & South, Inc.

——. *The Hoss.* Myerstown, PA.: JebFlo Press, 2003.

Weber, Max. *The Protestant Ethic and the Spirit of Capitalism.* New York: Charles Scribner's Sons, 1958.

Wert, Jeffery D. *From Winchester to Cedar Creek: The Shenandoah Campaign of 1864.* Mechanicsburg, PA.: Stackpole Books, 1997.

——. *Gettysburg Day Three.* New York: Simon & Schuster, 2001.

Williams, Thomas J. C. *History Washington County, Maryland.* 2 vols. Westminster, MD.: Family Line Publications, 1992.

Wise, Jennings Cropper. "The Boy Gunners of Lee." *Southern Historical Society Papers.* (December 1, 1916), 42, 158-159.

———. *The Long Arm Of Lee.* 2 vols. Lynchburg, VA.: J. P. Bell Company, 1915.

Wittenberg, Eric J. *Glory Enough for All, Sheridan's Second Raid and the Battle of Trevilian Station.* Washington: Brassey's, 2001.

———. *Protecting the Flank: The Battles for Brinkerhoff's Ridge and East Cavalry Field, Battle of Gettysburg, July 2-3, 1863.* Celina, OH.: Ironclad Publishing, 2002.

———. *The Union Cavalry Comes of Age: Hartwood Church to Brandy Station, 1863.* Dulles, VA.: Brassey's, 2003.

Index

A

B

command attacked Federal horse artillery on the Berryville Pike forcing
    them to leave in a short time, 264–265

company, first skirmish at Falling Waters, 21

day after wounded shot a Negro who had insulted his hostess, 257

death of Elizabeth Breathed Snodgrass (his aunt) on March 22, 283

death of Kitty Jones Lyles Breathed (his grandmother) on March 21, 283

died on February 14, 1870 of unknown cause, 296

elected to Lieutenant of Stuart Horse Artillery on March 23, 1862, 34

enlisted on April 1861 in what became the 1st Virginia Cavalry
    Regiment, 18

exemplary combat leader, 305

fight at High Bridge, various descriptions of, 347–348

fired his pieces into horse artillery of Capt. Alanson M. Randol, 158

first child of John and Ann who was born December 15, 1838, 2

horses had to be moved regularly to assure they had enough to eat, 119

led cavalry charge on June 24 against David Gregg's Division, 252–253

major of Breathed's Battalion, 209, 282

men left Richmond, crossed James River, bivouacking near Ream's
    Station, 263

men not accustomed to unlimited supplies of corn, 98

moved section to support 6th Virginia as it reached base of Miller Hill
    causing enemy to retire in great confusion, 155

moving grave to Hagerstown, 311

near Tunstall's Station used canister to flush out infantry in ambush, 56

not interested in transfer to Maryland Line, 211

oath of allegiance to Federal government took April 24, 1865 in
    Winchester, Virginia, 293

papers of, 301

promotion to major of, 205–206

proved himself a man of action who fought at front with his men, 34

rode with Fitz Lee's cavalry on June 29 when a trooper's pistol ball
    struck him in the abdomen and knocked him from the horse, 256

sick on the road from Patterson to Manassas, 22

Talley's farm, opened fire on enemy at, 140

went to Hancock, Maryland, home of sister Priscilla, 293

whenever he freed himself from studies he busily courted Mary Ragan
    Macgill (Mollie), 11

with Johnston's and Shoemaker's batteries rode with Fitz Lee in pursuit
    of Sheridan, 248

with Johnston's Battery joined Fitz Lee's troopers on May 7, 1864, 221

C

D

E

H

J

K

M

N

Pneumonia, James Breathed thesis on, 14

Poolesville, Maryland, 33, 81, 84

Pope, Major General John, 68–72, 76, 78

> attacked Jackson while Longstreet attacked the Union commander, crushing the enemy and driving him from the field, 72
>
> treated citizens of northern Virginia harshly, 69

Porter, Fitz-John, exposed corps north of Chickahominy River, 54

Port Royal, Virginia, 125

Priscilla, sister of James, had custody of Breathed's wartime artifacts, 312–313

R

Raccoon Ford, 69, 136, 187

Rapidan Station, Virginia, 110

Rappahannock Station, Virginia, 194

Reams Station, Virginia

> attacked from various sides the Union forces fled with many captured and others scattered on the road to, 255
>
> Wilson and Kautz, completely outnumbered had soundly routed at, 255

Rich, William W., Lt. Colonel of Phillips Legion, 108

Richmond, Virginia, 113

"Ride Around McClellan", needed to gain data about McClellan dispositions, 43

Ringgold, Major Samuel, Bai-Yuka built in 1825 for, 3

Rio Hill, north of Charlottesville horse artillery moved to for winter quarters, 196

Roberts, William P., Brigadier General of Roberts' Brigade, 282

Robertson, Beverly H., Brigadier General of 3rd Brigade, 64

> engaged only very briefly at Kelly's Ford and then withdrew, 334

Rockville, Maryland, Hampton captured Union wagon train by, 168–169

Rooney Lee's Brigade and Breathed Battery, contested advance of Union infantry until Breathed leapfrogged his guns back over road by which they had come, 241

Rosecrans, Major General William S., 185

Rosenberg, Henry, husband of Mollie Ragan Macgill, 312

Rosser, Thomas L.

> advance drove Custer's pickets and both sides fought all day without either side gaining an advantage, 219
>
> artillery company part of Stuart force to confront Colonel Isaac I. Stevens, 25

T

W